Economy and Class in Sudan

Edited by
NORMAN O'NEILL
Department of Sociology and Social Anthropology
University of Hull
and
JAY O'BRIEN
Department of Anthropology and Sociology
Lawrence University
Wisconsin

Avebury
Aldershot · Brookfield USA · Hong Kong · Singapore · Sydney

Published by

Avebury

Gower Publishing Company Limited
Gower House, Croft Road, Aldershot,
Hants. GU11 3HR, England

Gower Publishing Company
Old Post Road, Brookfield, Vermont 05036
USA

British Library Cataloguing in Publication Data
Economy and class in Sudan.
1. Sudan. Economic development
I. O'Neill, Norman, 1943- II. O'Brien, Jay, 1947-
330.9624'04

ISBN 0 566 05604 6

Printed and bound in Great Britain by
Athanaeum Press Ltd, Newcastle upon Tyne

Contents

Introduction

NORMAN O'NEILL AND JAY O'BRIEN

In most studies of the political economy of Sudan, as in the case of many other African nations, two subjects remain conspicuous by their absence: class formation, and the class structure of this post-colonial state.[1] These are not merely ideological omissions, unconsciously designed to ignore "imperialism" and the "class struggle"; they are also a clear reflection of uneven and combined development, in which, for example, the apparent "autonomy of the state" and "economic weakness of the indigenous bourgeoisie" are intimately related (O'Neill 1978). Similar features apply more generally in the "sociology of development". At one extreme the temptation is to argue that capitalism "underdevelops" Third World countries, while at the other, the argument is precisely the opposite (Frank 1967; Warren 1980). The fact is that capitalism has always developed unevenly (in both time and space), especially in the form of colonialism where economic planning was initially undertaken in order to satisfy the needs of the colonisers - whether in terms of the export of capital, the import of raw materials, or military strategy. The legacy of colonialism is therefore a malformed economy in which the primary export sector is usually dominant and often technologically advanced, alongside other sectors which remain economically and technologically impoverished. This penetration of advanced capitalism into non-capitalist formations inevitably poses a theoretical paradox in any attempt to postulate "stages of economic growth". This is because an obvious distinction needs to be made between the antecedents of capitalist industrialisation (the fact that capitalism developed out of European feudalism) and its subsequent development, on a global scale, through the agencies of colonialism and imperialism. In fact, the contemporary debate on the different political implications contained in the seemingly contradictory assertions that - crudely expressed - capitalism at once develops and underdevelops its periphery, has a parallel even in the works of Marx. Marx conceived of "modernisation" as a global process with contradictory results that included the possibility of "leaping stages" - a theme that was to prove politically crucial in the theory and practice of Bolshevism in contra-distinction to the rigid evolutionism of the Mensheviks (Marx 1973 and 1971).

Classical Marxism was exceptionally articulate if sometimes overly schematic, in delineating the course of European economic development (slavery being superseded by feudalism, and feudalism by capitalism), and analysed political conflict in terms of class struggle. Thus, political opposition to feudal absolutism was conceived as a class struggle between the rising bourgeoisie and landed aristocracy. The achievement of parliamentary democracy - based on free elections, freedom of speech, of assembly, and so forth, were all attributable to the emergence of the bourgeoisie as a progressive class. Similarly, free trade-unionism and the right to strike were related to the rise of the industrial proletariat in its class conflict with this same bourgeoisie. This latter struggle - of wage labour against capital - forms, of course, the basis of Marx's analysis of capitalism, and the revolutionary struggle for socialism. The bourgeois-democratic and socialist revolutions are therefore each conceived in terms of a specific class hegemony, and are theoretically distinct and historically disparate. The Mensheviks applied similar reasoning in arguing that the further development of capitalism in Russia would promote a progressive bourgeoisie, and a prolonged period of parliamentary democracy during which time the pre-conditions for socialism (in the form of a maturing labour movement) would materially progress. The Mensheviks thereby awarded - in advance - the leadership of the ensuing revolution to the Russian bourgeoisie. Events proved to be quite different. The success of the October Revolution was based on Lenin's theoretical premise that the unevenness of Russia's economic development rendered that bourgeoisie quite incapable of fulfilling the political task which the Mensheviks had ordained (see Mandel 1968).

Whatever the antecedent of capitalism and its subsequent extension through imperialism, economic penetration into those areas of the globe now euphemistically labelled the "Third" or even "Fourth World" (for in some, economic growth has been decidedly faster than in others) has exhibited the following general features: the gradual transformation of small-scale agriculture; land seizure and consolidation; the creation of a reserve army of migrant and unemployed labour; and, initially, the erosion or in some cases systematic destruction of handicraft industries that were in competition with those of the imperialist countries. This latter feature highlights the aforementioned paradox (i.e. of monopoly capital distorting, and unevenly developing indigenous capital) because for many years it limited (and in many countries continues to limit) the formation of an industrial bourgeoisie - the class which in Europe led the struggle for democracy.

Recognising that even in Russia this "national" bourgeoisie was too weak either to compete economically against imperialism (upon which it therefore necessarily came to rely) or to lead and sustain a genuinely democratic revolution, the Bolsheviks politically opposed "class-collaboration", collapsed the "bourgeois-democratic phase" into the "dictatorship of the proletariat", and, on seizing power, proclaimed the epoch of socialist revolution.

Failure of the revolution to spread outwards through Europe and beyond undoubtedly gave impetus to the notion of "Socialism in One Country", but Stalin's thorough revision of Marxism entailed not merely a re-evaluation of the role of the peasants (especially after the victory of the Chinese Revolution), but also of the "progressive" role of the "national" bourgeoisie in economically backward countries. This is ironic because in 1925-7 Chinese Communists had been instructed by the Communist International to join the Kuomintang under the leadership of Chiang Kai-shek, who subsequently sent thousands of them to their deaths. Despite this unpalatable truth, it has nevertheless become politically legitimate for many "Third World" Communists to seek "progressive" elements within their national bourgeoisie and to provide theoretical justification for it in terms of "Marxism-Leninism" - whether of the Chinese or Soviet variety. The result has been catastrophic defeat for Communists through the agency of such "bourgeois nationalists" as Premier Sukarno in Indonesia, General Kassem in Iraq, and - as Sudanese Communists need no reminding - of President Numeiri at home. It is therefore instructive to remind ourselves that a debate engaged in by Russian Marxists over 60 years ago, and in which they anticipated many of the essential arguments to be found in "development theory", has precisely the same political relevance today, as it had then: is there, or is there not, a progressive bourgeoisie with whom to collaborate in the struggle for social revolution? Also, what are the features and revolutionary capacity of the peasantry? In contemporary Sudan, these questions are of more than academic interest confined to social scientists; they pose vital theoretical issues having immediate practical implications in the current struggle for a national democratic revolution.

O'Neill (1978) has proposed a tentative answer to the first of these questions for Sudan which has been supported empirically in the extensive research of Fatima Babiker Mahmoud (1984). After assessing the class-interests and political behaviour of the Sudanese bourgeoisie, she concludes:

> This study has suggested that Sudanese capitalists are in fact a 'comprador' and dependent bourgeoisie. Given the repressive role their parties have played throughout the political history of the modern Sudan, and the personal role that some of those studied have played in opposition to radical change (to the extent of crushing governments in collaboration with foreign capital) these capitalists can in no way be classified as a 'national bourgeoisie' (Mahmoud 1984, p.152).

O'Brien (1985) has come to similar conclusions, but by way of a different route. Ibrahim Kursany (1983), however, presents a contrasting conclusion, arguing that sections of the bourgeoisie can be clearly identified as having a progressive role to play in the foreseeable future.

Closely related to this debate has been controversy over the class character of rural producers in Sudan, particularly concerning the political role of the large tenantry in irrigated agriculture (see chapters by Tait and by O'Brien and O'Neill in this volume). The Sudan Communist Party (SCP) enjoyed early success in organising tenants' unions in Gezira and other schemes and drew important support from them until Numeiri's re-organisation of unions under the Sudan Socialist Union (SSU) in the 1970s. The theoretical position underlying this political initiative has been variously expressed in the works of Barnett (1977), Founou-Tchuigoua (1978), and O'Neill (1978) in terms which represent the irrigated schemes as Taylorised "factory-like" organisations which employ tenants as disguised "de facto wage earners" behind a facade of "partnership" with capital and the state.

A movement within the SCP and the Gezira Tenants' Union (GTU) in the 1950s to organise non-tenant agricultural labour into the same union was defeated, leading to a Maoist split from the SCP which rejected the revolutionary potential of tenants and argued that they were in fact surplus takers and exploiters of the seasonal labour they hired. Similar arguments have been made by academics of varying orientations on the basis of a tenant "slave-owning mentality" and heritage or tenant "petty landlordism" (Al-Arifi 1975).

Recently, a more differentiated and historical class analysis of tenants in Sudanese irrigated agriculture has begun to argue that processes of class differentiation, beginning in the 1950s, have led to social and political heterogeneity among tenants, particularly in Gezira and other older schemes (see O'Brien 1984; Tait, this volume). These authors emphasise that to explain the political propensities of the indigenous bourgeoisie or different sections of the peasantry it is necessary to study not merely how merchants and rich peasants have become capitalists and whether peasants work in their fields or hire labour, but also to analyse the related processes of uneven economic development and class formation, wrought in conjunction with the penetration of foreign investment capital. This book offers a collection of studies of these issues by progressive Sudanese and expatriate scholars who share these broader concerns but differ in their assessment of the class capacities of the social groups they analyse and represent a broad range of the spectrum of progressive opinion in these crucial debates.

Sudan is Africa's largest nation state - being just under one million square miles, and extending across nearly 18° of latitude. Its geography and climate are of great significance in its history, and to its economic potential. The country extends 1,200 miles southwards from the southern borders of Egypt to Kenya, Uganda and Zaire, and 1,000 miles westwards from the Red Sea and Ethiopia to the Central African Republic and Chad, and to Libya in the extreme north-west.

Climatically much of the country is part of the savanna belt which stretches across sub-Saharan Africa - a large part being characterised by problems of inadequate water supply, due to unreliable and erratic rainfall. The Nile, which it shares with Egypt, is therefore Sudan's life-blood, and flows through extremes of contrast - from humid tropics in the south, to arid desert in the north. The Nile drainage system provides a physiographic unity to the country which makes it at once unique in Africa, and yet a microcosm of the continent. Alone among the savanna nations, Sudan includes a full range of bioclimatic regions, with a marked gradient from south to north, and from the Ethiopian plateau north-westwards.

Criss-crossed by the Nile and the main east-west cross-continental overland routes of the savanna, and abutting the Red Sea, Sudan has participated in or at least been affected by all the major developments in the old world, from the early stages of human evolution, through the neolithic revolution, to imperialism and the struggle for socialism. Settled agricultural communities flourished along the banks of the Nile in Sudan from at least 2500 B.C. and gave rise to the opulent Kushitic kingdoms, socially and culturally autonomous, but greatly shaped by intercourse and, periodically, rivalry with Pharaonic Egypt. Irrigators, iron workers, long-distance traders, and pyramid builders, the literate Kushites melded diverse peoples and cultural influences into a uniquely vital configuration which unified much of the Nile Valley - including imposing a dynasty over Egypt for a time - and drew the notice of European and Asian civilizations at least from the time of Herodotus. This Sudanese culture blended cultural and physical elements of Africa and southwest Asia into a diverse legacy which is still felt in Sudan today, both as a source of national identity and pride and as a source of tension and conflict.

Economic forms have emerged and been transformed; classes have risen and fallen; states have expanded and contracted; external links have been forged and broken. The ancient Kushitic kingdoms were succeeded by the Christian Nubian kingdoms on the Nile beginning in 543 A.D. Yet, already a century later, the Arabs and Islam overwhelmed Egypt, Sudan's important northern neighbour, and began to exert cultural and religious influences which culminated in the reunification of the Sudanese stretch of the Nile valley under the Islamicising Funj Sultanate beginning in 1504. Parallel developments led to the rise of the Keira Sultanate in Darfur and other states flying the banner of Islam to the west of the Nile. The rise and prosperity of these states, as with most of their predecessors, were intimately bound up with the long-distance trade linking Egypt, the Mediterranean and Asia with central Africa. The export of African slaves to the Ottoman empire gradually assumed a central role in this revitalised trade, introducing new elements into the class dynamics of Sudanese states (see Kapteijns and Spaulding, this volume).

Exploitation, together with resistance to it and, periodically, escape from it into autarkic local communities, has thus been a constant, if variable and changing, feature of Sudanese history for the past 4,000 years. New elements and discontinuities have been introduced, as with the medieval Arab immigrations, the Turco-

Egyptian conquest in the 1820s, the Mahdist revolution in the 1880s, and the British conquest in the 1890s (see O'Neill, this volume). Yet there are remarkable continuities as well. Many members of Sudan's contemporary dominant classes are descended from rulers of an earlier period and seek to use this descent and various cultural symbols associated with it to legitimise their modern dominance - even if their current power and the social content of its symbols have changed. On the other hand, there is also a rich - if sometimes contradictory and confusing - legacy of resistance to exploitation and oppression by subordinate classes kept alive and nurtured by Sudanese communities and organisations. It was not out of ignorance that many rural Sudanese called the British "Turks" and referred to the period of British rule as the "Second Turkiya".

In important ways then, contemporary struggles in Sudan represent a struggle for control over its rich cultural heritage; its rulers counter-posing the glories of empire to the mass traditions of resistance to oppression. This battle for control over Sudan's cultural legacy has in many ways mystified both academic analysts and political strategists, who have tended to accept the sectarian religious form of much contemporary political contention and to miss the class interests which lie behind the overtly religious alliances which appear to shape the dominant political parties. Both domination and resistance are, of course, genuine elements of Sudan's contradictory cultural heritage. Each has had its historical moments, but, except for a few interludes, such as the Mahdist triumph over foreign oppression and the popular revolutions of October 1964 and April 1985, the forces of domination have so far held the upper hand. Whether - or when - Sudan's democratic traditions of resistance to oppression will be liberated from the thrall of reactionary nationalism and appropriated by the Sudanese masses is a matter for practical politics, not academic speculation. The contributors to this volume share a commitment to helping that liberation through the demystification of the class forces ideology has obscured.

This political-intellectual project is in its early stages and accordingly suffers many handicaps. Research is lacking on many facets of Sudanese society and history and much of what has been done is inadequate. Research on contemporary problems has often lacked any sort of historical perspective and has tended to be dominated by the pragmatic developmentalist orientation of its main sponsors, while historical research has mostly had a distinctly antiquarian bent. In a country of such tremendous diversity, researchers and political activitists have often been too hasty to generalise or have retreated into the celebration of the particular. Research in the Southern Region was only possible for a total of about ten years in the past three decades due to civil war and the recent insurgency (see O'Neill, this volume). The repression of the Numeiri regime, especially in its last few years, prevented much important research from being carried out, or else made publication of its results impossible or dangerous to the researcher.

This volume assembles a collection of studies which document neglected aspects of economy and class in Sudan, propose useful models for research or strategies for organised action, or articulate key positions in the central debates about future directions for Sudan. We hope that progressive Sudanese intellectuals, as well as non-Sudanese, will find these studies informative and stimulating, particularly in the optimistic atmosphere of renewed open discussion which prevails in Sudan as we go to press.

The first two chapters by the editors attempt to develop a broad perspective on contemporary Sudan by placing current issues and events in their historical context and indicating the main lines of debate in progressive circles over their significance and the best way forward. Chapter Three, by Kapteijns and Spaulding, offers insights, rare in historical scholarship on Sudan, into the class structure and dynamics of precapitalist states in Sudan on the eve of foreign conquest and insertion in the capitalist system. In the following chapter, Tait takes a fresh look at the development of the profoundly important Gezira Scheme and takes a position in the debates concerning the social position and capacities of the tenants which breaks new ground. In Chapter Five Duffield builds on his earlier innovative analyses of the role of West African settlers in contemporary Sudan to specify the political and economic significance of the ideology of the "Fallata" as foreigners. O'Brien's analysis in Chapter Six traces the formation of a large seasonal wage labour force in capitalist agriculture from colonial times and documents its effects on peasant and pastoral systems and the character of capitalist production itself.

The following three chapters, by Bernal, Saeed and Faris, present rural case studies analysing the social character and impact of different experiences of capitalist encroachment. These studies are followed by a more polemical chapter arguing for a strategy for increased research in the rural sector and for rural transformation (Kursany).

Chapters Eleven and Twelve examine key urban problems. Al Shazali analyses the operation of urban labour markets, and Hale analyses the class content of ethnic networks in the towns. In Chapter Thirteen Galal-al-Din presents preliminary results of his investigations of the growing phenomenon of labour emigration to the Arab oil-producing states. Finally, Gruenbaum examines aspects of the subordination of women and the role in it of female circumcision and infibulation.

Note

1. Notable exceptions are: Issa G. Shivji, Class Struggles in Tanzania, (1976); Mahmood Mamdani, Politics & Class Formation in Uganda (1976); Fatima Babiker Mahmoud, The Sudanese Bourgeoisie (1984). See also, Carole Collins, 'Colonialism & Class Struggle in Sudan' (1976).

References

Al-Arifi, Salih Abdalla (1975), 'Landlordism among small farmers: The case of Gezira tenants in the Sudan', Sudan Journal of Economic and Social Studies, 1 (2) pp. 10-14.

Barnett, Tony (1977), Gezira: An Illusion of Development, Frank Cass, London.

Collins, Carole (1976), 'Colonialism and Class Struggle in Sudan', MERIP Reports, 46.

Frank, Andre Gunder (1967), Capitalism and Underdevelopment in Latin America: Historical Studies of Chile and Brazil, Monthly Review Press, New York & London.

Founou-Tchuigoua, B. (1978), 'De Facto wage-earners in the Gezira Scheme (Sudan)', Africa Development, 3 (1), pp. 25-50.

Kursany, Ibrahim (1983), 'The role of the national bourgeoisie in the national democratic revolution', Review of African Political Economy, 26, pp. 119-23.

Mahmoud, Fatima Babiker (1984), The Sudanese Bourgeoisie, Zed Press and Khartoum University Press, London and Khartoum.

Mamdani, Mahmood (1976), Politics and Class Formation in Uganda, Monthly Review Press, New York and London.

Mandel, Ernest, ed. (1968), Fifty Years of World Revolution, Merit Publishers, New York.

Marx, Karl (1971), Revolution and Counter-Revolution in Germany, Allen and Unwin, London.

--- (1973), 'The British Rule in India' in Surveys From Exile (Political Writings, Vol. 2), Penguin, Harmondsworth.

O'Brien, Jay (1984), 'The social reproduction of tenant cultivators and class formation in the Gezira Scheme, Sudan' in B. Isaac (ed), Research in Economic Anthropology, Vol. 6, JAI Press, Greenwich, Connecticut, pp. 217-41.

--- (1985), 'Sowing the seeds of famine: the political economy of food deficits in Sudan, Review of African Political Economy, 33, pp. 23-32.

O'Neill, Norman (1978), 'Imperialism and Class Struggle in Sudan', Race and Class, 20 (1), pp. 1-19.

Shivji, Issa (1976), Class Struggles in Tanzania, Monthly Review Press, New York and London.

Warren, Bill (1980), Imperialism: Pioneer of Capitalism, (edited by J. Saider), New Left Books, London.

1 Uneven development and class formation

JAY O'BRIEN AND NORMAN O'NEILL

The connected phenomena of devastating famine in Sudan in 1984 and 1985 and the fall of Numeiri's military regime in April 1985 have drawn unprecedented international attention to Sudanese economy and politics. Those who turn to the scholarly literature available on these subjects in English are unlikely to gain from it a satisfactory understanding of the sources of Sudan's problems. Economic analysis has been firmly situated within the problematic of "modernisation", in which imports of technology into such showcase exemplars of modern, large-scale production as the Gezira Scheme represent progress from backward subsistence production to advanced market production. Of course, progress has its setbacks, occasioned variously by bureaucratic mismanagement or bad weather - the famine being a particularly striking example. Such a view ignores, and in any case could not account for, the fact that Sudan escaped the famine that ravaged the Sahel from 1968 to 1973 despite experiencing similar rainfall shortages. Here, we shall take this as the central fact of contemporary Sudanese history to be accounted for and offer an explanation in terms of the dominance in Sudan, roughly from the late 1950s to early 1970s, of an agrarian bourgeoisie with a basis in large-scale food production for domestic markets (see O'Brien 1985). Progressive analysis, dominated by "dependency" perspectives, has insufficiently grasped the significance of the differences between fractions of Sudanese capital and the patterns of accumulation to which competition among them has given rise, and thus has also missed this fundamental point (but see Ali 1982).

The dominance of these economic interests in Sudan has largely escaped notice in political analyses, which have been resolutely constitutional and institutional in approach. These analyses (e.g. Al-Rahim 1969; Beshir 1974; Warburg 1978; Woodward 1979) have been overly influenced by the religious form of political association which has led to the affiliation of the major political parties with the predominant Muslim sects - the Umma Party with the Ansar, the National Unionist Party with the Khatmiya - in ways which cut across class lines. The programmatic differences between the parties are seldom seen to reflect any substantial differences in economic interests, but to represent essentially ideological and sectarian interests, often reduced to the sense of brute competition for power and spoils. Progressive political analysis (especially Mahmoud 1984) has advanced considerably beyond the limits of the institutional view, yet continues to assess sections of the bourgeoisie in the crude terms of predominant types of investment (e.g. industrial vs. commercial) or in terms of degrees of nationalism (compare Mahmoud 1983, 1984 and Kursany 1983, this volume).

In this chapter, we seek to develop an analysis of the formation of classes and shifting class alliances in Sudan in relation to patterns of accumulation and uneven development, including changing forms of foreign involvement in Sudan. From the pre-independence period under British supervision, contention between an agrarian fraction of the emergent bourgeoisie and a commercial (and increasingly bureaucratic) fraction has dominated Sudanese politics. With the rise of private mechanised sorghum production in the central rainlands in the late 1950s, the character of this struggle, and the pattern of accumulation it gave rise to, took on forms unusual in Africa.

The Expansion of Capitalist Food Production

The large-scale expansion of domestic food production in Sudan began with (a) the political ascendancy of the agrarian bourgeoisie following independence and (b) the concurrent decline in profitability of the cotton-producing pump-irrigated agriculture which had served as the basis of the initial accumulation of capital in Sudanese agriculture (Ali 1982, 1983; O'Brien 1980, 1981, 1983a; Ali and O'Brien 1984; see O'Neill, this volume). The recession in world cotton prices which set in during the late 1950s threw into sharp relief the disadvantages of having large amounts of capital tied up in the infrastructure of irrigated agriculture. In this context agrarian capitalists began to search for more favourable investment opportunities.

Partially mechanised sorghum production in the central rainlands provided an ideal opportunity. As a last colonial act, the British had established a highly profitable, state-supported pattern of mechanised production of sorghums in government-leased tracts of the fertile central clay plain. This pattern involved low levels of fixed investment and ecologically damaging cultivation practices which produced high rates of profit (see O'Brien 1983a).

Rapid post-independence expansion of capitalist agriculture boosted internal demand for commercial food crops to feed the large seasonal wage labour force, which was paid partly in kind. Such payments played a key role in keeping cash wage rates from rising as demand for seasonal labour soared (O'Brien 1980, 1983b). Thus capitalist production of sorghum enjoyed a buoyant internal market for its product which in turn provided a key to controlling wage rates and the labour force as a whole.

To support the pattern of investment dominated by rainfed mechanised agriculture which began to emerge in the late 1950s, the agrarian bourgeoisie in power used the facilities of the state to aid this sector, often at the expense of the mostly government-operated export (cotton) sector.[1] This class used its increasing control of the government to channel imports of machinery and spare parts, priority provision of fuel, etc., to private capitalist agriculture, often at the expense of Gezira and other government-operated cotton schemes. The result was that by the mid-1960s private rainfed farming dominated capitalist growth in Sudan. This growth received a further boost in 1968 with the 'Agrarian Reform Movement', which nationalised the private cotton pump schemes on generous terms, thus freeing agrarian capital to invest in sorghum production just at the time that the World Bank initiated its first project for assisting mechanised farming in Sudan (see O'Brien 1981, 1983a). The effects of these and related policies of the period on the export sector were severe. Starved of government resources and increasingly heavily taxed, government cotton schemes stagnated, leading to decline of government revenues and inevitable fiscal crisis. With stagnation of export revenues and a rising import bill for agricultural machinery, etc., severe balance of payments problems hit Sudan also in the early 1970s.

This pattern of capitalist growth led by food production differs sharply from the export-led growth pattern which has dominated in African and other Third World economies since colonial times. In a study of the agricultural production performance in 35 sub-Saharan African countries between 1961-65 and 1976-80, Hinderink and Sterkenburg (1983) found only two countries which showed a substantial growth in per capita food production at the expense of export crop production. These were Sudan and Botswana, in both of which per capita food production rose from an index of 100 to 112 while overall per capita agricultural output was virtually stagnant. Only five other countries in the study showed stagnation in food production as well as in overall agricultural output per capita, while output in the remaining 23 countries failed dismally to keep pace with population growth.

Impact on Rural Population

The overall structure of Sudan's rural economy led peasants to become oriented towards the production of food crops on their own plots, supplemented by seasonal wage labour, rather than towards the production of export crops as happened in the savanna zones of West Africa. Peasants did produce export crops, especially sesame, but generally within a framework which did not involve large-scale dependency on high-risk hybrids but was dominated by the criterion of self-sufficiency in grain (see O'Brien 1980; Ali and O'Brien 1984). This situation protected Sudanese peasants and pastoralists from famine during the period of the Sahelian famine of the late 1960s and 1970s in several ways, despite acute rainfall shortages and poor or failed crops. Many were able to maintain food reserves from their direct production. Slow development of rural market-orientation inhibited capitalist social differentiation from developing to the extent of undermining the ability of most people to produce substantial proportions of their subsistence requirements directly. This went significantly beyond simple food production to include - through maintenance of bush and forest fallow, etc. - the ability to provide other consumption needs, such as fuel and building materials, directly rather than through the market (see O'Brien 1985). When all else failed, there were plenty of opportunities to find wage labour, which usually included as a conventional component payment in the form of food - thus insulating seasonal labourers from some of the impact of price inflation. In addition, many cultivators produced sufficient grain surpluses in good years to maintain reserves, in the form of livestock as well as grain stores. Such reserves were a regular aim of production in many communities and helped enable peasants to survive frequent low yields due to fluctuations in rainfall.

These conditions can be attributed to the orientation of the most dynamic sector of the economy to the internal mass market and the overall dominance of agricultural development by large-scale projects employing seasonal wage labour rather than by peasant cash crop producers as in most of the areas in West Africa hit hard by the famine. It was also important that there was considerable room for expansion before the point was reached that capitalist agriculture and peasant agriculture came into direct competition over land. Many pastoralists were displaced from their pastures by the rapid expansion of the 1960s and 1970s, but either found open land to cultivate instead or maintained sub-optimal herding units through heavy reliance on seasonal wage labour to supplement herding incomes.

Crisis and Struggle

The effects of incorporation of rural populations into the wage labour force and the growing encroachment on their lands by spreading capitalist agriculture began by the mid-1970s seriously to inhibit the ability of the rural masses to meet their subsistence needs, especially for food, through their own direct production. Forest and scrub rapidly began to disappear as new schemes were cleared, commercial charcoal-making expanded to meet growing urban demand for fuel, and people - especially pastoralists - displaced by the schemes sought new land on which to settle. Cash needs began to increase rapidly as more and more people came to depend on markets to supply their needs for building materials, cooking fuel and other important items of consumption. As cash needs rose and rural producers felt increasing pressures to maximise cash returns to their labour time, ecologically important fallow and crop rotation practices came to be abandoned or attenuated - even where fallowland continued to be available (see O'Brien 1978; Ali and O'Brien 1984). Yields declined drastically in many areas, forcing even greater dependence on markets, both for income and for consumption. At the same time, the expansion of capitalist agriculture into new rural areas provided new opportunities for wage employment that made it increasingly difficult for kin-based production units to retain the labour of junior members.

In response to these conditions, seasonal wage labourers became increasingly aggressive in pursuit of higher cash wage rates. Increasingly, workers came to refuse payments in kind and to seek the highest available cash piece rates. By the mid-1970s, this pressure on wage rates, combined with growing problems of externally induced price inflation, deteriorating export performance and general fiscal and balance-of-payments problems, brought on a crisis of the agricultural labour force as a whole (O'Brien 1980, 1983b, this volume).

Heavy external pressure was also brought to bear on Sudan. Beginning about 1972, the World Bank became more insistent in pressing its arguments about Sudan's 'comparative advantage' lying in cotton production for export and against the policies which the government had pursued towards diversifying production in the irrigated schemes - including growing more import-substitution elite food crops such as wheat and rice. The World Bank's Third Mechanised Farming Project of 1978 halted Bank support for further expansion of this type of agriculture.

Foreign-Capital and the Restoration of Export Dependency

The IMF imposed an austere 'stabilisation plan' on Sudan in 1978, involving drastic currency devaluations, removal of government subsidies on food and other consumption items, a moratorium on new development projects and other draconian measures which rapidly depressed the living standards of both urban workers and rural producers.

Foreign Arab capital began, following the October War of 1973, to promote Sudan as the potential 'breadbasket' of the Arab world. Arab oil exporters agreed to guarantee Sudan's mounting debts and to provide short-term balance-of-payments support and development aid in return for Sudan's acceptance of the stringent terms of the IMF 'stabilisation plan' and Arab access to Sudan's agricultural resources for direct private investment. Saudi and other Arab capital - mainly private - took over further expansion of rainfed mechanised farming with the aim of using the sorghum and other products to feed livestock and poultry, and producing other foods for export to oil-producer markets.

The scope of planned investment was enormous (see O'Neill 1980). A multi-lateral Arab Fund, now known as AAAID or Triple Aid, was inaugurated in 1977 under the auspices of the Kuwaiti-based Arab Fund for Economic and Social Development. It envisaged a ten-year investment programme, costing over $6 billion, to finance a large number of interrelated schemes designed to bring the annual growth of Sudan's agricultural sector to an estimated six per cent.

Financial and infrastructural difficulties (and related doubts concerning the economic viability of very big schemes) delayed the implementation of Triple Aid's investment programme, but a start was made on the smaller and more manageable projects in the fields of horticulture, dairy processing, glucose production and poultry farming before the drought of the 1980s slowed things down. Companies were formed and equity distributed between the Sudan Government (37.5 per cent), Triple Aid (25 per cent), and the governments of Kuwait, Saudi Arabia and Iraq (12.5 per cent each). Tenders were issued and contracts awarded to Ritz Pompen of West Germany to supply water pumps for the $25 million vegetable scheme. Other European companies were earmarked for the construction of a slaughterhouse and packing plant for the $75 million Arab Sudanese Poultry Company, a $37.5 million starch and glucose factory, and the $88 million dairy plant for the Arab Sudanese Dairy Company. Furthermore, feasibility studies by HVA of Holland for a $92 million edible oils project and Sweco of Sweden for a $36 million feedmill scheme were made and tenders received from companies in Britain, France, Holland and West Germany for construction contracts related to phase 2 of Triple Aid's schedule. By the beginning of the 1980s, AAAID's total investment in Sudan exceeded $250 million.

The number of funding organisations in Sudan that have Islamic or Arab credentials has increased considerably since the mid-1970s and includes the OPEC Special Fund, the Kuwaiti based Inter-Arab Investment Guarantee Fund, the Saudi Development Fund and the Islamic Development Bank. The spectacular success of Saudi Prince Mohammed el Faisal's own Islamic Investment Company testifies to the extent to which an appeal to Islamic principles in banking can result in the accumulation of enormous financial reserves. Within the first four hours of its opening, the Faisal Bank in Khartoum took in ten million Sudanese pounds. By the end of its first year of operation, the bank's profits exceeded $45 million (O'Neill 1983).

European firms involved in recent projects in Sudan include Bonifica of Italy (to examine the feasibility of reviving Old Suakin as a Red Sea port), Rhein-Ruhr Industrie of West Germany (commissioned to study river transport) and a large number of French companies such as the Compagnie de Constructions Internationales (CCI) (Jonglei Canal and Juba airport), Rhone-Poulenc and Roussel-Uclaf (agriculture), Omnium Techniques de Pipelines (OTP), and Thomson-CSF (telecommunications - with Siemens of West Germany).

Assisting these projects, and their infrastructural support, is aid from the European Economic Community (which in 1981 increased its official aid grant under the Lome Convention to around $110 million for improvements at Khartoum Airport), the Islamic Development Fund ($39.3 million for petroleum products from Kuwait, $12 million for fertilisers, and $5 million for the Damazin Agricultural Development Company), the OPEC Special Fund ($7.7 million for the Kassala-Haiya road) and the Kuwait Fund ($4.7 million for the Sinnar-Damazin road and $5.2 million for the Rahad project).

Similarly, World Bank and EEC funds are supporting important rehabilitation work, and contracts have been awarded to, among others, British Leyland (for trucks), KSG Handels of West Germany (for pumping equipment), International Harvesters of Canada (for tractors) and Hunslet Engines of the UK (for engines for the Gezira Light Railway). Most of these contracts are related to rehabilitation work, currently being undertaken in the very large schemes. The aim is to boost agricultural production, not for local consumption but for export. Assistance to small, mixed farming projects, and to the subsistence farmers who make up the vast bulk of the population is very small indeed. Even here, however, foreign influence is dominant. Shareholding in the new Sudan Rural Development Finance Corporation (SRDFC) is weighted heavily in favour of Britain (the Commonwealth Development Corporation), France (Caisse Centrale Cooperation Economique), and West Germany (Deutsche Gesellschaft fur Wirtschaftliche), who between them hold a 60 per cent share of the capital, compared to the Sudan Development Corporation's 40 per cent. This ratio is clearly designed to encourage yet more external investment - particularly by Arabs, and by companies in the EEC and North America - and is supported by the 1980 Investment Act which codified existing investment guarantees and was specifically designed to remove any remaining constraints on foreign private investment.

Much of this investment finance derives from the accumulated surpluses of Arab oil production - either directly, or re-cycled in the international money markets - and through multinational companies. This is ironic because it is now clear that Sudan itself possesses considerable oil deposits. The fact that Chevron has spent over $1,000 million on oil exploration in Sudan ought to be sufficient to indicate that there is far more oil in Sudan than has previously been intimated. Of about 30 wells drilled up till 1983, 25 belonged to Chevron; but the tiny trickle of oil companies wanting a slice of the action soon turned into a small flood - another sure indication that oil experts have good reason to suppose that it is there in abundance. Phillips Petroleum of the US has secured an agreement to explore an area of 120,000 square kilometres northwest of Omdurman, Canada's Transpacific is looking at 70,000 square kilometres north of Port Sudan, and Sunmark, a division of Sun Oil of Texas, is investigating 170,000 square kilometres between El Damer and El Obeid. Other companies involved in exploration are the Texas Development Corporation of Geneva, Eastern and Union Texas, Burmah Oil of the UK and the Eastern Petroleum Company of the US. It was anticipated that Shell, Mobil, Atlantic Richfield, Elf and Enserch would all have joined in the search. As an indication of the known reserves, Chevron's Unity field has at least 23 million barrels, and some estimates put the figure as high as 400 million barrels.

All this will undoubtedly stimulate foreign investment, but the corresponding concessions on profit repatriation, wrenched by the multinationals, and the concomitant pressure on Sudan to develop its infrastructure to suit the needs of foreign capital, will tend to minimise even more the rate of rural development. It will also fuel inflation, and thereby price many small peasants out of the market.

Sudan remains one of the poorest countries in Africa in terms of per capita income. It has a huge balance of payments deficit, and a mounting backlog of debt. The balance of payments figures actually understate the seriousness of the problem, because many of the externally financed projects referred to above are recorded elsewhere. The credits are simply directly transferred from aid-donor to contractor without entering the country. Deficits in the balance of payments have frequently made it difficult for Sudan to pay for essential imports, such as pesticides and insecticides. Yet, luxury imports like motor cars jam the narrow streets of Khartoum and Omdurman, and the very latest stereophonic sound recorders and videos from Japan fill the shop windows, often giving foreign visitors to the country a superficial impression of affluence. Import controls have been a constant problem. In the recent past the Sudan government operated a so-called nil-value import system. This was designed to encourage expatriate Sudanese, who work in oil-rich Arab countries - a serious 'brain-drain' of professional and skilled workers (see Galal-al-Din, this volume) - to remit foreign earnings through the customs licence revenue paid on imported luxury goods. The result was a prodigious increase in these imports, which were subsequently sold at vastly inflated prices. The financial proceeds were frequently exported to foreign-based bank accounts via the currency black market.

In the early 1980s the government convened a special conference of expatriate Sudanese to reconsider the whole subject of customs and excise duties. The immediate outcome was the imposition of a 10 per cent tax on foreign earnings to be remitted to the Bank of Sudan. In return, various concessions on import duty were to remain, and others were to be extended. The government anticipated that the new arrangements would raise over $120 million in the short term and assist in closing the foreign exchange gap. The latter, combined with expectations of a poor economic performance, has on various occasions induced the IMF to insist upon 'austerity budgets' in which the Sudanese pound was devalued, subsidies removed on petrol, sugar, and other basic commodities, and the implementation of an economic programme (conceived in monetarist terms) that included an increase in import duties. These measures, always draconian in their effects, have at various times prompted protest strikes and demonstrations - involving, most notably, railway, factory and professional workers, and Gezira tenants (see O'Neill, this volume). It was demonstrations of this kind that led to Numeiri's eventual downfall.

The pattern is a familiar one. Economic measures inspired by the IMF result in opposition from the urban working class and rural producers (who suffer most from the immediate effects of devaluation and loss of subsidy) and opposition from the traditional religious groups who perceive these economic 'reforms' as being at odds with long-standing values born of Islam. Part of Numeiri's political skill, before he finally ran out of room to manoeuvre, was his stress on a personal commitment to Islam (thereby offsetting the influence of the Ansar and Muslim Brotherhood), while calling for 'modernisation' based on foreign investment capital, which corresponded to the economic needs of the indigenous commercial bourgeoisie. This class tends to oppose religious fanaticism as much as communism because concessions to either threaten its economic security; a security linked to the renewed penetration of foreign investment capital upon which it has come to rely. The greater this reliance, the fewer political options open to whatever regime forms the government - a fact evidenced by Numeiri's own shift from left to right. But concessions to international finance capital also serve at once to integrate and undermine traditional agriculture, making it a source of cheap migrant labour for technologically advanced agri-business. The latter is designed primarily to produce crops for export, and to enable those who invest in it the opportunity to realise enormous profits. These changes in the pattern of agricultural investment have created conditions in Sudan which leave its rural population, especially in the northern savanna zones, increasingly vulnerable to drought-induced famine.

Shifting Patterns of Capital Accumulation and Class Formation

The renewal of foreign investment and other foreign influences in Sudan played an important role in restructuring the economy but the reorientation of Sudanese agriculture during the 1970s and 1980s was not simply imposed on the Sudanese. The combined crises resulting in the early 1970s from the policies pursued by the hegemonic agrarian bourgeoisie brought about intense internal struggle among the fractions of the Sudanese bourgeoisie and their allied power blocs. Foreign intervention gave a decisive advantage in these struggles to the import-export oriented commercial bourgeoisie, which captured control of the state by 1972 (under the guise of Numeiri's shift from 'left' to 'right'), and has been gradually - and not without spirited opposition - consolidating its hegemonic position since, through establishing itself as the commercial agents in Sudan of foreign capital.

The two contrasting patterns of peripheral capital accumulation referred to correspond to what de Janvry (1981) has termed 'articulated accumulation' and 'disarticulated accumulation'. Capitalist expansion in Sudan during the 1960s occurred on the basis of a pattern of articulated accumulation in the sense that the leading sectors of the economy - under the control of the hegemonic agrarian fraction of the bourgeoisie - produced for, and therefore made their profits from, the internal mass market. Under such conditions famine represents the collapse of purchasing power and is thus very bad for business.

Patterns of disarticulated accumulation stand in stark contrast, because the welfare - or lack of it - of the producing population has little direct impact on the profitability of export production. The logic of capital accumulation within such a dominant pattern thus leads to the marginalisation of producers as consumers; profitability within the system does not depend in a significant way on the purchasing power of the domestic work force. Wages figure only as a cost of production which can be kept as low as prevailing social and political conditions allow without damaging profitability in marketing the products. Precisely the same feature applies in the dominant sector - cotton.

Even as late as the 1950s cotton still accounted for 80 to 90 per cent of the gross domestic product. Other sectors of the agricultural cash economy consisted of four main elements: gum arabic, camel meat and beef, vegetable cultivation and grains. In addition, oil seed cultivation - for processing into oils and oil cake - was increasingly introduced into the mechanised farms. As for industrial production, those factories then in existence, such as a brewery, soap and match factories, and a textile mill, made up only 2.5 per cent of the GDP at the time of Britain's formal withdrawal in 1956. As elsewhere in Africa, Sudan's indigenous industrial capitalist class was therefore very small, and in most cases dependent on foreign capital.

The primary source of domestic capital accumulation for other nascent capitalists was in agriculture, and especially in agriculture which involved the private pump schemes along the Nile. Three categories of people were in a position to invest their existing wealth in such schemes: the larger merchants, some tribal heads and especially the religious leaders. These latter were especially prominent. The Mahdi family of the Ansar sect and the Mirghani family of the Khatmiya were able to amass considerable wealth through the dues paid to them by their several million followers. Through a classic policy of divide-and-rule, British colonialism was able to encourage collaboration first with one and then with the other of these religious sects by offering various forms of economic inducement. Facilities were provided at various times for the Mahdi and Mirghani families to set up, develop and extend their farms - often on the basis of land granted to each of them by the colonial administration. To a lesser extent the same applies to tribal leaderships who possessed large herds. Merchants, too, were in a favourable position, and especially those tied up with increased trade in the Gezira.

Thus it was that these three categories - rich merchants, religious leaders and tribal heads - were able to consolidate their economic power prior to independence, and came to express their developing fractional class interests in agriculture and the import/export trade through their different political parties which came to dominate the political scene afterwards. Most political analysis of Sudan since independence (e.g. Al-Rahim 1969; Beshir 1974; Woodward 1979) has failed to penetrate the religious form taken by competition among bourgeois parties (i.e. Umma vs. National Unionist, etc.) to uncover the conflict between the agrarian capitalist interests of the Umma-led faction and the cotton-dependent commercial interests of the unionists (see Ali 1982; O'Brien 1985).

Corresponding to the emergence of these capitalists in industry, agriculture and foreign trade was the growing number of wage-labourers in the factories, on the farms and in transport - especially on the railways, where the Communist party was able to establish a strong industrial base before independence. Increasing numbers of workers were being drawn into capitalist property relations, either directly as permanent or seasonal labourers, or indirectly through the role of peasant farmers supplying crops for the market. The consequent imbalance of the post-colonial Sudanese economy has been further aggravated by the introduction of modern technology. Migrant labourers from outlying provinces and the so-called 'Fallata' from West Africa flooded into the cotton schemes, mechanised farms and urban areas in search of work. The outcome of this malformation, exacerbated by British colonial policy which encouraged a rigid divide between 'Arab' north and 'African' south and west, had been the formation of a separatist movement.

The indigenous industrial bourgeoisie, though small, flourishes in partnership with foreign capital, but as a class it is too weak to possess any long-term political significance on its own account. Commercial capitalists on the other hand are growing in number and political importance. Originally, many of them were Greek and Syrian traders who accompanied the British colonisers from Egypt, but most of these left Sudan during Numeiri's 'left turn'. The conversion to 'socialism' by many Sudanese merchants and state bureaucrats is now easily accounted for. Their support for nationalisation, and especially the expropriation of the 'foreign' petty bourgeoisie, paved the way for their own economic ascendancy. They are increasing in number in direct proportion to the penetration of foreign investment capital. Many of them are the direct agents for western firms, and they manage insurance companies, banks and export-import businesses. The unevenness of their different locations in the economy renders their politics extremely volatile, although being largely parastic to neo-colonialism. Family members from this stratum are frequently to be found in the state bureaucracy - entry into which generally comes through either the armed forces or the universities. They include military and civilian officials, the secret police, higher officers in the army, civil servants and some university personnel. In the lower echelons are the less powerful salaried officials, some professionals like doctors, engineers and lawyers, and beneath these the increasing number of clerical workers who form an expanding salariat.

The Sudanese trade unions were once among the best organised in Africa, and were led in strategic sectors such as transport and textiles by the SCP, which gave the party a substantial proletarian composition. This proletarian composition remains intact. The defection of prominent farmers (some of them party members) from the former SCP-led Gezira Tenants Union into organisations of the SSU had served to increase the proportion of working-class members in the Communist Party, while curtailing its broader political influence, although it still exercises some leadership over university and secondary school students, and has the support of sections of the intelligentsia. Where it has enjoyed less support is among the much more numerous lumpen proletariat of shoeshiners, porters, beggars and the rest, the urban migrant labourers and the broad mass of the heterogeneous peasantry.

The overwhelming majority of Sudanese - about 80 per cent - are farmers, farm workers or nomadic herdsmen. Most are peasants farming small plots and growing a limited variety of crops which, until the prolonged drought of the 1980s, kept them at the level of subsistence. A large number also depend partly or wholly on transhumant herding of livestock. This population has been especially hard hit by the famine. The 'middle peasants' are obviously of a different order. Some of them are retired army officers, many are developing commercial interests - especially through the introduction of machinery - and some own shops. Their political propensities vary roughly in accordance with their uneven development, but among the more wealthy the current regime enjoys a degree of support - especially in irrigated agriculture in the riverain communities of the north. This small segment of Sudan's rural population has recently become the target of so-called smallholder development projects aimed at 'modernising traditional agriculture' designed by the World Bank, USAID and various EEC aid agencies. The hope is that encouragement of agricultural investment among such middle peasants will lead to the expansion of rural markets and a political base of support for pro-Western regimes.

The pattern of capital accumulation typical of these farmers is not unlike that of others in the past, even though then, as indicated, the main source appears to have been the private pump schemes along the Nile, and, later, rainfed mechanised farming. Commerce had offered similar scope too, but on a smaller scale, and so had investment in real estate. All of these were to develop in importance, and to some extent become interrelated. The pattern for some emerging capitalists, for example, was undoubtedly accumulation in small-scale farming, leading to trade in the local markets; in some cases, to involvement in petty commodity production, thence to investment in urban real estate, followed by further investment - on a larger scale - in mechanised agriculture. It is a pattern that provided the initial accumulation for a small number of the presently most wealthy families and, partly for that reason, continues to serve as an ideological model with powerful attraction for farmers with upwardly mobile aspirations.

Tenants in Gezira and other irrigated schemes present even thornier analytical as well as political problems. Forming on the whole, but with exceptions, a strictly regulated aggregation of _de facto_ wage earners in colonial times, tenants organised some of the earliest and most militant unions in Sudan and were among the staunchest supporters of the SCP in the 1950s (see Barnett 1977; O'Neill 1978; Founou-Tchuigoua 1978). Through their unions they confronted not only the British colonial government, but also the leading Sudanese capitalists in the private pump schemes and, most dramatically, the first transitional Sudanese government (see Ali 1982; 1983; Ali and O'Brien 1984). The agrarian bourgeoisie and the governments of the period of transition to independence were able, however, to devise policies which gradually defused both the confrontation and tenant militancy in general. Tenants were given privileged access to social services and an important channel of upward mobility through the education of their offspring (Gruenbaum 1978, 1982; O'Brien 1984). Contracting of increased mechanical operations to private contractors provided scope for wealthier tenants to overcome limits imposed by a ceiling on tenancy size on their abilities to accumulate by opening an important new field for investment. Nationalisation of the private pump schemes as private capital shifted to rainfed agriculture removed the direct conflict of interests between the agrarian bourgeoisie and tenant farmers.

Establishing a principal basis of accumulation outside the cotton sector enabled the agrarian bourgeoisie, through control of the state, to increase the privileges and profits of a segment of the tenantry, thereby converting old enemies into allies.

An important result of these developments has been the growing scope allowed for processes of social differentiation and class formation within the tenantry, based primarily on off-farm investments but linked to the maintenance of tenancies (see Tait, this volume; O'Brien 1984; Sorbo 1986). Analysis and political strategy have been slow to catch up with these crucial developments and have continued to debate the social and economic character and revolutionary capacities of the tenantry as an undifferentiated mass. Just how great the political stakes involved are is indicated in proposals, first mooted by the World Bank in 1966, and now gaining increasing support in government circles, to raise or eliminate the ceiling on tenancy size, remove barriers to the sale of tenancies, and to contract out more of the technical services performed by the parastatal management body (the Sudan Gezira Board).

More generally, 'middle peasants' - including wealthy tenants among them - have trading interests that place them next to the rapidly developing indigenous commercial bourgeoisie. Some of them have been investing in mechanised agriculture, albeit generally without the government support afforded larger investors. Much of this activity is illegal and takes place on the grazing lands of pastoralists who lack the control over organs of local government frequently enjoyed by these 'middle peasants'. The areas farmed frequently take on the appearance of agricultural strip mining. Tree cover is destroyed, crop rotation neglected, and fertilisers ignored. Such criminal abuse as this bestows upon the land a productive life-span of five to seven years before its abandonment to desertification.

Similarly, faced with rising prices for a widening array of necessary consumption items for which they must pay cash, but unable to increase their wage incomes sufficiently to meet these needs, rural producers have been making adjustments which threaten to exacerbate their difficulties in the long term. Increasingly in direct competititon with capital for land, peasants and pastoralists adopt equally ecologically damaging practices which further reduce their abilities to provide for their own needs directly. As their crop yields decline and they come to buy a growing proportion of the food they eat, they lose the ability to maintain food reserves - whether in the form of grain or livestock. As they alter their crop selection to maximise cash returns rather than direct consumption requirements, they incur greater risks of crop failure in times of unfavourable rains and, in the long run, further impoverish their soil (O'Brien 1980, 1985; cf. Franke & Chasin 1980). As the surrounding forest and scrub recede, they also lose natural sources of food they used to fall back on in times of shortage. As more operations in the capitalist farms are mechanised, the main demand for seasonal labour is increasingly concentrated in a short peak season, increasing wage-competition among workers and reducing their ability to compensate for village crop failure through agricultural wage incomes (see O'Brien, this volume). In short, agricultural growth on the basis of a pattern of disarticulated accumulation in the conditions of the 1980s makes rural producers in Sudan dangerously vulnerable to starvation as the result of drought - a fact dramatically and tragically demonstrated in the terrible famine of 1983-85.

Limited industrialisation and the market imperatives of forms of capitalist agriculture in which output is destined for export and designed to ensure a high return on foreign investment suggest that conditions limit the emergence of a progressive nationalist fraction of the bourgoisie as a potential ally in the struggle for democracy. This is because where the economic interests of the commercial bourgeoisie become increasingly tied up with foreign capital, there is far less scope for the emergence of progressive elements within it. Awaiting bourgeois participation in the national democratic revolution seems an almost criminal folly when, during Numeiri's final months, leading Sudanese businessmen held their ships, bearing petrol and other key imports needed in the desperate race to relieve Sudan's starving millions, offshore in the Red Sea in anticipation of rising prices. This is particularly important to emphasise now, because the SPLM/A has - to quote John Garang's 26-27 May 1985 broadcasts - opened up "... channels of communication "with the Trade Union Alliance and other national democratic forces, not with the aim of negotiating with "Numeiri's Second Republic", but rather to create conditions for the forces from all parts, and work-places of the country to achieve a national democratic revolution. The form these "channels of communication" take could mean the difference between victory and defeat for Sudan's democratic forces.

Note

1. The research that documents this process has been carried out by T. Ali. Aspects of the early stages are analysed in Ali (1982), (1983) and Ali and O'Brien (1984).

References

Ali Taisier (1982), The Cultivation of Hunger: Towards the Political Economy of Agricultural Development in the Sudan, 1956-1964, PhD, University of Toronto.

Ali Taisier (1983), 'The Road to Jouda', Review of African Political Economy, 26, pp. 4-14.

Ali, Taisier and O'Brien, Jay (1984), 'Labour, Community and Protest in Sudanese Agriculture', in Barker, J. (ed.), The Politics of Agriculture in Tropical Africa, Sage, Beverly Hills.

Al-Rahim, Muddathir Abd (1969), Imperialism and Nationalism in the Sudan, Clarendon Press, London.

Barnett, Tony (1977), Gezira: An Illusion of Development, Frank Cass, London.

Beshir, Mohamed Omer (1974), Revolution and Nationalism in the Sudan, Rex Collings, London.

Founou-Tchuigoua, B. (1978), 'De Facto wage-earners in the Gezira Scheme (Sudan)', Africa Development 3 (1), pp. 25-50.

Franke, Richard and Chasin, Barbara(1980), Seeds of Famine, Allenheld Osmun, Montclair, New Jersey.

Garang, John (1985), A (typescript) statement made on 26-27 May to the Sudanese People on Radio SPLA on the Second Anniversary of the Bor, Pibor & Fashalla Resistance and Ayod Revolt.

Gruenbaum, Ellen (1978), A Study of Social Services in Gezira Province, Ministry of Social Affairs, Khartoum.

Gruenbaum, Ellen (1982), Health Services, Health and Development in Sudan: The Impact of the Gezira Irrigated Scheme, PhD, University of Connecticut.

Hinderink, J. and Sterkenburg, J. (1983), 'Agricultural policy and production in Africa: The aims, the methods and the means', Journal of Modern African Studies, 21 (1).

International Labour Office (1976), Growth, Employment and Equity: A Comprehensive Strategy for Sudan, ILO, Geneva.

de Janvry, Alain (1981), The Agrarian Question & Reformism in Latin America, Johns Hopkins University Press, Baltimore.

Kursany, Ibrahim (1983), 'The role of the national bourgeoisie in the national democratic revolution', Review of African Political Economy, 26, pp. 119-23.

Mahmoud, Fatima Babiker (1983), 'Indigenous Sudanese capital - a national bourgeoisie?', Review of African Political Economy, 26, pp. 103-19.

Mahmoud, Fatima Babiker (1984), The Sudanese Bourgeoisie, Zed Press and Khartoum University Press, London and Khartoum.

O'Brien, Jay (1978), 'How traditional is 'traditional' agriculture?', Sudan Journal of Economic and Social Studies, 2 (2) pp. 1-10.

--- (1980), Agricultural Labor and Development in Sudan, PhD, University of Connecticut.

--- (1981), 'Sudan: An Arab breadbasket', MERIP Reports, 99, pp. 20-6.

--- (1983a), 'The political economy of capitalist agriculture in the central rainlands of Sudan', Labour, Capital and Society, 16 (1), pp 8-32.

--- (1983b), 'The formation of the agricultural labour force in Sudan', Review of African Political Economy, 26, pp. 15-34.

--- (1984), 'The social reproduction of tenant cultivators and class formation in the Gezira Scheme, Sudan'. In B. Isaac (ed.), Research in Economic Anthropology, Vol. 6, pp.217-41, JAI Press, Greenwich, Connecticut.

--- (1985), 'Sowing the seeds of famine: the political economy of food deficits in Sudan', Review of African Political Economy, 33, pp. 23-32.

O'Neill, Norman (1978), 'Imperialism and Class Struggle in Sudan', Race and Class, 20 (1), pp. 1-19.

--- (1980), 'Investment and Development (Sudan)', Middle-East Yearbook, pp.219-27.

--- (1983), 'Recent trends in foreign investment and uneven development in Sudan', Review of African Political Economy, 26, pp. 60-5.

Sørbø, Gunnar M. (1986), Tenants and Nomads in Eastern Sudan: A Study of Economic Adaptations in the New Halfa Scheme, Scandinavian Institute of African Studies, Uppsala.

Warburg, Gabriel (1978), Islam Nationalism and Communism in a Traditional Society, Frank Cass, London.

Woodward, Peter (1979), Condominium and Sudanese Nationalism, Barnes and Noble, New York.

2 Class and politics in the modern history of Sudan

NORMAN O'NEILL

Sudan's geographical location - between east and central Africa in the south, and its Red Sea border and the east Mediterranean further north - is reflected in a unique amalgamation of Afro-Arab culture and ethnic traits that have deep historical and symbolic significance in the contemporary political consciousness of the Sudanese. The Nile Valley nucleus of Sudanese culture had assumed autonomous shape even in neolithic times, and Sudanese history has witnessed a process of class formation and state-building for over 4,000 years. Lineal antecedents of important elements of Sudan's contemporary classes can be traced back at least to the Funj and Keira sultanates - particularly to the struggles between rising merchant classes and royal authority in the eighteenth century (see Kapteijns and Spaulding, this volume). Somewhat paradoxically these class struggles which served to define the contending social forces, and the national arena in which they came to compete, also resulted - by the closing decades of the eighteenth century - in a political fragmentation which facilitated the first modern foreign occupations of Sudan, by the Turco-Egyptian forces of Muhammed Ali. Conflict and the decline of effective central authority in Sudan disrupted its long-distance trade, most importantly the supply of slaves to the Ottoman empire. It was the resuscitation of this trade, as much as any grand imperial design, which motivated the conquest of Sudan and the consequent fusion of its Nile Valley and western social formations. This chapter traces the history of class formation and politics from the moment of this conquest, through the Mahdist revolution, the second colonial occupation by British and Egyptian forces, to the post-independence period and the fall of Numeiri's military regime in 1985.

The Turco-Egyptian Regime

Muhammed Ali, Viceroy of Egypt under Ottoman suzerainty, had two principal objectives in conquering Sudan: to seek the legendary gold-mines, and to establish control over the growing slave-trade - both of which would have accorded him a degree of independence from the sultan in Istanbul. His failure to find large deposits of gold was more than compensated for by the plentiful supply of slaves; these, combined with high levels of taxation (of which payment in slaves formed a substantial proportion) provided the economic basis upon which Muhammed Ali established his empire in the Nile Valley. It was to last from 1821, when the remaining Sinnar sultans surrendered, until 1885 when Khartoum fell to the Mahdists.

Resistance was weak, partly due to lack of unity among the tribal territories into which the Funj sultanate had fragmented, and partly because of the obvious military superiority of the two invading armies. One, commanded by Ismail, Muhammed Ali's son, swept down through the northern and central regions, overwhelming what was left of the former Funj area. The other, under Ali's son-in-law Mohamed Bey, was equally victorious in the west. The conquerors had thus completed the initial stage of their strategy: to smash the independent power of the refugee Mamluks who had fled from Egypt, and to neutralise the tribes - especially the potentially powerful Shayqiyya confederacy.

Preparation was quickly made for the exploitation of the land of its peoples. Cattle, gum arabic, hides, grain, wool, ostrich feathers, slaves and ivory were all pillaged and exported in vast quantities. Onerous taxation followed. This was of a kind more accurately described as "confiscation" (MacMichael 1932, p. 420). Taxes were seldom paid in cash - specie being rare in Sudan at this time. Instead, payment was initially demanded in the form of slaves. In areas of riverain Sudan where slave labour made an important contribution, this created a debilitating drain on the labour force. Attempts by the indigenous Sudanese to replenish it became increasingly difficult because the Turco-Egyptian forces were themselves carrying out slave-raids, and on such a large scale that entire communities were often decimated. In consequence, the resident population became increasingly unwilling, and frequently unable, to meet the incessant demand for slaves dictated by the new regime's taxation policy. Early resistance among the Sudanese to this policy led to open revolt. The death of Muhammed Ali's son near Sinnar in 1822 at the hands of rebels was, however, brutally avenged by the slaughter of over 30,000 Sudanese - almost the entire population in the vicinity.

Defeated in battle, and with their subsistence economy constantly undermined, increasing numbers of peasants flocked into the market towns. Here, craft industries emerged, but their further development was hindered by continued social disorganisation. Iron smelting in Kordofan, and experimental plantings of cotton and sugar along the Nile were similarly affected. Such regional specialisation as this in agriculture, and in manufacture, underwent considerable modification and change, but not uniformly so. The general effect of rural depopulation, however, and the increasing incidence of slave raids were to break up the traditional agricultural communities, and to force a dwindling population to seek security in the bush.

Social differentiation among and within nomadic tribes was still, in the main, based on feudal-patriarchal property relations, although it should be emphasised that the tribes were scattered over vast distances, and since the decline of Funj authority over them in the eighteenth century, politically disconnected. The powerful Baggara Arabs, and others like them in terms of military superiority, were increasingly permitted to take over from the Turco-Egyptian forces the task of seizing slaves, destined to be sold to the European, Syrian and Turkish merchants whom the regime had encouraged to settle. This increasing penetration by foreign merchants engaged in the slave trade accelerated changes in the social organisation of nomads - the clan being superseded by a form of territorially-based nomadic feudalism over which presided a warrior aristocracy (Amin 1971, pp. 105-120).

Vast regions of southern Sudan soon came under the effective control of the slave traders or their Sudanese agents, even though in 1857 the Turco-Egyptian regime had boldly proclaimed the abolition of slavery. In reality, slaving proceeded as vigorously as before. Claims of mercenaries such as Charles Gordon who, possessed of a missionary zeal, campaigned in the name of the Khedive to subjugate the native Sudanese for the ostensible purpose of suppressing the slave trade thus rang hollow. The latter task would in itself have been an onerous one had it indeed been their sole preoccupation. As it was, by the 1870s, even maintaining law and order for the Khedive proved to be beyond their available resources.

Egypt, partly as a consequence of its share in the building of the Suez Canal which opened in 1869, became increasingly dependent upon foreign creditors - especially Britain, which already by this time was contemplating its military occupation. In 1877 Gordon progressed from having been responsible for the southern regions of Sudan to the position of overall Governor General over Sudanese territory claimed by Egypt. His own increasing autonomy corresponded with a weakening of Turco-Egyptian control. The greater financial restrictions imposed on Egypt by British and French creditors further diminished its authority in Sudan and by 1880 led to the closure of several military units there. Concurrently, Egypt's foreign debt led the regime to levy an even greater tax burden on Sudan, which, however, the Turco-Egyptian forces could no longer easily enforce. British colonial manoeuvres, the threatened increased tax burden, and the long experience of Turco-Egyptian despotism, all combined to promote a large-scale revolt that was religious in form, but nationalist in content. The Mahdist uprising in Sudan beginning in 1881 coincided with British intervention in Egypt and the growing opposition to it which culminated in the Urabi revolt of 1882. This opposition - organised around the army leader Urabi Pasha - was swiftly defeated by the British armed forces, and many Urabi troops were exiled to Sudan where, ironically, some of them joined up with the Mahdists to oppose foreign domination.

British policy, which the British government expected Gordon to implement (although he was nominally not acting as an Agent of the British government) was to negotiate Sudan's separation from Egypt, and possibly - in the light of subsequent events - to envisage the southern regions as an integral part of a British East Africa Federation (Oliver & Fage 1966, pp. 189). Though there is some doubt that the British had worked out a coherent strategy by this time, it is clear that Britain itself had no intention of financing a large-scale war against the Mahdi, and soon recognised that Egypt alone could not at this time provide the necessary resources. Hicks' defeat in 1883 at Sheikhan, south of El Obeid, was sufficient to convince the British that withdrawal was the most expedient option then available. Evacuation was therefore anticipated, and Gordon was expected to execute it. This Gordon refused to do, at the ultimate expense of his own life when the Mahdist forces completed their revolution with the taking of Khartoum in 1885.

The retention of Egypt became the central plank around which Britain was to handle its side of Africa's partition during the decisive years from 1886 to 1892. Certainly Baring (later Lord Cromer) - Britain's agent, and, as Consul-General in Cairo, the effective ruler of Egypt - assumed that Gordon would carry out the evacuation from Sudan as soon as possible. But the impetuous Gordon was to reply:

> I declare positively and once and for all that I will not leave the Sudan until everyone who wants to go down is given the chance to do so, unless a government is established which relieves me of the charge; therefore if any emissary or letter come up here ordering me to come down, I will not obey it, but will stay here and fall with the town and run all risks (Nutting 1967, p. 247).

So it was to be. When offered recognition merely as the sultan of Kordofan, not surprisingly the Mahdi indignantly rejected it, and in turning down any comparable deal with Gordon, prepared for battle. Gordon responded by calling for Indian troops to be sent to Sudan to "smash the Mahdi." The British House of Commons did not, at first, share Gordon's enthusiasm for further military adventures, but after much prevarication and a public outcry, Gladstone's government finally agreed to send a relief expedition. It arrived too late. News of the advance induced the national forces to attack Khartoum before the steamers arrived at their destination. All plans to save Gordon had failed. Instead, he and his forces fell victim in 1885 to Muhammed Ahmed, the proclaimed Mahdi (literally "saviour") whose Islamic state was to last for thirteen years.

The Mahdiya

The initial religious basis of the Mahdist movement was the Sammaniya, a sufist tariqa (religious brotherhood) brought to Sudan in the 1770s from Arabia. Similar tariqas had thrived towards the end of the eighteenth century, and were frequently built around the charisma of sufi fakis (religious men) some of whom led exemplary lives of austere asceticism while others of them put themselves in a position to engage in primitive accumulation - either as a result of dues paid to them by their followers, or through the acquisition of land. During the Funj period some fakis had received land grants. Their tariqas sometimes came to form the organisational basis for resistance to foreign domination. It is therefore not surprising that the Turco-Egyptian regime sought to diminish their status and influence, and sought to replace them by an official religious hierarchy centred on Cairo. In consequence, the Mahdiya has frequently been interpreted - in part - as a "... vehicle of protest by the indigenous and traditional Islamic leadership against the regime which had diminished their status," and more specifically as "a revolt of the fakis" whose leader "... very appropriately" was "... a holy man who had undergone the traditional education of the Sudan" (Holt 1967, p. 10). Mohamed Omer Beshir expresses it thus: "The Mahdist state was a continuation of that tradition of Sudanese national states which had existed in the Sudan since the days of Meroe and was only disrupted during the sixty years of Turco-Egyptian rule" (Beshir 1974, p. 15).

Not all the tariqas had opposed the regime (Trimmingham 1949). The Khatmiya, who were brought to Sudan in 1816, became closely associated with the Turco-Egyptian rulers who practised the same kind of divide-and-rule tactics later adopted by the British. The Khatmiya was to flourish under Turco-Egyptian rule, and it developed intimate ties with the official religious hierarchy (Beshir 1974, p. 13).

The Mahdi advocated a unified, non-sectarian Islamic state based on the Koran, preached Sufi asceticism (a devout life with few material comforts) and proclaimed a jihad (holy war) in defence of Islam and against corruption. The Sammaniya and other tariqas were to be merged into one true Islam, and the Mahdi and the adherents were dubbed the 'Ansar' or Helpers. Thomas Hodgkin (1971, p. 110) has suggested that Mahdism was "... particularly appropriate for 'the oppressed' in situations in which they have not only become conscious of oppression but are willing to respond to a movement which seems to offer a way out," and in quoting Lanternari, 'If the present belongs to the oppressors, the future belongs to us, the revolutionary community and outside the community there is no salvation and no future,' but unlike other ideologies, it develops in "... societies which have been fairly effectively Islamised over a period of time," and in which there exist an established body of Mahdist belief (ibid).

These beliefs reflect a recurrent and potent myth of Islam, which grows out of the division in Arab society between petty-commodity producers and merchants on the one hand, and bedouin nomads on the other. The former inhabit towns, grow relatively prosperous, become increasingly secular, and develop the sophisticated characteristics of urban civilization, while the latter remain relatively poor, cherish fundamental religious doctrine, lack sophistication, and maintain the austerity typical of life in the desert. It therefore frequently falls upon nomads to re-establish the true faith, under the leadership of a prophet or Mahdi, in purging Islam of corruption and religious deviation. The significance of Muhammed Ahmed was that his movement occurred during a period of foreign domination - with the Islamic but 'corrupt' Turco-Egyptian regime and Christian mercenaries like Gordon both being identified as the infidel. The result was that Mahdism in Sudan - unlike similar messianic movements elsewhere in Islam - drew enthusiastic support from peasants and disprivileged indigenous traders as well as nomads and became a national liberation movement. Its influence on the Egyptian masses was immediate, and soon evoked sympathy from within the ranks of the Egyptian army. Collaboration followed. A total of 53,000 Egyptian troops participated in battles in Sudan; 11,000 returned home; 12,000 were killed during Hicks' expedition; 30,000 remained. Of these, Wingate estimates that some 40 per cent were killed in battle (Wingate 1968, p. 353). Those remaining either joined up with the Mahdists or were scattered all over Sudan: some 18,000 troops - 60 per cent - therefore deserted en masse.

Many of the Nilotes of Bahr el Ghazal and Upper Nile also fought against the occupation, engaging in what may have been a tactical collaboration - Dinka chieftains having met with the Mahdi at Gebel-Gedir (Holt 1958, p. 70), although it remains uncertain as to what extent any explicit agreement was reached in regard to their political independence, and on the subject of slavery. But Smirnov quotes some evidence which does indeed suggest that the Mahdi sought to punish those who disobeyed an order not to seize slaves from among the Dinka (Smirnov 1974, p. 74), and later confidently declares:

> The Mahdi ... treated the Nilotic tribes of the South as allies in the fight for the complete liberation of the Sudan. He signed a number of decrees which strictly forbade the subjects of the Mahdist state to hunt for slaves among the Nilotes (Smirnov 1974, p. 74).

The aforementioned contrast between a sedentary population and bedouin tribesmen soon found ideological expression in an internal conflict among Mahdist supporters. The Mahdi's relatives represented the settled riverain Arabs whose economic ambitions and privileged position were to be disavowed by the Mahdi himself (Holt 1974, p. 92). His death, following an attack of typhus on 22 June 1885, occasioned a struggle for succession in which Abdallahi ibn Muhammad, leader of the Taaisha section of the feudal, slave-owning Baggara nomads, became supreme Khalifa. As head of these nomad warriors, the Khalifa Abdallahi undoubtedly conceived that he was re-enacting the drama of early Islam. Thousands of Baggara Arabs migrated from Kordofan and Darfur to Omdurman, the newly-created capital of the Mahdiya. They occupied newly-built houses in the vicinity of the Khalifa's court, established there a citadel, settled on the most fertile lands, and took over the best pastures for their horses and cattle. The state which they came to dominate was theocratic and centralised. By appointing Baggara nobles as deputies to the governors and commanders in all regions of Sudan and then gradually usurping their authority through these agents the Khalifa attempted to establish a national feudal aristocracy as his power base. Nevertheless, increased trade, prompted by a war economy that had stimulated the manufacture of gun-powder and cartridges, boots, shoes and clothing for the military, in addition to spears, swords and saddles, did serve to transform relations of production, and led to the introduction of a national currency. Trade in salt from Berber, grain from the Gezira, dates from Dongola and gum-arabic from Kordofan all seem to have developed correspondingly - but intermittent drought, cholera and malaria severely curtailed any possibility of sustained economic growth and accumulation. So did warfare.

Throughout its turbulent and short life, the Mahdiya was constantly at war: first with the Turco-Egyptian armies in 1885-6 (and again in 1891), then with the Ethiopians and Darfur sultanate between 1887-9, with the (British-supported) Italians in 1893-4, and with the Belgians in 1894. It is, therefore, not surprising that manufacture was restricted to small workshops - including a lithographic printing house, a mint, and of course an ammunition factory. The Anglo-Egyptian embargo also limited trade, but did in some degree serve to stimulate domestic textile production, once the importation of manufactured cotton goods from Egypt had ceased. Even so, despite all the enormous difficulties, the Mahdists were able to extend their administration - through a series of tribal alliances - to lay the foundation of the modern Sudanese nation.

In the European scramble for Africa, control of the Nile waters became a British colonial priority - especially once plans were made to expand cotton plantations in Egypt and in response to France's vision of a vast empire linking the Mediterranean, the Atlantic and the Indian Ocean (Oliver & Fage 1966, p. 190). A French occupation of the upper Nile would have threatened British interests in Egypt; and French troops were already converging on Lake Chad from the Congo, Algeria, and the upper Niger.

In 1896 the new Egyptian army - trained by Kitchener and under his command - began its southward advance. Sudan was in the throes of famine. Vast areas between Mongalla and Berber became depopulated; in the region near Shendi many had died of starvation, and the populations of Gallabat, Gedaref and Kassala were drastically reduced.

The Sudanese - literally - had no stomach for battle. They were finally defeated by the vastly superior firing power of the Anglo-Egyptian troops at Omdurman in 1898. At least twenty thousand Sudanese were slaughtered in the re-conquest: "The partition of Africa, as it approached its logical conclusion, was beginning to be a bloody business" (Oliver & Fage 1966, p. 192).

A week after the battle of Omdurman Kitchener was informed of Marchand's presence at Fashoda, and immediately confronted him with a vastly superior force. This - the "Fashoda incident" - brought France and Britain to the brink of war. Diplomacy prevailed. To prevent France's possible claims to Sudan, the British signed a "Condominium" agreement with Egypt that nominally placed Sudan under joint Anglo-Egyptian rule but in reality accorded Britain political domination.

The Anglo-Egyptian Condominium

Supreme military and civil authority was vested in the Governor-General - a nominee of the British. Nothing was said in the Condominium Agreement about the nationality of those holding the post, but it is a fact that all Governors-General from 1899 to 1955 were British subjects. The same can be said of the Provincial Governors and District Commissioners. The Agreement was also silent on the legal position of the two conquering powers - another feature which undoubtedly accorded the British considerable scope for diplomatic manoeuvre. If Britain's presence in Sudan was questioned by either France, Belgium or Italy, it could always be claimed that the British Government was acting on behalf of the Khedive. Similarly, if Egyptian nationalists objected they could always be reminded of Britain's role in the reconquest, and rebuked by the comment that "... the Mahdia was the direct consequence of sixty years of Egyptian oppression of the Sudanese" (Holt 1961, p. 111).

After Abdullahi's death in 1899 all co-ordinated resistance to foreign domination ceased, although local uprisings were common - especially in the South, including rebellions by the Nuer and Zande in 1901, the Dinka in 1919 and the Nuer again in the late 1920s. Piecemeal uprisings in the North were contained and undermined by the much improved communications infrastructure - particularly railways the British built on the basis of military requirement rather than economic criteria. By December 1899 Kitchener's military railway had been converted to civilian use, and extended to the Blue Nile opposite Khartoum, where the town of Khartoum North was soon to develop. The railways also created other towns such as Atbara and Port Sudan. These possessed enormous long-term economic and political significance, especially the new port because it made Sudan far less dependent on the trade route through Egypt.

In the years that immediately followed, the railway was taken to Khartoum, and thence southward through the Gezira to Sinnar, and from there westward across the White Nile to reach El Obeid in 1911. Concurrently, the British colonial regime was laying the foundations of what was to become a classic example of distorted and uneven economic development, through a dependency on cotton monoculture. It was the Manchester textile manufacturers organised through the British Cotton Growing Association (BCGA), who became the prime force behind this massive enterprise of primitive accumulation. Competition from the United States, Germany and China - especially at the coarser end of the trade - had induced Lancashire to specialise increasingly in fine cotton manufacture. This, however, required the longer staple varieties of cotton that were then grown only in Egypt, the United States, and, to a lesser extent, in Peru. Sudan was, therefore, conceived as an alternative source of supply - and one which could be controlled directly through a British colonial administration. In Egypt, high burdens of taxation had tended to drive the hard-pressed fellahin off the land. The British had no intention of witnessing a similar occurrence in Sudan.

The Development of the Colonial Export Economy

Only by divorcing the peasants from ownership or use of the land could the colonial administration force them to sell their labour power for low incomes. This was achieved in part through a series of Land Ordinances (1899, 1905 and 1921) in which legal sanction was given to what amounted to expropriation. Former peasant proprietors became tenants, forced to grow cotton on half their tenancies (Barnett 1977; Tait, this volume). Through this process of consolidation tens of thousands of Sudanese peasants were forced into the system of commodity production. They were told when, how and where to grow the cotton, under a system of inspection that resembled an enormous factory conveyor belt. The long-staple cotton was subsequently prepared for export to Lancashire - where manufacturers were able to maintain a competitive edge over their competitors in the United States and Germany.

The potential for cotton plantations in Sudan had been ascertained through the success of Leigh Hunt, an American entrepreneur, who in 1906, had begun experiments in cotton production with capital and land acquired through the British regime. The initial success of the cotton-growing experiments - particularly from 1911-14 - had prompted a loan of £13 million from the British exchequer to the so-called Sudan Government, as part of the project to dam the Blue Nile at Sinnar in order to irrigate a large portion of the eastern Gezira. Subsequent irrigation was facilitated by the favourable land-slope - from south to north and east to west - that enabled a large area to receive water by gravity-feed from a single dam. This process ultimately led to the formation of the Sudan Plantations Syndicate, which eventually came to manage the largest gravity-irrigated cotton plantation in the world - the famous Gezira Scheme. This scheme effectively "... sealed the bonds of Sudanese dependency on a cotton monoculture" (Collins 1976, p. 10). It also represented the most advanced agricultural area, in which migrant workers from other areas became employed as seasonal workers, receiving subsistence wages (see O'Brien, this volume). The fact that many of these workers were of a different ethnic origin from the mostly Arab tenants who employed them had, and continues to have, enormous ideological and political significance, in that it tends to disguise their increasingly uniform class interests (see Duffield, this volume).

In 1924, Huddleston, the Governor of the Blue Nile province, argued that:

> For any large extension of the Gezira Irrigated Scheme an assured supply of casual labour up to 50,000 men will be required. Local sources of supply will by then have been largely eliminated, and reliance will have to be placed on some Sudan source of supply, for example, the Nuba mountains, or the

greatly increased body of West African pilgrims (quoted in Duffield 1981, from National Records Office, Khartoum, Blue Nile Province, 1.25.176 f.10).

Between 1929 and 1932, effects of the global recession combined with cotton blights to produce crisis in Gezira. Many tenants abandoned their plots, thereby exacerbating the difficulties. An important aspect of the British response was to encourage settlement of West African immigrants, including assignment of vacated tenancies to some of them (Duffield 1981; O'Brien 1980, 1984). By 1936 the total number of Westerners in the Gezira Scheme was 28,300, of whom 8,000 were settled West Africans (Hassoun 1952, p. 84). Two decades later the governor of the same province expressed quite different sentiments, and the Civil Secretary was to order that there should be no mass applications of westerners for citizenship. These migrant workers were - in legal terms - defined as the tenants' wage-labour, but in essence, the income of both was in large measure derived from labour on behalf of capital, inasmuch as each group was effectively employed by the Sudan Plantations Syndicate (O'Neill 1978, p. 14). Thus, although the syndicate defined its relations with the tenants in terms of a "partnership," the reality was far different. Contracts enabled the syndicate to reduce the income of the tenants for "improper crop cultivation," without their consent, and although it was obliged to provide sufficient water for irrigation, tenants could not claim compensation when it failed.

Although the Gezira Scheme was beset by problems of cotton blight, labour shortage and the world depression in its early years, it proved very profitable to its investors and the government over the 25-yearspan of the SPS concession (1925-50). In assessing data examined by Gaitskell, Taha and Beshai, O'Brien concludes that:

> From the point of view of capital and the colonial government,the Gezira Scheme was an enormous success. The fixed capital investment, which totalled £15 million, or an average of £15 per irrigated feddan, had been remarkably small for such a vast enterprise ... (and) the government was able to amass a cumulative surplus of over £16 million on its direct Gezira share after debt service by 1950. Moreover from 1925 to 1956 cotton exports represented about 70% of Sudan's export earnings, over 80% of which came from Gezira. The total profits to the SPS (Sudan Plantation Syndicate) by 1950 also exceeded £16 million, with average annual dividends to its shareholders of 15% plus a capital profit of 25 shillings on every 20 invested upon liquidation and distribution of reserves (O'Brien 1980, pp.81-2).

The economic planning and organisation for the success of the Gezira scheme obviously required far more sophistication than was accorded by a purely military regime. Even so, martial law was in force until 1926. MacMichael describes the period as "autocracy on military lines for civil purposes" (MacMichael 1932, p. 108). This autocracy consisted of the Governor-General and his senior army officers, with Egyptian personnel in subordinate ranks, and an elite core of English district officials who formed the prestigious "Sudan

Political Service."

Colonial Administration and Resistance

Neutralisation of the religious sects was considered a military and political priority. Uprisings - often in the name of some aspirant Mahdi or "Nebi Isa" - were common features of the time, and even though in retrospect these may seem to have been insignificant, much the same had been thought, initially, about Muhammad Ahmad. It is therefore not surprising that the British took them very seriously indeed. They were also fearful that entry of the Ottoman Empire into the War on the German side (in November 1914) would undermine British authority over a Muslim population. Consequently, plans were made in 1915 to conquer the remaining independent sultanate of Darfur. These were finally executed in 1916 on the preposterous pretext that Sultan Ali Dinar was about to raid, if not to invade, Sudan (Holt 1974, p. 126).

Against the defeated Ansar sect, the Anglo-Egyptian administration at first favoured followers of the Khatmiya, whose political influence was later to grow in proportion to their accumulated wealth. Their developing economic strength lay in retail trade and the trade with Egypt, and was based mainly in the northern and eastern regions. These merchants constituted an embryonic commercial bourgeoisie. They were also a potential source of Arab nationalism. Their identification with nationalist resistance in Egypt in 1919 prompted the British to rehabilitate their mutual arch-enemy, the Ansar. Abdel Rahman el Mahdi, posthumous son of the Mahdi and spiritual leader of the Ansar, was granted lucrative contracts in connection with construction of the Sinnar dam and was subsequently given a licence to cultivate cotton on his 39,000 acre estate on Aba Island in the White Nile. In consequence, the Mahdi family re-emerged as a semi-feudal landed aristocracy which - in contrast to the Khatmiya slogan "Unity of the Nile" - later advocated Sudanese independence from Egypt as a means of safeguarding their economic interests. Britain continued to play off one sect against the other. It had also continued its manoeuvres in Egypt, where events were again to prove crucial for the political future of Sudan. Holt expresses it accordingly:

> As the Urabist revolution in Egypt had synchronized with the spontaneous Mahdist movement in the Sudan, so the revival of militant Egyptian nationalism after the First World War coincided with, and stimulated, the beginning of Sudanese nationalism (Holt 1972, pp. 129-30).

Its first leader of significance was Ali Abd Al-Latif, of Dinka origin, who formed the Sudanese United Tribes Society in 1921, and the first nationalist document - entitled "The Claims of the Sudanese Nations" - was published in the following year.

Ali Abd Al-Latif was promptly arrested, but after his release formed the White Flag League in 1924. His political perspectives had undergone a significant change. The League sought not an independent Sudan, separate from Egypt, but unity of the Nile Valley - freed from the British, and under the Egyptian monarchy. These contrasting political perspectives - between a Sudan fully independent of Egypt and one in which some form of integration was envisaged - continued to divide the nationalist movement, and each position at different times has received sympathetic support ever since. Their close association with the aforementioned tariqas and the different economic interests of those who formed their leaderships were also to shape the political alliances through support received from either Britain or Egypt. The latter's support for the White Flag League gave rise to much concern by the British, particularly after the June 1924 demonstrations in Omdurman and Khartoum, and even more so in August when an armed parade in the capital by the cadets of the Military School coincided with a mutiny of the Egyptian railway battalion stationed at Atbara. All these disturbances were brutally suppressed. The assassination in Cairo on 19 November 1924 of Lee Stack - the Governor-General of Sudan - accorded Britain the opportunity to evacuate Egyptian forces from Sudan. Troops of the 11th Sudanese battalion mutinied in solidarity with the Egyptians, and barricaded themselves in Khartoum's military hospital. The mutineers fought to the last man.

These events mark the turning point in the history of the Condominium. The pretence that Britain ruled Sudan in partnership with Egypt could no longer be seriously sustained - even though the Egyptian flag continued to be flown alongside the Union Jack and the King of Egypt nominally confirmed the appointments of British Governors-General. In the words of Muddathir Abd Al-Rahim, henceforth:

> ... relations between the Government and the small class of educated Sudanese,who were now seen as the collective enemy of the British, deteriorated rapidly and a period of intense bitterness began which lasted well into the thirties and was much aggravated by the Depression and the consequent retrenchment of salaries (Al-Rahim 1969, p. 65).

The departure of Egyptian civilian intermediaries, and Sudanese replacements of doubtful reliability, prompted the British to institute a system of Indirect Rule through the agency of tribal shaykhs and chieftains. This had already been tried, with success, among nomadic tribes. After 1927 it was to include settled communities, and as Sir James Currie was to comment "... the spectacle could be beheld of young administrators diligently searching for lost tribes and vanished chiefs, and trying to resurrect a social system that had passed away for ever" (Currie 1935, p. 49). Smirnov describes the result as "at once the conservation and artificial reconstruction of obsolescent social relations" (Smirnov 1974, p. 30). This description is not in the least far-fetched. The introduction of "Native Administration" in the North corresponded with the new "Southern Policy" - the principal objective of which was to prevent the spread of Islam and Arab influence in the southern region. The result was an even greater economic isolation of the southern provinces.

The British went to quite bizarre lengths to implement this policy of isolation. This is epitomised in a much-quoted instruction to Greek and other merchants from the District Commissioner at Bahr El Ghazal:

> I notice that in spite of frequent requests to the contrary, large quantities of 'Arab' clothing are still being made and sold. Please note that in future, it is FORBIDDEN to make or sell such clothes. Shirts should be made short with a collar and opening down the front in the European fashion and NOT an open neck as worn by the Baggara of Darfur. Also tagias (i.e. skull caps) as worn by Arabs to wind emmas (i.e. turbans) round are not to be sold in future. No more Arab clothing is to be made as from today: you are given till the end of February to dispose of your present stock. This order applies to all outside agents and owners of sewing machines (Beshir 1970, p. 52).

Henceforth, Southerners were discouraged from seeking work in the North, and those among them who had been given Muslim names, and who spoke Arabic, were induced to adopt their Christian equivalents and to speak English instead. Correspondingly, people in the South of Egyptian, northern Sudanese or West African descent were deported from the area, while a stringent system of permits and the "Closed Districts Ordinance" were designed to keep others out. Similarly with education; while it was curtailed in the North because educated Northerners were perceived as a political threat, in the South Christian missionary schools were encouraged as a means of combating Islam and the wider influence of Arab culture. These policies of divide and rule served to exacerbate North-South enmity, and in some measure contributed to the subsequent demands by Southerners for Southern separatism or independence.

The "Closed Districts" included Darfur, Bahr El Ghazal, Mongalla and Upper Nile, almost all of Kordofan, and parts of Halfa, Dongola and Kassala. They amounted to over 700,000 square miles (i.e. about two thirds of the country's area) and involved over half the population. Trade was strictly regulated, migration prohibited - unless special permission to travel had been obtained - and commerce was severely curtailed. The result was that a variety of pre-capitalist modes of production prevailed in all but the economically dominant regions of Khartoum, the Blue Nile Province and Gezira.

Frankel estimated that by 1936 foreign investment in Sudan (most of it British) had amounted to £43,352,000 - over half of which (£26,565,000) had gone into the construction of the railways, river and sea transport, and the Gezira scheme (Frankel 1938, pp. 158-9). The dynamics of this process of uneven economic development soon led to its description in terms of a dual economy consisting of an advanced modern sector in contrast to the backward traditional sectors that existed elsewhere. The policy of the "Closed Districts" therefore served to deepen and widen this familiar contrast.

The failure of the British even to consult the educated Sudanese (many of whom had graduated from Gordon College) about the legal status of the occupation which had received ratification in the

Anglo-Egyptian Treaty of 1936 prompted the formation of the Graduates' Congress two years later. The idea is believed to have been formulated initially by the Wad Medani Literary Society - one of the many that flourished as vehicles of legal political expression (Al-Rahim 1969, p. 125). The Secretary of the Congress was Isma'il al-Azhari, the descendant of a family of religious notables, and a mathematics teacher at Gordon College. Its title was inspired by the Indian Congress, and there is no doubt that Gandhi's advocacy of non-violent protest had a significant influence on some of the younger Sudanese nationalists at the time. The aims of the Congress as stated in its constitution were deliberately vague and seemingly innocuous: "to serve the public interest of the country and the graduates". Graduates included all former pupils of Sudanese schools above the elementary level, and - as a means of widening the circle of participation (which was undoubtedly part of the nationalist strategy) - those "Sudanese educated elsewhere," subject to the approval of the Executive Committee.

The British reaction was one of caution. Colonial officers recognised the Congress, but only on the understanding that it was "a semi-public organisation interested in philanthropic and public affairs and competent to hold and express opinions on such matters as come within its purview" (Henderson 1953, pp. 536-7). It was not to seek recognition as a political assembly, and not to claim that it represented any but its own members. The Second World War presented the Congress with an opportunity to contest these limitations. In 1942 it submitted a Memorandum demanding the abolition of the Closed Districts, unification of school syllabuses in North and South, and a declaration from the British that they would grant Sudan the right of self-government immediately after the war. The authorities refused to acknowledge the Memorandum, but in 1943 launched an Advisory Council for the North, and then in 1948 a Legislative Assembly for the country as a whole. In the meantime, Mahdist and Khatmiya-affiliated graduates split over strategies for independence. Khatmiya supporters (calling again for "Unity of the Nile valley") formed the Ashiqqa (Blood Brothers) Party in 1943, which was the forerunner of the 1952 National Unionist Party (NUP), and in 1945 the Mahdists (whose slogan was "Sudan for the Sudanese") formed the Umma (People's) Party.

After the Second World War Sudan's indigenous entrepreneurs were few, and in many cases dependent on foreign capital. Other nascent capitalists had invested in the privately-owned irrigated schemes along the Niles. Among these were rich merchants, leaders of the *tariqas* (or religious sects) and tribal shaykhs. Increasingly, they were able to consolidate their economic strength and came to express their developing class interests through the political parties that came to dominate the political scene at the time of independence. Corresponding to the emergence of these indigenous capitalists was the growing number of wage workers in the factories, on the farms and in transport - particularly on the railways, where the newly-created Sudanese Communist Party (SCP) was soon able to establish a strong industrial base among the 20,000 workers concentrated at Atbara and in Khartoum.

The colonial regime was reluctant to recognise the Workers'

Affairs Association (which was created in 1947 - the same year as the Sudanese Communist Party) because it feared the political implications of a militant labour movement. It had cause to fear such a movement, as subsequent events were to prove. A nation-wide railway strike in 1947 brought the WAA the recognition it demanded, and in 1949 it forged links with other workers through the Workers Affairs Congress, which in the following year became the Sudan Workers Trade Union Federation. This, the colonial regime would not recognise. Labour legislation - built up since 1946 - focussed mainly on conditions of employment, but it did acknowledge the right of workers to form individual trade unions. The Sudan Government was unwilling to extend such recognition to a federation of unions, and in 1951 refused the formal application for legal registration. This was interpreted by the unions as an abrogation of the spirit, if not the letter, of existing legislation, and they saw in it an ominous attempt to erode trade union rights. Political confrontation with the regime therefore became increasingly more likely, and in December 1951 the Federation amended its constitution to include political action. This was undoubtedly a victory for the SCP, whose members were determined to break down the institutionalised division between politics and trade-unionism that was, and is, a characteristic of the British model of industrial relations, and which the colonial regime sought to import into Sudan (Fawzi 1957).

The Federation adopted a firm anti-colonialist perspective. Encouraged by the unilateral abrogation of the Condominium Agreement by Egypt in October 1951 it eventually proposed a united front to fight for genuine economic self-determination. The response was almost immediate. The newly-created Anti-Imperialist Front included the SCP, the SWTUF, the Unionist Parties (NUP and others that called for unity with Egypt), the Students' Union, tenant farmers' associations, and the Sudanese Women's Union (which had been formed as early as 1946). In the ensuing months the Federation played a leading role in the nationalist struggle, but its influence was severely diminished as a result of the July 1952 Revolution in Egypt and its opposition to the Anglo-Egyptian Agreement of 1953.

The new regime in Egypt had declared its support for Sudanese autonomy, thereby undermining Britain's persistent claim that its continued presence was justified in terms of preventing a "unity with Egypt" which many Sudanese clearly opposed. Now - ostensibly - there was no formal diplomatic dispute. Both Britain and Egypt were each prepared to support Sudanese independence, and this prospect was incorporated in the agreement. It accorded the Sudanese the right of self-determination within three years, and as part of the preparations provided for the early evacuation of all British and Egyptian troops, and the Sudanisation of the police and civil service. Elections, supervised by an international commission, resulted in a victory for the National Unionist Party, whose leader, Ismail El Azhari, became the first Sudanese Prime Minister in January 1954.

The Mahdists - fearing that Azhari might still seek unity with Egypt - staged a massive demonstration at the official opening of Parliament on 1 March. In consequence, the scheduled ceremony - at which several people lost their lives - had to be postponed. Civil war in the North was therefore a serious possibility, and it became increasingly obvious that full political independence would serve to avert it. The South presented a more intractable problem. In late July, 300 Southern workers had been dismissed from the cotton factory in Nzara. Demonstrations ensued, in which the army shot at least twenty people. The following month the Southern Corps of the army mutinied, after rumours that it was to be disarmed and sent to the North. Further confrontations took place, and eight thousand Northern troops were airlifted to the South. Order was temporarily restored, but the political problem of integration - which had undoubtedly been exacerbated by Britain's Southern Policy - continued to bedevil all attempts to forge national unity. Before being prepared to vote for independence, Southern Members of Parliament insisted on an undertaking that their request for a federal form of government be given full consideration. This was agreed, and on 19 December 1955 Parliament unanimously declared Sudan an independent republic. It also resolved that a five-person committee exercise the powers of Head of State in place of the Governor-General. Full political independence was formally celebrated on 1 January 1956.

Independence and Crisis

Political independence could neither immediately remedy nor ideologically obfuscate Sudan's economic dependence on cotton - whose sharply declining prices on the world market in the years immediately following independence were to curtail government revenue severely. Furthermore, expenditure on social services, education (including the University College of Khartoum, which soon acquired independent status as a University), and extensions to the railway network south of Sinnar and west to Darfur, and the initial stages of the Managil extension to the Gezira Scheme - all contributed to an immediate drain on financial resources. In consequence, it soon became obvious that development plans for the first five years could never be paid for out of anticipated revenue.

The improbable Mahdist-Khatmiya coalition, led by Abdalla Khalil, which replaced Azhari's NUP shortly after independence came under increasing political strain, especially when Khalil sought American aid - which the Khatmiya-inspired People's Democratic Party had largely opposed - to make up for shortfalls in revenue.

The 1958 elections resulted in no appreciable change in the character of the coalition. Disaffected sections of the PDP had joined forces with the SCP, the SWTUF and Gezira tenants to demand - through a National Front - that the aid agreement be rejected. This temporarily united the Umma-PDP coalition against communists, militant students and trade unionists, but it was soon to dissolve through Saddiq al-Mahdi's attempted alliance with Azhari's NUP. Out of the ensuing quagmire came General Abboud's military junta of November 1958 - invited by Umma leaders to take control when they were unable to impose their will through parliamentary means. The military regime immediately arrested known communists and their sympathisers, brought their leaders before the courts, suspended the trade unions and imprisoned the leaders of the SWTUF. By 1960 union membership had been reduced by an average of at least 25 per cent, but even under these very difficult circumstances, wage demands were presented, and industrial struggles (mainly on the railways) became a focus of anti-government protest. In 1963 the junta itself sponsored a trade union conference in a manoeuvre aimed to contain industrial unrest, only to precipitate a spate of resolutions demanding an end to military rule. Similarly, attempts to control the Gezira tenants met with failure, in so far as their economic demands were eventually conceded.

Sections of the bourgeoisie were more supportive of the regime. General Abboud's expressed intention, after all, had been to restore political stability, as a pre-condition for economic development, and in this he was also to receive a degree of support from the two Sayyids, al-Mahdi and al-Mirghani. In terms of foreign policy the regime guaranteed to honour existing international commitments, pledged stronger links with other African and Arab states, emphasised its desire to improve relations with Egypt and Ethiopia, and accorded China full diplomatic recognition. But the most significant achievement of the military regime was the negotiation of a new Nile Waters Agreement in 1959 which made a larger share of the water available for expanded irrigation of cotton - still the basis of accumulation for the agrarian bourgeoisie.

Economic policy was to encourage diversification, but the legacy of Sudan's colonial past - in the form of Gezira and the pump schemes - rendered the 1962 Ten-Year Plan over-ambitious. The country was, and remained, dependent for its surplus revenue on cotton - whose fluctuating price was dictated by the vicissitudes of the world market. Various attempts to counter this market imperative, through a system of minimum price fixing, had been abandoned in 1959, and with some positive results. Part of the accumulated cotton crop backlog was subsequently reduced, and by the early 1960s government budgets were showing a surplus. This undoubtedly increased confidence, and encouraged further diversification. The government encouraged import substitution schemes, with match, soap, beer and glass factories being established. Textile production was also stimulated, and factories planned. Agricultural and Industrial Banks were set up to provide credit for farmers and entrepreneurs, loans sought from various international institutions, and aid was received from both the United States and the Soviet Union.

Much of this finance contributed towards the completion of the Managil extension, and the construction of the Roseires Dam on the Blue Nile and the Khashm al-Girba Dam on the Atbara. The latter was to irrigate land for the resettlment of the residents of Wadi Halfa whose ancient town had been submerged as a consequence of the new High Dam at Aswan (see Dafalla 1975). The Nile Waters Agreement was to provide Sudan with £S15 million in compensation - a figure,however, that fell far short of the £S26 million spent in resettlement. Sudan's water allocation amounted to 18,500,000,000 cubic metres, compared to Egypt's 55,000,000,000. Whatever prestige accrued to the signing of this agreement the domestic political costs were high, and had long-term repercussions because the grievances expressed by the Nubians involved "formed a rallying-point for opposition to the regime" (Holt & Daly 1979, p. 174).

Another source of discontent was rising inflation. Economic growth, in real terms, was reduced to less than zero, and by 1964 there was a £S214 million accumulated deficit in the balance of payments. Exacerbating these financial difficulties was the incessant drain on economic resources caused by the recurrent fighting in the South. Britain had left Sudan in the throes of civil war, and neither the civilian government nor the military regime was able to negotiate an agreeable settlement. Indeed, successive northern politicians relied on the tactic of taking advantage of tribal rivalries in the South, just as the British had, in order to maintain political control. This, combined with continued exclusion of educated Southerners from the civil service and other forms of racial discrimination, served to deepen Southern suspicions of Northern intentions.

Southern politicians had supported the concept of a united Sudan at the Juba conference of 1947, but, confronted by the Umma and PDP threat to establish an Islamic republic, it was not surprising that many of them began to advocate regional autonomy, or even separation. These politicians were mostly Christians, the products of an anti-Muslim and anti-Communist missionary education. So were the non-commissioned army officers, and many of the Southern troops who became the backbone of the 1955 mutiny. Their political propensities were to undergo no significant change, and in view of the subsequent behaviour of most Northern politicians, this is hardly surprising. Of the 800 or so positions vacated by the British, only 6 had been offered to Southerners, even though they made up a quarter of Sudan's total population.

Most of the southern Equatoria Corps that mutinied in 1955 fled into the bush to prepare for guerrilla war. They emerged in 1963 as the Anyanya ('snake-venom') secessionist movement. Once again "the South" was to become the central issue in Sudanese politics. In open defiance of military regulations, students at the University of Khartoum called a public meeting in October 1964 to debate the "Southern Question". The army intervened, shooting dead one student and injuring 31 others in the mass demonstrations that followed. The tactic of the general strike - which since 1961 had been advocated by the SCP - was adopted by all sections of the urban population, including students and academics, the Medical and Bar associations, the judiciary, as well as the SCP-influenced railway workers, and in the rural areas by the Gezira tenants. It was an enormous success. When troops and junior officers themselves plotted rebellion, the fate of the regime was sealed.

The October Revolution of 1964 and its Aftermath

General Abboud announced the dissolution of the Supreme Council and the resignation of the Cabinet on 26 October. Public celebration followed, but this could not "mask the difficulties facing the improvised Transitional Government, a coalition of mutually antagonistic groups" (Holt & Daly 1979, p. 183). The new coalition included representatives of the Umma, NUP, PDP and Muslim Brotherhood, but it was politically dominated by a strong Communist element in the leadership of the Professionals' Front and the Labour movement. In consequence, the SWTUF was re-established, and several unions were formed in the private sector. Fearing increased Communist influence the traditional parties began a counter-offensive, culminating in a huge demonstration of Ansar supporters who moved into the capital. Unwilling and unable to defend itself militarily, the government resigned.

A new coalition organised by Sirr al-Khalifa was dominated by the Umma, NUP and Muslim Brothers, with the SCP and PDP declining to participate. Steps were taken to deal with the South, but they fell far short of what was needed for a lasting resolution of the conflict. But the necessity and urgency of resolution was emphasised in the events of what came to be known as "Black Sunday". Southern residents in Khartoum had organised a demonstration to greet Clement Mboro, the Minister of the Interior, on his return from a tour of the South. A delay in his arrival corresponded with, and served to encourage, wild speculations over his safety - with the result that the demonstrators clashed with groups of Northerners, leaving several people dead in the streets. On 8 July 1965 northern troops attacked Juba, killing hundreds of its inhabitants, and set about destroying entire sections of the town. Three days later at Wau more killings occurred. One set of atrocities led to another, resulting in a determination on each side to secure a military victory. This proved futile, not least because of internal differences on both sides.

Personal animosity between Azhari, the President, and Muhammed Ahmed Mahgoub, the Prime Minister, resulted in a political crisis which was temporarily resolved by the mediation of the young Sadiq al-Mahdi, great-grandson of the Mahdi. In July 1966 he was to become Prime Minister. The Oxford-educated Sadiq represented a reformist wing of the Umma party, which planned to nationalise many of the private irrigation schemes and especially the unprofitable ones, controlled by his kinsmen. Much of the cash which the owners of these schemes eventually received in compensation was subsequently invested in rain fed mechanised farming and urban real estate. Politics had become increasingly more class conscious. In November 1965 the Communist Party was banned, and its members unseated from the Assembly. This was later contested in the courts, which in December 1966 ruled the action illegal - a judgement subsequently overruled, however, by the constituent assembly.

Merchants supporting the NUP also consolidated their economic power. Frequently their influence dominated the Ministry of Trade, and through it, the issuing of import-export licences and contracts. Sudan's commercial bourgeoisie was steadily advancing in the wake of foreign investment (Mahmoud 1984, p. 139), but in critical tension with the interests of the agrarian bourgeoisie.

From 1965-1969 economic conditions deteriorated. Cotton prices - the source of 70 per cent of Sudan's foreign revenue - plummetted, and after the Arab-Israeli War of 1967 foreign aid was considerably curtailed. By 1969 the foreign debt doubled to $260 million and the civil war was consuming nearly 30 per cent of the annual budget. The ensuing political crisis induced a military takeover.

The 'May Revolution' of 1969

On 25 May 1969 a group of 14 junior army officers led by Colonel Jafaar Mohammed Numeiri seized power in a virtually bloodless coup d'etat. A wing of the SCP mobilised in support, and two of its members joined the Revolutionary Council. Sudan was to be "democratic, socialist, and non-aligned." The new regime was populist in orientation and drew its inspiration from Egypt's Free Officers Movement. It manoeuvred with sections of the Left against the economically powerful sects by proclaiming that "the struggle against religious fanaticism was a social and economic necessity." The armed Ansar, the only force outside the army capable of mounting a serious military challenge to the new regime, suffered a decisive defeat in 1970 when thousands of them were killed at Aba Island and their leader, Imam al-Hadi al-Mahdi, grandson of the Mahdi, was killed. Soon afterwards, Sadiq al-Mahdi went into exile. The 'left' phase of Numeiri's programme was completed by the nationalisation of foreign banks and trading companies - 70 per cent of Sudan's banking system and 70 per cent of its foreign trade had been controlled by foreign capital.

Sudan's dependence on cotton necessitated a choice of economic policies that was soon to be reflected in the political differences between Numeiri and the Communists. The SCP's perspective of revolution by stages - first national democratic and then socialist - encouraged one faction to support both Numeiri's more moderate economic policies and his eagerness to dissolve the party into the newly-created Sudan Socialist Union (SSU). The veteran Communist 'Abd al-Khaliq Mahjub was opposed to this move, advocating instead an independent SCP in defiance of Numeiri's disbanding of political parties, but the faction led by Ahmed Sulayman and Mu'awiya Ibrahim engaged in open collaboration. This division created uncertainty among party rank-and-file and considerably weakened the SCP's leadership - a fact perfectly understood by Numeiri. Having dealt with the Ansar, he could now turn his venom on the Communists. Immediately after the slaughter at Aba Island, Mahjub was arrested, exiled to Egypt, and on his return to Sudan placed under house arrest. Then early in 1971 Numeiri boldly called upon the people to "destroy the Communist movement." It was a precipitous move, because the purges immediately preceding it had generated sympathetic support for communists from inside the army itself. But the 1971 coup d'etat attempted by pro-Communist army officers to reverse Numeiri's shift to the right was aborted by foreign intervention by Egypt and Libya - with the probable connivance of British intelligence. Thereafter Sudan was increasingly drawn into the capitalist orbit, and its foreign policy became more anti-Soviet.

Periodic purges of communists were to follow. Those executed immediately after the attempted coup had included Mahjub, who had stood out against collaboration, and Garang who had not. The latter, a prominent Southerner, had been instrumental in persuading Numeiri to advocate regional autonomy for the South, and this concern had perhaps obscured his political acumen. Also executed was El-Sheikh of the SWTUF.

Those in the SCP who implicitly rejected the "stages" theory of revolution for Sudan had all along been inclined to oppose any domestic alignment of the party with petty bourgeois politicians, and had therefore been critical of the SCP's earlier collaboration with the bourgeois Umma Party. There had, in any case, already been voices raised in party discussions as early as 1966 against the "politics of class-collaboration," when an influential faction advocated support for so-called progressive coups even in the absence of mass mobilisation. The debate on strategy had never been satisfactorily resolved, and this proved to be extremely damaging politically because, not only did it enable some communists to justify in theory and in practice support for what amounted to the party's liquidation, but some of them reportedly even went so far as to hand over to the security forces a list of party members. In the aftermath, Numeiri employed his own methods, and, in travelling the path already clearly laid out for him, set about banning the Communist Party and subsequently the trade unions. Opportunities for resistance were therefore severely curtailed by some of the very people who were expected to be in the forefront of the struggle. Communists in the army, and those who were employed by the government were dismissed and denied pension rights. In a frenzy of anti-communism over 1,000 SCP members or sympathisers were arrested.

With the SCP defeated, and the SSU having taken over the unions, Numeiri sought to shift the economy from one which was dominated by public enterprise and increasingly centrally planned to one in which the private sector could be considerably expanded. International investment capital was substantially encouraged, foreign companies previously nationalised were compensated, and legal commitments were undertaken to safeguard future foreign investment. The US alone immediately opened up $18 million worth of credit to Sudanese wheat importers and the IMF granted a $40 million loan, while Britain advanced $25 million, most of which, incidentally, never left the City of London because it was used to compensate British companies and banks (such as Barclays) which had previously been nationalised (O'Neill 1980, p. 223).

As a corollary, foreign policy changed dramatically and diplomatic relations were restored with the United States. A whole spate of loans from the US were subsequently earmarked for capital purchases from multinational corporations. But most significant of all was the massive Kuwaiti and Saudi financing of development projects (see O'Brien and O'Neill, this volume). Sudan was seen by the oil-producing Arab states as a potential breadbasket. Most of the projects were planned for the growing or processing of agricultural raw materials (textiles, sugar refineries, canning factories, tanneries, tobacco, and so on). The dream was that Sudan would one day meet a substantial part of the food requirement of the entire Arab world. It was estimated that Sudan contained well over three-quarters of the Arab Middle East's cultivable land. Projects included the Rahad Irrigation Scheme, the construction of the Jonglei Canal to by-pass the Sudd and to increase the Nile River flow, the Kenana sugar scheme (initially involving the British firm Lonrho) and the one million acre commercial cattle farm developed by AZL International, a subsisdiary of the Arizona, Colorado Land and Cattle Company. The marriage of Arab and western finance capital was also seen in deals like the 200 million Eurodollar loan arranged by Adnan Khashoggi - the Saudi financier with substantial interests in Sudanese industries involving textile, match, soap and glass factories. The Kuwaiti-based Gulf International, whose Sudanese director Khalil Osman came to own considerable real estate in Khartoum, became deeply involved in many of these projects. The marriage was also seen in Arab investment in firms such as Lonrho, which was acquiring raw material extraction interests in the Middle East and throughout Africa. Indeed, the location of the Arab Bank for Economic Development in Africa (ABEDIA) in Khartoum was explicitly conceived as a link between Arab oil money and the exploitation of African resources through the utilisation of capital goods purchased from the West. All members of the Arab League contributed to this fund, but most of the capital came from Kuwait and Saudi Arabia.

Settlement of the 'Southern Problem'

Little of this investment would have been forthcoming if the war in the South had continued. Nor could political relations with Arab states have been strengthened without an attempted solution to the "Southern problem". At first, as Holt and Daly emphasise, "Numeiri responded to the continuing Anyanya activity by recourse to a policy of suppression, which was, however, no more effective in 1969-70 than it had been under previous regimes" (Holt and Daly 1979, p. 201). Numeiri's regime then quickly moved from a strategy of confrontation to one of reconciliation.

In August 1967, Aggrey Jaden, who in 1962 had been involved with other Southerners in establishing the Sudan African National Union (SANU), had set up the Southern Sudan Provisional Government, but this was soon denounced by Jaden as a "Dinka clique" and, in consequence, it quickly fragmented. Then, two years later, the SSPG was superseded by the Nile Provisional Government under the presidency of Gordon Mayen, who had previously led the Southern Front in Khartoum. Joseph Lagu - a Madi from Equatoria and ex-captain in the Sudanese army - had supported the SSPG, but refused to participate in the new NPG. This resulted in yet further divisions. Subsequently, in July 1969 General Emedio Taffeng set up the Aniyidi State Government which embraced all factions not in the NPG. By 1971 Lagu, who was directly involved in bush fighting and contemptuous of the dissension among exiled leaders, increasingly began to challenge Taffeng's authority, and succeeeded in concentrating the Anyanya resistance in his Southern Sudan Liberation Movement.

Following this consolidation of the rebel fighting forces, Numeiri's strategy for a military solution crumbled. In July he appointed Abel Alier to replace Joseph Garang as Minister of

Southern Affairs and began secret meetings with Southern leaders in exile. The resultant Addis Ababa Agreement reached on 27 February 1972 was, on 3 March, translated into the Regional Self-Government Act for the Southern Provinces. This brought Bahr al-Ghazal, Equatoria and the Upper Nile Provinces into a self-governing Southern Sudanese Region, with a Regional Assembly and High Executive Council. The Khartoum government would control defence, foreign affairs, the currency, inter-regional communication, and general development planning, while devolved upon the assembly in Juba were control over regional education, public health, the police and mineral and natural resources. An important provision was a national force called the Southern Command composed of 12,000 officers and men of whom 6,000 were to be citizens of the Region and the other 6,000 from outside the region.

The President of the Republic was to appoint a president of the High Executive Council, and in consultation with that incumbent, its other members. An amnesty was granted, and Abel Alier became Vice President of Sudan and President of the Regional High Executive Council. The first Regional Assembly of 60 members was elected in November 1973.

Development plans for the South, when they were considered at all, were most enthusiastically supported by external funds only when they directly enhanced existing investment in the North. There were two especially blatant examples of the North benefiting from development schemes located in the South. One was the decision that petroleum extracted from the oilfield at Bentiu, in the South, would not be refined locally, but instead at Kosti further north. Numeiri also made an abortive attempt to redraw the boundaries between North and South so as to include the oilfields in the North. The other example was the Jonglei Canal project. The 175-mile canal, planned to run from the small town of Bor to a point south of Malakal on the White Nile, was designed to by-pass the Sudd swamps in which an estimated 32,000 million cubic metres of water are lost in evaporation each year, thereby increasing by an estimated 4,000 million cubic metres the volume of water flowing to the North. Southerners were doubtful that the expenditure was being carried out with their interests in mind, especially in the knowledge that Egypt was footing part of the bill in return for a substantial share of the increased water supply. Furthermore, some environmentalists expressed a fear that the ecology of the Southern Region (and perhaps even of East Africa) could be adversely affected, because the ensuing lack of evaporation from the Sudd might reduce general rainfall. More certain was that the lives of the Madi, Bari, Shilluk, Nuer, Dinka and others would be radically transformed - perhaps even disastrously, given their economic dependence on livestock. The full extent of Southern suspicions over the scheme was exemplified in the Juba riots of October 1974 sparked off by a rumour - improbable though it was - that over two million Egyptian fellahin were to be settled in the area as colonists. These two projects, at different times, were to be the targets of rebel attacks in the early 1980s.

In the meantime, efforts were being made in the South to resettle and rehabilitate the population displaced by the civil war, with the churches in particular seeking help from various international aid organisations. Some attempts, too, were made at settling nomads and in improving agricultural productivity. A training course was set up in Juba, and the vocational training school at Wau was extended. Elementary schools previously operated by the Anyanya were incorporated into an expanded regional system, and in 1977 Juba University was established to specialise in meeting the vocational training requirements of the South. Even so, economic recession in the North - all the more abrupt due to Sudan's increasing dependence on foreign investment - reduced the amount of capital expenditure on infrastructure, and the resultant decline in opportunities for speculation increased internal conflict among the Southern elites. Exacerbating their difficulties, and adding to their fears, was the war in neighbouring Uganda, whose refugees (many of whom were either prepared to sell or to use their arms for advantage) constituted a security problem. With the Southern masses deprived, and frequently armed, those who had been given key positions and attendant privileges by Numeiri in the military and civilian administration increasingly found themselves under threat. The immediate consequence, though, of Southern discontent was expressed through the ballot box. Vice-President Abel Alier and his team of ministers were defeated in the regional elections, and Joseph Lagu (the former Anyanya leader) was returned to the Assembly with a number of the "old guard", including Clement Mboro and Joseph Uduho as ministers. No sooner had it met, than accusations of corruption were levelled,cabinet reshuffles made, and Alier was again standing by to resume office.

The Collapse of Unity and Numeiri's Final Crisis

The settlement of the civil war through the Addis Ababa Agreement had been Numeiri's greatest political achievement. The Southern elites were appeased through incorporation into civil service and military posts and Numeiri found tremendous popularity among the Southern masses who saw him as responsible for restoring peace in their lives. Numeiri's ability to hold onto power came to depend upon this Southern base of support as he had permanently alienated the Umma-led faction of the right through the Aba Island massacre and the left through the crack-down on the SCP and attendant rightward shift. The remaining strength of opposition in the North was organised by right wing parties cloaked in Islamic fundamentalism and a history of hostility towards the South that led key segments of the bourgeoisie - which otherwise might have preferred them to Numeiri - to doubt their ability to maintain peace in the South. For a decade following the settlement of the 'Southern Problem', then, the South served as Numeiri's trump card in constant political battles.

After a decade had passed, however, with no discernible progress made towards economic development in the South, in-fighting among the Southern leadership intensified and opposition to Numeiri grew. In this context, Numeiri took advantage of the internal wrangles among Southern politicians, using them as an excuse to sub-divide the region into three regions as part of a general regionalisation of government nationwide. This policy was welcomed by Lagu, who was once more accusing the Dinka politicians of seeking political domination. Other Southern politicians, including Mboro and Uduho, departed from this view on the grounds that redivision effectively abolished Southern autonomy, and 21 of them set up a Council for the Unity of Southern Sudan (CUSS). This was in violation of the law, the SSU being the only legal party, and consequently all 21 were arrested, although all but Samuel Bol, the vice-chairman, were soon released.

At first, Numeiri proposed a referendum in the South on the issue of redivision, but then reneged by imposing it in May 1983. Another factor accentuating the crisis in North-South relations was the formal adoption of Sharia law. In part, this was to placate the growing influence of the Muslim Brothers, as Numeiri's Southern base of support eroded, and to some extent also aimed to please the regime in Saudi Arabia whose financial support was becoming increasingly indispensable. This connection was evident even in the mid-1970s. Aid from Saudi Arabia corresponded with the abolition of the State-run football pools; prostitutes were periodically driven off the streets, and bars were frequently closed. Most spectacular in the scenario had been the promotion of Hassan el Turabi, leader of the Muslim Brothers, from political prisoner in 1977 to Attorney General in August 1979.

Prior to 1977 Numeiri had sought to strengthen the SSU and to exclude the leaders of the traditional political parties from the political scene. His strategy was to reform local government through institutional links with the SSU that would increase his organisational hold over the rural areas. The legacy of British colonial rule had been to leave these rural areas in the hands of tribal leaders. These had proved to be a bulwark of support for the Umma party, especially in the West, and Numeiri was determined to break it. In response, the Umma sought an alliance with the National Unionist Party and the Muslim Brothers in the form of the National Front.

Allegedly supported at various times by Libya, Iraq and Ethiopia, the National Front made several attempts to depose Numeiri by force. One of these occurred in September 1975, but was quickly defeated, and its leader executed. Then, in July 1976, a more systematically-organised coup - described by Numeiri as an invasion planned in, and financed by, Libya - was attempted, but was also suppressed, with over one hundred of its participants being executed. Faced with a concomitant conflict with Ethiopia over support for Eritrean guerillas, Numeiri had been thankful to receive Egyptian military support. The resultant military defence pact with Sadat in 1977 led to renewed ties with Egypt and accounted for the regime's initial approval of the Camp David agreement. But Sudan's identification with Egypt soon became a political liability, and the regime made several tactical shifts in policy as Numeiri sought to placate the Saudis, hold on to his precarious support among Southerners (who were fearful of Egyptian influence), and to out-manoeuvre the National Front. In all this lies the political significance of Sudan's temporary rapprochement with Libya in May 1979. It served to emphasise, at once, the partial success of Numeiri's muted opposition to Egypt, and at the same time enabled him to defuse the opposition's political influence - a process which had begun in 1977 by a general amnesty, when over 1,000 political prisoners had been released.

Sadiq al-Mahdi, his death sentence having been rescinded, returned from exile in 1977, and joined the SSU; he resigned in October 1978, however, on the grounds that it was unrepresentative, and in protest at Numeiri's failure to condemn Sadat's foreign policy. Sharif al-Hindi, leader of the Democratic Unionist faction of the National Front, preferred to remain outside Sudan, opposing the regime until his death in January 1982.

On 8 August 1979, secondary school students in Khartoum staged a demonstration against rising inflation. Pressure from the IMF had induced the regime to withdraw the subsidy on wheat, and the price of bread increased by over 60 per cent. Later in the month the price of petrol rose by two-thirds, leading to higher bus and taxi fares. Taxation on tobacco and alcohol was also increased, and the price of sugar doubled. The effects were immediately felt in the urban areas. There were chronic food shortages throughout Khartoum. Street-fighting spread to neighbouring Omdurman and other towns, and several people died in clashes with the army. When the SCP-influenced railway workers staged a nationwide protest strike on 11 August, Numeiri quickly reduced petrol prices, and prepared to crack-down hard on the left once again.

The crisis had been heightened by the strike action of Gezira tenants against the imposition of a new water-rate which threatened their cotton harvest, and brought them into direct confrontation with government policy. There was an evident danger that these struggles would soon coalesce in an organised opposition to the regime, and therefore limit Numeiri's room for manoeuvre. He immediately reduced the SSU politbureau from 27 to 17 and the secretariat from 15 to four, all of whom became politbureau ministers. Abul Gasim, who had authorised payment to the railway workers, was the first to go in Numeiri's shake up. In a broadcast to the nation, Numeiri repeated his past strategy of blaming "communists and atheists" for the riots, and called upon good Muslims to purge their neighbourhoods and workplaces of communist influence. Known communists were subsequently beaten up and imprisoned by the authorities.

By the early eighties, relations with Libya had deteriorated again, partly because of the latter's increased involvement in the Chadian Civil War, which seemed to Numeiri to bring Gaddafi's armed forces perilously close, and also because of allegedly Libyan-backed attempted coups in 1982 and 1983. Relations between the two countries deteriorated even more in March 1984, when the broadcasting station at Omdurman was bombarded by an aircraft identified as a Soviet-built Tupolev TU-22 - allegedly deployed by Libya. This 'Libyan menace' met with a positive response in the Reagan White House, which accordingly increased military and economic aid to Numeiri.

Meanwhile, relations with Egypt improved considerably. Sadat's assassination in October 1981 - though greeted with mixed feelings in the SSU - nevertheless led to closer co-operation with Cairo; and, in October 1982, a Charter of Integration was signed between the two countries. It was planned to last for at least ten years, and provided for economic and political integration, and close association in terms of foreign policy and military security. The Charter set up a 120-member Nile Valley parliament, with a joint fund to administer its activities. Predictably, Sudanese politicians in the South saw ominous signs of a further diminution in their political role, while to the emergent rebel forces it merely confirmed what they had already anticipated. Their calculation was that the Sudanese masses, having witnessed a similar agreement in 1974 (which this one superseded), would greet it with either scepticism or indifference, if indeed they became aware of it at all. It was the military clauses contained in the Charter that understandbly bothered many of the Southerners. In them, they recognised the prospect of a collaborative invasion by "Northern forces" to "police the South". Egyptian pilots were already assisting the Sudanese Air Force in training personnel to operate its newly-acquired F-5 fighter bombers, and any further involvement of the Egyptians served to reinforce the aforementioned fears of fellahin occupation. This, plus the doubts over the Jonglei Canal project and the decision to pipe crude oil to Port Sudan implied to the Southerners a serious drain of their vital natural resources.

Never again was Numeiri to be greeted with enthusiasm in the South. On a tour in December 1982 he was confronted by demonstrations, and in Rumbek had to take cover in the local army barracks under a shower of stones. His immediate reaction was to order several arrests. When two prominent Southern politicians (Achuil and Ubor) were subsequently gaoled in Khartoum for having addressed Southern students in terms critical of the government, support in the South for armed opposition increased considerably. The munity at Bor in January 1983 was an additional symptom. For a combination of reasons (i.e. dependence on local plots of land to supplement their income, fears that they would be sent to Iraq to fight Iran, and concern over government plans for the South), Southern troops refused to be moved north, and after gaining a symbolic victory over their adversaries, joined forces with what had become known as Anyanya II. In April Numeiri sent an eminent career soldier, a highly respected Dinka, to reason with the mutineers. That soldier was Colonel (Dr) John Garang - who immediately joined the rebel forces, and emerged later as the leader of the Sudan People's Liberation Army, the armed wing of the Sudan People's Liberation Movement. Joseph Uduho, the veteran Southern rebel joined soon afterwards, and so did Martin Majier, a well-known lawyer and former Deputy Speaker of the Southern Assembly. The new movement - the SPLM - was clearly going to be considerably more broadly-based than the old Anyanya.

By the early 1980s Sudan was facing a severe economic crisis. The foreign debt amounted to $9 billion and the currency was repeatedly devalued while inflation climbed higher and higher. Between 1982 and 1984 the price of sorghum, the main staple of rural diets, rose 30 times, and the overall inflation rate was around 50 per cent. Numeiri responded to the simmering discontent with even more draconian measures, and in seeking religious justification for his repression, on 8 September 1983, imposed an extreme version of the Sharia Law, which included the amputation of limbs for law-breakers. This action was probably designed to forestall any influence that either the Muslim Brothers or Ansar (backbone of the Umma party) might derive from the wave of Islamic fundamentalism currently spreading throughout the Middle East. It also enabled Numeiri to imprison Sadiq al-Mahdi - who opposed amputation - for failing to endorse Muslim Law (he was released in the following year). More serious was the public hanging of Mahmoud Mohamed Taha, the aging leader of the Republican Brotherhood, for alleged heresy. This particularly outraged many liberal intellectuals who regarded Taha as a respected, harmless eccentric. In seeking to appear more Muslim than even the leaders of the conversative Muslim sects, Numeiri also further alienated the South. He was quickly running out of room to manoeuvre.

Adding to the economic difficulties and ensuing discontent that had prompted Numeiri into becoming increasingly more repressive, was the drought that had already hit Ethiopia and was by 1983 engulfing Sudan. By early 1985 about half of Sudan's 22 million people - many of them in Darfur and Kordofan were at risk of starvation. There were also over a million and a half refugees in Sudan seeking help. The war in the South was also a drain on resources, and was soon to cost nearly half a million dollars a day. Nor were there any immediate prospects of a military solution. Furthermore, realising the economic and symbolic significance of the Bentiu oilfield and Jonglei canal project, the SPLA forced them both to suspend operations. In a broadcast over the SPLA radio, on 24 March 1985, Garang made the following statement:

> The SPLM is determined to fight for a democratic and socialist Sudan where social justice, freedom and human dignity flourish. We fight for a socialist and democratic Sudan in which the nationality question ... is solved. We fight for a Sudan in which the problem of uneven development is solved so that all regions, especially the most neglected regions, receive a fair share and accelerated socio-economic development - a Sudan free from racism, a Sudan in which power is vested in the masses, exercised by them and in their interests, a Sudan in which there is no monopoly of power by any ethnic, religious, or regional group.

In the same month the US administration - which had hitherto pressured the IMF to be flexible in its terms of financial support - now suddenly sought to impose severe austerity measures as a pre-condition for releasing $67 million of aid money frozen under its 1983-84 package. This, as Richard Brown comments, "provided the final straw" (Brown 1985, p. 11), and, as he goes on to suggest, leads to one of two conclusions: either it was a big mistake, or it was a deliberate move to topple Numeiri.

The decision to raise food prices (bread by 75 per cent and petrol by 65 per cent) in response to IMF demands did indeed provide the initial impetus to the mass demonstrations on 26 March, which began as Numeiri was preparing to leave for Washington for a health check and aid negotiations. If ever senior army officers were to be given a "green light" this was it. Any serious moves to depose Numeiri would come from one of four sources: (i) a popular revolution organised by professional, skilled and unskilled workers with support from Gezira tenants - of the kind that toppled Abboud in 1964, but which would require either military support to sustain it, or an armed insurrection; (ii) a coup led by pro-Libyan/anti-American officers motivated by Islamic fundamentalism, (iii) a left-wing coup organised by radical army officers in cells similar to the Free Officers Movement that brought Numeiri to power in 1969; or (iv) a pro-Western coup, with Egyptian support, led by top army officers who would seek to re-establish the status-quo as soon as possible. There is no doubt whatsoever that - if Numeiri was to go - the latter is what the US administration most desired to replace him.

It is also clear that when the Sudanese masses took to the streets the army was restrained, either because the troops were unwilling to oppose the demonstrators, and/or (for these possibilities are not at all mutually exclusive) they were under orders not to do so. In any event, few arrests were made, despite large-scale riots, and only tear-gas was used to disperse the crowds. The emergent People's Alliance - which consisted of professional workers (university teachers, doctors, lawyers, and engineers) and trade-unionists - formed the spearhead of the popular movement, but it lacked a clear political strategy for the seizure of civilian power.

On 6 April 1985 army officers announced that Numeiri had been deposed, and that a military council led by the Commander-in-Chief, General Siwar el-Dahab, had seized control. Immediately there was talk in Khartoum of betrayal. Even the New York Times (9 April 1985) spoke of a pre-emptive coup to prevent more junior officers from taking over. John Garang labelled the new regime "Numeirism without Numeiri" and in broadcasts on 26 and 27 May 1985 made the following statements:

> Despite the continuation of Numeirism in a different uniform there have been positive aspects in the change of guards from Numeiri to his Minister of Defence and Chiefs of General Staff. Among these positive aspects are:
>
> You, the masses, have restored some of your rights and as a result there are now 40 political parties and 90 trade and professional unions that are able for the first time in 16 years to hold rallies and air their views in a new breeze of freedom. You have regained your ability to fight and bring down an unpopular regime which is a necessary prelude to realising the necessity to establish your own regime to safeguard your gains. Favourable conditions have been created for the struggle waged by the SPLA to converge with democratic forces in other parts of the country beyond the birthplace of the SPLA/M;

and,

> The SPLA/M will participate directly in the shaping of a new Sudan with other democratic and patriotic forces in the country. It is not a matter of a group of 15 generals seizing power in

Khartoum, forming a Military Council and their Civilian Cabinet and then calling on the SPLA to come in to take some reserved posts. No, we shall not take from anybody, we shall make the new Sudan together with other democratic forces in the country. Numeiri did precisely what the Junta is trying to do in offering the SPLA/M jobs in his Government except that he was more generous than his Minister of Defence; Numeiri offered the SPLA/M the First Vice Presidency, re-unification of the South under the SPLA and six ministerial posts in the Central Government. We answered Numeiri that we wanted 10,000 Ministerial posts, one for every SPLA soldier, but before he could respond, Siwar el-Dahab took over. The subject matter of negotiations is misplaced, and the SPLA is wrongly accused of refusing negotiations. The truth is that negotiations in the context of the so-called "Southern Problem" is against the national interest and a recipe for disaster. Suppose we solve the problem of the South, we will soon have to solve the problem of the Jebels (that is, the Nuba Mountains) because the Nuba can also take up arms; after that the problem of the Beja, and so forth. It is a national not a Southern problem that we must address.

This is a far cry from the old Anyanya leadership; the expressed goal now is not limited autonomy for the South, but a national democratic revolution. The direction in which the democratic forces respond to this call will be decisive in any forthcoming mass struggle. For, although the key to a successful conclusion to Sudan's uncompleted revolution undoubtedly lies in the South, its direction depends also on the democratic forces in the North. This is the full significance of the joint meeting held at Koka Dam in March 1986 between the SPLM/A and the National Alliance (consisting of representatives of the political parties, trade unions and professional associations) - but excluding the National Democratic Party, Khatmiya-based cliques, and the Muslim Brothers. The "two sides" agreed that the essential prerequisites for any immediate progress were:

a. A declaration by all political forces and the government of the day of their commitment to discuss the <u>Basic Problems of Sudan</u> and not the so-called problem of Southern Sudan and that shall be in accordance with the Agenda agreed upon in this 'Declaration'.

b. The lifting of the State of Emergency.

c. Repeal of the 'September 1983 Laws' and all other laws that are restrictive of freedom.

d. Adoption of the 1956 Constitution as amended in 1964 with incorporation of 'Regional Government' and all other such matters on which a consensus opinion of all the political forces shall be reached.

e. The abrogation of the military pacts concluded between Sudan and other countries and which impinge on Sudan's National sovereignty.

f. A continuous endeavour by the two sides to take the necessary steps and measures to effect a ceasefire (Khalid 1987, pp. 145-7).

"It is", reports Mansour Khalid, "no secret that the question of ceasefire was openly raised at the Koka Dam meeting ..." He goes on to explain that it was agreed that "this matter should only be discussed after the stage was set for the National Constitutional Conference, which means the abolition of the September Laws, military pacts and the state of emergency. Up to that point the continuation of war should be of surprise to nobody" (Khalid 1987, p. 115).

John Garang's opening speech at Koka Dam confronted the issue of a ceasefire directly, and concretely, in relation to Rumbek - the town which the government had only recently bombed using Libyan TU-22 aircraft. Referring to the fifth point of the Declaration, he argued:

> These agreements diminish our statehood, our sovereignty. These mutual defence pacts were made not for defence of the Sudan as such; we could not have had any quarrel with that, but for the defence of the May regime. Therefore, if the May regime has gone they should go with the May regime. As I talk to you now, and as a result of one of these two defence pacts, on 13, 14 and 15 of this month, March 1986, fifty bombs fell on us. These bombs were not thrown by Sudanese planes, not by Sudanese pilots, but by the implementation of one of these two defence agreements ... The May 11 regime is seriously fighting us ... we are going to be frank because I am going to leave you here to thrash this out and it is your historic responsibility (Khalid 1987, p. 133).

A quick military victory in the South, prior to the May elections, may have been hoped for by prominent members of the traditional parties, but it was not to be forthcoming, and it was incumbent upon other Northern politicians to allay the fears of Southern rebels, and seek agreement on constitutional guarantees before elections took place. The failure of the Transitional Military Council (TMC) and transitional government to abrogate the aforementioned military pacts with Egypt and Libya, and to abolish in their entirety the 1983 Sharia laws, made the SPLM/A even more hesitant towards supporting the forthcoming elections and then afterwards, unwilling to participate in a government under Sadiq el Mahdi, that had resulted from merely a partial election (Woodward 1987, p. 142).

In relation to Sharia Laws, the emphasis now being expressed in government circles is not so much on their abolition, as on laws which reflect "true Islam". Numeiri, it should be remembered, also claimed to support "true Islam" - as indeed, do the Muslim Brothers today, so whatever the religious affiliations of Southerners, they are unlikely to accept the proposition that Sadiq el Mahdi's coalition with the DUP and Nationalists, can legitimately impose upon the Sudanese, its own version of the Sharia. Their past experience of "true Islam" leaves them with little confidence that Sadiq's interpretation will be any more acceptable, either now or in the future.

But, as Mansour Khalid has recently argued, the question of the Sharia is not entirely one of religious conviction:

> Khartoum politicians are being harassed by the fundamentalists in a way that might erode the power base of some of them, so their wavering should only be understood in the light of this extortion and blackmail. Their action is guided by the sheer arithmetic of parliamentary power (Khalid 1987, p. 118).

The precise significance of Islam on politics in Sudan is difficult to predict (Woodward 1986, p. 6), but what is certain is that it will be inextricably bound up with Sudan's national identity - as will be the construction of its Arabism and Africanism. Those who falsely present Sudan as a contrast between Arab and non-Arab, or Muslim versus Christians, North against South, have given credence to those Sudanese politicians of the elite who seek closer unity with the Arab world often at the expense of the unity of Sudan. The response by non-Arabs has usually been to over-emphasise their African identity; while, Sudan as an entity in international relations has remained suspect among both African and Arab states for not being either sufficiently African ("the Sudanese are really Arabs") or Arab ("the Sudanese are really Africans"). Those who perpetuate this duality also seriously distort history, because the assimilation in Sudan of Arab-Islamic culture was the signal achievement of the two great African kingdoms of Fur and Funj. Sudan's heritage is both rich and potent, and its rediscovery will help forge a more cohesive nation.

Relations with Egypt, or Uganda, or with any African or other country, will inevitably be prefigured through the presentation of Sudan's own national character. One of the greatest achievements of the Addis Accord was also one reason why Numeiri survived for as long as he did: it presented to the world, and to the Sudanese themselves a vision of Arabism and of Africanism which was uniquely Sudanese. The Arab states had to acknowledge that devoutly Muslim Sudanese accepted a constitution which recognised the legitimacy of worship in other religions, and desisted from designating an official religion of state, thereby encouraging non-Muslims and female-Muslims to aspire to full citizenship. Correspondingly, other African nations could recognise in Sudan's Africanism a potential model of unity in diversity to which they in turn could aspire.

The unique amalgamation of Afro-Arab culture and ethnic traits alluded to at the beginning of this chapter, and which have deep historical roots, could and should be Sudan's strength in advancing and sustaining its national democratic revolution. The task is not an easy one, not least because Sudan's uneven development and correspondingly fragmented class-structure present enormous problems of political leadership. In this respect, the emergence of the SPLM/A is significant, because in alliance with other democratic forces throughout the country it has the potential to succeed.

References

Al-Rahim, Muddathir Abd (1969), Imperialism and Nationalism in the Sudan, Clarendon Press, Oxford.

Amin, Samir (1972), 'Underdevelopment & Dependence in Black Africa: Historical Origin', Journal of Modern African Studies 10 (4) pp. 503-24.

Beshir, Mohamed Omer (1970), The Southern Sudan: Background to Conflict, Hurst, London.

--- (1974), Revolution & Nationalism in the Sudan, Rex Collings, London.

--- (1975), The Southern Sudan: From Conflict to Peace, Hurst, London.

Breasted, James Henry (1906), A History of Egypt: From Earliest Times to the Persian Conquest, Hodder & Stoughton, London.

Brown, Richard (1985), 'A background note on the final round of economic austerity measures imposed by the Numeiri regime, June 1984 to March 1985', Development Studies Research Centre, Faculty of Economic and Social Studies, University of Khartoum, Khartoum.

Collins, Carole (1976), 'Colonialism and Class Struggle in Sudan', MERIP Reports, 46.

Currie, Sir James (1935), 'The Educational Experiment in the Anglo-Egyptian Sudan, 1900-1933', Journal of the African Society, 33, pp. 351-371 and 34, pp. 41-60.

Dafalla, Hassan (1975), The Nubian Exodus, Hurst, London.

Duffield, Mark(1981), Maiurno: Capitalism and Rural Life in Sudan, Ithaca Press, London.

Fawzi, S.E.D. (1957), The Labour Movement in Sudan, Oxford University Press, London.

Frankel, S.H. (1938), Capital Investment in Africa, Oxford University Press, London.

Garang, John (1985), A (typescript) statement made on 26-27 May to the Sudanese People on Radio SPLA on the Second Anniversary of the Bor, Pibor and Fashalla Resistance and Ayod Revolt.

Hassoun, Isam (1952), 'Western Migration and Settlement in the Gezira', Sudan Notes and Records, 33, pp. 60-113.

Henderson, K.D.D. (1953), The Making of the Modern Sudan: the Life and Letters of Sir Douglas Newbold, Faber, London.

Hodgkin, Thomas (1971), 'Mahdism, Messianism and Marxism in the African Setting' in Y. F. Hasan (ed.) Sudan in Africa, Khartoum University Press, Khartoum.

Holt, P.M. (1958), The Mahdist State in the Sudan 1881-1898, The Clarendon Press, Oxford.

--- (1961), A Modern History of the Sudan, Weidenfeld & Nicolson, London.

--- (1967), 'Holy Families and Islam in the Sudan', Near East Papers No. 4, Princeton University, Princeton.

Holt, P.M. and Daly, M.W. (1979), The History of the Sudan: From the Coming of Islam to the Present Day, Weidenfeld & Nicolson, London.

Khalid, Mansour (1987), Introduction to John Garang Speaks, K.P.I., London.

MacMichael, H. A. (1932), A History of the Arabs in the Sudan, Cambridge University Press, Cambridge.

Mahmoud, Fatima Babiker (1984), The Sudanese Bourgeoisie, Zed Press and Khartoum University Press, London, and Khartoum.

Nutting, Anthony (1967), Gordon: Martyr and Misfit, The Reprint Society, London.

O'Brien,Jay (1980), Agricultural Labor and Development in Sudan, PhD, University of Connecticut.

--- (1984), 'The social reproduction of tenant cultivators and class formation in the Gezira Scheme, Sudan', in B. Isaac (ed.), Research in Economic Anthropology, Vol. 6, JAI Press, Greenwich, Connecticut, pp. 217-41.

Oliver, Roland and J.D. Fage (1966), A Short History of Africa, Penguin, Harmondsworth.

O'Neill, Norman (1978), 'Imperialism and Class Struggle in Sudan', Race and Class, 20 (1).

--- (1980), 'Investment and Development in Sudan', Middle East Yearbook, I.C. Publications, London.

Smirnov, S.R. (1974), Africa as a Soviet Scientist Sees It, Nauka, Moscow.

Trimmingham, J.S. (1949), Islam in the Sudan, Oxford University, London.

Wingate, F.R. (1968) Mahdism and the Egyptian Sudan, Frank Cass, London (2nd edition, with a new introduction by P.M. Holt).

Woodward, Peter (1986), 'Islam and Politics', in M.A. Al-Rahim; R. Badal; A.Hardallo; P.Woodward(eds.), Sudan Since Independence, Gower, Aldershot, Hants.

--- (1987) 'Is Sudan Governable? Some Thoughts on the Experience of Liberal Democracy and Military Rule', in J. D. Latham, (ed.) British Society for Middle Eastern Studies Bulletin, 13, (2), St. Antony's College, Oxford.

3 Pre-colonial trade between states in the eastern Sudan c.1700–c.1900[1]

LIDWIEN KAPTEIJNS AND JAY SPAULDING

States arose at an early date in the region extending eastward from modern Chad to the Red Sea. This study is largely confined by its literature of sources to the century preceding the colonial conquest, approximately, the eighteenth century in the Nile valley and the nineteenth in the kingdoms of the west. It deals with the kingdoms of Ethiopia, Sinnar, the Shilluk, Taqali, Dar Fur, Dar Masalit, Dar Tama, Dar Qimr, Dar Zaghawa, Dar Sila, Dar Kuti, and Wadai. All the rulers of states in this region and period were supported primarily through the labour of their subjects in agriculture and animal husbandry: exchange played a significant but not a determinative role in the organisation of society.[2] Within each state society, several levels of exchange may be distinguished, including the face-to-face interactions typical of the local community and regional markets characterised by more formal transactions, a greater degree of state control, and the use of limited-purpose currencies (see Kapteijns 1984; Spaulding 1984). Trade between states constituted a third and distinct level of exchange; it was organised in response to a discrete set of economic realities and conducted according to its own peculiar set of rules. The institutions through which trade between states was conducted were shared by all the kingdoms within the area and period embraced by this study, whose burden will be to describe them. In doing so, we take issue with those who have asserted that the eastern Sudan played only a passive role in an international commerce initiated by others,[3] and with those who claim that the institutional forms through which this trade was conducted are irrelevant, being reducible to a naive reflex of abstract concepts of supply and demand or the alleged human propensity to truck and barter.[4] During the century preceding the colonial conquest, the states of the eastern Sudan attempted to accommodate numbers of foreign traders who brought with them the concepts and usages of commercial capitalism as practiced in the lands of the Mediterranean littoral. The present study examines the assault of these intrusive influences on the traditional system of trade between states, influences which most governments in the eastern Sudan succeeded in controlling until the scramble for Africa overtook them, but which contributed to the demise of the Nile-valley kingdom of Sinnar, where they arrived early and in force.

The internal organisation of the state societies of the eastern Sudan imposed constraints on the conduct of external trade. Prevailing social theory within each kingdom maintained that society was divided into two distinct classes - a hereditary ruling nobility and a legion of producing commoners (see Kapteijns 1985, pp.8-9, Brocchi 1843, vol. 5 p. 487). A fundamental constant in the political life of each kingdom was the ability and willingness of the former group to assert its authority over the latter, through non-violent institutions if possible but by force if necessary. Commoners usually appear in the historical record in groups - the "clans" or "tribes" of conventional discourse - each of which owed allegiance to a designated representative of the state and occupied an assigned geographical area. The cohesion of these groups derived in part from their internal organisation, notably kinship relations, but also from a threat imposed externally by the state. It was a fact of life that individuals who left the security of kin and community became masterless men, subject to robbery and enslavement. Such deviance was probably quite common, but so was the application of the corresponding penalties.[5] "In the past the Masalit used to beat up any stranger who came to their country and take his clothes," a Masalit informant said, while another asked rhetorically: "In whose country, by which road could one have traded? There were no roads, no secure roads" (see Kapteijns 1985, p. 36). Consequently the opportunities of commoners to trade outside their community were limited to those specifically conceded by their rulers, who sponsored and regulated the system of market-level exchange (see Spaulding 1984; Kapteijns 1985, pp. 31-2). But the existence of regional markets did not imply that the commoners who frequented them were therefore also licensed to undertake long-distance trade.

The commoners, as a rule, were not allowed to participate personally in the foreign trade of their respective countries, but their rulers obliged them to contribute to it indirectly. While the institutional details varied from state to state and often between regions of a single kingdom, each eastern Sudanic government stipulated that at least part of the tax burden it imposed must be paid in the form of precisely those locally-available commodities which were suitable for export, e.g., gold, civet, ivory, rhinoceros horn, slaves, horses, ostrich feathers, cattle, camels, honey, and butter.[6] This taxation policy insured that a preponderance of these goods would pass into the hands of the government, but it did not necessarily compel the recipient authority to export them; all had value within the kingdom itself, and a ruler might alternatively elect to consume them himself or to distribute them to deserving subordinates within the ruling class.[7]

The commodities imported into eastern Sudanic states were usually luxury consumption goods of low bulk and high value. The consumption of these imports within each society was limited by laws which specified precisely which material objects might be possessed and displayed by individuals of each social rank. In the Masalit Sultanate, for example, tea was an expensive luxury drunk exclusively by the nobility. The male members of the noble household drank the first two brews, one strong and one weaker cup; the third brew was for the women, while the remaining tea leaves - saturated with sugar - were given to the slaves "to eat" (Kapteijns 1985, p. 43, 158-9). Not only poverty inhibited commoners from buying imported luxury goods. They were also typically forbidden to wear sewn garments, headgear, imported fabrics, or even new and clean homespun. Noblemen enforced such rules, when challenged, by ripping the shirts off the backs of offenders, or beating the lowly wearer of clean linen, "for everybody must be miskin (common)" (Kapteijns 1985, note 99, 158-9; Nachtigal 1971, p. 248; al-Tunisi 1851, p. 371; Spaulding 1980). Less direct means of enforcement were also efficacious; to choose a fortuitously well-documented example from Sinnar, the nobility of one district forced some of their subjects to surrender firearms obtained in defiance of the rules by closing the regional markets upon which the offending commoners depended for salt (Schuver 1884, p. 5). Prolonged and systematic defiance of the traditional code was not possible.

Royal Exchange

Like other members of Sudanic society, the kings were involved in relationships with equals which were expressed in reciprocal gift-giving. Some of these gifts had a ritual character; for example, at the major rite de passage of the state, the death of its sultan, neighbouring rulers were obliged by custom to send a funeral offering (sadaqa), often consisting of livestock. At the death of Sultan Muhammad al-Husayn of Dar Fur in 1873, the sadaqa sent by the sultan of Wadai consisted of a number of cows which were sacrificed locally at Abesher, and some hundred camel mares, which were sent to al-Fashir (Nachtigal 1971, p. 236). Just as ritual had its commercial aspect, so commerce had its ritual aspect. The trading season between the sultanate of the Zaghawa Kobe and that of Dar Tama was ceremonially opened each year by an exchange of gifts between the two sultans (Tubiana 1980, p. 6). Most gifts were made for political and economic reasons. Their material value varied according to the size of the states and the status of the sultans involved, and according to political circumstances. The gifts exchanged between the heads of the larger sultanates could be substantial. Ibrahim Yusuf, sultan of Wadai from 1898 to 1900, sent fifty magazine rifles, three boxes of ammunition, six horses, and two concubines to Sultan Ali Dinar of Dar Fur, probably to win his support (or neutrality) in the civil war which wrecked his reign (NRO Khartoum, Darfur 1/33/170). The diplomatic gifts exchanged between Ali Dinar and the Sultan of Dar Sila, which consisted mainly of slaves, cloth, clothes and riding animals, also had an economic dimension; the Sila sultan, living close to the slaving grounds, had an abundance of slaves, while Ali Dinar, whose capital boasted workshops with fine craftsmen, could provide silver-ornamented spears and rifles (Kapteijns and al-Hadi 1981).

Reciprocal gifts were the language of diplomacy and expressed both the nuances and fluctuations of political relations between the states. Whereas the gifts exchanged between the larger states were expressions of goodwill between equals, those exchanged between neighbours of unequal strength and prestige expressed differences in status. For example, the gifts demanded by the ruler of Wadai from the sultans on his eastern border are referred to in the oral sources as _diwan_, an irregular tribute paid by an autonomous and nominally independent ruler to his overlord (Kapteijns 1985, pp. 111-2). Contemporary written sources - letters from the Wadai government to the smaller sultans - avoid the term tribute and refer rather to presents made for the sake of brotherhood and economic exchange, but the threats they contain confirm the political character of the "gifts" (see Kapteijns 1985, p. 120). The latter consisted of small numbers of horses and military slaves (_jihadiyya_), both important instruments of war. Gifts of ivory did not figure, possibly because they would have symbolised direct dependence. In return for their gifts and recognition of Wadai as their overlord, the smaller sultans received gifts of (imported) clothes and cloth, gunpowder, dates, and other scarce goods (Kapteijns 1985, pp. 111-2, 120-21). Refusing to send presents meant war or political and economic retaliation, as is evident from the letters of the Wadai sultan to Dar Tama; these contained ultimata which allowed the Tama sultan four to six days to send the horses demanded from him before relations between the two states would be severed (Kapteijns 1985, p. 122). Sending worthless presents was as serious an offence as sending none. The same Tama sultan provoked the anger of the sultan of Wadai by sending "such a worthless and imperfect horse that (even) my slave would not mount it" (Kapteijns 1985, p. 111). In 1896 the parvenu ruler of the recently-established Masalit Sultanate, who claimed equality with the neighbouring sultans, regarded a present of "old slaves, bad horses, and broken rifles" from his northern neighbour as a _casus belli_ (Kapteijns 1985, p. 120). A similar incident in the seventeenth century had precipitated war between Sinnar and Ethiopia (O'Fahey and Spaulding 1974, pp. 37-8).

Trade between the eastern Sudan and the Mediterranean world seems to have flourished at various periods throughout the region's long recorded history, but these ages of interaction were interspersed with long intervals when such contacts were considerably less prominent (see Adams 1977). The last precolonial era of increased trading activity began about the middle of the seventeenth century and continued until the colonial conquest.[8] Sudanic rulers of this period took the initiative in opening and organising trade between their lands and the Mediterranean world. In doing so they were certainly attracted by the diverse array of goods available in the north and may also have been motivated by an awareness of the profits to be won by excluding middlemen and sending their wares directly to northern markets. The method employed by the kings was to dispatch special emissaries to the north, initially as diplomats, and thereafter as leaders of caravans and "royal merchants".[9] Each caravan sponsored by an eastern Sudanic ruler bore evidence of its royal patronage - if only in the form of a written authorisation or the presence of a royally-designated guide - and some were further distinguished by the participation of prominent courtiers and accompanied by a military escort and the sets of kettledrums that symbolised royal authority (Krump 1710, pp. 176-9, 202, 220). The Dar Fur caravans were led by khabirs appointed by the sultan. The khabirs represented "the state's authority beyond its borders" (O'Fahey 1980:144). They were accompanied by bearers of royal kettledrums, and sometimes even carried the sultan's seal (Cuny 1954:95,102). The Shilluk kingdom seems to have been an exception in this regard. The reths did not organise expeditions to the outside world, but rather asserted their authority when foreign merchants approached; they fed and lodged the traders and concluded exchanges promptly (Brun-Rollet 1855, pp. 95-9). These exceptional characteristics of the reth's foreign trade reflect the fact that the Shilluk were not Muslims; their circumstances may perhaps provide a model of those under which the kingdom of Sinnar, for example, was said to have adopted Islam to facilitate trade with Cairo (Bruce 1805, vol. 6, p. 371).

The arrival of a Sudan caravan at a northern market tended to produce a temporary glut of southern commodities, while inflating the prices of goods the southerners would want to buy. Therefore Sudanic kings often found it useful to station members of the royal family or to appoint other trusted agents at the northern termini to make the royal purchases at opportune seasons and to warehouse the king's exports until they could be sold on advantageous terms (see Walz 1978a, 1978b, 1979a, 1979b; O'Fahey 1980; Burckhardt 1822, Leyden 1817, p. 290). Having thus made wise use of the fluctuations of the northern markets and minimised turnaround time, the caravan would reassemble and bear the king's imports back to the Sudan.

Goods obtained by a king through royal exchange or imported from the Mediterranean world could be used in several ways. Noblesse oblige in the eastern Sudan, and conspicuous consumption was one of the obligations of royal status. The king's horses were of a superior breed, his rifles the most sophisticated, his scented garments wide and flowing, and the food served in his antechamber and eaten in his compound was often exotic, and always richer and more abundant than anywhere else. Many of the goods procured through foreign exchange were redistributed by the king to his subjects, primarily but not exclusively among other members of the ruling class. Redistribution was an important aspect of the relations between government and subjects. A substantial part of the sultan's share of the country's produce, paid to him as taxes, was redistributed to faqihs, royal relatives or favourites, and needy commoners. Like this local produce, the goods imported from abroad were redistributed on many occasions, both periodic and impromptu (see Spaulding 1979; Kapteijns 1985, pp. 147-8; Nachtigal 1971, p. 176; al-Tunisi 1845, p. 110; Massari 1881, p. 821). One such occasion was the Feast of Fastbreaking at the end of Ramadan, when the king formally received his provincial governors and district chiefs and presented them with robes befitting their status and ample food. He also opened his stores for faqihs associated with the court coming to pay their respects, and for his slave soldiers. In Dar Masalit the latter received fancy clothes "so that people would be afraid of them". Depending on their free or slave status, members of the royal household were presented with high-quality cloth or homespun. People were what they wore: Sultan Abbakr of Dar Masalit (1885-1903) dressed the daughters of the founder of the sultanate, his father, in special imported garments "so that people would know who they were" (Kapteijns 1985, p. 159; cf., al-Tunisi 1851, p. 371).[10] Royal presents did not only reward noble status but also special services rendered to the king; the weeding of the sultan's fields by commoners or the mediation of the faqihs in spiritual affairs, for example, were occasions for redistribution as well.[11]

Private Traders

Kings of the eastern Sudan enjoined their royal merchants and agents abroad to induce foreigners with valuable trade goods or professional skills to come to the Sudan (see O'Fahey and Spaulding 1974, p. 56; O'Fahey 1972, 1980; Nachtigal 1971, pp. 57,245; Cuny 1954, pp. 94-5). Therefore, although caravans consisting primarily or completely of royal merchants and the king's goods were by no means unknown, it was more common for a caravan of the eighteenth or nineteenth century to comprise both royal merchants and private, often foreign, traders (see Nachtigal 1971, pp. 123,203; Browne 1799, pp. 249-50). These private traders were attached to the royal caravan at its termini and subjected to its discipline. In return for obedience and loyalty they received the protection of the caravan's royal insignia and force of arms, the expertise of its guides, and the assurance of free mutual assistance if the private trader's transport animals died or his food supply ran low.[12]

Some private traders may well have been tempted to enter the Sudan trade on their own terms as smugglers. The southern kings, to discourage such enterprises, balanced their protection of official caravans with a policy of licensing and encouraging attacks on smugglers, thus mobilising the combined vigilance and armed force of all their subjects in defence of the royal commercial prerogatives. This aspect of royal policy is particularly well illustrated in the case of Sultan Ali Dinar of Dar Fur, whose surviving correspondence includes specific instructions to the Simiyat, a group of subjects whose tribal homeland lay along an interstate trade route:

> We impressed upon you with the necessary emphasis not to open the road to those who, without a licence, cross your country on their way to Omdurman with slaves and other goods. This matter will shorten your life and cause your destruction, if God wills, for you ignored our injunction. You committed an offence, so prepare yourselves to die if, from this moment onwards, you allow anybody to pass through your country without a licence. When a traveller comes to you, stop him. If you find a licence on him, fine; if not, arrest him with all he has with him and send him back to us, to be detained ... (Kapteijns 1985, p. 116;

cf Kumm 1910, p. 85 on Dar Kuti).

Both the positive and negative incentives to obedience are evident in the same king's instructions of 1901 addressed to potential foreign traders coming to him via the Anglo-Egyptian government:

> If you have trade goods to send to my country, I want you to appoint from your side special people, who must come to us for that particular purpose. Impress upon them that they must not sell their trade goods anywhere until they have reached me. If God wills, I will meet them and treat them with respect. Whether they bring little or much, we will buy it from them to their satisfaction, and will send them back to you while they are full of praise and gratitude towards us, with the necessary letters ... However, if they linger on the country roads, which are unsafe, we fear that mishap may befall them from the hands of wrongdoers, and it would be painful for us to have this attributed to our country (Kapteijns 1985, p.116; cf.,Cuny 1954, p. 111).

The sultan's letter offers a textbook model of how, according to the viewpoint of an eastern Sudanic king, interstate trade should be conducted.

When a royally-sponsored caravan entered its homeland, a number of formalities were observed at the frontier. Often a medical inspection and period of quarantine were imposed in the hope of preventing the importation of dread diseases, notably smallpox (see Krump 1710, pp. 230, 238; Foster 1949, p. 101; al-Tunisi 1851, pp. 61-2). Royal customs agents recorded the names, nationality, and wares of the private traders, who were admonished not to trade along the route to the capital and warned that they would be held accountable for their inventory on arrival at the sultan's court (see Krump 1710, p. 238; al-Tunisi 1851, pp. 55-62; Browne 1799, pp. 189-191). Within the peaceful confines of the kingdom a caravan might disperse into smaller groups for convenience in travel, but it would often regroup for a formal entry at its destination. Throughout, the private traders remained under the protection and command of the king, and in return for surrendering the freedom to trade en route, they enjoyed extraordinary prerogatives. If a private trader was robbed, the king would make good his loss; if he killed a subject of the sultan, the king would pay blood-money to save his life; if he died, the sultan would act as executor of his estate, gathering and registering his goods for safekeeping and notifying his heirs or business associates abroad.[13]

The entry of a caravan into the capital (or other designated <u>bandar</u>, or entrepot for interstate trade)[14] was a festive occasion announced by volleys of gunshots and drumming; veteran traders were welcomed by relatives and old friends, while newcomers sought out their ethnic kinsmen or co-religionists (Krump 1710, pp, 219-221, 280; Cailliaud 1823, vol. 2, pp. 10-11; Kapteijns 1985, p. 159; Jennings-Bramley 1940, p. 176). The caravan commander went at once to the king to submit confirmation that all the private merchants who had entered the kingdom had also arrived at the capital with their wares, but the practical accommodation of the private merchants into local society preceded the opening of trade. Each Sudanic court designated certain trusted individuals to act as patron to foreign merchants; the patron provided his clients with lodging and storage facilities, represented his interests at court, supervised his exchange activities, and reported any irregular behaviour to the appropriate authorities. Each foreign merchant must have one such patron (Krump 1710, p. 281; Nachtigal 1971, pp. 55, 123; al-Tunisi 1851, p. 44; Kapteijns 1985, p. 157; O'Fahey 1980, p. 142). As time passed a foreign merchant was encouraged to marry locally and put down family roots; these ties gave the government additional leverage over his loyalty and behaviour both in the capital and while on the road. The private traders formed a distinct community within the kingdom, concentrated in the capital or trading entrepot; they enjoyed both internal self-government under their own community officials and a special socio-legal status superior to that of the commoner class.[15]

Private traders were assessed fees for their use of the royally-sponsored interstate exchange facilities, an obligation analogous to the market dues of the lower, regional sphere of exchange, paid by Sudanic subjects to the noblemen who sponsored regional markets (Cailliaud, pp. 3, vol. 3, 121; Browne 1799, p. 191; Cuny 1954, p. 118; Nachtigal 1971, pp. 201-2; Jennings-Bramley 1940, pp. 175-6). Most capitals of the eastern Sudan had large market-places, but interstate trade did not ordinarily take place there. Moreover, this difference in physical setting was only one of several institutional usages which distinguished foreign commerce from the regional level of exchange as practiced in the king's city. A foreign merchant's exchange activities began with the delivery of presents to the king. These "Royal Greetings" were chosen for their intrinsic value, rarity or uniqueness, and their appropriateness to the kingly ambience - typical examples would include full-length mirrors, sets of Venetian crystal, and saddles or repeating rifles inlaid with silver and gold.[16] The next two stages of trade were also exchanges between the private merchant and the monarch, but at this point the king often delegated his authority to the merchant's patron or other designated court official. Firstly, the king or his agent claimed possession of the merchant's entire stock of certain goods - for example, firearms and gunpowder - which only the king could legitimately purchase.[17] Secondly, the king or his agent exercised a right of first choice over the merchant's entire remaining stock, selecting the quantity and quality desired of all his wares (see Kapteijns 1982; Bjorkelo 1976; Brun-Rollet 1855). The king or his agent would then give the merchant Sudanese commodities in payment for the imported wares selected - though often payment was made only after a rather prolonged delay (see Nachtigal 1971, p. 202; O'Fahey 1973, pp. 31-7). A wise king endeavoured to send the private traders away content:

> The goods which he (Makk Nimr of Shendi) selected were exchanged by his vizier who was under instructions to behave with justice and in no way to compromise the interests of his friends as he called the merchants (Santi and Hill 1980, p. 75).

Meanwhile other members of the royal family and state officials would take their turns in visiting the merchant to accept presents appropriate to their rank and to select wares from what the king had left behind. When the high officials had completed their selection, the king might allow the merchant to expose his wares to all and sundry, or even to travel from place to place in the kingdom to dispose of his remaining goods. At this stage even a commoner could buy, if he had sufficient wealth and if the merchant had goods which individuals of lowly status were allowed to own (Kapteijns 1982, pp. 183, 186; Machtigal 1971, pp. 82-3). In other cases, however, the king exacted a further charge on the private trader (and guaranteed the observance of sumptuary rules among his subjects) by obliging the merchant, before passing out into the countryside, to exchange all his imported wares at royally-determined rates for local currencies such as homespun cloths - which had previously been collected as taxes by the king and stored in his treasury (see Santi 1965, p. 87; Krump 1710, p. 288). If any subject, high or low, failed to pay a private merchant for goods taken in purchase, the king undertook to enforce the terms of the transaction:

> When in Wadai the time has come for the departure of a caravan to the north, and some of those who want to travel have not succeeded in collecting their debts, they turn to the king who does not delay in announcing clearly to the negligent debtor, whether a high official or a slave, 'If you have not satisfied your creditor by such and such a date, you will go with him as a slave as a substitute for the money you owe him' (Nachtigal 1971,p.52; cf., Kapteijns 1982, p. 181; Ohrwalder 1892, p. 236).

When a private merchant had disposed of all the imported wares he had (or could expect to sell) and had received Sudanic goods in payment, he began the process of departure. The king or his agent advised the merchant as to which goods would be most suitable for importation on future journeys, and bestowed a farewell present (see Krump 1710, pp. 352-5; Nachtigal 1971, p. 374). Sometimes the farewell present was small and of primarily symbolic value, but in other instances the authorities obliged the merchant to accept the advance of quantities of export goods,thus co-opting his services and in effect transforming him into a "royal merchant".[18] In either case, when the negotiations were complete the king granted the merchant permission to depart, often couched in the form of a written laissez-passer.[19] The merchant would join an outward-bound caravan and leave the kingdom, as he had arrived, under the royal aegis. The laissez-passers often prescribed the route the caravan was to take, and by specifically recommending it to both the local governors and the neighbouring sovereigns through whose territories it was to pass, the king attempted to extend the system of royally-administered trade beyond the state boundaries.

Implicit Tension in the Mediterranean Trade

When an eastern Sudanic king opened trade with the Mediterranean world, he tended to assume that at the other end of the route could be found a counterpart to himself, a ruler who regulated foreign trade according to precapitalist principles similar to those which he shared with his fellow sultans of the south. In the eighteenth and nineteenth centuries this assumption was not correct, for the Mediterranean governments of the day endorsed quite different economic principles, typical of commercial capitalism, which placed far fewer political limitations on the right of subjects to travel and to trade. Thus when Ali Dinar extended the invitation to trade cited above, the Anglo-Egyptian authorities possessed no institutions of government-sponsored commerce through which they could have responded positively. Many of the private traders trained in the expectations and customary usages of the Mediterranean world, for their part, must have shared the revulsion expressed by one nineteenth-century merchant as he sailed quickly past the Shilluk kingdom in order to purchase ivory from the more malleable stateless societies further south. While the reth also had ivory to sell, it was preferable not to risk one's capital in a realm where only one customer existed, and therefore where "the merchant's loss or gain is entirely dependent upon the caprices of the king, or the hostile or welcoming disposition of his courtiers" (Brun-Rollet 1855, p. 96). Resignation rather than revulsion was expressed by the trader Yunus Badis, whom the sultan of Dar Sila compelled to return a slave woman he had just bought:

> The woman did not want to return, nor did I want to give her up, but as the sultan was the only man through whom I could sell my merchandise, I thought it best to give way (Jennings-Bramley 1940, p. 176).

The implicit conflict between precapitalist Sudanic and capitalist Mediterranean institutions of foreign trade manifested itself during the last century of the eastern Sudan's independence as a series of acrimonious rivalries - between the king's subjects and the royally-sponsored foreigners, between the king's traders and private merchants, between the king and his subordinate governors, and between the king and his royal neighbours.

One source of tension lay in the favoured status of foreign traders and the opportunities for enrichment accorded them by the kings. Many southern subjects of the eighteenth and nineteenth centuries must have shared the recorded views of would-be ivory merchants among the Shilluk during the period from 1840 to 1865, who regarded their king's monopoly of the trade and collusive favouritism towards selected foreigners as tyrannical. Shilluk of the northern districts of the kingdom, who had made common cause with newly arrived Arabic-speaking immigrant traders from the north, openly expressed an eagerness to be "emancipated from the tyranny of the Reth and his counsellors" (Beltrame 1881, p. 86). But the clearest record of popular resentment against foreign traders comes from Wadai:

> The higher the esteem in which the king with his partiality for trade and commerce held the foreign merchants, and the greater the profit gained by them from their activities in the country, the more unpopular they were with the natives. With their boundless fear of the king, the natives indeed tolerated the foreigners, but nevertheless looked on them as intruders and

parasites who live sumptuously at their expense (Nachtigal 1971, p. 59; cf., Cuny 1954, pp. 88-9).

A king could respond to such pressures either by curtailing the trade and expelling the envied foreigners, or by allowing at least some of his subjects to enjoy similar opportunities. While a few instances of expulsion are known (see Gray 1961, p. 76; Nachtigal 1971, pp. 51,57), most rulers made the latter choice.

The rise to prominence of private traders of southern origin may be documented in the Nile-valley kingdom of Sinnar by a change, over the course of the eighteenth century, in the nomenclature used to designate a private merchant. In earlier times the accepted term was khawaja, a word that carried connotations of pale complexion and foreign origin (Brocchi 1843, vol.5, pp. 317,330; Bruce 1805, vol. 6, p. 362; al-Shatir Busayli 1961, pp. 17-18). By the nineteenth century a more common term for private merchant was jallab, which might well mean "foreigner" in some contexts, but which did not imply non-Sudanic origin. During the nineteenth century the jallaba of the Nile valley joined private traders of Mediterranean origin as agents in the conduct of the foreign trade of the western sultanates, and in the twentieth, men of western origin who aspired to the vocation of private trader often adopted their ethos and label of identity.[20] In the precolonial western sultanates, comparative paucity of towns and the considerably smaller scale of the market in food grains reflected the weakness (in some cases even the absence) of an indigenous merchant class, a condition favourable to the survival into the twentieth century of royally-administered trade. In the eastern kingdoms, however, the development of an indigenous merchant class had profound social implications, most of which lie beyond the scope of this essay, which is confined to an examination of precolonial trade between states.

A second set of tensions arose between the king's merchants and the private traders who attached themselves to a royal caravan. The ideology of caravan organisation, as expressed (for example) in the oath of obedience and mutual support which the members of a Sinnar caravan swore on departure, asserted that all the members of a royal caravan were engaged in a single common enterprise (Krump 1710, p. 369; Foster 1949, pp. 94-5). In practice, however, the interests of the royal merchants and the private traders were by no means always identical, and this divergence of interests became increasingly acute as the native-born jallaba gradually eclipsed the khawajat in importance. For, if some of the jallaba, in functional terms, were simply khawajat with dark skins, many were much poorer individuals who intended to conduct a fundamentally different kind of commerce. The origins of this second commerce must be sought in the details of royal caravan practice.

As a royal caravan traversed its homeland, the private merchants - who, unlike the royal agents, had no claim on the state revenues in kind hoarded at intervals along the way - were obliged to enter the regional markets and even the local sphere of exchange in order to obtain supplies. Anecdotal evidence suggests that such interactions formed an important channel for introducinig foreign products of comparatively low unit value (e.g. soap, beads, or nails) and occasionally even foreign coinage into the lower spheres of exchange.[21]. The poorer jallaba joined a royal caravan with the intention of trading in these lowly commodities, a traffic which may be viewed in analytical terms as an extension of the regional level of exchange to the Mediterranean market. The interests of these petty traders were best served by freedom of schedule and geographical mobility, and the avoidance of government representatives, who expected presents and seized forbidden goods. While participation in a royal caravan conferred some important benefits - it was the only safe and legitimate way to enter and leave the country - it did not always serve their interests.

A dramatic example of the clash between the conflicting interests of royal merchants and private traders is afforded by the case of the northward-bound Sinnar caravan in 1702. When confronted by insecurity on the road to Egypt, the well-capitalised royal merchants preferred to wait at their national border until the safety of their passage could be assured. Such a delay spelled ruin for the private merchants with their more limited resources, and this conflict was probably a common feature of mixed private/royal caravans:

> Most of the jallaba were in such a state of misery and want due to the loss of so many camels and the purchase and maintenance of new ones that they were forced to sell their wares, slaves and other belongings for a joke. It went so far that they bartered even their lances, their one weapon with which to oppose their enemies, to obtain food for their camels. Some of them, with the loss of their camels, were forced to leave their wares here (Krump 1710, pp. 378-80).

When the private traders took matters into their own hands and "resolved to enter the high desert in a few days, (trusting) in the name of God and their false Prophet", the sultan's caravan commander imposed strict discipline:

> Therefore, the whole caravan was summoned to a general council, and the royal merchants from Sinnar decreed that whoever moved from here before confirmation of the security of the roads would be declared a rebel against the king (Krump 1710, pp, 378-80).

Not surprisingly, "the tempers of both factions became so embittered that it might easily have led to an exchange of lances ... it would have only taken a little to bring them against each other with weapons in hand" (Krump 1710, pp. 378-80). While the pressure of delay bankrupted khawajat as well as jallaba, it bore more heavily upon the latter because, as a rule, they were poorer.[22] Or again, the caravans sponsored by the nineteenth-century government of Dar Fur imposed the regulation that upon arrival in Egypt, all goods whatsoever - including those of private traders as well as royal merchants - must be exchanged exclusively by the king's caravan leader: "no one among the jallaba may sell individually what belongs to him - it is a right reserved to the khabir" (Cuny 1954, p. 103; cf., Browne 1799, p. 225). The perceptive observer Charles Cuny felt that this monopolistic policy would soon collapse, however:

for the vices of the present system are too visible and too contrary to the interests of the private merchants ("particuliers") to require enumeration ... if each of the jallaba had been able to sell these elephants' teeth in smaller units as he saw fit, they would surely have been sold at a considerably greater profit (Cuny 1954, pp. 103-4).

The commercial interests of the Fur sultan, conversely, were best served by the maintenance of the monopoly, which insured that the king's wares could not be undersold.

Political authority in the states of the eastern Sudan was usually decentralised geographically, and a third set of tensions arose between the sultan's government which sponsored the royal caravans and the lesser authorites whose territories they traversed. While these tensions were common to all states of the eastern Sudan, they were most conspicuous in the case of Sinnar. It was accepted practice that the lesser lords should receive presents from passing merchants, which was often accomplished with dignified ceremony (see Krump 1710, pp. 304-5; Burckhardt 1822, p. 347; Nachtigal 1971, pp. 231,242), but they were allowed neither to open a trade with the royal merchants nor to sponsor caravans of their own. The fact that many lesser lords found this to be a grievance may be inferred from the lengthy record of their misdemeanors in regard to foreign trade. In some cases they attempted to open and examine cargoes destined for the sultan himself (Krump 1710, pp. 236-44). They extorted additional presents from merchants through such devices as threatening to report the presence of smallpox in the caravan, or simply through personal intimidation or the robbery of selected individuals (for incidents, see Krump 1710, pp. 230-45,265,271,382; cf., Cuny 1954, p. 87). They delayed each passing caravan as long as possible so that private merchants would be obliged to barter their trade goods for food and supplies at ever-inflating prices (Krump 1710, pp. 230,278-80; Burckhardt 1822, pp. 282-3; Kapteijns 1985, p. 195). In more extreme cases, a lord blessed with a suitably impregnable base of operations might adopt the vocation of robber baron, systematically looting the caravans of his betters (Cailliaud 1823, vol. 2, pp. 68,120; Krump 1710, pp. 231,256-7,264-5,369; Burckhardt 1822, pp. 151,224-6). (He might judiciously allow the merchants who did not resist to travel on with a portion of their wares so that the trade might continue.) Alternatively, an advantageously-situated lord might transform his people into a tribe of smugglers.[23] In the early eighteenth century the sultans of Sinnar found themselves obliged to allow two of their subordinate territorial lords to send their own official merchants - complete with the vassals' kettledrums - along with the royal caravan (Krump 1710, pp. 220, 262). It was not enough; by the end of the century most of the northern vassals of Sinnar had established their own commercial and diplomatic agents abroad, and were engaged in wholesale smuggling in systematic defiance of the sultan's prerogatives (Burckhardt 1822, pp. 2, 233).

A final set of tensions that may be attributed to the opening of royal trade between the states of the eastern Sudan and the Mediterranean world arose from the geographically-determined differential access of these states to the north. While kingdoms such as Sinnar, Wadai and Dar Fur were in direct contact with the North African trading centres, other states could conduct their Mediterranean trade only by passing through the territories of these sovereigns, who were therefore in a position to exploit this dependence on their goodwill. The conflicts which erupted periodically date back to early times; one cause of the first Sinnar-Ethiopia war, for example, was the alleged hindrance by the Funj king of a caravan bringing a new bishop to Ethiopia from Egypt (O'Fahey and Spaulding 1974, pp. 59-61). Most notorious for using commercial sanctions as a political weapon was Ali Dinar, ruler of the restored Dar Fur Sultanate from 1898 to 1916. Those states which challenged his conviction that they were part of Dar Fur and ignored his command not to submit to the French conquerors saw their communications with North Africa (and Mecca) cut off. Ali Dinar imprisoned or enslaved all merchants and pilgrims going north and stopped all caravans heading for the south and west (Kapteijns 1985:, pp. 76, 195-7). In 1911 the following colourful anecdote was related in the Nile valley:

> A certain merchant sold an English spring mattress to a native Sultan in the Bahr-el-Ghazal, and the fame of this article of luxury spread abroad even unto the kingdom of Dar Fur. Thereupon the merchant received shortly afterwards a letter from Ali Dinar, asking why the bed had not been offered to him, as he could have paid twice the sum. The merchant hastened to reply that he would himself bring a similar bed to Dar Fur without delay. Accordingly he set out, but no sooner had he arrived, after many days' toilsome journey, than he was summoned into the presence of Ali Dinar, violently reproached for having given first choice to a negro potentate instead of to an Arab Sultan, and then cut up into several hundred pieces (Stevens 1912, pp. 229-30).

Apparently Ali Dinar carried his jealous attempts to control the foreign trade of the small states south of Dar Fur so far that he avenged without mercy even minor slights to his prestige.

Royal Trade in Eclipse

The royally-administered commerce of the western sultans survived into the twentieth century; however, the corresponding sphere of exchange in the Nile-valley kingdoms experienced the cumulative impact of the tensions enumerated above at an early date (Sinnar) and in acute form (the Shilluk). Evidence derived from the period around the fall of Sinnar (in 1820/21) reveals the survival of many of the external forms of the old sultanic commerce. However, these vestigial institutions no longer possessed major economic significance when compared with the flourishing efflorescence of private enterprise, and in many cases showed evidence of corruption through the commoditisation of relationships previously upheld by fiat or by force.

One concession wrested by private merchants from the king was the right to compete with his tribute-collectors in the acquisition of

Sudanic goods for export. Pioneer entrepreneurs from Sinnar (1770s) penetrated the gold-producing districts of Fazughli (Abu Salim n.d.:I,doc.22; Triulzi 1981), and bands of private traders from Dar Fur and Wadai (1840s) sought out the gold of southern Kordofan (Brun-Rollet 1855, p. 131). While evidence is lacking, a private trade in ivory, civet, and similar commodities probably developed simultaneously and along similar lines. Kings were able to compete effectively with the private traders in the exceptionally dangerous activity of seizing slaves. In Dar Fur private traders advanced the capital to finance slave raids but played a subordinate role in slave acquisition (O'Fahey 1973, pp. 31-37). Similarly, in late Sinnar private merchants were allowed to follow the raiding armies into the field and to make their purchases at a discreet distance behind the lines.[24] But the growth of a free market in slaves often tempted rulers to abuse their power by enslaving and selling the more vulnerable of their subjects - at the ultimate cost of their own legitimacy.[25]

The last kings of Sinnar also sacrificed their monopoly over the organisation of caravans to the outside world. Periodic royal caravans still set out, but the relative significance of these ventures dwindled towards the vanishing point amid the private commercial boom (see Walz 1978a). The organisation of a private caravan superficially resembled that of a royal one, but there were important differences. Private caravans received neither leaders nor armed escorts from the king; the role of caravan-guide became a private entrepreneurial profession (it was judicious to pay his fee, but not essential to obey him), and the sale of protection to caravans became a major industry among strategically-located groups such as the Ababda (see Burckhardt 1822, pp. 153, 191, 326). A caravan member whose pack animal died underway could still expect the assistance of his fellow-travellers in transporting his goods to the next settlement; but in contrast to the usage of the olden days, he could now also expect to pay handsomely for this service (see Burckhardt 1822, p. 164). The role of the king as the guardian of commercial probity underwent a corresponding transformation; in theory a dissatisfied creditor could still seek relief by appealing to the king, but the fact that by 1814 long-term credit arrangements among import-export traders had virtually disappeared strongly suggests that such appeals were not generally believed to be efficacious (see Burckhardt 1822, p. 266). When a king recovered stolen property for a merchant, he now expected to be paid for the service (Burckhardt 1822, pp. 253, 333). The kings preserved some of the time-honoured techniques for extracting a profit from private traders; they still expected "greeting" presents and sometimes exercised the right of option over exotic imported goods they particularly desired.[26] An important indirect form of taxation available to the king lay in the temporary closure of the market to private traders whenever the king had import or export goods to sell.[27] This practice reveals that by 1821 the value of royal commodities was determined by market mechanisms rather than royal fiat. Finally, the king no longer bestowed a farewell present on departing merchants as an investment and gesture of good will; rather, he demanded that they give something more to him (Burckhardt 1822, pp. 229, 233). In summary, a Sudanic ruler who had once organised and dominated the foreign trade of his country could now aspire no higher in this regard than to remain one prominent businessman among many others. For a variety of reasons not directly related to the question of trade between states, however, even this limited ambition was to prove excessive.

The experience of the Shilluk kingdom may serve as an exemplary model of the political consequences of the socio-economic themes discussed above. As late as the 1840s a system of administered trade between the reth's agents and a few, specified foreign merchants remained intact. Over the next two decades an influx of foreign private traders was tolerated, and Shilluk political opinion divided into a party of conservatives who wanted the foreigners expelled and a party of liberals who advocated the extension of trading privileges (and the right to own firearms) to Shilluk commoners. The accession of a conservative reth and his subsequent expulsion of foreigners in September, 1860 precipitated civil war; by 1862 the liberal faction and their jallaba allies had prevailed, but the final victory was not to be theirs. The neighbouring Turkish government in Khartoum found the turmoil a suitable occasion to send troops, and in 1863 Shilluk independence was extinguished (see Gray 1961, pp. 33-4, 53, 74-8).

Conclusion

The eastern Sudan has a long tradition of state societies. These states were organised according to precapitalist principles up to the eve of the colonial conquest, and were thereafter transformed to permit incorporation into a capitalist-dominated world. This chapter has explored one dimension of this transformation, that which concerns the institutions through which the states of the eastern Sudan conducted their external trade during their last century of independence (approximately, the eighteenth century along the Nile and the nineteenth farther west). The kingdoms of this region shared a common set of institutions governing the conduct of their mutual interstate exchanges. This precolonial interstate trade was organised by the kings and carried out by their agents, not because the common people of the eastern Sudan possessed a psychology different from that of other people, but because the society of each kingdom was specifically structured to prevent their participation in foreign trade either as agents or as consumers of imports (except under very unusual circumstances), while compelling them to produce a quantity of goods suitable for export and to deliver them as taxes to the government. The goods exchanged between precolonial rulers of the eastern Sudan consisted of luxury items of local provenance such as horses, ivory, and slaves. One may infer that the precolonial trade between kingdoms was not essential to their existence, but that it played a significant secondary role by enhancing the superiority of the ruling elite, and particularly the kings.

A series of trade routes from the eastern Sudan to the Mediterranean world were opened (or reopened) beginning as early as the mid-seventeenth century but assumed much greater prominence during the eighteenth and nineteenth centuries. A comparative wealth of source material permits a rather detailed description of this particular form of commerce. The kings who opened the Mediterranean trade expected to conduct it according to familiar principles, and they assumed - in most cases, correctly - that their governments were strong enough to absorb an influx of foreign traders, foreign goods, and foreign ideas. However, a close examination of the royally-initiated Mediterranean commerce reveals that it introduced a series of problems peculiar to itself, the presence of privileged foreigners antagonised southern subjects who, when allowed to join the royal caravans, began an altogether different types of commerce and joined the foreigners in chaffing at the restrictions imposed by the government. Members of the lower echelons of the ruling elite rebelled in various ways against their exclusion from the unprecedented opportunities of the Mediterranean trade, which also nourished rivalries between those kingdoms that enjoyed comparatively easy access to the outside world and those that did not.

The problems mentioned above may be summarised as a challenge presented to the traditional Sudanic institutions of royally-sponsored interstate trade by commercial capitalism as practiced in the Mediterranean world. This challenge did not affect all the kingdoms of the eastern Sudan equally, nor at the same date, nor was it by any means confined to the limited issue of trade between states with which this essay is concerned. The Nile-valley kingdom of Sinnar experienced the challenge first; her royally-sponsored trade withered during the eighteenth century, eclipsed by private enterprise, and her jallaba of capitalist persuasion set out to evangelise their western and southern neighbours during the nineteenth century. But the difficult course and ultimate success of their mission, as the case of the Shilluk kingdom exemplifies, must be understood within the context of the advance of Turkish, French, and British colonialism into the eastern Sudan. An illustrative example of the termination of royally-administered trade by a conquering colonial power may be found in the treaty by which the sultan of Dar Sila surrendered to the French in November, 1909 (quoted in translation from Arabic original in Kapteijns 1985, p. 182):

> The French will be the protectors and we the rulers in our country. The roads will be open for the traders and for all the commoners. Slaves will not be sold anymore.

Notes

1. The original version of this article, supplied with correct diacritical marks for non-English transliterations, appeared in African Economic History, 11 (1982), pp. 30-62. We are grateful to the editors for permission to reprint this material here.

2. Our viewpoint may be contrasted with the "African Mode of Production" proposed by Catherine Coquery-Vidrovitch, the defining characteristic of which was that it was "based upon the combination of a patriarchal agrarian economy with a low internal surplus and the exclusive ascendancy of one group over long-distance trade;" see Coquery-Vidrovitch (1978, p. 106). Terray (1974, pp. 316-8) summarises a number of similar viewpoints.

3. The most eloquent and extended defence of this interpretation may be found in Terence Walz (1978a). A recent study of Dar Fur by R.S. O'Fahey (1980, p. 132) has also concluded that the foreign trade of the sultanate was "responsive to market forces and was largely under the control of the merchants themselves," while the Keira government played only a subordinate and facilitating role. A similar though slightly more differentiated point of view is expressed in A.J. Bjorkelo (1976, p. 175). The attitude of these scholars seems to perpetuate a longstanding North African prejudice in regard to the rulers of the Sudanic belt. When the Governor-General of Tripoli in ca. 1870 gave Gustav Nachtigal a personal letter of introduction to the sultan of Wadai, the latter considered this to be an insult, "and found it quite strange that a pasha of Tripoli should wish to teach the king of Wadai how he should conduct himself with strangers" (Nachtigal 1971, p. 130). We share the indignation of the king.

4. An able defence of the former, "formalist" viewpoint in the West African context may be found in Hopkins (1973). An unusually belligerent exposition of the latter, psychologising approach is offered by Lamberg-Karlovsky (1975).

5. For examples, see the fate of the refugees from war in western Dar Fur in the period from 1874 to 1890 as described in Kapteijns (1985, pp. 50-2) and Carbou (1912, vol. 2, p. 124); the fate of the refugees from drought in Wadai in 1912/13 as described in Kapteijns (1985, p. 52) and SHAT (France) Tachad, Carton 3, dossier 2, Capt. Simones, 17/2/1914; and the fate of those who had committed a crime for which their kinsmen were unable or not willing to pay compensation (Kapteijns 1985, p. 141).

6. The general principle involved was expressed well by the informants of Lorenzo d'Anania, who explained that the Tunjur king of Uri (Dar Fur, ca. 1580) "is supplied with arms by the merchants of Cairo who come there because of the quantity of gold found there. The prince does not wish this gold to be used in his country in order that the people will not, out of

avarice, become greedy for the metal, nor that it will be lacking for trade, so that the merchants will no longer come. He therefore wishes that they use barter" (Lange and Berthoud 1972, pp. 342-45). For Shilluk examples of a similar royal logic, see Luzarche d'Azay (1904, pp. 95-6). For similar practices among the hunting peoples of Sinnar see Myers (1876, pp. 152, 185-186, 208, 214). The Masalit sultan, like the sultans of Wadai and Dar Fur, had a right to one of the two tusks of every elephant found dead or killed within the state's boundaries (Kapteijns 1985, pp. 119, 160). See also Nachtigal (1971, pp. 181-2, 359) for the diwan paid to the Wadai sultan in the 1870s and Kapteijns (1985, pp. 111-2) for that paid to him in the 1890s. For a discussion of a region where gold rather than animal products was the preferred form of tribute and most highly-desired export commodity, see Spaulding (1980).

7. For Shilluk examples see Brun-Rollet (1855, pp. 96-7). For examples from Sinnar, see Montano (1948, vol. 2, p. 423), Krump (1710, pp. 299-300), and Bruce (1805, vol. 6, p. 291). In Wadai, ostrich feather standards and an ostrich feather fan belonged to the regalia; see Nachtigal (1971, pp. 128, 173, cf., p. 343)) and El-Tounsy (1851, p. 372)..

8. This periodisation, based largely one evidence from the Nile valley, may require qualification in regard to the region to the west. Individual Egyptian merchants penetrated parts of the northeastern Sudan during the age before the opening of the royal caravan trade, relying upon the guidance and protection of border tribes; for a discussion, see Walz (1979, pp. 211-33).

9. An example is afforded by the reopening of the trade route between Wadai and Benghazi by Sultan Muhammad Sharif of Wadai in 1836; see Cordell (1977, pp. 21-36). Krump (1710, p. 171) described Abdin, the leader of his caravan, as "the commander and guide"; he was apparently not familiar with the title of khabir, "guide" commonly applied to such an official. Krump added that Abdin "was the foremost of the merchants, not only because he was an old, highly-experienced man, but also because he had been sent by the king of Sinnar to Egypt to purchase things for him and necessities for the kingdom". Abdin was accompanied by a number of men whom Krump called "royal merchants". This term meant "the merchants who carry the goods of the king of Sinnar" (Krump 1710, p. 229) or, more precisely, who accompanied the caravan on the backs of horses or donkeys and gave orders to the "servants" on foot (Krump 1710, p. 220) who conducted "the camels of the king of Sinnar" (Krump 1710, p. 219), which latter actually bore the royal burden.

10. Kapteijns 1985, p. 159; cf., al-Tunisi 1851, p. 371. Among the Shilluk (1841), only the leaders of villages and higher-ranking officials were allowed to wear cloth garments, which were imported from abroad by the reth and distributed by him to lesser dignitaries. See Werne (1848, pp. 462, 492, 498).

11. Many examples of such donations by kings to holy men may be found in the Tabaqat of Wad Dayf Allah, a contemporary compilation of biographies of religious dignitaries. See Yusuf Fadl Hasan (1971). For Masalit examples, see Kapteijns (1985, p. 150).

12. The oath of agreement by which private merchants were attached to a royal caravan was recorded by Krump (1710, p. 369): "On the sixth (of August, 1702) Abdin, the guide and commander of the caravan, had all the jallaba called together before sundown by the customary beating of the kettledrum. After prayers, they placed themselves in a circle on the bare earth, with feet crossed over each other, and he made a speech concerning the four following points. Firstly, tomorrow he intended that they should enter the very dangerous Bayuda Desert, full of Arabs and rebellious subjects ... Because the enemy was very strong each and every one should fight well with weapons; if there was an encounter, they should fight and defend themselves like knights to the last man. To this they bound themselves by their customary oath, wa-Allahi, that is, 'By God'. Then he ordered the caravan, which was more than two thousand five hundred camels strong and could offer stiff resistance to the enemy, that they should not separate far from each other, but should rather march at all times together. Finally, he added that if one or another of the jallaba was not completely ready for the journey he should openly say so, so that everybody could help him and he would not be prevented from making the journey. Under such circumstances no one abandons his fellow. Everyone assented to this speech ..." Specific examples of mutual aid were recorded by Krump on several occasions (1710, pp. 204, 206, 214, 216-7). One may compare Cuny's statement (1954, p. 119) that members of a Dar Fur caravan, before re-entering their homeland, often took an oath that they would not inform the king of anything that the khabir decided to keep from his knowledge.

13. For the compensation paid by the sultan when traders were robbed in his kingdom see Kapteijns 1985, pp. 157-8, 166 and Hasan b. Shawir, "Wadih al-bayan fi muluk al-Arab bi'l-Sudan", NRO (Khartoum) Miscellaneous 1/20/232. Of Wadai sultan Dud Murra (1902-1909) it was said: "If a merchant is killed the Sultan is sure to revenge him, and should the merchant kill a native the Sultan himself would pay the blood-money", NRO (Khartoum) Intelligence 2/5/125. See also Nachtigal (1971, p. 54), to whom Sultan Ali of Wadai explained that "the gifts he received or claimed from foreign travellers were ... in the nature of a tax for which as a counterpart he undertook to guarantee the security of their property and person." For the role of the Sinnar sultan as estate executor see Spaulding (1977, p. 414 and note 8).

14. In states which used numerous terms of discourse borrowed from the Islamic heartlands an authorised centre for the conduct of foreign trade was often called a bandar. From the perspective of Egypt, for example, the town of Sinnar was a bandar (Douin 1944, vol. 1, p. 95). Funj legal documents usually referred to

the town of Sinnar as a madina, "city", a term implying elevated status which also incorporated the concept of an authorised centre for the conduct of foreign trade. Among the other places of origin of Funj legal documents, only Qarri ever employed the title madina (Abu Salim 1967, p. 124), and Qarri was more commonly termed a bandar. The fact that Qarri (along with Old Dongola and Sinnar itself) was one of the three authorised centres for the conduct of royal trade abroad in 1700 may be substantiated from the testimony of Krump (1710, p. 220). During the course of the eighteenth century, several of the new towns of the Funj kingdom arrogated to themselves the title of bandar: al-Halfaya (Abu Salim 1967, p. 108), al-Timayd (Abu Salim 1967, p. 142) and Shandi (Abu Salim n.d., vol. 2, no pagination, two examples). In some cases the authorised foreign trading centres of the western sultanates were also designated bandar: al-Fashir (NRO (Khartoum) Mahdiyya 2/5 I 321) and Dirjayi (Kapteijns 1985, p. 335, Interview 27). Nachtigal distinguished between the authorised international entrepots and the regional markets of Wadai: "The wholesale (foreign) trade of Wadai, if it can be so described, is carried on in the capital Abeshr, and in Nimro, the town of the merchants; public (regional) markets are held in only three or four other places" (1971, p. 203).

14. For the distinct trading communities in Dar Masalit, Wadai, and Dar Fur, see respectively Kapteijns (1985, p. 157); Nachtigal (1971, pp. 61-2); and Cuny (1954, pp. 88,108). "This is a free city," wrote the European Krump (1710, p. 285) in Sinnar, "and men of any nationality or faith may live in it without a single hindrance." See also Spaulding (1977, pp. 413-14). By the 1840s even the Shilluk kingdom had its community of Muslim traders, whom the reth allowed to settle near his capital (Brun-Rollet 1855, p. 94).

15. Krump (1710, p. 284). In 1820 the khabir of a caravan in Dongola bound for Kordofan (at that time under the rule of Dar Fur) expressed his delight at the gift of a box of matches and a bottle of sulphuric acid from the explorer Cailliaud; he was sure that these unusual gifts would bring him a rich reward from the "Sultan of Kordofan" (Cailliaud 1823, vol. 2, p. 14). In 1873 Nachtigal tried to impress the sultan of Wadai with a telescope; the sultan, however, found the device useless and returned the gift. Nachtigal eventually disposed of the telescope by giving it to the sultan of Dar Fur, who also received a music-box (1971, pp. 54, 370). For the greeting-presents given to the Wadai sultan by Tripolitanian traders, see Nachtigal (1971, p. 130).

17. See Jennings Bramley (1940) for the royal monopoly on gunpowder in Wadai, and Kapteijns and al-Hadi Ahmad (1981, pp. 62-3, 70) for the sultanic prerogatives in regard to the trade in firearms and ammunition. In the Mahdist State, the government undertook to disarm the population by buying up all the firearms, possession of which had become common during the Turkish period, and then imposing severe penalties for individuals who had not turned in their weapons through the established channels; see

Ohrwalder (1892, p. 223). A similar policy applied to suits of armour.

18. We feel that the extension of an obligatory credit relationship, be it great or small, was implicit in the institution of the king's farewell gift to a foreign merchant upon his departure. While direct evidence from the eastern Sudan is perhaps not conclusive, travellers in sixteenth-century Ethiopia very explicitly documented this method of royal involvement in foreign trade: "This town of Manadeley (near modern Maqalle) is a town of very great trade, like a great city or seaport. Here they find every kind of merchandise that there is in the world, and merchants of all nations, also all the languages of the Moors, from Giada, from Morocco, Fez, Bugia, Tunis, Turks, Roumes from Greece, Moors of India (who are like inhabitants there), Ormuz and Cairo; also they bring merchandise from all parts. While we were in this country the Moors, inhabitants of this town, were complaining, saying that the Prester John (the Ethiopian emperor) had by force thrust upon them 1,000 _ouquias_ (ounces) of gold, saying that he was lending them for them to trade with, and that each year they were to give him another 1,000 _ouquias_ interest, and that his own 1,000 should always remain alive." See Beckingham and Huntingford (1961, vol. 1, p. 187). The kings, for their part, were sometimes disappointed by the services of less-than-reliable agents thus recruited. For example, a _jallab_ named Khalifa al-Hajj Dalil, having visited al-Fashir, Kafia Kinji, and N'dele, won the confidence of Sultan Bakhayt of Dar Sila, who entrusted him with seventy oxen and forty-four donkeys to go trade at Kafia Kinji. The _jallab_ returned with empty hands and excuses, but again won the sultan's trust. In March 1912 Bakhayt sent the trader out with a princely consignment of four hundred kilos of royal ivory and rhinoceros horn - only to be betrayed again (SHAT (France), Carton 3, dossier 2, Capt. Mongelous, 8/7/1913).

19. These "exit visas" constitute one of the oldest genres of written documents in Arabic from the Sudan. In the 1630s the sultan of Sinnar gave such a document to the Ethiopian traveller Zaga Christ, though the text has not survived. See Crawford (1950, pp. 287-96). A German translation of Krump's exit permission of 1702 may be found in Krump (1710, pp. 355-56), and an English translation of three such documents issued to James Bruce is appended to Murray (1808, pp. 226-28). An early eighteenth-century letter of Pasquale da Montella described the function of such a document; it afforded protection from exactions by the sultan's subordinates and obliged them to supply the bearer with travel necessities (Montano 1948, p. 480). For _laissez-passers_ issued by various rulers of the western sultanates see Kapteijns (1985, p. 117 and note 150) and Nachtigal (1971, pp. 372, 394).

20. For some discussion of the nineteenth-century _jallaba_, see Spaulding (1982). Doornbos (1984) explores the adoption of _jallaba_ identity by people of southwestern Dar Fur.

An instructive comparison may be drawn with Baier's (1972) treatment of the external trade of late nineteenth-century Damergu. The protagonists of Baier's study are familiar: noble (Tuareg) caravan-masters, immigrant merchants from the Mediterranean world (Tripoli, Ghadames, and elsewhere), and upstart indigenous commoner entrepreneurs. Several of Baier's major themes would seem to recall the experience of the eastern Sudan. He argues convincingly that the commoner entrepreneurs responded to the advance of the capitalist market and the eclipse of their precolonial political masters over the course of the nineteenth century by opening a foreign commerce in mundane commodities, the full potential of which was not realised until the colonial reorganisation of the area's economy. Some important differences would seem to have existed between Damergu and the eastern Sudan. These include the comparatively diffuse character of political power as exercised by the Tuareg masters of Damergu ("a geographical expression rather than a territory under unified political control", p.47) in contrast to the highly-centralised states of the east, the precise nature of the new mundane trade by commoners (the export of natron, salt, and livestock would be more representative of the east than the tanned goatskins of Damergu; imports of cheap cotton cloth were important in both cases), and the specific chronology of the decisive encounter with the Mediterranean world. We do not agree with Baier that formalist staple theory in general or the slave trade/legitimate commerce "framework of analysis worked out by Hopkins" in particular constitute the best conceptual tools with which to interpret our data, if only because the very class of commoner entrepreneurs who initiated a petty but "legitimate" trade in the eighteenth century went on to conduct the burgeoning slave trade of the nineteenth.

21. "Except for dealings among the jallabs of the caravan", wrote Krump in Dongola (1710, p. 223), "coinage is not accepted in these lands, nor is it even found at all. In the villages it is as the Latin proverb says, 'do ut des', or, 'give me little nails, pepper, needles, spikenard, blue-coloured wool, white sandalwood, rings drawn of buffalo horn (which women wear on their fingers and arms, as is frequently done in Cairo) and other similar gew-gaws - in return, I will give you this or that, say, a pigeon, sheep, dates, fodder for the camels, firewood, milk, kisra (bread), eggs, and whatever it may be."

22. Krump (1710, p. 380) described the ruin of an Egyptian khawaja: "There was a certain Turk (in Krump's usage, "Turk" meant "Muslim") of Cairo in our caravan who had marched out of Sinnar with fourteen camels and had lost them all; he was forced to entrust his wares to a Barbarin (a Dongolese Nubian) here until he could come to get them another year. Since he could not go on foot he bought himself a donkey, and took service with the royal merchants to earn his maintenance." cf Browne (1799, pp. 225-26) for hard feelings among the jallaba of the Dar Fur caravan, which was held up by the king.

23. For example, the Masalit of the borderlands between Wadai and Dar Fur were notorious for attacking caravans plying between the two kingdoms (Kapteijns 1985, pp. 21-2; Nachtigal 1971, p. 239).

24. Lapanouse 1802, p. 97. The earlier eighteenth-century sultans of Sinnar, like the Mahdist state to follow, made slave acquisition a government monopoly and obliged private merchants or would-be slave owners to make their purchases from the government authorities at the national bandar (Mahdist terminology: bayt am-mal). See Krump (1710, pp. 285-86) and Ohrwalder (1892, pp. 150-51, 231, 273-74). Ohrwalder emphasised the distinction between the free private commerce in slaves typical of the Turkish period and the policies of the Mahdist State - a distinction, however, that did not survive Reginald Wingate's translation of Ohrwalder into English. According to Ohrwalder the Mahdist army was the only major source of slaves, which were delivered to the bayt al-mal in Omdurman. Most male slaves were incorporated into the army, and only a modest and predominantly female surplus was sold by auction to private persons for use or export. Private purchasers were careful to obtain certificates stating that their slaves had been purchased legally from the bayt al-mal. Similarly monopolistic policies were established with regard to ivory and gum Arabic, and during the ascendance of Ibrahim wad Muhammad Adlan as amin bayt al-mal, steps were taken to open an authorised trade in these commodities with Egypt and the Red Sea. These initiatives of the amin Ibrahim, a member of the family of Hamaj wazirs who had ruled Sinnar from 1762 until the Turkish conquest of 1821 and the son of the last prominent Hamaj leader, the manjil al-kabir ("Generalissimo") Muhammad Adlan, may be seen as an attempt to re-establish an administered "sultanic" export trade on the model of Sinnar. These policies died with the amin in 1890, however, and thereafter smuggling by private traders flourished. For a smuggler's participant account, see Youssef Bedri and George Scott (1969).

25. An illustrative incident from the Shilluk kingdom was recorded by Brun-Rollet (1855, p. 196): the reth found himself obliged to execute a kinsman who had been caught selling Shilluk children to Arab slave merchants. In the long run, the fact that this particular reth resisted the temptation to allow the enslavement of his own subjects is less important than the fact that his subordinate nobleman had not. A generation later the would-be slave traders in alliance with foreign jallaba overthrew a conservative reth, and the massive enslavement of the Shilluk began. The imposition of tribute in the form of slaves by the Turks provided a powerful new incentive for surviving traditional rulers to overcome their residual squeamishness about enslaving their own subjects (see Spaulding 1980, pp. 16-18).

26. For the forcible purchase of firearms from traders by makk Nimr of Shandi and other kings, see Burckhardt (1822, pp. 254-56). "The fact is", wrote the traveller, who lost his own gun to the royal option, "that traders are afraid to carry them, lest they

should excite the cupidity of some or other of the chiefs; and it is not to be supposed, that until they are more numerous, they can be taken to market like other goods, or be paid for at a regular price."

27. At the time of the Turkish conquest of Sinnar, Cailliaud (1823, vol. 3, p. 121) described this practice: "Only after the malik (of Shandi) has himself sold his merchandise to the caravans are the merchants given permission to traffic in theirs. It is the same in Sinnar (town)." For confirmation of the practice in Sinnar town in 1814, see Burckhardt (1822, p. 282).

References

Abu Salim, M.I. (n.d.), Sadat al Majadhib, National Records Office, Khartoum.

Abu Salim, M.I. (1967), al-Funj wa'l-ard: watha'iq tamlik. University of Khartoum, Khartoum.

Adams, William Y. (1977), Nubia: Corridor to Africa, Princeton University Press, Princeton.

Baier, Stephen (1972), 'Trans-Saharan Trade and the Sahel: Damergu, 1870-1930', Journal of African History, 18, pp. 37-60.

Beckingham, C.F. and Huntingford, C.W.E. (1961), The Prester John of the Indies ...Written by Father Francisco Alvares, Hakluyt Society, Cambridge.

Bedri, Youssef and Scott, George, eds., (1969), The Memoirs of Babikr Bedri, Oxford University, London.

Beltrame, G. (1881), Il fiume bianco e i Denka, Drucker & Tedeschi, Verona.

Bjorkelo, A.J. (1976), 'State and Society in Three Central Sudanic Kingdoms: Kanem-Bornu, Baghirmi and Wadai', Unpublished Hovedoppgave, University of Bergen (Norway).

Brocchi, G. B. (1843), Giornale delle osservazioni fatte ne'viaggi in Egitto, nella Siria e nella Nubia, 6 vols., A. Roberti, Bassano.

Browne, W.G. (1799), Travels in Africa, Egypt and Syria, T. Cadell Junior and W. Davies, London.

Bruce, James (1805), Travels to Discover the Source of the Nile, 2nd edition, Archibald Constable and Co., Edinburgh.

Brun-Rollet, Antoine (1855), Le Nil Blanc et le Soudan, L. Maison, Paris.

Burckhardt, John Lewis (1822), Travels in Nubia, 2nd edition, John Murray, London.

Cailliaud, F. (1823), Voyage a Meroe, Imprimerie royale, Paris.

Carbou, M. (1912), La region du Tchad et du Ouaddai, 2 vols., Ernest Leroux, Paris.

Coquery-Vidrovitch, Catherine (1978), 'The Political Economy of the African Peasantry and Modes of Production', in P.C.W. Gutkind and I. Wallerstein (eds.), The Political Economy of Contemporary Africa, Sage, Beverley Hills.

Cordell, D. (1977), 'Eastern Libya, Wadai and the Sanusiya, a Tariqa and a Trade Route', Journal of African History, 18 (1) pp. 21-36.

Crawford, O. G. S. (1950), 'The Strange Adventures of Zaga Christ', Sudan Notes and Records, 31 (2), pp. 287-96.

Cuny, Charles (1954), 'Notice sur le Dar-Four, et sur les caravanes qui se rendent de ce pays en Egypte et vice versa', Bulletin de la Societe de Geographie (4th ser.), 8, pp. 81-120.

Doornbos, P.A. (1984), 'On Becoming Sudanese. Aspects of ideological transformation in rural Sudan',(unpublished).

Douin, Georges (1944), Histoire du Soudan Egyptien, Societe royale de geographie d'Egypte, Cairo.

El-Tounsy, El Cheikh Mohammed Ebn Omar (1845), Voyage au Darfour, translated by H. Perron, Benjamin Duprat, Paris.

El-Tounsy, El Cheikh Mohammed Ebn Omar (1851), Voyage au Ouaday, translated by H. Perron, Benjamin Duprat, Paris.

Foster, William (1949), The Red Sea at the Close of the Seventeenth Century, Hakluyt Society, London.

Gray, Richard (1961), A History of the Southern Sudan, 1839-1889. Oxford University Press, London.

Hasan, Yusuf Fadl, ed., (1971), Kitab al-Tabaqat...ta'lif Muhammad al-Nur b. Dayf Allah, University of Khartoum Press, Khartoum.

Hopkins, Anthony G (1973), An Economic History of West Africa, Longman, London.

Jennings-Bramley, W.E. (1940), 'Tales of the Wadai Slave Trade in the Nineties, Told by Yunes Bedis of the Majabra', Sudan Notes and Records,23, pp. 169-83.

Kapteijns, Lidwien (1984), 'The Organization of Exchange in Precolonial Western Sudan', in L. O. Manger, (ed.), Trade and and Traders in the Sudan, University of Bergen Occasional Papers in Social Anthropology, 32, Bergen.

--- (1985), Mahdist Faith and Sudanic Tradition. The History of the Masalit Sultanate, 1870-1930, Routledge and Kegan Paul, London.

Kapteijns, Lidwien and al-Hadi Ahmad (1981), 'The Chado-Sudanese Frontier on the Eve of Colonial Conquest', Sudan Texts Bulletin 3, pp. 56-74.

Krump, Theodoro (1710), Hoher und Fruchtbarer Palm-Baum des Heiligen Evangelij, Georg Schulter und Martin Happach, Augsburg.

Kumm, H. Karl W. (1910), From Hausaland to Egypt through the Sudan, Constable, London.

Lamberg-Karlovsky, C.C. (1975), 'Third Millennium Exchange and Production", in J. A. Sabloff, and C. C. Lamberg_karlovsky, (eds.), Ancient Civilization and Trade, University of New Mexico Press, Albuquerque.

Lange, D. and Berthoud, S. (1972), 'L'interieur de l'Afrique occidentale d'apres Giovanni Lorenzo d'Anania', Cahiers d'Histoire Mondiale, 14, pp. 342-45.

Lapanouse, J. (1802), Memoire sur les caravanes du Darfour et du Sennaar, Arthus Bertrand, Paris.

Leyden, J. (1817), Historical Account of Discoveries and Travels in Africa, George Ramsey, Edinburgh.

Luzarche d'Azay, R. (1904), Voyage sur le Haut Nil du Caire au Congo Belge, Lahure, Paris.

Massari, A.M. (1881), 'La Spedizione Borghese, Conferenza di A.M. Massari tenuta alla Societa Geografica il giorno 18 dicembre 1881', Bolletino della Societa Geografica Italiana, pp. 812-37.

Montano, G. M. (1948), l'Etiopia Francescana nei Documenti dei secoli xvii e xviii, 2 vols., Collegio di S. Bonaventura.

Murray, Alexander (1808), Account of the Life and Writings of James Bruce of Kinnaird, A. Constable, Edinburgh.

Myers, Arthur B.R. (1876), Life with the Hamran Arabs, Smith, Elder & Co., London.

Nachtigal, G. (1971), Sahara and Sudan, IV, Wadai and Darfur, trans. A.G.B. Fisher, and H. J. Fisher, University of California Press, Berkeley and Los Angeles.

NRO (Khartoum) refers to archival materials kept in the National Records Office, Khartoum.

O'Fahey, R. S. (1972), 'The Affair of Ahmad Agha', Sudan Notes and Records, 52, pp. 202-03.

O'Fahey, R.S. (1973), 'Slavery and the Slave Trade in Dar Fur', Journal of African History, 14, pp. 29-43.

O'Fahey, R.S. and Spaulding, J.L. (1974), Kingdoms of the Sudan, Methuen, London.

O'Fahey, R.S. (1980), State and Society in Dar Fur, Hurst, London.

Ohrwalder, Joseph (1892), Aufstand und Reich des Mahdi im Sudan, Rauch, Innsbruck.

Santi, Paul, ed. (1965), Memoire d'un voyage en Haute-Nubie en 18511 d'apres un manuscrit anonyme, Institut de Lettres Orientales, Beirut.

Santi, Paul and Hill, Richard eds., (1980), The Europeans in the Sudan, 1834-1878, Clarendon Press, Oxford.

Schuver, Juan Maria (1884), 'Reisen im oberen Nilgebiet', Petermanns Mirtteilungen, Erganzungsheft.

SHAT (France) refers to archival materials kept at the Service Historique de l'Armee de Terre, Paris, France.

al-Shatir Busayli Abd al-Jalil (1961), Makhtutat Katib al-Shuna fi ta'rikh al-sultana al-Sinnariya wa'l-idara al Misriya, al'ammiya li'l thaqafa, Cairo.

Spaulding, Jay (1977), 'The Evolution of the Islamic Judiciary in Sinnar', International Journal of African Historical Studies, 10, pp. 408-26.

--- (1979), 'Farmers, Herdsmen and the State in Rainland Sinnar", Journal of African History, 20 (3), pp, 329-47.

--- (1980), 'Toward a Demystification of the Funj: Some Perspectives on Society in Southern Sinnar', Northeast African Studies, 2 (1), pp. 1-18.

--- (1982), 'Slavery, Land Tenure and Social Class in the Northern Turkish Sudan', International Journal of African Historical Studies, 15, pp, 1-20.

--- (1984), 'The Management of Exchange in Sinnar, c. 1700', in L. O. Manger, (ed.), Trade and Traders in the Sudan, University of Bergen Occasional Papers in Social Anthropology, 32, Bergen.

Stevens, E.S. (1912), My Sudan Year, Mills and Boon, London.

Terray, E. (1974), 'Long-Distance Exchange and the Formation of the State: the Case of the Abron Kingdom of Gyaman', Economy and Society, 3 (3), pp. 315-46.

Triulzi, Alessandro (1981), Salt, Gold and Legitimacy, Instituto Universitario Orientale, Naples.

Tubiana, M.-J. (1980), 'Nouveaux apercus sur le structure du pouvoir au Dar For', paper presented at the colloquium, "l'Esprit de Decouverte", Valbonne.

al-Tunisi, see El Tounsy.

Walz, Terence (1978a), The Trade Between Egypt and Bilad as Sudan, 1700-1820, Institut Francais d'Archeologie Orientale du Caire, Cairo.

--- (1978b), 'Asyut in the 1260s (1844-53)', Journal of the American Research Center in Egypt, 15, pp. 113-126.

--- (1979), 'Trading into the Sudan in the Sixteenth Century', Annales Islamologiques, 15, pp. 211-233.

--- (1979a), 'Family Archives in Egypt: New Light on Nineteenth-Century Provincial Trade', in L'Egypte au XIXe siecle, Centre National de la Recherche Scientifique, Aix en Provence, pp. 15-33.

--- (1979b), 'Abd Allah al-Kahhal and the Northeast Africa Trade of Egypt, 1880-1920', paper presented at the American Research Center in Egypt Conference, Philadelphia.

Werne, Ferdinand (1848), Expedition zur Entdeckung der Quellen des Weissen Nil, G. Reimer, Berlin.

Yusuf Fadl Hasan, ed. (1971) Kitab al-Tabaqat...ta'lif Muhammad al-Nur b. Dayf Allah. Khartoum: University of Khartoum.

4 Capitalist penetration and the geneology of the capitalist mode of production in the Gezira scheme

JOHN TAIT

The Transformation of the Land Tenure System

Colonial rule in Sudan acknowledged, in principle, the right to private property or, in the case of collective utilisation of land, to prescriptive rights. However, the control of the land was restricted: sale, lease, loan or cession of property needed the consent of local government, which also had the right to expropriate land not utilised or withheld from planned public utilisation. The aim of the measures in the official reading was

> to secure the best possible development of the land (and) to prevent merchants and persons with no local connection from acquiring them solely for investment or speculation (Sudan Government 1948, p. 42).

As 90 per cent of the Gezira land was private property of various size, the colonially-imposed land tenure system played an important part in providing the extra-economic measures for penetrating the existing modes of production. By law, all proprietors could be compelled to lease their land to the government at nominal rents fixed at the rates of non-irrigated land. At the same time they were given the right to become tenant farmers on their own land to a limit of 40 feddans (1 feddan = 1.038 acres) and to nominate tenants on their property exceeding this margin.

Contrary to Barnett, who argued that land and labour were thus turned into productive forces of capitalism, colonial intervention in land tenure seems in fact to have prevented land from becoming a fully capitalist commodity (Barnett 1977). Gezira land became a factor of production within a capitalist-dominated mode of production without the capitalist mode of distribution concerning rent and lease taking effect. The Gezira landlords neither received rent in relation to the growing profits of the cotton syndicate (the annual rent having been fixed at 10 pt per feddan) nor could they receive an equivalent for the growing value of their land. The only economically reasonable option remaining for the landlords was to accept the tenancy contract offered to them. To understand this mechanism as part of the process of socio-economic formation of production and the central role the landlords were to play in it, we must consider the other problems colonial capitalism had in establishing its mode of production: (i) the problem of mobilising a labour force from the ranks of the pre-capitalist subsistence modes of production; and (ii) the establishment of a system of capitalist commodity production through the separation of the producers from their means of production.

The Mobilisation of a Capitalist Labour Force

The mere transformation of land tenure in itself would not suffice in providing labour for the Scheme. The decimated population of Sudan after the turbulent events of the Mahdia and the difficulties of rapid integration of the nomadic and semi-nomadic population of the region into the wage labour system posed severe problems as far as the satisfaction of the growing labour demand of the Scheme was concerned. This, by the way, is the background to British colonial encouragement of the 'Fallata' settlement in the Sudan, which by the time of World War II was to solve the gravest labour shortages (Duffield 1979, 1981). At the time of the inauguration of the Scheme, however, the only solution to the problem - and to many others, as we shall see later - was the incorporation of the landlord-based mode of production into the capitalist mode of production (CMP).

For the specific labour problems of the Gezira - stemming from the irregular needs of cotton cultivation - the terms of production achieved established two preconditions:

1. The mode of the tenancy contract bound the landlords and other leading social groups to the land and thus to the production process in a double sense: on the one hand by limiting the magnitude of economic benefits to be drawn from agricultural production through the limit on the maximum size of holdings permitted and thus curbing possible expansion; and, on the other hand, by providing conditions for a modified continuation of the very mode of production on which their social status and orientation were based.

2. By providing acceptable conditions and incentives for landlords and important religious or political families to stay in the Scheme and to take up agricultural commodity production, the CMP attained access to productive resources not otherwise available to it: namely, members of the

extended family, the tribe or other persons in some kind of dependent relationship, e.g. the tenants nominated by the landlords for a holding or ex-slaves.[1]

With the rapid geographical expansion of the Gezira scheme turning more and more resident labourers into tenants, the dependency of the scheme on non-capitalist relations of production increased at the same rate as the demand for seasonal labour. The extension of labour recruitment into regions not yet dominated by the capitalist mode of production put the tenants into a unique position, as only they could provide for the relations of production necessary for the mobilisation and integration of the migrant labour into the production process of the scheme. These are relations of production in which the tenants maintained personal, not exclusively wage-dominated, relations to the labourers. This was expressed through giving presents and advances in cash and kind during the recruitment procedures in the home villages of the labourers, and in the provision of housing, food and water during the period of work in the Gezira.

The Tenancy Contract: The Alienation of Producers from Their Means of Production

The backbone of the tenancy contract is the so-called "triple partnership" between the government, the Sudan Gezira Board (SGB, which replaced the Sudan Plantation Syndicate in 1950), and the tenants. By this arrangement, the government provides water and land, the SGB supplies the means of production (seed, tractors, fertilisers) and management (cultivation control, processing and marketing of cotton), while the tenants organise labour for cultivation and harvest. Even more decisive than this separation of producers from their means of production is the alientation of the producers from the control over their products manifest in the policy-making structure of the scheme. The management alone determines which products to grow, by which methods, in which crop rotation and at which time. The uniformity of measures respecting their execution is controlled by local inspectors equipped with the right to sanction deviations from these regulations to the point of expelling tenants.[2]

Independent of this partnership arrangement, even if subjected to the basic requirements of crop-rotation, were the tenant subsistence crops of sorghum and lubia, together adding up to half the area devoted to cotton production. Thus, until 1965 when diversification started, the Scheme developed on the basis of a division into:

(i) an organised capitalist sector in which cotton was produced for the world market according to international standards for which alone managerial services and, in the course of development, modern inputs (fertilisers, insecticides, tractors) were provided;

(ii) a non-capitalist sector for the production of subsistence crops, in which, other than the observation of general rules of cultivation (e.g. crop-rotation, cleaning of fields after harvest), no norms of production existed and to which modern inputs only very rarely were applied.

This divorce of production sectors shows the CMP in dominance, reflected in the fact of heavy capitalist investments in irrigation infrastructure. For reasons already given, the forces and relations of production were not subjected to complete displacement by capitalist forms. The dominance is manifest rather in the form and mechanisms of reproduction in the Scheme. We find the mode of surplus distribution and the mode of circulation of commodities, including labour, to be organised according to the reproductive needs of the CMP. The conditions of the 'joint account' between the tenant, the government and the management provide for a division of profits after the management has deducted all its costs, but in which costs of the tenant for wages and family labour are not reckoned. This means that only the reproduction of the management is secured at a profit level in the capitalist sense, but not that of the tenant. His cotton-derived income more closely approximates a wage or even subsistence standard.

The fact that tenants continue to produce under these conditions necessarily leads to the conclusion that their economic reproduction cannot be totally governed by the capitalist logic of profitability. Rather, production strategies determining the utilisation of resources are simultaneously related to village-based relations of production. Various aspects of these relations have been analysed by among others, Barnett (1977), Al-Arifi (1975) and Culwick (1955). The conventional critical approach explains the coexistence of capitalist commodity production and non- or semi-capitalist relations of production as pertinent for a specific form of capitalism in which heterogeneous relations of production are the very condition for over-exploitation: the overall level of individual reproduction is kept low and thus labour increments are valued below their real price calculated as world market commodities.

No doubt, these mechanisms of exploitation exist, but the question is whether capitalism can alone be held responsible for the state of things. If we choose to attribute the structural heterogeneity of relations of production in the Gezira to capitalist development, as Barnett (1977) does, I find it hard to accept the proposition that the magnitude of counter-productive contradictions in the Scheme in the last two decades can really be explained by the functional operation of one mode of production according to its structural properties and reproductive needs.

To exemplify this hypothesis, the following analysis will be based on the notion of possible articulation of the CMP with other modes or reproductive units of non-capitalist origin. The idea is that although capitalist forms dominate the essential parts of production (e.g. commodity production and extraction of surplus value), a complete transformation of the economic base is retarded by inter-systemic contradictions between the CMP and the social formation into which commodity production was installed by extra-economic means. The cornerstones of this analysis will be: (i) the already indicated historic-genetic conditions under which capitalism takes root via landlord involvement in the Scheme; (ii) the specific social, legal and economic measures colonial rule took to launch capitalist production by tapping and not eradicating pre-capitalist modes of production and their productive forces; (iii) the extent to which pre-capitalist social formations could adapt to capitalist penetration without loss of internal socio-economic coherence; (iv) the amount of state intervention to maintain established political and social structures; and, finally, (v) the specific conditions under which the CMP operates in general in agricultural production.

This last point sheds some light on the problem of managerial control over individual producers and the frequently criticised reluctance of the SGB to convert the inspectorate system to an extension service. If our impression is right that commodity production is predominantly enforced by juridico-political sanctions - namely eviction of the tenant from the Scheme if cotton production were rejected by him - then the precipitate abolition of the inspectorate system would have indeed resulted in a widespread relapse to subsistence and petty commodity oriented production. The failure of capitalism to determine tenants' production preferences is reflected in somewhat contradictory development policies. The general managerial strategy has been to submit the Gezira to quasi-industrial relations in which a gradual separation of the tenants from the control over their means of production has been effected by the continuous expansion of managerial responsibilities in conjunction with mechanisation. The complete failure of this policy to increase productivity is not really surprising if we realise that not even agricultural production in the industrial capitalist centres is completely subjected to capitalist relations of production. In contrast to the industrial relations of production, agriculture is based on farmers who remain in possession of the means of production and work, to some extent, within family-based relations of production in which subsistence continues to play a part. In other words, for its reproductive needs in agriculture, capital depends to a great extent on a form of agricultural production in which only the commodity circulation is dominated by capitalist laws of motion. Whether this only constitutes a transitional historical stage in the relations between industrial capital and the forms by which agricultural commodities may be produced, or, as some authors would argue (see Vergopoulos 1974), agricultural production poses a 'natural barrier' to the expansion of capitalist relations of production, cannot be our subject. But, in any case, it underlines the fact that agricultural development under capitalist dominance was based on the transformation of the reproductive structures of small-scale, family-based production units which provided the pre-requisites for the development of the forces and relations of production and not vice versa. Appropriate pre-requisites to promote production in the Gezira would be adequate price and market conditions which would allow a continuously enlarged scale of capitalist reproduction based on profitability.

I am aware of the fact that agricultural diversification in the past two decades has provided a genuine market orientation for tenants, but this is paralleled by the continued effects of administrative dirigism on production. The outcome of this struggle will be discussed in the closing section of this paper on the basis of contemporary empirical data.

The Pre-capitalist Mode of Production and Its Reproductive System

Unfortunately, little has been published on the subject of the modes of production in the Gezira preceding the irrigation scheme. Randell (1958, p. 30), one of the exceptions does at least describe some of the elements of production and reproduction for El Gedid village. According to him, production was based on rainfed sorghum cropping (and, when possible, additional cultivation of the Nile banks), livestock, and a limited trade in surplus agricultural products. The relations of production in a predominantly settled tribal community were based on various forms of co-operation (e.g. the nafir system) in agriculture and handicrafts. This tribal mode of production, very similar to present-day peasant agriculture in Um Fila east of the Blue Nile not far from the Gezira Scheme (see O'Brien 1980; Ali and O'Brien 1984), was probably very common in the whole Gezira, existing side by side with feudal, semi-feudal and nomadic modes.

Whether any kind of dominant relationship existed between these different pre-capitalist modes of production is difficult to establish. The point is that capitalism was faced with the problem of satisfying its reproductive needs for labour and agricultural products,and was confronted with a closed socio-economic system, yielding neither a surplus product nor a surplus population for wage labour. Therefore, capitalist penetration could only have taken place through extra-economic measures; e.g. by implantation of private property in land, by introducing taxation, seizure of land and livestock or by sheer state force. The articulation of capitalist structures with analogous existing structures of production and appropriation - those of feudal landlords - is an obvious solution minimising social friction and offering access to rural labour.

The necessities of commodity-based production in the Scheme seem to have ruled out an articulation with modes of production of communal or co-operative nature for two reasons: First, the juridical and financial conditions of commodity production necessitated a personal assessment of production performance to maintain certain productive standards and to enable individual penalties. In addition the amount of agricultural work at harvest time exceeded the total work potential of the villages and made additional wage labour necessary. For the management this had the advantageous effect that the tenant was compelled to earn cash by cotton cultivation to a much larger extent than his individual monetary needs would otherwise have forced him.

The structure of the established articulation can therefore be seen as the result of the double operation of industrial capital:

on the one hand it blocked the reproductive systems of tribal and nomadic modes of production through the installation of commodity production, surplus production, and, to some extent, relations of production based on wage labour; and, on the other hand, it acknowledged the right to private property and established relations of production signifying private appropriation of surplus production, thus reinforcing elements already in existence within the feudal mode and leading to dominance of landlords within the Gezira village social structure.

Although these landlord-based relations of production no longer exist as a direct feudal appropriation of surplus, certain mechanisms of non-capitalist appropriation obviously continue to prevail. In many cases landlords who no longer reside in the village are found nominating wakils (agents) to run the tenancies - the wakil merely receiving a fixed salary, while a production-related rent is appropriated by the landlord. Elsewhere, tenants who have obtained their holdings through nomination by the landlord are subjected by their sponsors to some kind of tribute. In addition, other forms of redistribution exist to the benefit of families who are considered religious or tribal leaders. Most frequent are privileged access to labour - which, in general, is recruited collectively by the village tenants - or by privileged access to irrigation water (see Barnett 1977, pp. 101-15).

It is only from these historic-genetic conditions that the further development of the Scheme may be logically reconstructed not as straightforwardly capitalist, but as development which must be understood as resulting from an articulated social formation in which social relations of non-capitalist origin play an important part. For the analysis of the second stage of development in the Scheme, in which village structures are submitted to increasing capitalist pressures - with commodity relations undermining traditional social relations - the concept of 'displacement' is crucial. Displacement refers to a mechanism in which village resources bestowed on individual members of the community as rent, tribute, or redistributable funds designated as welfare or material aid, are subjected to private capitalistic utilisation. Thus, in contrast to the material conditions for the acquisition of village-produced resources - which signify social relations of mutual benefit - the impact of capitalism may in fact enhance their manipulation by individuals into private appropriation and capitalist exploitation.

The extent to which these mechanisms of displacement may materialise within the distributive structure of villages obviously depends on three factors: (i) the possible scope of capital accumulation and the prospects for lucrative private investment; (ii) the ability of the village community to integrate capitalist relations into the system of communal reproduction; and (iii) the extent to which capitalist entrepreneurs continue to depend on non-capitalist forms of appropriation for their accumulation processes.

Historically, the conditions of production did not enable tenants on small holdings (15 feddans or less) to produce at a profit. Even today, between 30 per cent and 50 per cent of these tenants depend on a production credit to cover the considerable advances needed to pay for wage labour (Adam and Apaya 1973; Humeida and Mubarak 1976). Therefore, tenants who had additional sources of income (rent or tribute) or who, due to their larger holdings or privileged access to cheap labour, could produce with profit and accumulate money capital often attained a strategic position within the expanding system of capitalist circulation - that of money-lender. The credit system practiced is that of shayl, which is based on the advance sale of crops, generally at a rate of about half their value at the time of harvest.

Although interest as a capitalist form of appropriation soon displaced tribute as the dominant element in the reproductive structure, this did not necessarily give rise to a contradiction between the foundations of the mode, the forces and relations of production, and its reproductive form. Tribute and interest are forms of private appropriation which may co-exist without contradictions under certain conditions of distribution. Moreover, the greater accumulative potential of capitalist interest can be controlled to the extent that the laws of motion and mechanisms of communal reproduction determine the distribution of the appropriated surplus. Considering the fact that in all pre-capitalist formations the ideological or political factors dominate the structure of reproduction, it would be quite wrong to underestimate this element for the Gezira. Although it is difficult to quantify their precise contribution, family-based ideologies and religious aspects are expressed in the social superstructure of the villages. Here we find that the social structure closely corresponds to a mode of distribution in which interest has become the dominant mechanism of reproduction in a non-capitalist mode of production.

Given the low level of Gezira productivity, the fragmentation of holdings and the absolute limits of redistributable village resources, I would argue that the relationship between the upper and lower strata of the villages can be conceived as a form of patronage. The economic conditions for patronage are provided by the fact that the appropriable surplus is confined to the productive potential of the village, thus setting defined limits of exploitation by a potential financial elite. Furthermore, the social relations of village members are bound within the regulative system of traditional Islamic welfare, which works to redistribute excess wealth for the benefit of village members in need, thus preventing ruin, either from shayl contracts or from the economic conditions of the tenancy contract. It is in this context that the villagers do not conceive shayl as usury, as only the patron's credit enables the continuation of production by impoverished tenants and protects them from Gezira Board sanctions.

Finally, the phase of transformation of the non-capitalist mechanisms and laws of motion can be said to begin with the Korea War boom in the early 1950s, which, for the first time in the history of the Scheme, provided high incomes for all tenants, rapidly expanding capitalist commodity exchange and circulation. However, the extension of economic activities of various groups from the upper strata into local trade and transport does not contradict my conception of intra-village relations being predominantly non-class relations. Trade and transport have tended to develop in direct conjunction with agricultural activities or along the lines of division of labour within a tenant family. This, and the fact that village-based merchant's capital has prevented capitalist penetration from outside, seems to have contributed to the survival of non-capitalist mechanisms of reproduction and the patronage system, despite the growing dominance of the CMP outside the Scheme. Basically, capitalist activities operating from the villages are still confined to the redistribution of village-produced surplus, which, in most cases, does not provide a substantial base for 'take off' of capitalist accumulation.

The Field Study - Problems and Results

The Sampling Procedure

Important criteria for our research design were provided by Barnett's study (1977) of Nueila village in which he found first indications of changes in the socio-economic situation of the village leading to the emergence of a new type of agricultural producer. This development must be seen in close conjunction with increased mechanisation and diversification, which enlarged the economic reproductive basis for some tenants to include contracting of agricultural machinery or the marketing of newly introduced crops. The latter implies commercial advantages for villages located in the vicinity of urban centres such as Khartoum and Wad Medani.

A research strategy of village comparison could be deduced from this information which was not orientated to criteria of general representability (e.g., by random selection of villages) but rather to the principles of a proportional stratified sample. This sampling technique secures the representativeness of relevant factors in accordance with our research hypothesis derived from the analysed structure of articulation in the Gezira. Thus, our sample was to include:

1. Two villages of comparably advanced level of development; one developed through favourable marketing conditions (Darwish), the other developed to a certain extent under conditions of an extension experiment of the Sudan Gezira Board (Bortubeil).

2. Two villages which, according to the criteria of social services (schools, social clubs), agricultural services (extensions), level of productivity, market location and general level of development (indicators: number of shops, handicraft, transport, etc.) are below average for Gezira; one from the North (El Fagadab) and one from Managil (Goz el Ruheid).

The manner in which some of the variables were assessed is self-evident where yields, costs or simple frequencies could be established by simple questioning. Other variables, however, could only be measured by scales constructed on the basis of various indirect measures derived from a sample survey of 141 households I carried out in these villages in 1978.[3] The scales relevant to the present analaysis are: the level of the tenant's agricultural qualifications; the standard of the tenant's information about prices; the tenant's innovativeness; the degree of the tenant's commercial orientation; a socio-economic index of the tenant's position; the tenant's readiness to move (mobility); and the tenant's degree of satisfaction with village life in the Gezira.

Factor analysis of the empirical results of my survey, including the scaled variables, showed quite clearly that the non-capitalist mode of intra-village redistribution still functions to the benefit of privileged groups. This analysis will not be reported in detail here (see Tait 1983, p. 101), but results pointing to the central importance of the tenant's socio-economic status in determining productivity and general agricultural performance must be mentioned to make the village configurations analysed below understandable. The factor analysis found cotton, wheat and sorghum yields to be closely correlated with one another and with the scales measuring tenant socio-economic status and agricultural qualification. Farm size, amount of family labour, commercial orientation, total expenditure on picking and weeding and other variables showed no relation to yields for these crops. The deviation of groundnut yields from this pattern seems to be explained by its competing demand on the tenant's cash resources with cotton and the fact that it is most preferred by tenants owning large herds - for which the plant's greens serve as an important fodder.

In general, the availability of cash and a tenant's ability to avoid the ruinous terms of shayl contracts - factors in the index of socio-economic status - proved to be central determinants of tenants' agricultural performance, as has been noted in other studies (cf. Sorbo 1977; Ali and O'Brien 1984). This is, however, not merely a matter of possession and timely expenditure of cash resources, for large-holding tenants often spend less money on wages due to their ability to mobilise labour at lower rates through non-market mechanisms associated with their dominance of patronage networks.

These and other findings of the factor analysis suggest that the social structures of tenant villages are crucial in determining agricultural performance. Previous surveys obscure the operation of this factor through collecting data on the basis of block or plot surveys which compare regions of the scheme, tenancies of different size classes, etc. In contrast, the following analysis takes the village as its unit of analysis and seeks to develop types of village configurations representing important differences in village social structure as they affect production in the Gezira Scheme.

Three Configurations of Villages in Stagnation and Transition

Two of the villages in my study still fit into the pattern of the conditions of production which have dominated the Scheme for 50 years, while the two other villages are in a process of transition. To be more precise, the economic prosperity of Darwish and Bortubeil coincides with institutional innovations implemented in the early 1960s, such as: diversification of agricultural crops to include new marketable products for the tenant and to meet the urban demand for wheat, rice and vegetables; agricultural extension experiments; and technological and mechanical intensification of production.

The connection which obviously exists between innovation and development cannot, as we have seen, be explained satisfactorily by single, isolated independent variables, i.e. factor markets, market conditions (despite a slight advantage of the 10 per cent of tenants who are allowed to grow vegetables in Darwish and Bortubeil for nearby urban markets) or by individual tenant features such as age, education, size of family, etc. My hypothesis is rather that the innovations have a distinct capitalist bias. In other words, their potential can only be realised by tenants under two conditions: 1) they must be able to accumulate money or be able to borrow money at terms which are not prohibitive to profitable production as production becomes more capital intensive and, 2) the overall socio-economic context of the village must permit the development of capitalist forms of production which necessarily contradict the dominance of a non-capitalist mode of production. Both of these conditions can be assessed by the existence of certain tenant fractions which may be classified according to their scale of reproduction: enlarged reproduction, based on a predominantly capitalist production strategy striving for profit; simple reproduction dominated by traditional, non-capitalist production orientations; and, negative or dependent reproduction based on small scale subsistence production dependent on subsidies from rich tenants (welfare) or from members of the family. Sub-classifications into concrete tenant fractions will be introduced in the village contexts.

Darwish

The first configuration is that of the village of Darwish, in which a social polarisation between tenant fractions has developed based on enlarged reproduction and simple reproduction. Pre-conditions for this development were provided by very considerable potential additional economic resources offered by the growing nearby urban market for vegetables as well as by SGB services, such as an animal insemination programme and the introduction of high yield cotton and sorghum varieties.

Prior to this polarisation, the village social structure was based on an above-average large-holder tenant population (39 per cent of holdings 30 feddan or larger) which constituted a tenant group was able to realise an enlarged reproduction under traditional conditions. Shayl and trade provided them with important sources of revenue to supplement extensive agricultural production with low family labour inputs. The control of trade, favourable marketing conditions, privileged access to labour and ready capital as dominant features of large-holders are all attributable to a social position already attained under the dominance of non-capitalist social structures, thus predisposing this group to be early adapters to a capitalist mode of reproduction. Furthermore Darwish is, as yet, the only village within the sample in which a fraction of petty capitalist entrepreneurs has emerged among the ranks of the large-holders. The new sources of revenue commanded by the petty capitalists are the contracting of agricultural machinery and transport and profit-oriented farming. The shift of the main revenue sources of both of these groups from tribute and interest drawn from the middle tenant and the small-holder fractions to profit from trade, agriculture and contracting, has distorted the traditional social relations of the village as they existed under non-capitalist dominance.

The traditional middle tenant derives revenue exclusively from agriculture on a simple scale of reproduction and does not systematically attempt to realise a surplus. Such a tenant finds his position undermined by the new conditions in two ways. First, economically he finds himself cut off from all potential additional sources of revenue, as he can neither obtain the capital needed to start some kind of off-farm activity in the village nor is he allowed to grow vegetables. Furthermore, the shayl credits on which this tenant group relies to finance cotton and groundnut production have become less readily available as the creditors are now inclined to utilise their capital for capitalist investments. This capital constraint is clearly expressed in the fact that the average income from cotton is only £S 17.70 on a 15 feddan holding compared with £S 171.50 on a large holding. Secondly, the middle tenant is deprived of his traditional social orientation towards the village patrons who were originally the heart and motor of community activities, but who now give priority to private interests. For example, a planned co-operative for combine harvesters was prevented by the withdrawal from the project of the patrons - who today, however, privately own and contract out this same machinery.

The SGB has in no way supported the middle or the small-holder in developing an appropriate adoption strategy. The considerable number of these tenants now taking up a second occupation in town may therefore be interpreted as an inhibition from agriculture as a primary source of income, with predictably negative effects on their future production standard.

Bortubeil

Under similar developmental pre-conditions as in Darwish - i.e. belonging to the same production group and located in the vicinity of urban markets - Bortubeil has attained an even higher overall standard of productivity. An enlarged scale of reproduction is now realised by virtually all tenants, including the small-holders. The social relations between large-holders and the mass of what we now must call productive small-holders (67 per cent of holdings not more than 20 feddans) here are essentially non-capitalist and non-exploitative. The dominant features of the recently emerged fraction of productive small-holders are: intensified agricultural production with an optimal utilisation of family and wage labour; very little surplus invested in cattle despite the relative wealth of the tenants; and only small reductions from agricultural revenue through redemption of crop mortgages (the still considerable number of shayl contracts seem to work on better terms than usual in the Gezira). Furthermore, we find a certain tendency to concentrate on the production of cotton, sorghum and wheat, while groundnut production is often sub-let at favourable terms.

The background to this development is the political mobilisation of small-holders in conjuncture with the popular mobilisation following the May Revolution of 1969, which disrupted the authority of the shaykh and led to close contact between the local SGB representatives and the new village elite. This rather exceptional relationship was rewarded by selecting Bortubeil and the adjoining villages of the Medina block for an extension service experiment from 1971 to 1975. Data on cotton production before and after these events (see Tait 1980) indicate a complete change in production patterns in comparison with Darwish and Goz Ruheid. Whereas cotton yields, assessed in productivity groups, have remained unchanged in Goz Ruheid and declined in Darwish, the majority of the tenants in Bortubeil have moved from the low productive group to the high productive groups.

There are some contradictions in the SGB extension policy which must be considered in this connection. The Gezira Scheme was very slow to adopt extension, and experimental implementation was only tackled under the persistence of the FAO and World Bank (see IBRD 1966, p. 39). After encouraging initial results (which have never been systematically analysed), the experiments were stopped in 1975. This can only be explained when we realise that extension has not only to do with agricultural productivity, but is closely related to vital political and social interests in the scheme. Firstly, the natural target group of extension efforts are the middle tenants and the small-holders, but any developmental policy directed at these groups bypasses the dominant social relations within the scheme, which are based on the rich large holders. It is the rich tenant who represents the tenants in the Tenants Union and on the Board of Directors of the SGB and who is the patron of the village. It is evident that certain central aims of the extension concept - e.g. the direct target group approach of developmental measures, or teaching these tenants how to organise their production (which might make them independent of shayl) - are contradictory to the interests of rich tenants who fear a loss of control over village resources. The other group which fears losing its influence is the SGB itself. The increase in production has obviously had a considerable impact on the social perception of the villagers of Bortubeil. No other village population perceives the deficiencies in services and in consumption so severely as that of Bortubeil - the village within our sample which is best equipped with these services. In direct comparison with El Fagadab (data in parentheses below) the perception of the 'biggest problem in the village', expressed as a percentage of total answers, in Boutubeil was: consumption 33.8 per cent (8.1 per cent); credit/services 24.6 per cent (0 per cent); infrastructure 15.4 per cent (75.7 per cent); and no problems 6.2 per cent (8.1 per cent). Therefore I have the strong impression that the continuing reservations of the SGB concerning extension may now, to some extent, be based on the realisation that projects which change the authoritarian structures established in the scheme quickly advance to the point where the tenants begin to reject the general relations of production altogether.

El Fagadab

The situation in the village of El Fagadab is characterised by the domination of a non-capitalist mode of reproduction and its corresponding social relations. The hierarchy of social relations is determined by large-holders who still maintain patrongage functions. This is expressed, for example, in the perception of the small-holders as to which group has done "most for the development of the village in the last 10 years." According to the results of the survey, these were perceived as the rich tenants (22.2 per cent), the shaykh (22.2 per cent) and the merchants (22.2 per cent) - that is the patrons - whereas only 11.1 per cent named the government. In contrast the perception of small-holders in Darwish were: SGB 17.6 per cent; village council 35.3 per cent; merchants 5.9 per cent; and government 41.1 per cent.

Despite a certain tendency of patrons to utilise their non-capitalist privileges, such as access to cheap labour and better marketing conditions, in accordance with capitalist mechanisms of reproduction, the growing incomes of a few large-holders are still seen by other tenants to be part of the tribute due to them and not as an erosion of non-capitalist reproduction in the village. In the absence of productive small-holders and petty capitalist fractions in the village, the tenant fractions corresponding to the large-holder patrons are the middle tenants, small-holders and dependent small-holders. All of these groups share the basic socio-economic values and orientations of the large-holders, the difference being the actual scale of reproduction. But whereas the middle tenants are able to achieve simple reproduction from agriculture, this is not the case with all small-holders. Although the dominant non-capitalist laws of motion have prevented a widening of the income gap between large and small-holders - the per feddan returns being even higher for small-holders - they are not without problems for the social coherence of the village. Egalitarian as they may be, their stagnant character tends to frustrate the potential agricultural innovators, who are to be found primarily among the small-holders taking up off-farm occupations. Potential agrarian innovators, who, finding it impossible to develop a productive small-holder strategy under the dominance of a strong large-holder fraction, are the first to take up off-farm occupations.

Lastly, the dependent small-holder benefits from the dominance of non-capitalist reproduction. This type of tenant, frequently elderly, is only able to achieve a low level of productivity, although a concentration on subsistence crops (sub-letting the others) usually takes place. But high costs of labour and large <u>shayl</u> expenses make simple reproduction impossible without remittances from employed family members or grants for repayment of debts by the patron creditors.

Omitting the social structure of Goz Ruheid - which is still in the process of formation in accordance with the mode of production in the Scheme - it is possible to draw the following conclusions concerning the alternatives of development. We must recognise that there are two basic developmental problems, the first concerning the transformation of the stagnant non-capitalist mode of reproduction, which then immediately merges into the second problem of uneven capitalist development at the village level. One of the lessons to be learnt from the Gezira is that the egalitarian conditions under the dominance of non-capitalist laws of motion in no way predetermine the structure of reproduction once the capitalist laws of motion have become dominant. Rather the large-holders are placed in the position of being able to utilise non-capitalist mechanisms of appropriation to sustain capitalistic reproduction. The income of large-holders in Darwish may seem impressive to some development planners, but it is based on the exploitation of small-holders by capitalistic means, leaving these with an income which is no better than that of comparable tenant groups in non-capitalist dominated villages. The social destabilisation and the de facto inhibition from farming of these groups in the course of such a development have already been pointed out. As something like 70 per cent of Gezira villages are probably still dominated by non-capitalist reproduction, the question becomes vital as to which forces are able to accomplish an alternative development to that of Darwish, which I take to be the prototype of development if the economic dynamics of capitalist penetration and transformation are left unchallenged. Bortubeil is an example in which a political mobilisation has proved successful. However, this was achieved in a conjucture in which large-holders were weak and small-holders were organised and motivated - circumstances which are not very common in the Gezira. Besides, strong tendencies exist in the villages to isolate explicit political or agricultural reformers, thus making large-scale mobilisation an unlikely prospect.

The Stagnation of Productivity and Production Relations in the Gezira Scheme: Organisational Problems and Management's Concepts of Reform

In a memorandum by the new manager of the Scheme, and in a detailed background story in Sudanow in March 1980, the hitherto latent crisis of the Gezira Scheme was admitted in public. According to figures of the Sudan Gezira Board, the tenants' money income dropped by 45 per cent between 1951 and 1973. The yields of all crops are not only considerably below those obtained at the research farm (46 per cent for cotton, about 50 per cent for wheat, and even 66 per cent for sorghum) but they have also shown a marked tendency to decline further since the mid-1960s. Cotton yields declined from a five year average of 4.7 kantar per feddan between 1970-71 and 1974-75 to only 3.3 kantar per feddan between 1975-76 and 1979-80 - the lowest yields since World War II! At the same time, wheat yields sank from 0.5 tons per feddan (Sudanow 1980, p. 37). The declining yields coincide with an increase in the costs of production per feddan of cotton from by 48 per cent between 1961-62 and 1979-80 (as derived from figures of the joint account of state, Gezira Board, and tenants). In just four years, costs rose from

£S77.50 per feddan of cotton in 1976-77 to £S102 in 1979-80. Not only soaring world market prices for agricultural inputs, particularly for fertilisers and insecticides, are responsible for this trend, but also the multiplication of input-intensity in the Gezira. Whereas in 1950 it was sufficient to spray cotton with insecticides once per season in order to achieve complete protection, by 1980 this operation had to be repeated seven times per season. Whereas formerly one unit of fertiliser per feddan was sufficient, in 1980 six were needed in order to compensate for the decreasing fertility of the soil due to the intensification of production (omission of fallow) and the introduction of wheat as another crop dependent on fertiliser. But above all, it is the ecological instability of the region following from the monocultural structure of land use and the great susceptibility to pests and diseases, which necessitate spending 85 per cent of costs of production on insecticides. Pest control, amounting to £S 14.2 million per season, thus far exceeds the entire picking costs of £S 8.2 million incurred by the tenants (Sudanow 1980, p. 36).

Since the beginning of the diversification measures, the organisational problems of the Scheme seem to have multiplied, too. Although the personnel of the Sudan Gezira Board has doubled in number during the past ten years, the additional administrative capacity has not sufficed to cope with the new organisational and agro-technical problems brought about by the introduction of wheat and groundnuts. The great majority of the additional staff is occupied with administrative work only, and thus contributes to the administrative inflexibility of the board (roughly one third of the personnel in the middle and at the head of the board are accountants). Above all, there is a grave lack of agriculturally-trained field personnel. For example, when wheat was introduced the whole agro-technical advice made available to the tenants consisted of sending a booklet of eight pages containing the most important rules of wheat cultivation to each block inspector.

Since production was diversified, co-ordination problems have multiplied with respect to three key areas: provision and distribution of seeds, fertiliser and insecticides; control to ensure that the co-ordinated dates for seeding and harvesting are met; and co-ordination of seeding, thinning, weeding, etc., with the centrally fixed dates for watering. The rigid administrative manner in which the management of the Scheme tries to cope with these problems - e.g. the fixed dates of seeding are strictly adhered to even if this means seeding on a smaller surface than projected - fails to address the underlying problems. This is also true for the proclamation of the new guideline of the return to "discipline, diligence, hard work and the rule of law" (Manager, SGB, quoted in Sudanow, 1980, p. 37).

Concrete supportive measures for the tenants to overcome capital bottlenecks and to compensate for declining incomes are also under discussion. This involves paying more attention to those crops which are not under the control of the SGB, such as sorghum and groundnuts[4] and the introduction of a system of incentives to raise cotton production. This consists chiefly of a new way of sharing profits between tenants on the one hand and the state and the SGB on the other. If a tenant produces more than 4 kantar per feddan, he gets a higher share. If he produces more than 8 kantar per feddan, he gets the total net profit. In addition there are plans to improve the marketing conditions through adequate infrastructural measures. Today, only the system of incentives to raise cotton production is being put into practice. In the main, it will benefit the richer tenants, and so aggravate the already existing disparities between the different groups of tenants. It is furthermore doubtful whether the other supportive measures mentioned - which are indeed much better adjusted to the main production problems of the small and middle tenants - are to be given more than lip service. Despite the promising results of extension experiments in parts of the Gezira such as Bortubeil it is obviously not planned to draw far reaching conclusions from the current production crisis of the Gezira. Yet, the maintenance of an organisational structure whose rigid regulations and controls bear the marks of the colonial past cannot be entirely explained through referring to the often cited economic importance of the Scheme for the Sudanese budget and the country's reserves of hard currency - which is held to discourage experimentation. An organisational reshuffle, however, would result in a cut-back in the established privileges of the Gezira bureaucrats and the large-holders - which they would certainly oppose. This makes clear that the discussion about possible mobilisation strategies in the Gezira is closely interwoven with the socio-economic functions of the existing mode of production.

The Prospects of Contemporary Capitalist Penetration in the Gezira Scheme

This analysis has not examined the laws of motion behind the contemporary capitalist mode and production (CMP) as a world system and their impact on the Sudan, which has become a part of this system. To do this comprehensively is beyond the limits of the present analysis. Nevertheless, there are two points in which the structure of external domination of the CMP in the Sudan can be made apparent:

1) in the utilisation and application of technology in the Gezira, which is almost exclusively imported from the world market; and,

2) in the impact of the reproductive needs of world capitalism in the Gezira concerning raw materials, markets and labour in which the existing structure of articulation in the social formation is being either reinforced or dissolved.

Utilisation and Application of Technology

The mechanisation of agricultural operations (land preparation, fertiliser application, weeding and harvesting) has increased continuously in recent years. For example, tenant outlays for hire of labour in cotton operations were reduced by nearly 50 per cent between 1961-62 and 1971-72 (ILO 1976, p. 257). However, the general strategy of mechnisation is not simply guided by aims concerned with the reduction of production costs, the improvement of standards of agricultural operations or the elimination of quantitative or qualificational deficiencies in the labour market. The recent expansion of mechanical operations by the SGB Mechanical Engineering Department to include sowing, application of fertilisers, spraying of herbicides, etc., and experiments on the extraction of cotton stalks, all imply use of machinery at times within the agricultural calendar which do not coincide with peaks in labour demand. The driving force behind this development - resulting in an ever-increasing technological input (fuel, spares) dependency on the world market - is the apparent strategy of the Gezira Board to solve the production problems of the scheme solely in the expansion of SGB responsibilities. In the conception of agricultural planners, mechanisation of production becomes the alternative to structural or organisational reforms, although all available economic data contradict this decision. The problem behind the SGB mechnisation strategy is that it has not been implemented as an economic measure to complement labour - that is, it is not applied selectively in areas where costs for manual labour are high - but as a policy of general substitution for labour in the production process with irreversible effects.

Migrant labour is available in accordance with the Scheme's demands because the cotton harvest coincides with the off-season of the labourer's own subsistence production. Resident labour must, however, meet the Scheme's labour demand throughout the entire irrigation season, and thus cannot be replaced by migrant labour; lacking its own subsistence it is dependent on having a degree of job and income continuity within the Scheme. If mechanisation is extended irrespective of these reproductive needs, this will necessarily lead to an eviction of large numbers of resident labourers. In other words, uncoordinated mechanisation may aggravate rather than solve certain labour problems, as the Rahad example shows (Heinritz 1982, pp. 69-87). Moreover, every additional step in mechanisation of production impairs the chances of the extension concept to replace the inspectorate system because, if no agricultural operations remain for which the tenant must take decisions, an agricultural advisory system becomes senseless. Even though this policy will, in the long run, lead to a complete degradation of the tenants to the status of contract-workers, not much opposition is to be expected from the Tenants Union. The tenant groups which represent this union either have a direct agrarian capitalist interest in the expansion of private contracting of agricultural machinery or, as is the case with the large-holders, are generally not interested in production policies which impute family labour.

The Reproductive Needs of Capitalism and the Structure of Articulation

The SGB mechanisation strategy exemplifies the fact that technology is by no means a neutral medium only corresponding to productivity and division of labour. It is rather directly related to the social relations and, in the case of the Gezira, actually promotes the separation of the producers from their means of production to the point that the self-conception of the tenants as 'farmers' becomes fictitious. But mechanisation of the Scheme is only one part of capitalism's reproductive needs in providing a market for technical equipment additional to that for imported consumer goods.[5] No doubt the expansion of capitalist markets to the Gezira brings to bear a strong element of dissolution on the existing forms of reproduction, but a full scale capitalist development would in fact contradict the dominant reproductive need of capitalism within the Gezira. There are at least three elements of the production process which will exert a strong tendency to reinforce the basic structure of articulation in the Scheme for some time. First, large scale, monocultural and labour intensive production of long staple cotton sets certain demands on labour input and utilisation that could not be met other than by something like the existing combination of heterogeneous relations of production and by the different terms of individual labour's reproduction it must draw on. The profitable realisation of the extremely discontinuous labour demand of 35,000 pickers for no longer than three months would not be possible without the existence of the subsistence production of these labourers which meets the reproduction costs during the rest of the year (see O'Brien 1983). Given the scale of cotton production and the continuance of long staple varieties which cannot be harvested mechanically, neither a capitalist wage labour system which would have to reproduce its labourers continuously (all year round) in a capitalist production process, nor full mechanisation can be considered alternatives to the existing relations of production.

The subsistence production on the tenancy and the tenancy system itself provide similar preconditions of production which could not be established or maintained by the CMP alone. The tenant is bound to his farm and thus to the capitalist production process independently of the prevailing income situation. Thus, without a guaranteed revenue base from capitalist commodity production, the tenancy system ensures for this same production an immobile, readily available local labour reservoir. Of the up to 500,000 persons engaged in the production of the Scheme, not more than 2,500 - the staff members of the SGB - are fully integrated into the capitalist wage-labour system, i.e. are subjected to the conditions of the so-called formal labour sector of the state.[6]

The second element lies in the fact that the non-capitalist mode of reproduction provides social relations between the tenants, in the form of patronage and communal solidarity, which cushion the economic disparities among the tenants inflicted by capitalist commodity production. Much the same applies to the relations between the tenants and the various forms of labour. The non-capitalist elements of labour recruitment and the semi-personal relationship between labourer and tenant separate and isolate the labourers from one another, thus preventing organised wage demands corresponding to the value added to the product by their work. The wage level is therefore still largely determined by the reproductive costs of the subsistence sector, a factor which contributes substantially to the maintenance of favourable production costs of cotton in the Gezira. A certain rise in labour costs in recent years after a very long period of stagnation seems to be attributable to growing competition between the expanding irrigation schemes and to the high inflation rate in Sudan (see O'Brien 1983).

Thirdly, the capitalist mode of distribution, established in the conditions of cotton production as a joint enterprise of the state, SGB, and the tenants, conceals the character of tenants' labour as part of capitalist surplus production. The profits appropriated by the state and the SGB are conceived by the tenants as a form of rent for the supplied means of production (land and water) and the right to cultivate other crops. An analysis of the concrete proportions of appropriation reveals the fact that, in cotton production, the state realises extra profits while the average tenant is not even able to cover his or her running costs from cotton production. Under prevailing yields, most tenants receive only the guaranteed minimum price for cotton, which, after the deduction of tenants' costs, leaves a small-holder (15 feddan) a net revenue of £S17.60 (see Table 4.1).

Table 4.1

Cotton Proceeds and Costs per Feddan (£S)

	at 5.5 kantar/ fed.	at 4 kantar/ fed.
State:		
Proceeds from joint account	5.30	2.80
Proceeds from export tax	14.00	10.20
	19.30	13.00
Subsidies for groundnuts and wheat	-2.10	-2.10
Total Proceeds	17.20	10.90
Tenants:		
Proceeds from joint account	26.50	25.00
Costs for labour	-21.50	-21.50
Total Proceeds	5.00	3.50

at minimum price paid from tenants' reserve fund.
Source: Ministry of Irrigation, 1977.

According to my sample data, cotton production, which consumes most of the tenant's outlays and most of her or his own labour, contributes approximately only between 9 per cent and 15 per cent of the tenants' net revenues. Furthermore, we must take into account that the tenant carries the whole financial risk in case of crop failure for all labour costs, which are not part of the joint account. The situation for the state is quite different, as we can conclude from Table 4.1. At a time when most tenants are making net losses from cotton production (if the interest payments on shayl contracts are considered part of the tenant's costs), the state is pocketing an annual £S5.5 million from the Scheme - mainly in the form of export taxes. Even taking into account the fact that the state has had to subsidise the SGB and the tenants' reserve fund in order to maintain the minimum price for cotton, we can deduce from the fact that cotton production is continued in all irrigation schemes despite heavy real losses by the tenants, that the state is able to extract considerable profits. The effect of this share-cropping arrangement has been to exempt cotton production from any law of value with assessable relations of costs and benefits on behalf of the tenants. Not surprisingly, cotton was rated rather unanimously by tenants as the least important crop for their income, with wheat and sorghum in prime position (see Tait 1978). This negative image of cotton will probably prove to be an injurious heritage for production even under the recently introduced system of land and water rent for all crops.

Governmental Policies and the Emergence of Social Formations in the Gezira: Some Conclusions

Even after half a century of capitalist dominated production in the Gezira the process of class formation in accordance with the established economic structures is still far from being conclusive. On the one side we might agree with Founou-Tchuigoua's conclusion that tenants are '*de facto* wage-earners' (Founou-Tchuigoua 1978). But the exploitation experienced by many at the hands of the large-holders and the petty capitalists, together with their sense of powerlessness to control their own conditions of production, has by no means led to the formation of a wage-earner class consciousness among tenants. On the contrary, the self-assessment of the majority of tenants is still very much that of 'petty landlords' based on a system of social values which has its roots in feudal ideologies and in Islamic social traditions (see Al-Arifi 1975; Culwick 1955). As we have seen, the economic base for this type of social order still exists in the more traditional villages where communal forms of reproduction and redistribution according to the village hierarchy prevail. In a certain equilibrium to this traditional form, and not in contradiction, we find forms of reproduction more closely related to the capitalist attitude of private profit appropriation. In these cases social status becomes determined by the individual level of consumption and the possession of commodities with status value (see Nugdalla 1973, p. 91). Both systems seem completely compatible within the village structure to the extent that differentiation often even takes place within one family - the father being the patron for the more traditional tenants, the tractor or lorry-owning son being the representative for the fraction of innovators in the village.

But the inertia of traditional social relations in the Gezira despite changing economic conditions is not only evident in intra-village relations: in maintaining the cleavage capitalist development has driven between tenants and labourers, the tenant's attitude of 'petty landlordism' functions as sheer ideology. To explain this, we must look back to the beginning of the Scheme. The conditions of production, requiring surplus production of commodities in an otherwise completely subsistence-based agricultural sector, put tenants in a conflicting situation. On the one hand the operation of the tenancy necessitated the extension of labour recruitment into work resources of the subsistence sector not accessible other than by traditional social mechanisms of work co-operation, e.g. the nafir system. Therefore the principal base of social relations to hired labour was one of reciprocity even though work could only be repaid in kind or money. On the other hand the relations of the tenant to the colonial capitalist management required his integration into a system of commodity production in which profits could only stem from the retention of reciprocal relations in the recruitment and remuneration of labour and the exploitation of these relations at the same time. Little wonder that the colonial policy of indirect rule fell on fertile ground in the Gezira: when tribal leaders were made agents of local colonial government, this not only reinforced the social position of shaykhs and landlords and the social order on which their authority was based, but, inevitably also gave rise to a 'petty landlord' self-identification for the mass of tenants. This, we may conclude, is indeed the equivalent ideology of legitimation appropriate to the form of labour-exploitation capitalist production imposed on tenants.

But of course political and ideological state interventions in support of an installed traditional social order necessarily produce contradictions with the capitalist laws of motion. The selection of rural Gezira as one of the centres of education in Sudan can only be explained by the supplementary part it was to play in solving some of the emerging political and economic problems of the Scheme: inaccessibility of newly irrigated farm land, the prohibition of partition of inherited tenancies, and the deficiency of jobs with adequate status for tenants' sons, all point to contradictions between the stimulated high social aspirations and the real economic development at village level. The introduction of formal education in the Gezira in 1934 and the rapid expansion of school enrolment after independence provided an escape from some of these disparities, as social mobility towards urban jobs was made possible. In fact, the rate of enrolment of Gezira children in primary schools - 64.7 per cent in 1977-78 - is matched only in urban Khartoum.[7]

More generally, indirect rule, an urban standard of educational facilities, and the rather privileged provision of social infrastructure of all kinds to the Gezira can be conceived as an important moment in the development of the social identity of tenants (see Gruenbaum 1978). Although income development has not kept pace with the urban sector, Gezira tenants can consider themselves a socially privileged and politically influential group in Sudanese society. This is not so much due to the economic success of tenants in general as tenants, but is rather the result of the political interventions of the Sudanese state to stabilise the economic base of production and, last but not least, to stabilise the ideological superstructure of the Scheme.

What then are the conclusions for the future development of the Scheme? At the beginning of this paper I questioned the notion that the established relations of production in the Gezira and the subsequent development of class formation may be satisfactorily explained as linear expressions of a 'dependent capitalism' in relation to the reproduction of a capitalist world system. Rather, the futile attempts to raise the standard of productivity and to promote the commercial 'instincts' of the mass of tenants in the past two decades seem to contradict popular notions about the propensity to auto-development of capitalism under certain historic conditions. Rey (1973) has proposed an alternative concept of development under capitalist dominance which not only fits the course of historical fact in the Scheme but also provides a structural-genetic explanation for the contemporary economic crisis and conflicting policy options. As Rey points out, in the event of colonial subjugation no amount of political or military dominance may transform the existing conditions for production other than by the gradual process of destruction of the existing modes of production. In the course of this process the pre-conditions for the CMP appear: the division of producers from their means of production and subsequent availability of labour, agricultural surplus production, and accumulation of capital. Taxation, the introduction of private possession and expropriation of communal possession, the decomposition of existing trade and markets by imported commodities, etc., all work to enlarge the base for capitalist production when imposed on natural economies. But in the case of late 19th century colonialism, with a home industry hungry for raw materials, there was no time, and penetrating capital resorted to basing its production on pre-capitalist forces and relations of production if capitalist dominance by extra-economic means seemed feasible. The result - as in the case of the Gezira - has been a transitional mode of production, the development of which, however, may not be seen as structured by inter-systemic contradictions between capitalism and pre-capitalism alone. In addition to this we have contradictions of an intra-systemic nature stemming from the specific form of appropriation and exploitation capitalism employs in the production process. If capital is unable to install production with direct control over the immediate producer as in wage labour relations, then capitalist dominance must involve a double system of appropriation: (i) the appropriation of non-capitalist origin (in our case that of tenants) taking place in accordance with the conditions for mobilisation and extraction of surplus from pre-capitalist forms or modes of production in the manner already described, and (ii) the capitalist appropriation which imposes dominance in the conditions by which the management and the state extract the product and forward it to the capitalist commodity market. This explains why the formation of class or nacent class relations in the Gezira in accordance with the installed mode of production increasingly became structured not only by wage labour relations, but additionally by the emergence of an intermediate social group of non-capitalist appropriators under the direct auspices of capitalism.

Hence, we finally arrive at an assessment of developmental policies within a conflicting frame of reference. From the logic of capital, policies in the Scheme were slow in developing the forces of production which advanced rather in accordance with the dominant forms of appropriation. The centralisation of technology-based means of production together with the agro-industrial organisation of production (fixed crop rotation, schedule of production, etc.)

beyond control of the tenant, have worked to maintain a low standard of productivity in the relations of production involved at the level of the immediate producers. It is from the perspective of an advanced capitalist development which extracts relative surplus value from a higher level of productive forces rather than absolute surplus value from over-exploitation, that the activities of the IBRD in the Gezira may be adequately understood. These range from the 1966 proposals to modify the inspectorate system to direct intervention in the case of the recent rehabilitation programme to modernise infrastructure and to re-adapt production to export orientation (see Wall Street Journal, Europe, No. 69, 1983).[8] The actual policies in the Scheme under capitalist dominance from 1965 to 1980 - introducing diversification of crops, must however be seen in relation to intra-systemic contradictions of capitalist development within the established social formation. As the structures of appropriation and village redistribution were left untouched, the policy necessarily failed its aim to generally boost incomes and productivity. On the contrary, as an innovation with a 'capitalist bias', diversification worked selectively for those tenants who were able to draw on the redistributive system of the village community, giving rise to a new socio-economic configuration in the villages; the petty capitalists not only coming out on top of the village hierarchy but simultaneously advancing into the status of de facto or potential class allies of the capitalist class. This last point is probably illustrated most distinctly in the SGB-bank securities bestowed on these tenants for the acquisition of agricultural machinery, which, contracted out, helps to overcome the insufficient base for capital accumulation agriculture alone provides. Needless to say, this binds the representatives of the tenants in a very materialistic way to the very strategy of production which seems the least appropriate to reinstall the producers in control of their means of production.

The solution to the production problems of the mass of dependent small tenancies would seem rather to be a fundamental restructuring of the Scheme which would include at least the following measures: rehabilitation of the groundnut marketing co-operatives under administrative control of the SGB or other forms of access to agricultural credit as alternatives to shayl; reorganisation of the joint account to reflect the actual production costs of the tenant (including wage labour), thus making cotton a real cash crop in the eyes of the tenant; improvements of the general standard of agricultural qualification through specific extension work; the introduction of a concession for each tenant to produce for local markets on part of his or her tenancy; the development of programmes to integrate animal husbandry by tenants; a more flexible SGB strategy which is adapted to the socio-economic situation of the villages within an extension concept, in which the local SGB-personnel are equipped with the facilities and the administrative competencies to implement locally adapted development measures; and, supplementary to management decentralisation, tenants' rights of co-determination at the local level.

As the target group of all these measures would be the small-holders and not the large-holders, I have no illusions concerning the chances of realising such a policy, which undermines established economic conditions. The present policy of the SGB of supporting the emerging capitalist farmer only nourishes expectations that the general productivity deadlock might be broken. I have found no indications that their example can stimulate other tenants. On the contrary, the economic practices of capitalist farmers have only disrupted the social relations in the village - with negative effects for the overall average level of village yields. Lastly, and of greatest importance, there are strong indications that the capitalist entrepreneurs emerging from the ranks of large-holders are inclined to develop a mode of reproduction along the lines of merchant capital: their ultimate aim is not the maximisation of surplus production through the development of productive forces but the maximum extraction of profit from monetary circulation in the Gezira through trade, transport, contracting of machinery, etc. (see Sellin 1980; O'Brien 1977).

If we extend the present determinants of production into the future, the scenario after the CMP has completely disrupted the communal-based relations of production in the villages will not be a rapid development of productivity and the establishment of an expanding reproduction for all tenants. Rather, the reshuffle of the social equilibrium with the petty capitalists as the new dominant class in the village will give rise to a fierce struggle for the redistribution of resources. The losers in this struggle will no doubt be the disoriented, non-adapting middle tenants and small-holders who - as the only group depending on agricultural production - are the backbone of the Gezira Scheme. The stagnation and decline of average yields in the Scheme in the last few years may indicate that this process has already advanced far.

Appendix

Summary of Empirical Results of the Comparative Village Analysis

Village	Institutional Framework	Profile of Social Development
El Fagadab	No schools; no club; not electrified, no particular extension services; mill for sorghum and wheat available	Continuity of traditional tribal structure with dominance of the Shaykh and traditional families; poor tenants integrated in coherent village community; political opposition isolated; innovators not completely integrated, often with second occupation besides farm work; total rate of additional occupations in the village: 30 per cent mainly with lower stratum of tenants as a substitute for insufficient income from farm.
Goz el Ruheid	Primary school and club with TV set available; not electrified; no particular extension services or other institutional services through SGB.	Old social structure based on semi-nomadism is dissolving; formation of a new type constrained by poverty. Social structure relatively homogenous apart from very small upper stratum. SSU-members isolated. General commercial, innovative and qualification level of tenants very low. Rate of school attainment very low, together with high degree of utilisation of family labour for agricultural production.

Village	Structures of Production	Comparative Situation of Production
El Fagadab	Predominance of extensive subsistence production. Access to production factors, situation of yields, conditions of marketing and wages in favour of high status tenants. A small faction of commercially oriented tenants is the SGB-representatives' target group for modernisation.	Unfavourable conditions of labour market lead to deficient weeding. Favourable yields only with sorghum. Very bad returns from cotton due to picking costs above the average. Annual income* from: 15-feddan-tenancy: £S203.40 30-feddan-tenancy: £S341.00
Goz el Ruheid	Factor markets and marketing conditions similar for nearly all tenants. Strong labour bottlenecks for weeding due to unfavourable situation of labour market are reinforced by restricted access to <u>shayl</u> credits. Labour bottlenecks can often only be overcome through intensive use of family labour. Subletting is frequent. Differences in tenants' individual productivity positively correlated with social stratification.	Generally strong disadvantages for agricultural production through periodic lack of canal water. Lack of capital and credit facilities as well as unfavourable conditions for hiring labour out of the harvesting season cause worst returns of all villages; net losses with cotton. Annual income* from: 15-feddan-tenancy: £S118.80 30-feddan-tenancy: £S216.00

Village	Institutional Framework	Profile of Social Development
Darwish	Village included in an artificial insemination programme of the SGB. HY-varieties of cotton and sorghum. Primary and secondary school established through self-help. Club with TV-set available; electtrification planned.	Strong commercialisation of production since 1960 caused the emergence of a fraction of agrarian capitalists, which developed from the traditional elite. Strong tendencies to undermine the coherence of the village community. Proportion of young tenants oriented towards innovation and commerce is above the average. Despite social frictions between poor and rich tenants, the SSU-opposition is communally isolated. High rate of formal education and qualification of tenants. High rates (33.3 per cent) of additional occupations in the tertiary sector (income diversification of the medium and high strata of tenants).
Bortubeil	From 1969 to 1973 village was the site of an extension experiment of the SGB. HY-varieties of cotton and sorghum. Primary schools for boys and girls. Public club with TV-set; electrified since 1977.	Since 1969, change in the social structure in direction of productive smallholders without destroying solidarity of the village community. Relatively close co-operation of smallholders with SGB in matters of production and self-management. Very high degree of dissatisfaction with living conditions due to social sensitisation. SSU-members sponsored by local SGB-representatives, e.g. through concessions to grow vegetables. Tenants' rates of education low, but high aspirations as to education for children. Rate of tenants with additional occupation: 10 per cent.

Village	Structures of Production	Comparative Situation of Production
Darwish	Factor markets and marketing are largely egalitarian. Salient correlation of high productivity and high social status. Extensive cropping strategy still widespread, as well as rudimentary orientation towards subsistence production in terms of extensive uncommercial animal husbandry. In general, low utilisation of family labour.	Higher amount of working capital available to most of the tenants permits hiring of sufficient labour. Good and continuous access to the labour market, particularly for weeding. Favourable returns from groundnuts which must be seen in conjunction with the high degree of animal husbandry. Annual income* from: 15-feddan-tenancy: £S203.60 30-feddan-tenancy: £S625.50
Bortubeil	Conditions of production and marketing equal for all groups of tenants. Highest level of productivity within the existing production relations has been reached; tendency to withdraw from parts of produciton (sub-letting). Subsistence orientation not very accentuated, savings for working capital, not for animal husbandry.	Average access to labour market, but as capital inputs for labour are 25 per cent higher than in the other villages, Bortubeil has the best yields per feddan of cotton, sorghum and wheat (for 15-feddan-tenancies) Annual income* from: 15-feddan tenancy: £S382.90 30-feddan-tenancy: £S563.00

* For basis of calculations see Tait 1983, pp. 123-7.

Notes

1. The existence of these groups, even the former existence of a slave based mode of production in the Gezira is denied by Founou-Tchuigoua (1978). However, anyone who has been in the Gezira will have no difficulties in finding semi-feudal village structures. See also O'Fahey (1973).

2. There are, of course, some differences between the Plantation Syndicate and the SGB, but aside from the participation of tenants on the Board of Directors of the SGB, little has changed in the basic structure of policy-making.

3. The methodology, construction of the scales used, statistical procedures employed, and comprehensive results are described in Tait (1980).

4. Wheat counts as a tenant's crop, too, but is mainly produced with SGB-owned and operated machinery. It is also marketed by the SGB using a procedure whereby a large share of the harvest must be delivered to the SGB to cover the production costs incurred.

5. See Barnett's table of origins of consumer goods in the Gezira (1977, p. 176).

6. This is to include minimum wage regulations, old age pensions, health insurance, regulations pertaining to job termination and promotion, etc.

7. Figure obtained from Ministry of Education, Gezira Province.

8. This was specifically the case with wheat production,which, highly subsidised by the government, and expanding at the cost of cotton, must be considered a political, income-adding concession to tenants and to the newly developing tenant-contractors who hire out combine harvesters to the SGB for wheat production.

References

Adam, Farah Hassan and Apaya, William Andrea (1973), 'Agricultural Credit in the Gezira', Sudan Notes and Records, 54, pp. 104-15.

Al-Arifi, Salih Abdalla (1975), 'Landlordism among Small Tenants - The Case of the Gezira Tenants in the Sudan', Sudan Journal of Economic and Social Studies, 1 (2), pp. 10-14.

Ali, Taisier and Jay O'Brien (1984), 'Labor, Community and Protest in Sudanese Agriculture', in J. Barker, (ed.), The Politics of Agriculture in Tropical Africa, pp. 205-38, Sage, Beverly Hills.

Barnett, Tony (1977), The Gezira Scheme: An Illusion of Development, Frank Cass, London.

Culwick, Geraldine (1955), A Study of the Human Factor in the Gezira Scheme, Sudan Gezira Board, Barakat.

Duffield, Mark (1979), Hausa and Fulani Settlement and the Development of Capitalism in Sudan, PhD, Centre of West African Studies, University of Birmingham.

--- (1981) Maiurno: Capitalism and Rural Life in Sudan, Ithaca Press, London.

Founou-Tchuigoua, B. (1978), 'De Facto Wage-Earners in the Gezira Scheme (Sudan)', Africa Development, 3 (1), pp. 25-50.

Gruenbaum, Ellen (1978), A Study of Social Services in Gezira Province, Ministry of Social Affairs, Khartoum.

Heinritz, Gunter (1982), Problems of Agricultural Development in the Sudan, Edition Herodot, Gottingen.

Humeida and Moubarak (1976), Rural Credit in the Sudan Gezira Scheme, Dept. of Rural Economy, University of Khartoum, Khartoum.

IBRD (1966) Gezira Study Mission: Main Report, International Bank for Reconstruction and Development, Washington, D.C.

ILO (1976) Growth, Employment and Equity: A Comprehensive Strategy for the Sudan, International Labour Office, Geneva.

Ministry of Irrigation (1977), Blue Nile Waters Study, Ministry of Irrigation, Khartoum.

Nugdalla, Sid-Ahmed (1973), The Sudanese Political Leadership. PhD, University of Manchester.

O'Brien, Jay (1977), 'Primary Export Production and the Structures of Underdevelopment' in Ali Mohammed El Hassan (ed.), Essays on the Economy and Society of the Sudan, pp. 69-87, Khartoum University Press, Khartoum.

--- (1980), Agricultural Labor and Development in Sudan, PhD, University of Connecticut.

--- (1983), 'The Formation of the Agricultural Labour Force in Sudan', Review of African Political Economy, 26, pp. 15-34.

O'Fahey, R.S. (1973), 'Slavery and the Slave Trade in Darfur', Journal of African History 14 (1), pp. 29-43.

Randell, John (1958), 'El Gedid - A Blue Nile Gezira Village', Sudan Notes and Records, 39, pp. 25-39.

Rey, Pierre-Philippe (1973), Les Alliances de Classes, Maspero, Paris.

Sellin, Harald (1980), 'Die Entwicklung der Handelsbourgeoisie im Sudan', in Rainer Tetzlaff and Karl Wohlmuth (eds.), Der Sudan: Probleme und Perspektiven der Entwicklung, pp. 610-41, Alfred Metler Verlag, Frankfurt am Main.

SGB (Sudan Gezira Board) (1969), Socio Economic Survey 1969 - Wad el Naim, SGB-Archives, Barakat.

Sorbo, Gunnar M. (1977), 'Nomads on the Scheme - A Study of Irrigation, Agriculture and Pastoralism in Eastern Sudan, in P. O'Keefe and B. Wisner (eds.), Land Use and Development, pp. 132-50, International African Institute, London.

Sudan Government, (1948 approx.) The Sudan: A Record of Progress 1898-1947, Sudan Government, Khartoum.

Sudanow, (1980), Gezira - What Future? Sudanow 3, pp. 33-9.

Tait, John (1978), 'Diversifizierung, Mechanisierung und Kapitalisierung der Produktion im Sudan Gezira Scheme: Auf dem Weg zur Uberwindung kolonial deformierter Agrarstrukturen?', Afrika Spectrum 13 (2), pp. 165-178.

--- (1980) 'Die "Modernisierung" der kolonialen Produktionsweise im Sudan Gezira Scheme' in Rainer Tetzlaff and Karl Wohlmuth (eds.), Der Sudan: Probleme und Perspektiven der Entwicklung, pp. 431-609, Alfred Metler Verlag, Frankfurt am Main.

--- (1983) 'The Modernization of the Colonial Mode of Production in the Gezira Scheme', in Peter Oesterdiekhoff and Karl Wohlmuth (eds.), The Development Perspectives of the Democratic Republic of Sudan, pp. 81-136, Weltforum Verlag, Munich.

Vergopoulos, Kostas (1974), 'Capitalism deforme: Le cas de l'agriculture dans le capitalisme', in Samir Amin (ed.), La question paysanne et le capitalisme, Maspero, Paris.

Wall Street Journal Europe, 1983, No. 69 (1983).

5 The Fallata: ideology and the national economy in Sudan[1]

MARK R. DUFFIELD

The word 'Fallata' is popularly used in the Niles region of northern Sudan as a derogatory generic term loosely applied to the numerous Westerners and their descendants there, regardless of whether they have originated from Darfur, Chad, Central African Republic, Cameroun, Nigeria or Niger. Because the term is, however, practically useless as a descriptive category - there being marked socio-economic differences between the groups so distinguished - it is more important, and profitable, to examine it from the point of view of its ideological content. The term 'Fallata' (sing. 'Fallati') in the Niles region is implicity associated with migrants and migration, with a state of being 'non-Sudanese' and, moreover, with the performance of specific economic tasks, especially the more arduous and unrewarding aspects of unskilled urban and agricultural work. That 'Fallata' has achieved a wide degree of popular usage, despite its connotations of transiency and non-belonging, indicates that the groups and occupations so designated have, indeed, had a long historical association in this region. Here, I will not examine the nature of this association in detail (see Duffield 1981) but will concentrate on the place that the 'Fallata' ideology, as opposed to an empirically existing group, occupies in Sudan society and the manner in which it contributes to the expansion of Sudan's capitalist economy.

In those societies where capitalism has gained a position of dominance, of which Sudan is one, the role of the politico-ideological superstructure is to help support and maintain capitalism's economic reproduction. From this point of view, ideology is inseparable from specific and corresponding forms of political practice. Since economic production, like political practice, is a real and concrete thing, it follows that ideology, in supporting this intervention, defines an equally real field of experience. Ideology is not based on misunderstanding or false consciousness. In terms of the particular interests it represents, ideology defines how those interests appropriate and control the world of which they are part (cf. Hirst 1976).

With Sudan's recent history of regional and internal dissension (O'Neill 1978), the notion of 'national unity' became the main ideological form in which the Numeiri regime attempted to resolve the inherent contradictions of the capitalist economy over which it presided.[2] The 'Fallata' ideology is significant since, by defining what is not Sudanese, it delimits the boundaries, as it were, of this unity and thereby strengthens it. What is more important, however, is the fact that the 'Fallata' do not represent an easily identifiable and unified group in the Niles region. Indeed, in terms of physical appearance many of those so categorized are indistinguishable from the natives of this area. Thus, to say the 'Fallata' are ostracised on the Niles is only meaningful when it is understood that what is not in question is an empirically existing cultural or racial group. Rather, it is those menial and arduous occupations of porterage, gum cleaning, groundnut decorticating, cotton picking, heavy agricultural work, and so on, which are identifiable, and which are ideologically associated with the 'Fallata', that are being delineated and set apart.

This restatement of the situation is illuminating since it suggests that Sudan's post-colonial state is incapable of mediating all the contradictions engendered in the development of capitalism. Those aspects of production which the 'Fallata' ideology separates out, and hence that broad category of unskilled migrant labour which usually performs them, are not secondary or insignificant; on the contrary, they are of primary economic importance. The ideological (hence political) ostracism of the 'Fallata' is, at the same time, an attempt to negate the importance of migrant labour, regardless of its origin, to the Sudanese economy. Thus, popular ideology has it that the primary reason why migrant labour is present in Sudan is not due to the requirements of capitalist development, but to problems arising outside its borders and internal to the migrants' countries of origin. Are we also to believe that the jobs migrants do have also been imported? This ideological negation of the necessity of migrant labour reveals its specific character. If migrant labour is to play its allotted role in the expansion of capitalism in Sudan - requiring that it be cheap and malleable - it must be divested of all economic and political rights. In other words, migrants and the tasks that they perform can never be a factor of 'national unity' - they must, at the level of ideology, remain alien and contingent. In order to analyse how the 'Fallata' ideology aids the reproduction of Sudan's capitalist economy I will briefly outline how this ideology has evolved over time since the beginning of large-scale Westerner immigration and settlement.

Immigration and Settlement

Westerner immigration and settlement did not begin to assume numerical and economic importance until after the British conquest of Sudan in 1898. During the colonial period Westerner immigration can roughly be divided into several stages. Until the end of the 1920s the bulk of immigrants were mainly of Nigerian origin, whilst after this period Chadians and Darfurians assumed numerical ascendancy. With regard to Nigerians, the Fulani were originally most numerous but, by the end of the First World War, the Hausa began to predominate. Since the 1950s the migration and settlement of non-Sudanese Westerners (I will deal with Darfur below), has, with the structural changes in their respective home economies and increasing restrictions on free movement across the border, steadily declined with the result that Nigerian settlement, for example, has all but ceased. The outcome of this prolonged immigration is that nearly fourteen per cent of northern Sudan's present population, or roughly one and a half million people, have originated from outside Sudan's western borders. Nigerians and their descendants, being about a million people, form the bulk of these, with the Hausa constituting the largest single group. This non-Sudanese Westerner population is not uniformly distributed over northern Sudan but, with the exception of the predominantly Hausa urban settlements, is concentrated in the agricultural districts of its central and eastern areas (Duffield 1979).

Prior to British colonisation at the turn of the century, the term 'Fallata' in Sudan related specifically, and in a non-derogatory manner, to those Fulani religious shaykhs or other notables of West African origin who, either alone or with their followers, had been settled in Sudan since the eighteenth century (Duffield 1977). These settlers, whose easterly limit is the Blue Nile, together with many Bornu, form part of that broad group known popularly as Muwallid, meaning that they have been 'born in Sudan'. The direct historical antecedents of the contemporary 'Fallata', however, are not these Fulani groups but those 'black Muslims' from Wadai and Darfur who, as contemporaries of the Muwallid, established both urban and rural settlements in the central and eastern areas of northern Sudan on the overland pilgrimage route to Mecca (Burckhardt 1822, pp. 365-66, 373). These pilgrims, many of whom were from the faqih class of religious teachers and diviners, were known in this region as Takarir, this being the generic term common throughout the Middle East for black Muslims from West Africa (Al-Naqar 1969). Because the Takarir were popularly acclaimed as religious healers and charm makers, and were thus potential rivals of the riverain faqih class (an important repository of 'public opinion') together with the fact that as Muslims in an area in which domestic slaves were usually black, they occupied an anomalous social position - they were commonly regarded as vagabonds and thieves and consequently disliked and feared (Hill 1970:172, 215; Werne 1852, p. 75).

Colonisation, in laying the foundations for the development of capitalism through the eventual outlawing of domestic slavery, radically transformed existing social structures and so created the context in which modern migration has taken place. It is in this context that we must seek the origin of the contemporary usage of the term "Fallata'. One of the initial consequences of the abortive resistance of the Fulani aristocracy to the British conquest of northern Nigeria (1900-1903) was to set in train a major out-migration of Fulani groups, the majority of them originating from the eastern areas of northern Nigeria, which lasted for over a decade and has been estimated as involving more than 25,000 people (Tomlinson and Lethem 1927, p. 9). The result of this large and relatively sudden out-migration was to swamp the existing Westerner settlements in northern Sudan and radically change the meaning of 'Fallata'.

The majority of the Fulani groups entering Sudan originated from an area in which 'Fallata' was commonly used amongst them as a term of self-ascription. Moreover, these groups were not light-skinned nomadic Fulani. Many had been sedentarised for some time and had inter-married with the Hausa peasantry with the result that they were very often indistinguishable from other black Westerners (Palmer 1919a; cf Radclyffe-Dugmore 1924, p. 194). The consequence of this immigration was to inaugurate the popular association of the 'Fallata' in the western and central areas of northern Sudan with the Fulani and, more importantly, with the Hausa who eventually surpassed the Fulani in numbers. Thus, by the end of the First World War the 'Fallata' in this broad area collectively comprised all of those groups, including Bornu, originating from roughly northern Nigeria - the most important area of out-migration at the time. In western Sudan the term still retains this meaning, whilst on the Gash and in the far east the term Takarir to describe Westerners has, until quite recently, remained in popular usage. It is in the Niles region that the most significant changes have occurred.

In the Niles region Nigerian settlement, initially at least, was concomitant with the displacement of the inferior and anomalous status of the earlier Takarir onto the 'Fallata'. In 1909, for example, it was recorded that the inhabitants of Omdurman were of the opinion that "... Allah took away our slaves but sent us the Fallata" (Reports 1909, p. 55). Not only were the 'Fallata' disliked (Tomlinson and Lethem 1927, p. 36), they were disliked as a result of the specific economic niche that they came to occupy. Without understanding the nature of this niche the evolution of the 'Fallata' ideology cannot be grasped. In establishing the colonial economy the British were faced with a serious 'labour problem'. It was not until two decades of colonial rule had elapsed that the socialisation of the sedentary and semi-sedentary inhabitants of the Niles region into a dependence on wage labour had begun to make headway (cf., Scarcity of Labour 1918). In this context the thousands of Hausa and Fulani who had been annually travelling across Sudan since the beginning of the colonial period and who had broken their links with a subsistence economy, and thus had little choice but to work for wages, were quickly realised as offering a solution to the problem. In 1912 Wingate expressed the opinion that,

> When settled down they (the Nigerians) are hard working and law abiding people, and it is for the general good of the country

that they should be encouraged to make it their permanent home. (Reports, Vol. II 1912, p. 23)

Until the end of the Second World War such sentiments remained the basis of British policy and, through gifts of land, tax concessions, monetary inducements and direct coercion, 'Fallata' settlement was actively promoted. Although in many areas, notably those which were relatively underpopulated, land was made available for settlement, it is important to realise that an integrated subsistence economy was not allowed to reform. Rather, a colonial peasantry, existing on cash-crop production and casual wage labour, was created in the countryside, whilst in the towns reserves of unskilled manual labour were formed.

Thus, although the inhabitants of Omdurman saw a resemblance between the 'Fallata' and the slaves of an earlier period, the resemblance was nonetheless misleading since the 'Fallata' were slaves not to any person, but only to their dependence on wage labour. This is why ideas which attempt to understand the subordinate position of the 'Fallata' in contemporary Sudan through the persistence amongst indigenous Sudanese of a 'slave owning mentality' (e.g. McLoughlin 1962) have no basis in the social structure.

It was as cash-crop producers and wage labourers that the 'Fallata' were encouraged by the British to settle, and thereby to help lay the foundations of Sudan's present capitalist economy. Thus, by the end of the 1920s the 'Fallata' - at this point mostly Nigerian settlers - had become Sudan's strategic weapon in combating the colonial labour shortage. Within the first few years of this century the 'Fallata' were already indispensable in the flood irrigation schemes on the Gash and at Tokar. Apart from meeting the bulk of the demand for urban casual labour, they quickly colonised the under-populated rural areas of the Blue Nile and by the beginning of the 1930s they were being used to 'open up' the Gedaref region. Finally, the Gezira Scheme - the single most important economic development during the colonial period, which became operational in 1925 - was heavily dependent upon 'Fallata' labour for its initial development and later expansion.

At the end of the 1920s the situation started to change. The labour demand created by the continuing expansion of the Gezira Scheme and the development of the Gedaref area began to outstrip that which was available from Nigerian settlement. It is from this date that other Westerners, notably from Chad and Darfur, began to assume numerical importance in the Niles region. Moreover, at the same time sedentarised and semi-sedentarised riverain groups came to form an increasingly important part of the migrant labour system (cf., General Reports on Gezira Labour 1929-1932).

The effect of this proliferation of labour supply was twofold. Firstly, given the growth of the labour market through the entry of increasing numbers of Sudanese, it was concomitant with the fixing of the Westerners' role as the backbone of the unskilled manual labour force, especially with regard to the more demanding tasks. The only major exception was the granting of tenancies on the Gezira

Scheme to Nigerians as a consequence of the depression. Although the 1930s saw a growing number of White and Blue Nile Arabs seasonally migrating to the Scheme to pick cotton they generally brought their animals and thus remained on the scheme's edges. Unsettled Westerners monopolised all the arduous tasks and being mobile and unencumbered could be found all through the scheme (Fawzi 1957, pp. 6-7). The second effect of the expansion of the labour market in the Niles region, especially the increasing number of Chadians and Darfurians entering and settling there, was to change the popular conception of who the 'Fallata' are. From referring specifically to Nigerians, the term 'Fallata' came to encompass all Westerners, indeed, often any black non-riverain African.[3] Moreover, uneven economic expansion in the area also resulted in a growing regionalism as to what the characteristics of the 'Fallata' were said to be.

The 'Fallata' ideology is, as I have already mentioned, essentially a popular Sudanese ideology on the Niles. It is this popular status which underlay the difference between it and the view of Westerner settlement held by the colonial state. Indeed, the colonial view can be seen in many respects as the antithesis of the general experience. Colonial officials thought of Westerner migration and settlement in a functional manner, that is, as a natural and inevitable phenomenon, unconnected with the existence of colonialism and the demands of the colonial economy.[4] In general, colonial officials regarded Westerners as better cultivators and harder workers than the riverain Sudanese and saw their settlement on the Niles as part of an inevitable easterly spread of hardy agriculturalists into this fertile though relatively underpopulated region. With regard to Nigerians, a more definite explanation presented itself in the form of the overland pilgrimage to Mecca which, for the Hausa majority, provided a framework in which the settlers themselves perceived their own migration. The pilgrimage, understood as a free individual choice belonging to the emotions rather than the intellect, was viewed by the British not as an effect of the colonial re-organisation of Nigeria but rather as a consequence of the positive role that colonialism was argued to have played in guaranteeing the security of the overland route and providing opportunities for pilgrims to earn money along the way (e.g. Palmerb, 1919, pp. 6, 11; Tomlinson and Lethem 1927, p. 32; Nadel 1940, p. 8).

The colonial regime viewed Nigerian settlers, who if no longer the most numerous of Westerners at the end of the colonial period were certainly the most cohesive and widely distributed, as honest Muslims and industrious and diligent workers. In this respect it is interesting that the self identity which arose amongst Nigerian settlers, which I have called the 'Takari identity' since it involved the adoption of this term as a means of self ascription (Duffield 1983), reproduced in all its essential features the colonial viewpoint. The Takari (a name adapted from <u>Takarir</u>), were in their own eyes hard-working and pious Muslims awash in a sea of indolence and religious heterodoxy. The form of this identity and its coincidence with the colonialist view can only be understood through a consideration of the class structure which emerged amongst Nigerian settlers and the relation of its various components to the colonial state.

Social Differentiation Amongst Nigerian Settlers

The main cleavage amongst Nigerian settlers during the colonial period can be briefly summarised as that between the 'old established' and the 'newcomers'. It is this division which provides the real clue to the nature of the Takari identity. It was amongst the old established settlers that the colonial regime recruited its quarter shaykhs, village shaykhs, labour agents, overseers, informants, interpreters, and so on. Newcomers, on the other hand, supplied the bulk of the unskilled labour force and were, in many cases, dependent for advice, patronage and shelter upon their more established brethren. The Takari identity, in fostering the idea of equality, served to hide the relationship of exploitation, especially in the urban and more developed rural areas, which the old established settlers enjoyed over the newcomers and so helped to further the interests of the former. Since it was the old established who were the agents of the colonial state and the medium through which the 'Fallata' were administered, it can be argued that the Takari identity reproduced the colonial regime's view of the 'Fallata' because the old established settlers were themselves part of the administrative apparatus of the state. Through the planned distribution of shaykhships, the supervision of settlement and other forms of intervention, the position of the old established was directly maintained and, through them, the strategic role played by the 'Fallata' in the colonial economy organised. The Takari identity was an ideology of incorporation and control which, in the last analysis, reproduced the colonial mode of exploitation.

Because the self-identity of the more privileged class of Nigerian settlers was basically an extension of the ideas held by the colonial regime, this identity stood in direct opposition to the popular riverain view of the 'Fallata'. This difference is itself indicative of the divide and rule nature of the colonial labour strategy and consequent specialisation and fragmentation of the labour market during this period. The growth of nationalism as a popular movement first made clearly manifest the contradictory and anomalous position of the 'Fallata' in Sudan. Since the old-established amongst the 'Fallata', the only class capable of mobilising Westerners on a large scale, were associated with the colonial state, the 'Fallata' played no direct part in the nationalist struggle. On the contrary, the 'Fallata' question was made a focal point of much nationalist agitation (cf., Hassoun 1952) and, during the course of the struggle, the 'Fallata's' ideological role as the external threat - the antithesis of national unity - was consolidated.

It is interesting to note that, although the British view of Westerner settlement and that of the Sudanese nationalists were opposed, their contrariety was expressed within a shared functionalist framework in which any problems or contradictions within the system are seen as originating outside of, or as being unconnected with, the existing order of things. Crime, poverty and prostitution, for example, are commonly thought of in Sudan as being brought in from 'outside' and to be the work of 'foreigners'. The agitation for, and eventual promulgation of, Sudanese nationality laws clearly marks the superstructural response to the development of the post-war capitalist economy and the attempt to define it in national terms - an event which marks a definite break with the colonial mode of production. The first of the laws enacted was the 1948 Sudan Ordinance which defined as 'Sudanese by descent' any person who had been resident, or who had ancestors resident, in Sudan before 1897, the year in which the Anglo-Egyptian invasion of Sudan began. The Minister of the Interior could, by grant, also naturalise any applicants who had been resident in Sudan for at least ten years, providing they were of good character and had an adequate knowledge of Arabic (Laws 1956, pp. 149-50). The Nationality Act of 1957, which repealed the Sudan Ordinance, did little to alter the basic substance of the law (Legislative Supplement 1957, 82-7).

Given the fact that some sections of the nationalist movement were adamant that, regardless of the law, they would refuse to recognise any 'Fallata' as Sudanese, it is clear that the British were embarrassed by the fact that along the Blue Nile, for example, "hundreds, perhaps thousands" of Westerners were eligible for Sudanese citizenship. In order to avert a potentially dangerous situation,

> The Civil Secretary .... ordered that there should be no mass application (for citizenship) of Westerners. No special publicity was therefore given to the new Ordinance and there have, in fact, been few if any applications (SCR/39 8.2.1951).

The first major issue fought by the nationalist movement concerning the question of nationality and legitimacy arose in the Gezira Scheme, one of the most developed rural areas in Sudan. Agitation to prevent tenancies passing into the hands of 'Fallata', or the heirs of former 'Fallata' tenants, began in the latter half of the 1940s (Fawzi 1957, p. 7; Hassoun 1952, p. 100). Since it was apparent to the British that the bulk of Westerners settled in the scheme were entitled to Sudanese citizenship, the Governor of the Blue Nile Province, within which the Gezira Scheme lay, advised against any encouragement of Westerners to apply for citizenship since it would "raise an outcry from local tenants who are very greatly in the majority" (SCR/39 4.4.1951). In June 1952 a meeting of the Sudan Gezira Board passed the following resolution;

> That non-Sudanese tenants be allowed to retain their tenancies only until such time as they die, desert, or are evicted for inefficient work, when their tenancies will revert to local Sudanese inhabitants; and that no non-Sudanese be considered hereafter for tenancies which fall vacant (SCR/39 18.7.1952).

This decision, although not officially accepted, remained *sub judice* and, in order to allay any criticism, the Civil Secretary indicated that he would, with regard to applications for Sudanese nationality, exercise the discretion given to him by law in "...

refusing any applications from Westerners until the ... whole question has been debated by the Sudanese" (SCR/39 18.7.1952). It is now contrary to the regulations of the Scheme that a tenancy should pass into the hands of non-Sudanese. Although the overwhelming majority of all Westerners and descendants settled in the Gezira are eligible for Sudanese citizenship, it still remains the case that, owing to the way the nationality laws are put into effect and the strength of local opposition, many "non-Sudanese" Westerners find difficulty in obtaining their rights. The result has been a certain amount of out-migration of settled Westerners from the Scheme.

As one of the most developed of rural areas of the country, the Gezira Scheme is an example of the uneven development of capitalism in Sudan. This unevenness is reflected in the marked variation within the 'Fallata' ideology on the Niles. In general, the ideology varies according to the nature of the dominant form of production in each area. In Khartoum and its environs, for example, where casual work takes the form of heavy porterage for men and clothes-washing, gum cleaning, groundnut decorticating and other occupations of low remuneration for women, the 'Fallata' are regarded as beggars, vagabonds and thieves. Rather than contributing to the economy, they are seen as a drain on existing resources and services. In the Gezira Scheme, on the other hand, where the arduous tasks associated with the production of cotton provide the basis for casual employment, the 'Fallata', although often acknowledged as hardworking, are regarded as dirty, disease-ridden and fond of poor food. In relation to the last characteristic, it is common along the banks of the Blue Nile, where Nigerian settlers and their descendants are a very important element in the river fishing industry, for Sudanese to claim that the 'Fallata' eat nothing but fish. Apart from the assertion that all 'Fallata' are pilgrims and are only just passing through, regardless of how long their settlements have been established, another feature which is common to the 'Fallata' ideology in general (and which I will elaborate below) is the idea that they are shifty and conspiratorial and, whilst keeping much to themselves, are nonetheless out to further their own interests.

The nationalist victory and the fixing of the 'Fallata' as an external threat to national unity simultaneously saw the emergence of two new contradictions. In the first place, many of those subsumed by the Sudanese under the heading of 'Fallata' have played an important role in the expansion of capitalist production in Sudan. Secondly, capitalist expansion did not mean the end of Sudan's need for cheap unskilled labour. In fact, the opposite has occurred and since independence in 1956 the demand for labour has greatly increased at the same time as the number of Westerners entering and settling in Sudan has declined. The increased demand has largely been met by the growing participation within the system of labour migration of Sudanese groups which had previously not been involved.

The descendants of Westerner settlers, especially those living in towns and the more developed rural areas, have in no way been isolated from capitalism's post-war expansion in Sudan. Indeed, as practitioners of the skilled personal services, such as tailoring, barbering and watchmending; or as lorry and taxi drivers, mechanics, and metal workers, and in other areas of tertiary production, they have played an extremely important part. In some towns, such as El Obeid, Gedaref and Kassala, the 'Fallata', the majority of whom are second or later generation, form a large proportion of all the tailors and barbers working there (Duffield 1983). Sudan's nationality laws are, through the connected licensing and employment regulations, directly related to Sudan's post-war economic expansion and define an important aspect of its ideology. In general terms, and with the obvious exception of expatriate businessmen, in order to be anything other than a small peasant farmer or manual unskilled labourer you first have to obtain proof of Sudanese citizenship. Nationality restrictions even exclude non-Sudanese from most forms of factory work. Amongst the descendants of Westerners in the towns and more developed rural areas the possession of legal proof of Sudanese nationality has become a socio-economic necessity. This is not the case in the more isolated rural areas however, where, owing to a different occupational structure and the prevalence of manual techniques of agricultural production, nationality is not such a pressing issue.

Given that the nationality laws operate within the framework of the 'Fallata' ideology, it can be appreciated that the application for citizenship by many Westerners can meet with resistance, if not outright refusal and intimidation on the part of the authorities concerned. One of the most significant amendments in the nationality laws occurred in 1963 when the power to confer citizenship was taken out of the hands of the Minister of the Interior and given to the Chief of Police in the district or area where the application is made (Legislative Supplement 1963, p. 6). This has meant that the ease or difficulty of obtaining Sudanese citizenship has, to a large extent, been regionalised. In general terms it tends to be easier to obtain citizenship in urban as opposed to rural areas. This is especially the case in towns west of the Niles. In Khartoum and to the east, however, the situation can be more difficult. In Khartoum, for example, according to recent information, the authorities there have stopped issuing naturalisation papers to "non-Sudanese" Westerners altogether. In the countryside the main areas of difficulty are in the large agricultural schemes, such as the Gezira Scheme, or in areas like that between Ed Damazin and the Ethiopian border where Westerners, here mostly of Nigerian origin, form the bulk of the peasant population. The relative ease for town dwellers in obtaining Sudanese nationality lies as much in their different social relations as in the more liberal attitudes of the administration. In the towns, Westerners are able to utilise contacts within the state bureaucracy or muster other forms of patronage; not least of all, owing to the existence of more lucrative forms of employment, they are more able to afford the bribes that the granting of nationality often involves. In the countryside, on the other hand, the Westerner peasant has no political patronage on which he can rely nor does his economic activity realise a surplus with which his rights can be purchased.

The split, which roughly corresponds to a town/country division, amongst settled Westerners on the question of the necessity of taking Sudanese nationality is indicative of the profound socio-economic changes that have occurred amongst them since the Second World War. These changes can be most clearly seen in the urban and the more developed rural areas of settlement. In these localities new classes based on the transport and services sectors have emerged around commercial capital (Duffield 1981,1983). Through higher education a growing number of the descendants of Westerner settlers are also entering the professions, including the police and the armed forces, or taking up administrative and clerical positions. Since social mobility in northern Sudan necessitates one becoming 'Sudanese', these developments have been concomitant with a change in identity, or to be more precise, a change in ideology amongst the more affluent strata of Westerners. This is especially true of the professionals and bureaucrats amongst them who are Sudanese in outlook and affiliation, if we take this to imply the life-style and aspirations of the middle classes of the Niles region.

Owing to the pervasiveness of the 'Fallata' ideology however, and the pressure to become 'Sudanese', the price of social mobility is often to hide one's 'Fallata' background from workmates, colleagues and other associates. To disclose one's heritage can have effects varying from a cooling of relations to the damaging of career prospects and open abuse. These eventualities, however, should not be seen as the result of some form of innate riverain Sudanese or Arab racism. Rather, it is an effect of both the manner in which cheap labour is being reproduced and controlled in northern Sudan and the attempt by the riverain middle classes to maintain their hegemony of the state apparatus. The contradiction is clear. For the 'Fallata' to have a significant presence in clerical and official positions indicates their long association with Sudan, yet the 'Fallata' ideology maintains that they are migrants of menial status. To explain why 'Fallata' are to be found in such jobs ideology frequently resorts to a 'conspiracy theory', this being the only logical way to explain the jump, say from unskilled labourer one day to police officer the next, in which the devious and scheming 'Fallata' are attempting to infiltrate and subvert the state.

Although the derogatory stereotypes of the 'Fallata' operate more clearly at the point of production, it is the conspiracy theory, since it relates directly to the riverain monopoly of the state, which is dominant in the media and which provides the framework for casting the 'Fallata' as one of Sudan's foremost political scapegoats. In December 1974, for example, President Numeiri, in his monthly address, accused the 'Fallata' of being guilty of economic sabotage following the widespread rioting of secondary schoolboys occasioned by the rise in the price of sugar. Accusation, however, was not enough and many 'Fallata' were rounded up in various towns, including Khartoum. In a number of instances, after being forced to sell their belongings, people were deported to the Chadian border (cf., al-A'yam 7.1.1975). Since then the 'Fallata', quite without foundation, have been linked in the media with several attempted coups and disturbances (Al-Nasr 1978, p. 38) and 'Fallata' areas in the Three Towns (Khartoum, Omdurman and Khartoum North) are frequently cordoned off and the inhabitants harassed during the course of searching for arms. Inflamatory and xenophobic articles often appear in the press which, despite the documented decline of immigration, usually take the line that Sudan is in danger of being swamped by 'Fallata' immigrants unless immediate steps are taken (e.g. al-A'yam 18.7.1976, 21.8.1978, 6.2.1979; al-Sa'arfa 2.1.1979).

So far we have seen that the 'Fallata' ideology can be divided into two related aspects. On the one hand, it helps in the reproduction and control of cheap migrant labour since by maintaining that all 'Fallata' are migrants and foreigners it denies this labour any economic or political rights. Secondly, it helps the Sudanese riverain bourgeoisie in maintaining their hegemony over the state apparatus in the face of competition from the descendants of Westerners, their only serious rivals in the north. The 'Fallata' ideology, however, in dividing the labouring masses by isolating important sections of migrant labour, also hinders the struggle for democracy at the same time as it enhances capitalist production. In this respect the 'Fallata' ideology, in simultaneously operating at several levels within the social structure, illustrates the efficiency and economy characteristic of ideology.

The significant decline in the numbers of Westerners entering Sudan in recent years corresponds to structural changes in the economies of their homelands and has been matched by a steady increase in the scale of internal labour migration within Sudan. One estimate suggests that more than a million people are annually on the move across Sudan in search of work (ILO 1976, p. 91). The western region of Darfur is an area of continuing importance in supplying large numbers of migrants to the central and eastern regions of northern Sudan. Lumped during the colonial period with other Westerners as "non-Sudanese", Darfurians are now regarded as Sudanese in the popular and legal sense of the term. Such a change has been necessary to maintain the ideological coherence of the notion of national unity. A result of this change and the continued operation of Sudan's nationality laws is that Westerners can now be divided into "Sudanese" and "non-Sudanese". Unlike "non-Sudanese" Westerners, Darfurians can enter many of the more lucrative areas of employment, such as the skilled or semi-skilled aspects of factory work, government corporations or the armed services. "Non-Sudanese" Westerners living in Sudan, however, especially those from the more isolated or outlying rural areas, are still numerically and economically important. Whereas capitalist expansion has allowed a not insignificant skilled labour force to emerge - a development from which many "Sudanese" Westerners have profited - the arduous, unskilled and less remunerative tasks upon which the profitability of new areas of production depend are still to a large extent the work of "non-Sudanese" Westerners. This is not a result of Sudanese racism or the heritage of a slave-owning mentality. It is a consequence of the expansion and reproduction of the capitalist mode of production and the character of the state - together with its associated classes - which has arisen from this mode and which presides over it.

Notes

1. The fieldwork upon which much of this article is based was carried out in Sudan amongst Nigerian settlers and their descendants between December 1973 and February 1975. In October 1976 I returned to Sudan for three years in the capacity of Research Fellow at the Institute of African and Asian Studies, University of Khartoum. This gave me opportunity to explore further the themes outlined here.

2. For the place of ideology in the development of the Tanzanian state see Goulbourne 1978.

3. Colonial reports, however, continued to remain fairly specific with regard to the division of migrants and settlers into ethnic or regional groups.

4. Thus, functionalism, as an anthropological paradigm, as is sometimes asserted, can instead be seen as an extension of the colonial experience itself. This is a further illustration of the fact that ideology is not simply false consciousness or an inadequate understanding of reality, but, in fact, occupies the place of real experience.

References

Al-A'yam, 7.1.1975, 18.7.1976, 21.8.1978, 6.2.1979.

Al-Naqar, U. (1969), 'Takrur, the History of a Name', Journal of African History, 10, pp. 365-74.

Al-Nasr, A. A. M. (1977), Maiurno of the Blue Nile: A Study in Oral Biography, PhD, University of Wisconsin - Madison.

Al-Sa'arfa, 2.1.1979, Scarcity of Labour, National Records Office, Khartoum.

Burkhardt, J.L. (1822), Travels in Nubia, John Murray, London.

Duffield, M.R.(1977), 'Mahdism and Revisionism in Sudan: Hijra or Compromise with Colonialism?', Paper presented to Third International Conference,'The Central Bilad at Sudan: Tradition and Adaptation', University of Khartoum.

--- (1979), 'A Note on the Demography of Nigerian Settlement in Sudan' in M. A. Galal al-Din, (ed.), Immigration and Internal Migration in the Sudan, Khartoum University Press, Khartoum.

--- (1981), Maiurno: Capitalism and Rural Life in Sudan, Ithaca Press, London.

--- (1983), 'Change Among West African Settlers in Northern Sudan', Review of African Political Economy, 26, pp. 45-59.

Fawzi, S.E.D.(1957), The Labour Movement in Sudan, 1946-1955, Oxford University Press, London.

Goulbourne, H. (1978), 'Some Aspects of Ideological Functions in the Development of the Post-Colonial State in Tanzania'. Africa Development, 3 (2), pp. 57-73.

General Reports on Gezira Labour, 1929-1932, Blue Nile Province, 1/20/125 National Records Office, Khartoum.

Hassoun, I.A. (1952), 'Western Migration and Settlement in the Gezira', Sudan Notes and Records, 35, pp. 60-113.

Hill, R. trans. and ed., (1970), On the Frontiers of Islam, 1822-45, Oxford University Press, London.

Hirst, P.Q. (1976), Problems and Advances in the Theory of Ideology. Cambridge University Press, Cambridge.

International Labour Office (ILO) (1976), Growth Employment and Equity: A Comprehensive Strategy for the Sudan, ILO Geneva.

Laws of the Sudan, 1956, Vol. 1 Titles I-III, Khartoum.

Legislative Supplement to Sudan Gazette, 1957, 1963, Khartoum.

McLoughlin, P.F.M. (1962), 'Economic Development and the Heritage of Slavery in the Sudan Republic', Africa, 32, pp. 355-91.

Nadel, S.F. (1940), 'Report on West Africans in El Obeid', in Immigration and Emigration, General Policy and Rulings, 1929-1943, Kassala Province, 1/55/204, National Records Office, Khartoum.

O'Neill, Norman (1978), 'Imperialism and Class Struggle in Sudan', Race and Class, 20 (1), pp. 1-19.

Palmer, H.R. (1919a), 'Note on Fallata in Sudan', in Notes and Reports on Control of Fallata, 1911-1922, Blue Nile Province, 1.31.224, National Records Office, Khartoum.

--- (1919b), Report on a Journey from Maidugari, Nigeria, to Jeddah in Arabia, Reports List, 2/1/5, National Records Office, Khartoum.

Radclyffe-Dugmore, A. (1924), The Vast Sudan, Arrowsmith, London.

Reports on the Finance, Administration and Condition of the Sudan, 1909 Reports List, 2.1.6, 1912 Vol. 11, Reports List, 2.7.24 National Records Office, Khartoum.

Scarcity of Labour, 1918 Intelligence Reports, 4.5.41, Nationl Records Office, Khartoum.

SCR/39 Roseires Sub District 39. Legal A. General, 1951-1952 Roseires Town Council, Uncatalogued.

Tomlinson, J.F. and Lethen, G.J. (1927), History of Islamic Political Propaganda in Nigeria, Mss. Brit. Emp. S. 276, Box 7, Rhodes House, Oxford.

Werne, F. (1852), African Wanderings, Longman, London.

6 The formation and transformation of the agricultural labour force in Sudan[1]

JAY O'BRIEN

The development of capitalist agriculture in Sudan since colonial times has depended upon the formation of a large seasonal wage labour force. Commentary on this labour force in discussions of Sudanese agriculture has been rigidly limited to debates over whether or not it is large enough and what should be done if it is found to be too small for desired expansion. Between 1.5 and 2 million seasonal workers, mostly peasants and pastoralists for the rest of the year, work in weeding or harvesting operations in state and private plantations annually. More than 300,000 of them pick cotton in the Gezira Scheme alone. Yet, when the British occupied Sudan in 1898 there was virtually no wage labour market at all. Thus, in a very real sense, the story of the development of capitalist agriculture in Sudan has been the creation of the agricultural labour force. Viewed from the historical perspective of the formation of this labour force, the question of labour shortage immediately becomes more complex than head-counting, and is revealed as a social and economic question having to do with the circumstances under which non-wage producers became wage workers. It is the purpose of this essay to describe and analyse what these circumstances have been and how they have changed in recent years, to illuminate the structure and dynamics of the labour force which resulted, and to sketch the contours of a major transformation of the structure and dynamics which has occurred since 1975.

The focus of concern here is with the period of rapid expansion of capitalist agriculture and the seasonal labour force in Sudan since independence in 1956, culminating in the crisis of the late 1970s in

Sudanese agriculture and the simultaneous appearance of transforming trends in the dynamics of the agricultural labour force. The required historical background of the development of capitalist agriculture in Sudan and the initial stimulation of a labour supply to fuel it is outlined in the following two brief sections (for more detail, see Chapter 1 above).

Before proceeding, however, it is important to note that the development of the agricultural labour force in Sudan since the British conquest has passed through three distinct phases, and by 1975 was entering a fourth phase. These phases have each been characterised by distinct policies towards labour and agriculture and by different patterns of expansion of both agriculture and the agricultural labour market. The development of the agricultural labour force should thus be approached within the framework of a periodisation of its principal phases.

Phase 1: 1898–1925

British strategic goals in occupying Sudan dominated policy in all fields. Agricultural development was limited to small-scale experimentation with cotton cultivation and was rigorously supervised by government. Out of fear of renewed nationalist uprisings, the use of taxation and other classical colonialist methods of stimulating labour supply was severely restricted.

Phase 2: 1925–1950

Ensuring a secure supply of seasonal labour to the Gezira Scheme, opened in 1925, and the pump-irrigated private cotton estates opened later dominated all labour policy, and virtually all other economic development was restricted. The settlement of large numbers of West African Muslim immigrants in and around the Gezira area as a supply of agricultural labour was encouraged by the British. This phase corresponds to the concession period granted to the Sudan Plantations Syndicate (SPS), a British corporation, for management of the Gezira Scheme.

Phase 3: 1950–1975

This period began with the nationalisation and Sudanisation of the Gezira Scheme and saw a rapid expansion of capitalist agriculture, both irrigated and rainfed, including the beginnings of large-scale private Sudanese investment in agriculture. The corresponding expansion of the seasonal labour force was accomplished through an elaborate system of recruitment and resulted in the formation of a labour force which was highly segmented into virtually distinct markets for different agricultural tasks.

Phase 4: 1975 to the present.

Deepening economic crisis accompanied by accelerating inflation beginning in 1973 began to have noticeable effects on agricultural labour markets by 1975, when wage rates began to rise sharply. The recruitment system and the barriers between segments of the labour market began to break down. The significance of these events and tendencies can only be assessed in the context of a full analysis and is examined below.

The Development of Capitalist Agriculture

The development of large-scale capitalist agriculture under the British in Sudan was preceded by some centrally organised estate agriculture during the periods of the Funj and Keira sultanates and Turko-Egyptian rule. These earlier forms, however, exploited predominantly resident or settled captive populations through tax/tribute, direct labour service and/or chronic indebtedness. Markets for agricultural wage labour on the large scale fostered by the British did not exist (see O'Fahey and Spaulding 1974; O'Fahey 1980; Hill 1959; O'Neill, this volume).

The Sudanese economy has been dominated by cotton since the British opened the Gezira Scheme in 1925 based on a three-way 'partnership' involving the colonial government, a British company known as the Sudan Plantation Syndicate (SPS), and several thousand households of tenant cultivators (see Gaitskell 1959, and chapters 1 and 4, this volume). The area of cotton planting in Gezira rose from 80,000 feddans (1 feddan = 1.038 acres) in 1925 to over 200,000 feddans by the late 1930s, with demand for seasonal labour growing accordingly. Sudan assumed second place, behind Egypt, as a major supplier of long staple cotton to the world market. All other agricultural developments were tightly restricted until independence out of fear of disrupting the vital supply of seasonal labour to Gezira.

Gezira remained unrivalled as an agricultural production complex. Even after other schemes began producing cotton, it still produced over 80 per cent of Sudan's cotton and dominated all aspects of the economy and related policy. By independence in 1956, the colonial administration had nationalised the management function under the Sudan Gezira Board (SGB), and the total irrigated area had been raised to a million feddans. Within a few more years, a new dam was built on the Blue Nile and the irrigated area doubled.

An explosive expansion of capitalist agriculture outside the Gezira Scheme followed independence. Wealthy Sudanese, attracted by the soaring cotton prices of the Korean War boom, invested heavily in pump-irrigated schemes along the White and Blue Niles. Even extended recession in world cotton prices in the late 1950s did not slow this expansion for another decade. By then an attractive alternative had emerged and an obliging government freed capital invested in the foundering pump-schemes by nationalising them on generous terms.

The alternative was mechanised farming of sorghum, the main food crop, in the central rainlands. The beginnings of rainfed mechanised agriculture date back to 1943, when the British had started a small project near Gedaref to feed troops stationed in the region. By 1953, the government had reduced its role in this project and begun to lease large plots to private Sudanese investors for operation on a commercial basis. This enterprise proved so profitable to the Sudanese petty bourgeoisie and the budding agrarian bourgeoisie that crop areas expanded to 1.2 million feddans within five years and 8 million feddans by 1977 (see O'Brien 1983b; Chapter 1, this volume).

The Stimulation of a Seasonal Labour-Supply

The colonial regime mobilised all its powers to meet the large demand for wage labour in the Gezira Scheme. With the regime securely entrenched and the countryside pacified, taxes were raised and more rigorously collected. The time of rural tax collection in key labour supply provinces was shifted from the end of the dry season (May-June) to the beginning of the cotton-picking season (January-February) by 1943 in order to ensure that peasants and pastoralists were relieved of their cash at the most opportune time. The regime aggressively pushed the marketing of Manchester cotton goods, tea, coffee and sugar into new areas and vigilantly monitored their sale and manipulated their supply and price in relation to local crop yields and grain and livestock prices. In times of critical labour shortage (e.g. 1942/43 cotton harvest) they stopped supplies of consumer goods to rural districts and channelled them through the administrative offices of the Gezira Scheme (see Labour Board 1943; O'Brien 1980). Traditional handicraft production which withstoood the effects of competition from manufactured goods came under direct assault, as when the British banned and then destroyed cotton cultivation (and thus independent cloth production) in provinces abutting the Gezira (see O'Brien 1980, 1984a).

A form of recruitment was developed in the 1930s which came to assume an important role in the elaborate recruitment system which developed in the 1950s. Village shaykhs and other local notables were contracted to supply agreed numbers of labourers from among their followings in return for a per capita fee, and were given the responsibility to ensure that those agreed numbers showed up in the fields and remained picking throughout the harvest. The field staff of the colonial administration were used for this purpose as well as general propogandising in the countryside on behalf of the Gezira Scheme. In times of labour shortage in the scheme reduced rail fares were made available for passengers to Gezira stations.

Most significantly, the British took advantage of the Hausa exodus from the Fulani sultanates, encouraging and facilitating the immigration and settlement in and around the Gezira Scheme of these and other West African groups.[2] In the 1930s, dwelling sites were allocated to these settlers, subsidies made available to build their huts, and small rainland plots set aside for them to cultivate grain crops for household consumption. A sparsely populated region to the southeast of the scheme was set aside as a <u>dar</u> (tribal homeland in the Native Administration structure), under the shaykhship of the Fulani Sultan Mai Wurno, where West African immigrants were encouraged to settled (see Duffield 1979 1981).

The settlers within the scheme area provided a virtually landless pool of cheap labour available year-round for sowing, weeding and other operations in addition to cotton picking. This group in particular was used by management to insure tenant discipline. Any tenant failing to carry out an operation on the cotton crop to the satisfaction of the field inspector risked having the work done by locally recruited settled labour at double wages charged against his cotton account. Tenants who regularly failed to give satisfaction or who absconded (as many did during the lean depression years) were replaced by West African settlers. Meanwhile, Mai Wurno's dar provided a nearby pool of cheap seasonal labour on a migratory basis (see Abdel Hamid 1966).

Unlike many indigenous Arab Sudanese cultivators, most of these West African settlers had long become accustomed to hard agricultural labour under conditions of systematic exploitation and low incomes. The fact that they were such hard competitors in the labour market combined with their use by management against the tenants in the scheme to create great resentment against them on the part of Arab Sudanese and to enhance the ability of capital and government to manipulate the labour market through them. The term Fallata by which all such groups are known in Sudan indiscriminately has since become a strongly pejorative one, which most of them reject in favour of the term Takari (see Duffield, this volume).

Another practice which was developed by the tenants for attracting cotton picking labour came to be reflected in SPS policy. Many tenants found that they could attract pastoralists from surrounding areas to pick cotton by offering grazing in their fodder plots to pickers' animals as part of the wage payment. Thus many pastoral family groups came to spend the dry season picking cotton in Gezira where their animals had ample grazing and water in the months when these were scarcest elsewhere. Although the SPS staff preferred to eliminate the fodder crop from the rotation because it made their job of protecting the cotton crop from diseases more difficult, the role the crop played in attracting labour forced them to accept it as a permanent component of the agricultural regime, particularly in the border areas of the scheme.

The System of Seasonal Labour Recruitment

The organisation of labour recruitment involved a number of participants, including scheme managements, government bodies, tenant committees, growers' associations and private contractors. In the Gezira Scheme about 75 per cent of cotton picking labour came to be recruited by tenant committees assisted by management (Galal-al-Din 1978). Representatives of these committees would travel to principal labour supply areas to make contacts and recruit labour. In some cases independent labour contractors or hired agents undertook recruitment on behalf of such committees or management. Generally, recruiters would make a trip a few weeks before the harvest began in order to negotiate arrangements with a group of migrants. Advances would be paid at this time to the contracted workers and arrangements would be made to send lorries to pick them up for the trip to the scheme at an appointed later date. Usually, negotiations took place through an influential member of the local community, sometimes the village shaykh, but frequently through persons not holding any formal position but known simply as "shaykhs of migrants" for the roles they played in recruiting and organising parties of workers. In addition to negotiating the wages to be paid to the migrants, the shaykh of migrants would negotiate his own reward for supplying workers, usually a per capita commission for each recruit of 5 pt or 10 pt plus a small cash grant or loan. The pattern was similar in other irrigated schemes.

In the rainfed schemes, the management of the state farms followed similar procedures in recruiting seasonal labour. In the private schemes, recruitment was generally carried out by the growers' association of each project area, a task which was one of the main functions of such associations. In many areas, self-recruiting labour would assemble in the major towns near schemes, where labourers were contacted and employed by recruiters who then trucked them out to the schemes.

Such recruitment of course added an important non-wage component to the total wage bill - roughly one quarter of a million pounds annually for the Gezira Scheme in the 1970s (Galal-al-Din 1978). However, a central feature of the pattern of demand for seasonal agricultural labour which undoubtedly made the recruitment strategy less expensive to capital in the long run than raising wages would have been is the fact that the demand for seasonal labour fluctuates widely from year to year in response to variations in yields and crop prices. Accordingly, the common practice in the schemes was to estimate the volume of each season's crop shortly before the harvest and to calculate recruitment goals on the basis of estimates of how much labour is needed to harvest a crop at that anticipated yield level. Reliance on spontaneous market forces to supply labour to the schemes would very likely have resulted in relatively unstable wage rates - especially when the additional complicating factor of the influence of peasant yields on propensity to migrate is taken into consideration. Furthermore, wages would have had to be sufficient at the level of the labour market as a whole to cover the costs of transportation incurred by labourers coming from great distances. Without large-scale organised recruitment, wage rates for seasonal agricultural labour would undoubtedly have risen considerably more between 1950 and 1975 than they did.[3]

In effect, a critical inelasticity of demand for seasonal labour in capitalist agriculture came to play an increasingly important role in the expansion of the seasonal labour market after 1950. Although the actual number of labourers needed varied considerably from year to year, a stable supply was required which could meet the demand created by high yields in any given year. The impact of this inelasticity was muted in the early years when the labour market was dominated by tenant-based agriculture where tenants had the ability to replace hired labour by family labour instead of paying higher wages if sufficient labour failed to come forward at the going wage. But in the years following 1950 the spread of educational opportunities (and their consequences) for tenant offspring and other factors reduced the availability of family labour in tenant-based agriculture while the expansion of capitalist farming in the rainlands restructured demand for seasonal labour. Consequently, the proportion of the seasonal work force which could be replaced by family labour dwindled to insignificance as far as the dynamics of the agricultural labour market were concerned (see O'Brien 1984b; Tait, this volume).

Coupled with systems of recruitment, wage-setting policies practiced by scheme managements helped to keep wage rates stable. Before each season the SGB, for example, announces the rate of the picking advances it will give to the tenants per guffa (basket) and disburses to the tenants or recruitment committees advances to cover the costs of recruitment. The tenants, whose cotton incomes have been low, of course try very hard to keep negotiated wages within the amounts advanced to them. Their ability to do so throughout most of the history of the Gezira Scheme was enhanced by the general stability of wage rates over long periods of time. When a conventional wage rate, announced by the SGB, prevailed from year to year, workers were unlikely to hold out for a higher wage unless they had reason to believe that a general rise was imminent and other recruiters likely to visit their village, or else had more attractive comparable alternatives.

It is hardly possible to overestimate the historical importance in the formation and regulation of the Sudanese agricultural labour force of the mediating role between labour and scheme management played by the tenants (see O'Brien 1980, 1984b). In this role they have served as foremen, supervisors and agents for disciplining the work force. Instead of one 2.1 million feddan plantation under a single central management unit negotiating with a labour force of over half a million, the Gezira Scheme, for the purposes of labour relations, is broken down into nearly 100,000 autonomous units, each of which hires a handful of workers and separately negotiates wage rates. Moreover, the managers of these small units depend for their livelihood on their ability to hold the wage bill down to the absolute minimum, by means which include doing a variable portion of the work themselves. Apart from the obvious economic advantages for management, this situation creates an element of antagonism between tenants and seasonal labour which acts as an obstacle to the emergence of solidarity of the two groups against management. Furthermore, the tenant (or an agent) is present in the field supervising the work of a small number of hired labourers to ensure that they maintain the productivity, both quantitatively and qualitatively, which is so vital to the tenant's own well-being, given the structure of the scheme which sets returns to tenants on cotton yields in proportion to world cotton prices.

Expansion of the Labour Supply 1950–1975

The strategy of expanding labour supply through aggressive recruitment after 1950 reinforced on a larger scale patterns of seasonal migration which had emerged in the previous period. The agricultural labour force continued to have a core, or rather several cores, of regular participants and a periphery of irregular migrants who sought seasonal wage labour in some years but not others, depending on village yields, livestock prices, incidence of special expenses for marriage, circumcision, and so on. With the vast expansion of capitalist agriculture, the growing agricultural labour force in Sudan came to be highly segmented in a number of cross-cutting ways.

Government policies discussed earlier combined with the effects of spreading capitalist agriculture in penetrating village economies to stimulate and expand cash needs. Although local productive systems were altered by the decline of traditional handicrafts, increased cultivation of cash crops and participation in wage labour, many of them remained basically self-sufficient peasant and/or pastoral communities in the limited sense that local production of subsistence and cash goods, irregularly supplemented by wage labour, generally was sufficient to reproduce the community from one year to the next. When local production was insufficient to meet all needs, seasonal labour was resorted to in order to make up the difference. The frequency with which this was necessary varied from community to community.

However, the wholesale disarticulation of domestic economies was not widespread in this early period and was mainly restricted to the core labour supply areas of Blue Nile Province and central Kordofan. But even in these areas it was not generalised. Such disruption seems first to have affected nomads and relatively recently settled former nomads more than others, especially in the drier areas. Many pastoralists found the availability of dry season grazing and abundant water for their animals in the Gezira very attractive, and began from the start to work in cotton picking, with grazing rights to irrigated fodder crops as part of their wage payment (cf Abdel Hamid 1966).

Also from an early date a process gained momentum in which unsuccessful nomads, unable to meet rising cash needs and maintain the minimum viable herding unit, settled in thinly populated areas adjacent to the schemes. Many of these former pastoralists had long regarded cultivators with contempt and regarded heavy agricultural labour as degrading (see Spaulding 1979). The practice was adopted by many of them of cultivating small plots sufficient to meet only family needs for part of the year and then spending the entire cotton-picking season in the schemes picking cotton, where food was provided as part of the wage payment. Not only did they thereby save the crops they had cultivated for consumption during the rainy season, but they used the cash wages they earned to buy meat and other food to supplement their diet and to meet other recurrent cash needs such as for clothing. In addition, they were saved the rigours of digging dry season wells to supply themselves with water. The productivity, and consequently the cash wages, of such groups tended to be relatively low, as the food, water and grazing with which they were provided were the primary things they were interested in, and small amounts of cash were sufficient to meet other needs, particularly as in most cases several of the members of a family were working.

An alternative response to new and increasing cash needs, particularly in higher rainfall zones, was increased effort in local production. That is, peasant cultivators could avoid migrating annually for wage labour by expanding household agricultural production and growing cash crops through extending and intensifying the working day and the working season as a whole. This option was pursued by some peasant communities in which no stigma was attached to hard agricultural labour and a high value was placed on maintaining local autonomy. This was not merely a matter of sentimental attachment to peasant independence, but involved fundamental questions of the maintenance of patriarchal authority and intergenerational axes of appropriation within the household. In such villages, migration for wage labour was generally irregular, and usually took place as a result of poor harvests or high consumer prices.

These alternative responses illustrate but do not exhaust the range of variation in responses to the development of capitalist agriculture in Sudan by different communities based on the internal characteristics and local conditions of these communities. What is important in this context is that the development of the peripheral capitalist economy in Sudan, and of the agricultural wage labour force in particular, proceeded in such a way that the manner and extent of incorporation of individual communities depended largely on their location and internal characteristics.

A consequence of this condition of the agricultural labour force was a diversity of forms of incorporation which allowed continued reproduction of the organising social relations of specific communities. This in turn led to the emergence of a variety of patterns of labour migration. These patterns varied along a number of axes, including frequency and duration of migration, composition and organisation of the work group, pattern and intensity of work, social relationships to employers and the type of work done (see O'Brien 1980; Ali and O'Brien 1984). The main principles involved can be illuminated through the description of the two primary patterns of labour migration in Sudan.

Primary Patterns of Labour Migration

One of the most salient features of the agricultural labour force in Sudan until 1975 has been the operation of virtually separate markets for cotton picking on the one hand and sorghum and sesame harvesting on the other hand. The labour force for cotton picking was dominated by family groups, including women, children and old people, migrating and working together. In contrast, sorghum and sesame harvesting was dominated by men migrating and working without their families.

Cotton picking is less arduous work than harvesting (including threshing) sorghum and sesame, and even children 10 to 12 years old work as productively as most adults. In contast, sorghum and sesame harvesting is difficult not only for children but also for women who are pregnant or encumbered by small children and for old people to carry out productively.

Although extensive data on wages in seasonal labour are lacking, such figures as do exist from a variety of limited studies strongly suggest that the average daily wage in sorghum and sesame harvesting in the rainfed mechanised schemes was generally on the order of 50 per cent higher than the daily wage in cotton picking. It would be a mistake, particularly in light of the post-1975 developments which are discussed below, to view this difference as a simple reflection of any essential difference in the quality of the types of work involved. Rather, this wage differential derived primarily from the differential costs of the social reproduction of the specific labour forces involved. Put simply, cotton picking wages were relatively low because so many of the cotton pickers worked in family groups in which several family members earned incomes to meet the consumption needs of the family. Conversely, wage rates in the rainfed schemes were relatively higher because the work force there was composed principally of individuals who left their families at home and went out in search of an income to help meet the family's consumption needs (see O'Brien 1980).

This difference arose from differences in the social organisation of production within peasant and pastoral productive systems. Where women traditionally participated prominently in agricultural work and public life the migration of the whole family for wage labour in the slack season was a possibility. Where the traditional division of labour excluded women from some or all types of agricultural work, especially when this exclusion was accompanied by a more or less strict seclusion of women within the homestead, the requirements of the reproduction of the village productive system as a viable site for the reproduction of a seasonal labour force restricted the availability of women for wage labour (see O'Brien 1980; Ali and O'Brien 1984).

These contrasting requirements of village reproduction explain why labour from the latter type of village had to be paid a higher wage than labour from the former type could be satisfied with in order to ensure the reproduction of the village economy as a source of seasonal labour. It does not, however, suffice to explain why it in fact came to receive such a higher wage. The fact that higher wages have been paid to the latter type of labour is the result of the conjunction of the specific historical processes of the expansion of capitalist agriculture and the penetration into village economies. New schemes, even to some extent new cotton schemes, established during the period of rapid expansion had to pay somewhat higher wages initially than the going rate in order to attract labour. Because the labour the rainfed schemes attracted was a different type of labour with different reproduction requirements, higher wages had to continue to be offered in the context of continuing expansion in order to attract it. Thus, the fact that these workers could command higher wages than the current rates is not surprising. What needs to be explained is the fact that the market for cotton picking labour remained relatively isolated from the influence of these increased wage rates for two decades.

This can only be explained by reference to the historical process of penetration of peasant and pastoral systems of production. The bulk of the labour force that was most successfully and regularly recruited to seasonal wage labour in the period from the opening of the Gezira Scheme until about 1950 was made up by what could be called "reluctant cultivators", and secondarily by members of communities which had been disrupted and/or uprooted in the preceding period of turbulence. Many (but not all) of the "reluctant cultivators" were sedentarised or partially sedentarised nomads who regarded heavy agricultural labour as undignified but found themselves confronted with the necessity of cultivating. Some of these were members of groups whose animal wealth had been confiscated or otherwise seriously depleted during the Mahdia. Others were from individual pastoral units which found themselves unable to maintain minimum viable herding units. The numbers of such units would of course have been increased significantly by colonial taxation policies, for a pastoral unit is inherently more vulnerable to such measures due to its dependence on animal reproduction rates not immediately governable by expenditure of labour power, and its dependence on the sale of animals - its main productive assets - in order to raise cash. Furthermore, the threat of herd sizes declining below the optimum was sufficient to induce many nomads owning viable but dangerously small herds to seek wage labour as an alternative source of cash to selling animals.

These groups shared an aversion to heavy agricultural labour as well as, in many cases, a traditional division of labour in which women did some agricultural labour, sometimes taking complete responsibility for regular small-scale cultivation of grain crops. The first characteristic predisposed them to look more favourably on the relatively light work of cotton picking than the arduous work in the rainfed schemes. The second made it easy for women to be involved in agricultural wage labour along with men. The two characteristics combined made it more desirable from their point of view to work in family groups in cotton picking than to have individual members have to work harder to earn enough for all.

The response to the growth of seasonal demand for labour and the expansion of cash needs by established peasant cultivators was quite different. In most rainland areas cultivable land was abundant, at least until recently. Thus, for most rainland peasant cultivators the sale of agricultural land was neither a necessity nor a possibility as a means of meeting new and growing cash needs. On the contrary, they had the possibility of increasing their commitment of family labour to their cultivations and extending the area cultivated to meet these needs. Thus, initially, they had only to resort to wage labour when low rainfall, pests or other factors reduced their harvests in bad years. Of course, they did also have the alternative of engaging in regular seasonal wage labour instead of increasing local production, and some did, especially those living in areas close to the schemes. But many such groups seem to have preferred to increase local production and to resort to wage labour only when they experienced shortfalls in local production.

Whether the migration for seasonal labour of members of such groups was in family groups or by individual adult men depended to a great extent on the traditional division of labour in each group, and secondarily on the location of their homes in relation to the schemes. Groups which practiced a strict seclusion of women - most especially rural Takari and related groups - generally kept women and children at home and sent only adult men out in search of wage labour - usually in sorghum and sesame harvesting, unless cotton picking was available much closer at hand.

This broad characterisation of two dominant patterns of involvement in seasonal wage labour is only indicative of the extent to which the market for agricultural labour in Sudan has been segmented. Within each of these patterns additional factors produced further variation segmenting the market. The boundaries between the various segments of the agricultural labour market were defined in the first instance in ethnically identifiable terms, modified to a greater or lesser extent by geographical location. That is, knowing an individual's ethnic identity was the single most reliable indicator of the manner and type of his or her involvement in agricultural wage labour.

The Formation of a National Labour Market in Agriculture Since 1975

Significant changes in the character of agricultural labour markets in Sudan began to become apparent in 1975. The chief visible sign of these changes was the rapid rise in wages for agricultural labour which occurred in the late 1970s after two decades of relative stability of wage rates. By 1978/79 the standard piece rate in Gezira for cotton picking had risen to 30 pt per guffa (about 35 lb) from 10 pt, and rates of 45 to 60 pt were not uncommon. Similar rises were evident in other irrigated schemes. Data for wages in the rainfed schemes are harder to come by, but indications there also suggest significant though less dramatic increases in the same period (see O'Brien 1980).

Of greater signficance to the structure and dynamics of the agricultural labour force than the overall rising trend of wages was the tendency for wage rates in the segments of the market outlined above to converge. Wage rates in cotton picking increased by a greater proportion than wage rates in sorghum and sesame harvesting. Moreover, wage rates in smaller local markets tended to increase by greater proportions than wages in the big schemes, thereby making them more comparable to wage rates in the wider market. These processes of increasing wages and the equalisation of wage rates across the traditional boundaries of the segmented agricultural labour market cannot be accounted for in terms of growing labour shortages or simply by reference to the general inflation in the economy. Rather, it is my contention that they reflected a fundamental restructuring of the previously highly segmented market for agricultural labour towards the formation of a truly national labour market. This restructuring was not complete by the onset of the 1983-85 famine, which, despite attendant disruptions of market processes, seems to have accelerated the transformation.

The Breakdown of Market Segmentation

The most suggestive indication of the nature of this process is given in the trajectories of wage rates for agricultural labour of different types. What it suggests is that the boundaries between the various segments have largely broken down and that labour is flowing across them, particularly the boundary between cotton picking and sorghum and sesame labour markets, as labour moves more freely between types of work. This and related changes which began to take place in the late 1970s are intimately bound up with the effects which expansion of involvement in wage labour had on peasant and pastoral productive systems during previous periods and must be analysed in that context. These effects can be summed up in terms of the spread of capitalist penetration to all areas of the country and the beginning of the rapid wholesale disarticulation of domestic economies as self-reproducing systems - a process apparently completed in most parts of the north by the famine.

Until the 1970s the dominant process of penetration and incorporation of peasants and pastoralists into the capitalist economy operated on the basis of absolute surplus value rather than relative surplus value. That is to say, surplus value was extracted from them, either directly through wage labour in the schemes or indirectly through taxation and the market, by creating conditions which required them to extend their working day and/or their working season. Thus, their contribution to the national and international economies was obtained through increasing the amount of time they had to work beyond what had been necessary to produce their own requirements. This entailed drawing out surplus labour from peasant and pastoral communities in such a way as to maintain their ability to produce most of these requirements on the basis of existing patterns of division of labour and organisation of work. The limits of absolute surplus value which could thus be extracted were therefore largely defined by the flexibility required to allow family group labour in one type of work and the individual labour of one or two male representatives of each family in another. The first form enabled more surplus labour to be extracted from each family unit involved, while the second captured more labour from each individual drawn into the market. However, the conditions of reproduction of this sort of labour force did not allow the two to be combined on a large scale.

The processes which began to dominate the dynamics of the labour force after 1975 are breaking down this last barrier to absolute surplus value and increasing the importance of relative surplus value. This can best be seen in recent trends in the migration of family work groups for cotton picking. Heads of migrant families have been facing a declining ability to mobilise large family groups for work in cotton picking at the same time that the ability of family groups to earn sufficient incomes working at the old relatively low wages obtainable in cotton picking has been declining. Their children, particularly sons, have found growing opportunities for earning an income at an earlier age and it thus has become difficult for parents to get their children to work with the family group, much less to contribute all of their incomes from this work to the general household budget.

Those smaller numbers of family members picking cotton have had to lengthen and intensify their periods of wage labour or seek other higher paying jobs. It has become increasingly common, for example, for male members of such families, particularly those between about 18 and 45, to work in sorghum harvesting while the rest of their families pick cotton. As increasing numbers of cotton picking families began to succumb to these pressures, wages for cotton picking had to rise sufficiently to retain their labour against this competition.

An important consequence of this sort of shift is a tendency of the agricultural labour market to become more uniformly a market for the labour power of individuals, and for more members of all families to be pressed out in search of wage labour, regardless of traditional divisions of labour or practices of female seclusion. Thus, by the late 1970s there was evident a rapid rise in the participation of women and children in agricultural wage labour generally. Among many groups from which only men had previously migrated for wage labour, male household heads continued to harvest sorghum and sesame while their families began to go to the cotton schemes without them.

While wage rates for different tasks appeared to be converging and more men - as well as significant numbers of women - were moving into the heavier tasks, we should not necessarily expect wage rates to reach full parity or all differences in work group composition according to task to disappear. It seems rather more likely that some differences more directly reflecting the differences in physical effort required by different tasks will remain. Thus, wage rates in sorghum and sesame harvesting seem likely to remain somewhat higher than in cotton picking, but not by anything like as much as previously. At the same time, the shift in composition of the respective labour forces appears to be moving towards the concentration of the able-bodied and unencumbered - meaning women without small children as well as men - in the heavier tasks, while the cotton picking labour force - which formerly closely reflected the age and sex structure of the general population - draws more heavily on the aged, young children, and women encumbered by small children. A survey of cotton-picking labour in 1980 already showed a large preponderance of female labour in Gezira (see Aricanli 1983a, 1983b).

The Breakdown of the Recruitment System

As classical market mechanisms began to operate more freely in the movement of seasonal wage labour, the chief non-market mechanisms organising this movement started to break down. In particular, the effectiveness of elaborate centralised systems of recruitment has declined. By 1978 the managements of several large irrigated schemes, including Gezira, had suspended cotton picking labour recruitment activities. As cotton picking wage rates destabilised in the mid-1970s, migrants increasingly elected to finance their own travel to the scheme areas in order to negotiate the highest rates they could find. In turn, tenants and other employers of seasonal labour, facing mounting costs, began to employ the increasingly available self-recruiting labour and sought to trim their wage bills by reducing or eliminating recruitment and transportation expenses.

As this trend gained momentum, many migrants found, as Tait (personal communication) discovered in visits to a number of villages in the traditionally important recruiting ground west of Tendelti in December 1978, that they no longer could count on being recruited in their villages and transported to the schemes.

The costs of finding work and travelling to the place of work, which had previously been a separate part of the wage bill incurred by employers, are now entering into the general labour market as elements of the wage rate. Paradoxically, the formation of a national labour market thus entails a regionalisation at the same time, as workers seek to cut costs by finding work as close to home as possible.[4] Regional disparities in wage rates persist, but only within limits regulated by costs and risks of employment-seeking travel between regions. In addition, large, but uncounted, numbers of villagers from the outlying provinces in which employment opportunities are fewest, particularly Darfur, have been resettling on empty - often marginal - lands in the regions where the big agricultural schemes are concentrated. In the rainfed mechanised farming schemes where plots generally go out of commercial production after five to seven years, migrants from other areas often settle on the land as share-croppers or renters. In the areas around new irrigation schemes, new settlers often take over fields abandoned by local inhabitants who have become tenants in the scheme. During the famine in Sudan and Ethiopia and its aftermath, wide local swings in wage rates have occurred as the result of local differences in crop failure and patterns of flight of refugees from the hardest hit areas.

These changes do not mean that recruitment activities of all kinds are necessarily disappearing altogether. Rather, recruitment seems to be becoming decentralised and shifting to more open market arenas. Recruitment seems to be undertaken more often - as I found in the Rahad Scheme - by individuals or small groups of tenants. Instead of travelling to distant villages, they seem instead to be going to small regional market towns, sometimes within the schemes themselves, where numbers of migrants collect and negotiate with several potential employers.

The Disarticulation of Peasant and Pastoral Productive Systems

These transformations which have been occurring in the nature of the agricultural labour market are part of broader changes in the national political economy which affect peasants and pastoralists in a variety of ways that make them increasingly dependent on markets in general and wage labour markets in particular (see Chapter 1 above). At a time when small producers are facing rapidly deteriorating terms of trade everywhere, peasants and pastoralists in Sudan have been facing serious problems of declining productivity. As large projects encroach on grazing and fallow lands, as ecologically sub-optimal production units are enabled to persist with the help of wage labour, and as relative prices come to dictate crop and livestock selection in place of ecological considerations, crop yields per unit area in peasant cultivations and animal off-take rates in pastoral herds have been declining. Accompanying these trends and the expansion of large-scale clear-cutting plantation agriculture have been accelerating processes of desertification and deforestation. These lead to difficulties in supplying villages with wood and straw for fuel and building materials, thus creating new markets and expanding cash needs among rural producers. The commercialisation of some key household tasks, particularly those of women, has had similar consequences. The spread of mechanical flour mills and of government wells (which charge money) and commercial water carriers not only increases cash needs, but, by supplying a cheap substitute for two of the previously most time consuming tasks of women, makes many women both available for and dependent on wage labour.

This last named change points to the really fundamental aspect of overall transformation which has been disrupting peasant and pastoral productive systems - the transformation of traditional divisions of labour and the destruction of autonomous systems of social reproduction. With the disruption of traditional divisions of labour between the sexes and the undermining of patriarchal authority over wives, sons and sisters, large extended family production/consumption units become dissolved by commodity relations. The clear tendency in Sudan's rural areas is towards the nuclearisation of production units producing a narrower range of goods and facing increasing economic individualisation within them and greater dependence on wage labour to make ends meet. Stripped of their imbrication in local circuits of social reproduction and transformed in a multitude of ways, peasant and pastoral units have increasingly been subsumed by a generalising process of expanded reproduction of labour power and capital. The attendant destruction of ecological and kinship regimes set the stage for the famine which accompanied the drought in the mid-1980s (see O'Brien 1985).

Implications of the Transformation of the Agricultural Labour Market

The transformation in Sudan's agricultural labour market which I have described constitutes a restructuring of the labour force on a new basis, a shift away from the predominantly ethnic structure of the labour force mobilised through extra-economic mechanisms. The development of a national labour market which operates freely on the basis of unfettered market forces would, of course, be disastrous for capital in a cheap labour economy such as that of Sudan. However, such development has not been unfettered. It is rather the nature of the constraints and the level of the economy at which they operate which has been changing. A series of key government policies pursued in the late 1970s is important in this regard and has had profound effects on the evolution of the labour market in the decade following 1975.

In particular, policies related to the Nationality Act of 1948 and its narrowly restrictive definition of Sudanese nationality have assumed a broader role in the stratification of the labour force (see Duffield, this volume). Access to government employment, trading licenses, charcoal-making permits, etc., is restricted to holders of valid Sudanese nationality certificates. Descendants of West African immigrants and members of a number of other non-Arab groups are systematically discriminated against with respect to certification of nationality and its benefits, as well as in de facto if not de jure access to schooling. On another level, the provisions of the Nationality Act have been used in the programme to resettle Eritrean and Ethiopian refugees in and around major agricultural schemes as permanent pools of wage labour. The status of these people as statutory foreigners in perpetuity ensures that they cannot securely own land or cultivate more than small plots in some resettlement schemes, take other employment or gain adequate access to schools. The effect of such policies is to foster hostility between sections of the labour force and a primary stratification of the labour force into groups defined as "Sudanese" and "foreigners". In the process, the earlier ethnic structure of the labour force which integrated various cultural groups into different sectors based on their varied internal characteristics is replaced by a specifically social structure defined ideologically in the first instance by nationality.

Another vital government policy has been technical in form but carries tremendous social consequences. This is the policy of capitalisation - particularly mechanisation - of key agricultural operations, especially the introduction of mechanical picking of medium staple cotton, mechanical harvesting and threshing of sorghum, and chemical and mechanical weeding. This has been taking place in spite of the demonstrated fact that the costs involved are frequently much higher than when performed manually - as in Rahad, for example, where experiments showed that mechanical cotton picking costs on the order of five times as much as manual picking. Moreover, the prevailing justification for such expensive changes in methods - the threat of long-term labour shortage - was manifestly baseless at a time when, as I have indicated, the number of peasants and pastoralists being thrown onto the labour market was expanding rapidly.

It is only an appreciation of the transformation of the agricultural labour markets in Sudan occurring since the late 1970s (together with an understanding of the broader arena of class struggles in Sudan in articulation with the interests of international capital) that can make sense out of such seemingly irrational policy within the framework of the Sudanese political economy. From this perspective, the importance of agricultural mechanisation lies in the thousands of jobs it eliminates in a context of abundant labour supply in an increasingly competitive labour market and in the way it concentrates labour demand into a relatively compact harvest season. In other words, the significant consequence of mechanisation is not the elimination of labour shortages (conceived as absolute shortages of labourers) but the creation of unemployment and underemployment. The result is that structured unemployment and underemployment together with increased competition among workers replace the recruitment system and other extra-economic devices in regulating the supply of cheap labour to the agricultural schemes. In this context, famine is merely a temporary acute manifestation of increasingly chronic food shortages acting as an additional spur to participation in cheap labour.

Notes

1. An earlier version of this essay appeared in Review of African Political Economy in 1983. Portions of that version are reprinted here with permission. Research was carried out in Sudan 1974 to 1979 with support from a Ford Foundation grant to the Manpower Research Project of the Faculty of Economic and Social Studies, University of Khartoum, and from the Economic and Social Research Council, National Council for Research, Khartoum. Additional logistical support and release time was provided by the Department of Anthropology and Sociology, University of Khartoum, and the Faculty of Economics and Rural Development, University of Gezira. I was assisted in various phases of the research by the following individuals: Salah al-Din Shazali, Haj Musa Kuku, Mohamed Yousif Ahmed el Mustafa, Mohamed Azim Abu Sabah, Mohamed Abdalla el Dukhari, Abdel Rahman Abdel Rahim, and Abdalla A. Abdalla. The analysis here owes much to the critical comments of James C. Faris, Mohamed El Awad Galal-al-Din, Ben Magubane, Mark Duffield, Ellen Gruenbaum, Taisier Ali and Robert Johnston. To all of these individuals and institutions I extend my thanks.

2. Muslim West African settlement in Sudan is a phenomenon of long standing, traditionally associated with the overland pilgrimage traffic to Mecca. However, both the scale and principal causes of this migration changed qualitatively in the early twentieth century, as Duffield (1979, 1981) has documented. This change followed the British conquest of northern Nigeria and the break-up of the Fulani sultanates, which resulted in the emigration from that region of large numbers of poor Hausa peasants and captives, many of whom eventually settled in Sudan (See Duffield, this volume).

3. These features of the agricultural labour "market" reveal that it did not, at least until the late 1970s, properly constitute a true market. The term is thus used in this discussion in a general sense in order to avoid cumbersome expressions.

4. Such regionalisation of labour markets is, of course, not unique to Sudan, but characterises labour markets in the large advanced capitalist countries. The idealised model of capitalist markets employed by Abedlkarim (1985) in his critique of my thesis (as presented in O'Brien 1983a) on the basis of the persistence of wage differentials between Gedaref and Gezira misses this fundamental fact. Ironically, the author's data confirms my predictions concerning the trajectory of the transformation of the labour market by showing the extent to which regionalisation of wages and recruitment has occurred (See O'Brien 1987).

References

Abdel Hamid, Ahmed (1966), The Agricultural Labour and the Gezira Scheme, Musaad, Social Research Section, Social Development Department, Sudan Gezira Board, Musaad, Sudan.

Abdelkarim, Abbas (1985), 'The segmented agricultural labour market in Sudan', Review of African Political Economy, 34, pp. 46-54.

Ali T. and O'Brien, J. (1984), 'Labour, Community and Protest in Sudanese Agriculture', in J. Barker (ed.), The Politics of Agriculture in Tropical Africa, pp. 205-38, Sage, Beverly Hills.

Aricanli, Ali Tosun (1983a), 'The second report on the findings of a research project on Gezira Scheme village census of demographic, occupational and health status', unpublished paper.

--- (1983b), 'Sources and changes of agricultural labour force in the Sudan', unpublished paper.

Duffield, Mark (1979), Hausa and Fulani Settlement and the Development of Capitalism in Sudan, with Special Reference to Maiurno, Blue Nile Province, PhD, Centre of West African Studies, University of Birmingham.

--- (1981), Maiurno: Capitalism and Rural Life in Sudan, Ithaca Press, London.

Gaitskell, Arthur (1959), Gezira: A Story of Development in the Sudan, Faber & Faber, London.

Galal-al-Din, Mohamed El Awad (1978), Population Dynamics and Socio-economic Development in Rural Sudan, Development Studies and Research Centre, Khartoum.

Hill, Reginald (1959), Egypt in the Sudan, 1820-1881, Oxford University Press, London.

Labour Board (1943), Minutes of the eighth meeting of the Labour Board, in unnumbered file labelled 'Minutes of the Meetings of the Labour Board 1943-1946', Sudan Gezira Board Archives, Barakat, Sudan.

O'Brien, Jay (1980), Agricultural Labor and Development in Sudan, PhD, University of Connecticut.

--- (1983a), 'The formation of the agricultural labour force in Sudan', Review of African Political Economy, 26, pp. 15-34.

--- (1983b), 'The political economy of capitalist agriculture in the central rainlands of Sudan', Labour, Capital and Society, 16 (1), pp. 8-32.

--- (1984a), 'The political economy of semi-proletarianisation under colonialism: Sudan 1925-50', in B. Munslow and H. Finch (eds.), Proletarianisation in the Third World, pp. 121-47, Croom Helm, London.

--- (1984b), 'The social reproduction of tenant cultivators and class formation in the Gezira Scheme, Sudan', in B. Isaac (ed.), Research in Economic Anthropology, Vol. 6, pp. 217-41, JAI Press, Greenwich, Connecticut.

--- (1985), 'Sowing the seeds of famine: The political economy of food deficits in Sudan', Review of African Political Economy, 33, pp. 23-32.

--- (1987), 'On Segmented and National Labour Markets', Review of African Political Economy, 38.

O'Fahey, R.S. (1980), State and Society in Dar Fur, St. Martin's, New York.

O'Fahey, R.S. and Spaulding, Jay (1974), Kingdoms of the Sudan, Methuen, London.

Spaulding, Jay (1979), 'Farmers, herdsmen and the state in rainland Sinnar', Journal of African History, 20 (3), pp. 329-57.

7 Continuity and contradiction: the maintenance of peasant production – the destruction of peasant economy in a Blue Nile Scheme village

VICTORIA BERNAL

The literature on peasants[2] has often underestimated the importance of non-agricultural economic activities in peasant household economy. Friedmann, for example, while emphasising "the variety of social and economic contexts of agricultural household production" does not include the possibility of households selling some of their labour or launching entrepreneurial enterprises outside of agriculture (1980, p. 159). The eight authors in Smith and Welch's (1978) volume on African peasants give short shrift to peasant participation in the labour market. As Long and Richardson note:

> There is a large body of literature in economic anthropology which examines household organisation and decision-making, and which explores relations between units of production and consumption. Much of this work, however, treats peasant economies as relatively isolated from other sectors. It therefore does not often deal with multiple employment strategies which extend beyond agriculture and thus ensure the survival of peasant households (1978, p. 206).

Economic activities outside of farming are often assumed to be of secondary importance in household economy when this is a subject for empirical investigation. As Cook (1984, p. 14) puts it, researchers have been prone to "agrarianise the countryside, that is, to study and write about rural peoples and their problems as if these involved exclusively agricultural pursuits."

Much of the research on Sudanese agricultural schemes is similarly biased. Management and independent researchers have long recognised that Sudanese tenants and their families participate in wage labour and trade. Yet rarely do their analyses reflect the integration of household agricultural production into a larger household and regional economy.

Sudanese agricultural policy has suffered from this narrow view. As Hoyle has writen in reference to the Khashm al Girba Scheme:

> In the planning context the scheme was regarded as an entity in itself and not part of a wider context, whereas the responses of the settlers have emphasised the need to take into account such a wider context (1977, p. 128-9).

There is, however, a growing body of research on the Sudanese schemes that suggests that off-farm opportunities for income and investment have consequences for tenants' agricultural strategies (Sorbo 1972, 1977; Taha 1973; O'Brien 1980, p. 279). Olsson and Keddeman, for example, write that:

> The availability of (off-farm investment) opportunities reduces on-farm family labour-supply as farmers engage in such activities as trading, transport, construction, etc. and hire workers for cultivating the land or even sub-lease their tenancy (1978, p. 24).

This study explores the interplay between agriculture and participation in trade and wage labour in a Blue Nile village. The implications for household economy, peasant production strategies, and regional economic development are considered.

Research focussed on individuals - as labour migrants, traders, or farmers - has tended to obscure the interaction between farming and off-farm economic strategies. Looking at the household we find that farmers, wage-workers and even merchants or other entrepreneurs are often contributing to the same common economic entity - the household. Furthermore, as Long and Richardson observed in Peru, "Households frequently develop livelihood strategies involving members in qualitatively different relations of production, both capitalist and non-capitalist" (1978, p. 186). Yet the consequences of such diversified household economies for peasant production have not been thoroughly studied.

I argue that we must examine the full spectrum of household economy and its integration into regional economic systems if we are to understand peasant agricultural strategies. That is, peasants' decisions as farmers are affected by the other relations of production in which their households participate, whether or not they as individuals are directly employed in the commercial/wage labour economy. My study suggests that participation in labour and commodities markets has a number of consequences for the organisation of household agricultural production (Bernal 1985). This paper will focus specifically on: 1) the subsidy of farming through trade and wage labour; 2) the composition of the household agricultural labour force; 3) the role of agricultural production in household economy; and 4) the place of household agricultural production in the regional economic system. While these villagers are tenants on a government scheme which determines many of the conditions in agriculture, it is hoped that the findings can suggest directions for understanding peasants in other situations as well.

Methodology

This study was conducted in the village of Wad al Abbas located between Wad Medani and Sinnar on the east bank of the Blue Nile in the Blue Nile Province. Wad al Abbas has a population of about 7,000 comprising approximately 1,000 households. The local irrigated agricultural scheme is administered as part of the Blue Nile Scheme.

Data were collected over a two-year period from 1980 to 1982. Methods of data collection include: long-term residence and participant observation in the community, interviews, and a random sample survey of 53 households.[3] Forty-four of these households (83 per cent) had tenancies on the Blue Nile Scheme at the time of research. The quantitative analyses in this paper include only those households. One of the 44 had to be eliminated due to incomplete data, reducing the sample size to 43 households. Survey questions covered: land size, crops planted, area planted, use of hired labour and/or sharecroppers, cash expenditures for agricultural production, and crop yields and sales. Data on two consecutive agricultural years - 1980-81 and 1981-82 - were gathered in one survey.

Local practices of polygyny and uxorilocal residence[4] mean that households do not always coincide exactly with the unit of production in agriculture. The separate households of polygynous tenants are one unit with regard to agricultural production, while co-resident male affines farm separately. For these reasons, the 43 households translate to 37 agricultural production units. Twenty-eight of these are households, while nine do not coincide exactly with the boundaries of a single household.

Subsidy of Farming Through Off-farm Work

A body of literature has emerged dealing with the role of peasant production within peripheral capitalist economies (Vergopoulos 1978; Bennholdt-Thomsen 1982; Taylor 1979). The idea that subsistence agriculture contributes to the reproduction of wage labourers and can thus be said to subsidise the capitalist economy has become common currency (Meillassoux 1981; Bodemann & Allahar 1980; Goodman & Redclifft 1982). I argue here that the farming household's dependence on cash from commercial and wage labour activities is the other side of the coin. Where items of household consumption and/or inputs to agricultural production have become commodities, agriculture itself may be subsidised through the commercial and wage labour activities of household members. This subsidy is both direct - in the form of cash inputs to agriculture,

- and indirect - through the support of the agricultural producers as dependent household members.

Agriculture at Wad al Abbas

The Blue Nile Scheme at Wad al Abbas is organised along the same general lines as the Gezira Scheme, which has been the subject of much research (Gaitskell 1959; Barnett 1977; Tait 1978; O'Brien 1984). Farmers are required to grow cotton and are given land on which they can plant a crop or crops of their own choice, usually their subsistence crop, sorghum.[5] A standard tenancy on the Blue Nile Scheme is 15 feddans. (1 feddan = 0.420 hectares or 1.038 acres). Each year, five feddans are under cotton, five feddans under sorghum, and five feddans fallow. A cost-sharing and profit-sharing arrangement operates between farmers and management on the cotton crop. The scheme provides technical inputs to cotton production and controls the ginning and marketing of this crop. Charges for these services are deducted from the farmer's share of cotton profits. The farmer is primarily responsible for the labour input to cotton production. Except for irrigation, the sorghum crop is solely the responsibility of the farmer and the scheme receives no share in it.

Cotton

Cotton production at Wad al Abbas is characterised by little profit and much risk. Water shortages, pests, crop diseases, rainfall variation, weeds, technical breakdowns and labour shortages are common problems. Cotton yields and prices have not kept pace with rising costs of production. Farmers find it increasingly difficult to cover the production charges assessed against them by the scheme. Unpaid charges are carried over to successive years' accounts. Thus, many farmers not only receive no cotton profits, but begin the agricultural year with a negative balance. Many farmers have not received cotton profits in years. For example, of 1,597 tenants in the area including Wad al Abbas, only 6 received any profits for the 1979-80 cotton crop, according to scheme records. The remainder were in debt to the scheme. Scheme personnel and farmers alike stated that 1979-80 was no aberration, but quite typical of conditions on that scheme. In 1982 a tenant expressed it this way:

> I will tell you so you understand about this cotton. 'Farmer' means death. I go to the island in the river and cut thorns and sell them for 10pt and 20pt to feed my children. My name is 'farmer'. This cotton, you go and work on it all year and finally they tell you you're in debt.

Farmers must cultivate cotton, however, or they lose access to the irrigated subsistence plot.

Not only is cotton production unprofitable for most farmers, many must actually spend money to cultivate it. Cotton cultivation is labour-intensive. According to calculations for the Gezira where production takes place under similar conditions, cotton requires 82 person-days/feddan/year as compared to only 13 for sorghum (ILO 1976, p. 259). Households' holdings vary considerably as do their labour resources, and agricultural labour requirements peak at several points during the year. Furthermore, the division of labour by gender is such that women and girls generally do not participate in agricultural operations other than cotton picking. Picking is not carried out on a household basis in any case, but by groups of paid pickers. The only unpaid household labour in agriculture, then, is that of men and boys. Hired agricultural labour is thus a necessity for many households. In practice, households do not devote all their labour resources to farming, creating even greater shortages of family labour.

Hired agricultural labour is expensive. In the 1980-81 agricultural year at Wad al Abbas, labourers were generally paid £S2[6] for a customary day's work with an additional pound for an extended workday. As one farmer said:

> The hired workers are better off than the farmers. Where can a farmer get that money?

Some cash credit is provided by the scheme for these expenses. But the amount is fixed per unit of land rather than geared to a farmer's actual needs or expenses. And, no credit is provided for sorghum production which competes for households' cash and labour resources. Even family labourers, though not paid cash wages, must be provided for. In order to sustain production, households must be able to provide for themselves and even generate some cash for inputs of hired labour. If cotton generally yields no profits, where indeed can a farmer get money?

Sorghum

Sorghum production at Wad al Abbas is characterised by low yields and high risk. The sorghum crop is plagued by many of the same problems as cotton. Figure 7.1 shows the distributionofsorghum yields for the 27 production units[7] in the sample that planted sorghum in 1980-81. The mean sorghum yield in the sample was 1.4 sacks/feddan in 1980-81. The mean yield was 1 sack/feddan, the mode was zero. Yields ranged from 0 to 6 sacks/feddan.

The most striking thing about the 1980-81 sorghum yields is the prevalence of total crop failure. Ten (37 per cent) of the 27 production units that planted sorghum in 1980-81 got nothing at all. If these levels of crop destruction or failure are representative it means that more than one in three production units that planted sorghum that year harvested no food crop at all. As some production units represent the multiple households of polygynous men, an even greater number of households are affected.

The following year was slightly better. The mean yield in the sample was up to 2 sacks/feddan and the median yield was 2.4 sacks/feddan in 1981-82. But the crop failure rate was still high, afflicting slightly fewer than one in three production units (i.e. 8 [31 per cent] of the 26 that planted sorghum).

Figure 7.1 Distribution of Sorghum Yields

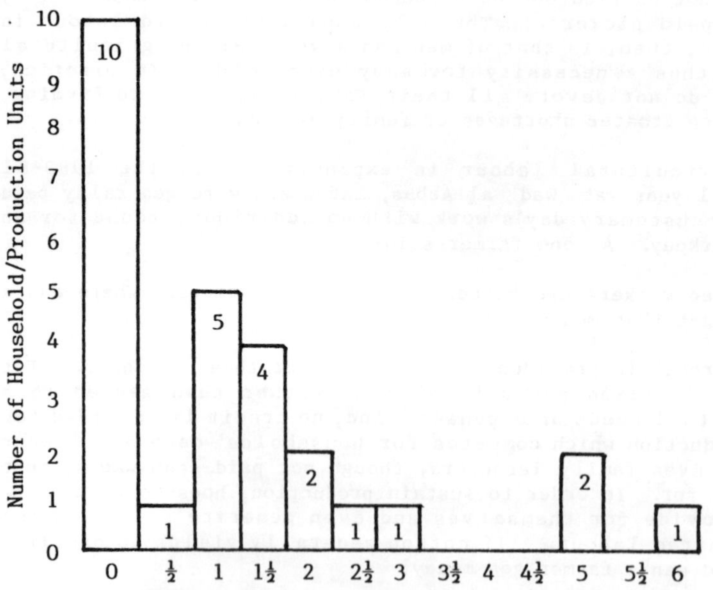

Yield in sacks per <u>feddan</u>
(rounded to nearest half sack)

1 sack = 7.5 <u>kayla</u> = 210 <u>rotl</u> = 208 lbs.   N = 27

Generally, then, households cannot even count on their sorghum crop to meet their basic consumption needs. Even higher average yields provide little security if the risk of crop failure remains high. Many Wad al Abbas farming households purchase much of their subsistence grain. Even those with somewhat better yields often supplement home-produce with purchased grain to meet their consumption needs.

At present, then, local agriculture neither assures the subsistence of the agricultural producers and their families nor generates cash for household needs and for reinvestment in production. Agricultural production at Wad al Abbas is not a self-sustaining system. Household agricultural production there is dependent upon inputs from off-farm economic activities, usually trade and wage labour.

There are references to this type of situation elsewhere. I believe it is common. Murray, writing on South Africa, makes the important observation that: "agriculture and migration are not in fact alternatives, since agricultural output partly depends on cash investment for migrant earnings" (1979, p. 342). Halim writes of sharecroppers in Malaysia: "Without wage work, it is doubtful if the rural structure based on extraction of labour tribute can survive for long" (1983, p. 266). Hill's study of what she calls the "dry grain mode" of farming in Nigeria and India found that:

> a great proportion of households are obliged to follow non-farming occupations, their grain production being altogether insufficient for household needs and farm-labouring being a highly seasonal occupation ... (1982, p. 141).

Scott (1976), in his treatise on peasant moral economy, refers to the "labour-exporting village" and notes that such a village is more affected by conditions in the wage labour market than by prices of agricultural commodities or a poor harvest. O'Brien (1980, p. 261) writes of Sudanese peasants and pastoralists in general: "The availability of wage labour has given sub-reproductive production units a new ability to maintain production due to the income earned by family members elsewhere" (cf. Duffield, 1983, p. 57). But if off-farm economic strategies help perpetuate household agricultural production, they also change it. Before examining the nature of such changes in agriculture at Wad al Abbas, it is necessary to look at villagers' non-agricultural economic activities.

Non-agricultural Occupations Among Wad al Abbas Households

Women's economic activities are for the most part restricted to unpaid domestic services. Their opportunities to earn cash are very limited. Men make up the household agricultural labour force and are the off-farm income-earners as well. Outside of farming, the men of Wad al Abbas are involved in a range of occupations. Many men engage in some type of trade. They range from petty traders who buy small amounts of produce, for example, and resell it in the village market, to wealthy merchants. Some of the latter own trucks and even employ a hired worker or two. Their enterprises are based outside the village in towns. They are often involved in long-distance and import trade.

There are some craftsmen and artisans at Wad al Abbas. They include: shoemakers, saddle-makers, angareb (traditional bed)-makers, butchers, tailors, carpenters, and builders. These men are all based in the village and almost without exception their operations are very small-scale, one man working alone. Other men work as wage or salaried employees. Most of the men from Wad al Abbas engaged in such work could be classified as skilled or clerical workers and some as professionals. These jobs virtually always necessitate migration from the village. Migration to Saudi Arabia and other Arab oil-exporting nations is not uncommon. Comparatively few men work as unskilled manual labourers or hired agricultural labourers.

In the 43 tenant households surveyed there are 93 adult men. Seventy-four (79.6 per cent) were employed or self-employed at the time of the survey. The remaining 19 include men in school or training and those who have ceased to work as well as those temporarily unemployed. Table 7.1 shows the breakdown by occupation of the men in the sample.

Table 7.1

Men's Occupation in Tenant Households

Occupation	Number of men	Percentage of working men	Breakdown
Trader	29	39.7	Wide range
Farmer	20	27.4	8 full-time 12 part-time
Wage or salaried worker	13	17.8	8 in Sudan 5 abroad
Crafts	5	6.9	1 shoemaker 1 carpenter 1 butcher 2 builders
Other	6	8.2	3 soldiers 1 taxi-owner/driver 1 bakery owner 1 private agri-cultural scheme owner
TOTAL N = 3		100.0	

*Note: data from 43 tenant households.

Trade is the most important occupation, accounting for 29 (39.2 per cent) of the men. And even more men actually trade since many of the part-time farmers are petty traders as well. Wage labour accounts for 14 men (19 per cent) - fewer men than either farming or trade when part-time farmers are included. But all these wage labourers are employed full-time and two of the part-time farmers also work for wages as agricultural day labourers.

Significantly, out of 74 working men in the 43 tenant households surveyed, only eight (11 per cent) are full-time farmers. (There are, in addition, three older women in the households sampled who do some farming.) Only slightly over one in every ten working men, then, is engaged in full-time agriculture at Wad al Abbas. Another 12 men in the sample farm part-time. Thus, of 20 men who do some farming, twelve (60 per cent) have another occupation as well. This is one indication of how distorted our picture of Wad al Abbas would be if we focussed exclusively on farming. Yet such a bias is not uncommon in research on the Sudanese schemes. Indeed in 1980 Voll went so far as to state: "most of the cash in the Gezira comes directly from cotton," though she presents no data to support this

(1980, p. 279).

Table 7.2 shows the number and percentage of sample tenant households that have members engaged in the various occupations. In these tables adults engaged in farming at least part-time are listed as farmers rather than by their other occupations. Their non-agricultural occupation, however, is not necessarily secondary in terms of time or income. Fifty-six per cent of the households have a member engaged in farming, but many of these farmers are also part-time traders or craftsmen. Over half the households have at least one member engaged in full-time wage work. (In Table 7.2 and Figures 7.2 and 7.3 polygynous men are counted in each of their households, since their income contributes to each of them.)

Table 7.2

Occupational Participation by Household

Occupation	Number of households with at least one member	Percentage of tenant households
Farmer	24 (includes 3 women)	55.8
Trader	22	51.2
Wage or salaried worker	15 (includes 1 woman)	34.9
Crafts	5	11.6
Other	4	9.3

N = 43 tenant households

*Note: As these categories are not mutually exclusive, column totals exceed the sample.

Many households have more than one income-earner. Figure 7.2 shows the number of employed and self-employed members per household at the time of the survey. With the exception of three women who do some farming and one woman employed as a teacher, women are not counted as income-earners, due to the limited and intermittent nature of their cash-oriented activities. The range of income-earners per household is from zero to four. Two households have no internal source of support. They are dependent upon relatives in other households. Twenty-three households (53.5 per cent), or over half of the sample have more than one income-earner. Thirteen households (30.2 per cent) have more than two. As shown in Figure 7.3, only one household has more than one adult farming. Households tend, then, to allocate at least some of their labour to off-farm strategies rather than concentrate labour in farming. Nineteen households (44.2%) allocated no household labour to farming. (The table only shows adults, but the households without adult farmers also have no children farming.)

Figure 7.2 Income-Producers Per Tenant Household

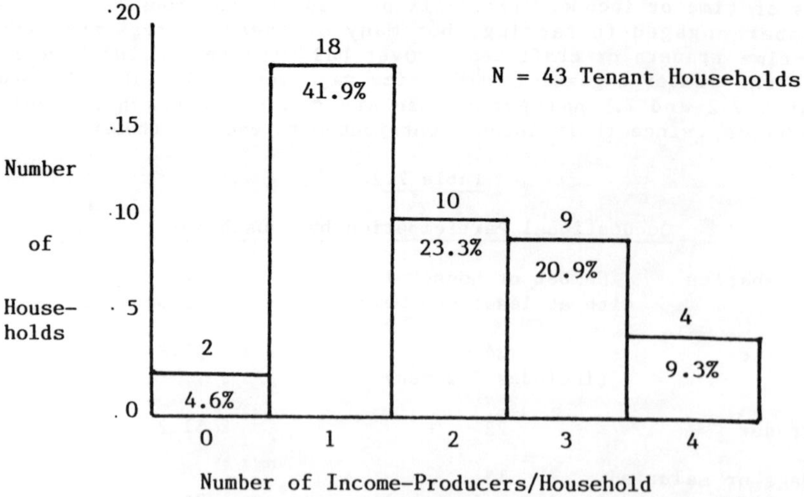

In sum, these data indicate that non-agricultural occupations are an integral part of household economy at Wad al Abbas. Households depend to a great extent on incomes generated through participation in commerce and wage labour. Income from these off-farm activities is channelled into agriculture indirectly through the support of household members who do the farming and indirectly by providing the necessary cash for other inputs such as hired labour and tractor rental.

Over twenty years ago researchers on the nearby Gezira Scheme noted:

> There are signs that (non-agricultural occupations, at one time secondary to the running of a tenancy, are becoming the primary occupations of the villagers concerned who now often employ a manager (<u>wakil</u>) to run the tenancy for them (Brausch et al., 1964, p. 90).

This transformation of the basis of peasant household economy has profound consequences for the organisation of household agriculture production.

Figure 7.3 Adult Farmers Per Tenant Household

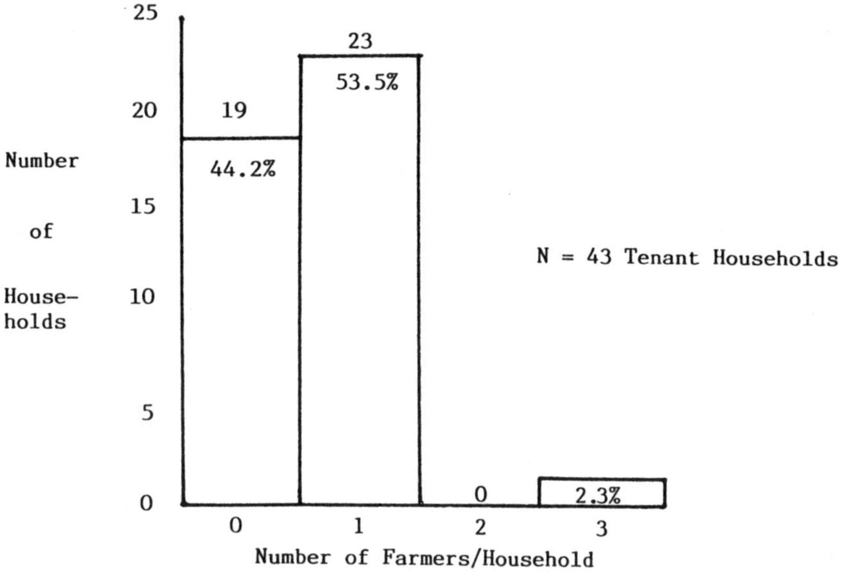

Composition of the Household Agricultural Labour Force

Rural agricultural producers are increasingly participating in labour and commodities markets. A debate has grown up around the very conceptualisation of peasantry, peasant small-commodity producers, peasant-workers, and rural proletariat, etc., showing perhaps that the complexity and variety of real economic forms have outstripped our classical concepts (see, for example: Lebrun & Gerry 1975; Orlove 1977; Roseberry 1978; Cohen, Gutkind & Brazier 1979). By and large this has not meant the complete disappearance of household forms of production. Such production continues but under altered conditions.

Minge-Kalman found that Swiss peasants' involvement in wage-labour had consequences for the family labour unit:

> The children eventually cease to be part of the family labour group and the parents' resources, including their own labour time, are reallocated from strictly food production to preparing children for wage jobs which require more education (1978, p. 195).

However, she views such households as merely experiencing the "peasant-to-worker transition." While this may be true in Europe, evidence from third world economies indicates that these hybrid economic forms can be very persistent. Peasant communities are not necessarily faced with impending proletarianisation so much as with an imperfect and partial integration into capitalist relations of production.

Rothstein (1983) mentions that in Central Mexico, farmers involved in wage labour employ more hired labour on their farms than do other peasants. But, she uses this to emphasise a dichotomy between peasants and wage-workers rather than to examine the consequences of participation in capitalist relations of production for peasant agricultural production. Kahn notes that in West Sumatra there is a

> good deal of flexibility of the co-operative group involved in subsistence cultivation - the labour intensity of cultivation varying according to rates of migration, degrees of involvement in commodity production and the like (1974, p. 2).

Yet, analyses of peasant production have often placed disproportionate emphasis on household development cycles and demography (e.g., Chayanov 1966; Barnett 1977; Durrenberger 1984; see Guyer 1981 and Donham 1981 for critiques of this approach). Buttel and Gillespie point out that:

> Despite the crucial role of the internal structure of the household, family forms of agricultural production are rooted in the larger economy and society as well. Phenomena external to the household but which affect the structure of household production include factor markets (i.e. for capital, labour and land inputs), product markets, non-farm labour markets, and public policies (1984, p. 185).

Even the partial integration of peasants into the market economy has consequences for their production strategies.

I argue that one effect of the market for non-agricultural labour is to raise the opportunity cost of farm labour within the household. In using his and his family's labour on the farm, the peasant is foregoing the rewards that labour would generate on the market. The particular conditions in farming and the opportunities for non-agricultural employment set the terms of this trade-off in each case.

In Sudan, incomes outside of agriculture are generally much higher than those possible in agriculture (McLoughlin 1963, p. 357; Affan 1977; ILO 1976, p. 356). This sheds light on the seeming paradox of labour shortage, rather than underemployment, in Sudanese agriculture alongside rural-urban migration. Rural underemployment is often cited as a cause of migration. However, at Wad al Abbas agriculture is labour-intensive. It is not a question of underemployment, but of undercompensation. The ILO found that:

> All in all, the evidence shows that migration depends on the level of farm income in the sending area, or rather the difference in earnings between the sending and receiving areas, and not on the degree of underemployment in traditional agriculture (ILO 1976, p. 103).

At Wad al Abbas participation in wage labour and trade reduces the household labour available for farming. One farmer says, "I used to farm with my sons, now they are gone. Now, alone, I pay people from outside - it's all money." Another says:

> In the past you wouldn't find a soul from Wad al Abbas outside. They were all here farming and the suk (market) was good. Now they've all gone out. The reason for that is the agriculture here. The scheme doesn't benefit the farmer anything. The traders too have moved to Sinnar and other places. Now there can't be fewer than 300 or 400 sons of Wad al Abbas outside.

Households that use hired labour to replace family labour face increased costs of production. This, in turn, reinforces their dependence on wage labour and trade to provide cash. But, not only is the absolute quantity of household labour reduced, the quality of household agricultural labour is affected as well. I found that the labour market for non-agricultural labour has become a determining factor in the composition of the household agricultural labour force at Wad al Abbas.

Analyses that focus on options often fail to address adequately the constraints under which people operate (Asad 1974). Access to wage employment or commercial enterprise is not evenly distributed. Skills, education, capital, and even connections are prerequisites in various degrees for different occupations. The attempts of Wad al Abbas men to find jobs and to go abroad are not always successful. As one woman stated, "If it weren't so hard to get papers and visas (a process which often entails both the use of personal contacts and large cash expenditures) all of the men would be over in Saudi Arabia."

Agriculture associated with poor returns pressures households to allocate their labour elsewhere. In the competitive labour market, the more skilled, educated, youthful labour becomes wage or salaried labour or enters commerce.[8] The rest of the population is effectively marginalised. The commercial/industrial economy cannot absorb it directly. This "surplus" labour, then, by its characteristics, is not so much a reserve industrial labour pool as it is a reserve labour pool for the least productive, least developed element of the economy - agriculture. In one villager's words, "The young men leave since there's no work here but the hawasha (tenancy), and that doesn't give money. The older people are left to farm, and the young ones leave and send money." At Wad al Abbas farmers are often those who have no market outlet for their labour.

The impact of the labour market on household agricultural labour at Wad al Abbas is reflected in the characteristics of farmers as compared to men in other occupations. By and large those household members who farm at Wad al Abbas are old, uneducated men. Table 7.3 shows the association of educational level and occupation for adult male members of the 43 tenant households. Since elementary school is six years of study at Wad al Abbas, this is one logical break-off point in looking at men's educational backgrounds. While there are a total of 74 employed or self-employed men in these households, lack of data on some men's education reduced the sample size to 58 men here. Traders have the largest percentage of elementary school graduates (54 per cent) with wage and salaried workers the next highest (50 per cent), followed by craftsmen (40 per cent) and farmers with none.

per cent) and farmers with none.

Table 7.3

Education of Wad al Abbas Men in Various Occupations

Occupation	With six years or more education Number	Percentage	N =
Wage & salaried workers	7	54	13
Traders	16	52	31
Craftsmen	2	40	5
Farmers	0	0	15
(Data from 53 households)		N = 64	

Given the small sample size and the fact that some of the men in the original sample could not be included for lack of data, there is probably a large margin of error here. But, certainly the educational gap between farmers and those in other occupations is clear. None of the 15 farmers whose educational level was known had completed six years of education. In fact, none had completed more than three years. In addition, almost all (13 out of 14) of the farmers stated they could neither read nor write. In contrast, the majority of traders (28 out of 31) and wage and salaried workers (11 out of 13) claimed or were reported to be literate.

Education is a prerequisite for many salaried jobs. The fact that many of those in trade also have an education is due in part to the higher returns possible in trade as compared to a fixed wage and to the relative tightness of the wage labour market as compared to the more open mercantile sector.

Table 7.4 shows the age-group distribution of men in the various occupations. It clearly shows that farming is the work of old men. Nearly three quarters (73.7 per cent) of the farmers are 50 or over. Wage and salaried workers, at the other extreme, are young. Eighty-six per cent of them are 30 or younger. Trade also has a large number of young men: 57 per cent of traders in the sample are 30 or younger. But, unlike wage-workers, only 7 per cent of whom are over 50, 29 per cent of the traders are in this age-group. Eighty per cent of the craftsmen are in the youngest age-group, none are between 35 and 45, and only one is 50 or over. While the sample is subject to the same limitations mentioned above, the difference between farmers and those in other occupations is evident. Both these tables support conlcusions drawn from participant observations and informal interviewing as well.

Table 7.4

Ages of Wad al Abbas Men in Various Occupations

Occupation	Age: 30 or younger No.	%	35-45 No.	%	50 or older No.	%	N =
Wage & salaried workers	14	87.5	1	6.25	1	6.25	16
Craftsmen	3	50.0	2	3.33	1	16.7	6
Traders	18	54.5	5	15.2	10	30.3	33
Farmers	2	10.5	3	15.8	14	73.7	19
							N = 74

*(Note: Ages are estimates rounded to the nearest 5 years)

To summarise, the profile of an average farmer is old, uneducated, illiterate. The profile of an average wage-worker is young, literate with some elementary education. Four (33 per cent) of the 12 wage-workers whose education was known had high school education or more. Traders have a broader age distribution than either farmers or wage-workers. And, while over half of them have elementary education, only 4 (14 per cent) of the 28 traders whose education was known had secondary school education as compared to one-third of the wage-workers. This distribution also reflects generational differences as access to education was limited until the 1960s. Conditions in agriculture have also deteriorated over time, so the pressures to move into other occupations were not as great in the past (Bernal 1985). The data indicate, however, that at present farming is an occupation of last resort. Those who can market their labour or engage in trade do so. Those members of the household who farm are those with no other productive outlet for their labour. They are almost without exception old men. Young boys, in off-hours from school, also help out. They, too, would otherwise be idle. The household agricultural labour force is thus largely shaped by the market for labour outside of agriculture.

Lewis (1981) found a similar transformation of the agricultural labour force in Mali. And, Kahn found that in Indonesia:

> The migrants tend to be the young, especially young men. The people left behind to cultivate rice and to keep irrigation systems and earthworks in good repair are the less efficient producers, particularly old men and women who cannot find work as migrants (Kahn 1975, pp. 150-1).

Elsewhere this process has resulted in a largely female labour force in household agricultural production (Arnould 1984, p. 158).

The participation of rural people in national and international labour markets, then, is not only a question of peasants becoming workers or merchants. Such participation alters the conditions under which household agricultural production takes place and has consequences for the size and composition of the household agricultural labour force. This research further suggests that this process has consequences for the place of agriculture in household economy and in the larger regional economy.

Agriculture in Household Economy

Agriculture at Wad al Abbas offers poor returns and is characterised by much risk. Under such conditions, it is not surprising that villagers have moved into other occupations. What may be more puzzling, given the conditions in agriculture at Wad al Abbas is why households continue to farm at all. The reasons are not the same for all households. And they do not all pursue the same agricultural strategies.

We saw in figure 7.3 that some households had ceased to allocate any household labour to farming. These include households whose land is cultivated by sharecroppers or exclusively by hired labourers, or in a few cases lent to relatives. Table 7.2 and figures 7.2 and 7.3 show that there is variation among households in terms of participation in trade, wage labour, and farming. Households' agricultural and non-agricultural strategies vary; and they impact on one another. For example, the use of large amounts of hired labour is only possible for wealthier households. At the same time, wealth can give access to alternative avenues of investment more attractive than farming. Some poorer households may continue to farm for lack of any such alternative. Others may even be too poor to farm, for as pointed out earlier, farming requires resources. Use of sharecroppers offers little return at Wad al Abbas, but requires no cash input. Hired labour is costly, but intensive farming can result in higher yields. These, and reliance on household labour, represent alternative agricultural production strategies, each with its own rationale in household economy.

Elsewhere I have considered the variation in households' agricultural labour strategies and argued that they are largely determined by the household's access to income from trade and wage labour (Bernal 1985). Here, I would like to focus on those households that continue to farm with at least some household labour. Both participant observation and the survey data indicate that this is the most common strategy at Wad al Abbas. Twenty-four households in the sample (55.8 per cent) have at least one member farming. Since households of polygynous tenants have joint holdings, they must be counted as one unit of agricultural production. The 43 households make up 37 farm units. Of these, 27 units (73 per cent) cultivated their land with some unpaid household labour, in both 1980-81 and 1981-82 agricultural years.

I suggest that it is the interaction of the market economy and the non-market aspects of household economy that causes these households to maintain agricultural production in spite of absolutely low and perhaps even diminishing returns. Their agricultural strategies are shaped largely by the exigencies of participation in the market economy. Many researchers have noted the tendency of peasant producers to work for very low returns. This may be a characteristic of household enterprises generally (Millar 1970). Chayanov (1966) has written of "self-exploitation" among independent peasants who must continue to labour to satisfy their own needs regardless of diminishing returns. The Chayanovian peasant household continues to work until "an equilibrium has been achieved between needs and the drudgery of ... effort" (Kerblay 1971, p. 152). However, when peasants become integrated into a market economy and must purchase some of their subsistence needs and/or inputs to production, this balance between satisfaction and drudgery is altered.

> Capitalist enterprises ... must earn the average rate of profit on capital in order to remain in production. Peasant enterprises, in contrast, with the subsidy towards reproduction given by family production of use-values, may continue to produce and release 'surpluses' for the market even when the market price falls below the actual costs of production and (imputed) wages. In this struggle to secure the reproduction of peasant enterprises, the living standards of peasant families may decline to 'a physical minimum' (Goodman & Redclifft 1982, p. 92).

Once the peasant household is no longer self-sufficient, it may have to labour more and more intensively to satisfy the same needs. When costs of production and/or costs of reproducing producers increase, peasants face what Bernstein (1977) calls "the simple reproduction squeeze". He argues that the simple reproduction squeeze

> is one of the mechanisms of intensifying the labour of the household to maintain or increase the supply of commodities without capital incurring any costs of management and supervision of the production process (1977, p. 65).

Bernstein warns that costs of production may be raised "by rural development schemes which encourage or impose more expensive means of production ... with no assurance that there will be increased returns to labour commensurate with the costs incurred" (1977, p. 65). This certainly applies to the agricultural scheme at Wad al Abbas.

Wad al Abbas households have also come to depend on the market for many basic items of consumption, including, as we have seen, even their subsistence grain. They face rising costs of food, clothing, and other necessities. As one villager put it, "Before people here had few things and they were cheap. Now we have many things but they require a lot of money." Similarly, Barnett found that on the Gezira Scheme: "Almost every object consumed in the home is purchased" (1977, p. 175). He adds that:

> The tenant is highly dependent on purchasing food and consumer goods from the shops because the Scheme within which he works has removed from him to a considerable degree the possibility of producing for his own subsistence and that of his family (1977, p. 179).

The dependence of rural producers on purchased foodstuffs and consumer goods, however, is not limited to the Sudanese schemes. Anthony et al (1979, pp. 97-8), cite studies showing that many rural households in Nigeria and Ghana purchase between 50 per cent and 60 per cent of their food alone. Ghai and Radwan (1983) report that throughout Africa the rural poor are often net purchasers of food. It is in this context that we can begin to understand the role of agricultural production in household economy at Wad al Abbas. I argue that many households intensify their labour output by struggling to maintain agricultural production as well as having members participate in commerce and wage labour.

The labour market places values on certain types of labour - not all labour-power is equally rewarded or equally saleable. The household, in contrast, supports (or seeks to support) all its members, even the very young, the aged, and the ill who cannot labour. The old men and boys that make up the household agricultural labour force at Wad al Abbas must be provided for regardless of their productivity. Their labour has no alternative productive outlet. If not engaged in farming, they would otherwise be idle. Their labour thus has no cost in household agricultural production. If the other expenses of farming can be minimised, returns do not have to be good to attract households' "surplus" labour. As we have seen, households at Wad al Abbas continue to maintain agricultural production in spite of very poor returns.

At Wad al Abbas agriculture has shifted from a primary to a secondary role in household economy. Agriculture is subsidised - through the support of the agricultural producers as dependent household members and through direct cash inputs to production - by household members' participation in trade and wage labour. This has changed the goals of household agricultural production. The vast majority of households can expect no income from their cotton crop, and many actually spend money to produce this crop. The irrigated sorghum crop is the sole benefit they receive for participating in the scheme. We have seen that sorghum production at Wad al Abbas is plagued by low yields and crop failure. Many households rely heavily on purchased grain. For example, the 27 production units that planted sorghum in 1980-81 account for 31 households. Twenty-three of these households (74 per cent) purchased at least part of their grain that year. And, at least 19 of these purchased half of their yearly grain consumption or more. For the majority of households, sorghum production is not aimed at self-sufficiency or at market profits. Rather they produce sorghum to reduce household expenditures for grain.

Chibnik (1978, p. 562) argues that "a 'sensible' farmer will value crops consumed at home considerably higher than market price." Hart asserts to the contrary that "pricing subsistence activities by their current market equivalences <u>inflate the money value of</u>

nonmarketed goods and services" (1982, p. 129, emphasis original). I suggest that the value placed on subsistence goods and services is directly tied to the degree of integration of the subsistence economy into the market.

I argue that Wad al Abbas households value the sorghum they produce at approximately what it costs to purchase sorghum at peak prices when grain supplies are short. Thus, they overvalue their crop in terms of its market value right after the harvest when prices are low. But, as market prices rise to their peak in the pre-harvest season, this gap is narrowed. The imputed value of home-produce is further enhanced by the fact that it is secure. In contrast, the market price of sorghum fluctuates and is subject to inflation. Households can never be sure at what price they may be forced to purchase grain on the market. As one villager remarked in reference to a farmer who had received cash compensation for livestock damage to his sorghum crop: "What is money? Grain is better than money."

In the October 1981 pre-harvest season, sorghum was selling for £S23/sack at Wad al Abbas. When households run short of grain they often buy in smaller amounts, by the kayla. A kayla was selling for £S4 in October 1981, bringing the equivalent sack price to £S30.

High market prices for food and the competitive labour market which restricts alternatives for some household labour, pressure households to attempt to produce a subsistence crop. Because sorghum is expensive, households can conserve cash by producing at least some of their own grain, even with low returns to labour and poor yields. Sorghum production at Wad al Abbas, however, is tied to cotton production. Failure to grow cotton can lead to the loss of the land altogether. The cotton crop competes for households' labour and cash resources, but, there is little or no incentive to invest in it. From the perspective of the household, cotton production is simply an added expense of sorghum production. If the household relinquishes any hope of cotton profits, as many have, they can reduce labour and cash inputs to cotton production. They need only make the minimum effort required to pass inspection. If costs of cotton production can be kept low enough, home production of sorghum is still economical given the availability of some "surplus" household labour and the high market price of grain.

Many households at Wad al Abbas pursue this strategy. Often lacking the resources to hire sufficient labour to cultivate cotton with any degree of success, they have little alternative. Researchers report the following behaviour among Gezira tenants:

> The tenant then tends to carry out all operations properly at the edges of the cotton hawasha so as to assuage the field inspector, while the bulk of the plants in the middle of the field receive very little or no care at all (Adam & Apaya 1973, p. 112).

Without the high labour demands of cotton, the reduced family labour force may be nearly sufficient for sorghum production. The cash credit from the scheme for cotton production can be used to hire some additional labour for cotton and/or sorghum. In addition, a tractor must be rented for furrowing the sorghum plot. This cost £S10/five feddans in 1981. As we have seen, a single sack of sorghum was worth up to three times that amount that year. And, in a good year, five feddans of sorghum could yield 25-30 sacks.

The organisation and goals of household agricultural production at Wad al Abbas are largely determined by the household's dependence upon the labour market for employment, upon commodity markets for food and necessities, and upon the scheme for access to irrigated land. Household strategies, in turn, also have consequences for the regional economy.

Household Agricultural Production in the Regional Economy

Wad al Abbas households are linked to the regional economy both through their direct participation in trade and wage labour and via the government which owns the agricultural scheme. Because subsistence production at Wad al Abbas is tied to mandatory cotton cultivation, those members of the household employed outside agriculture effectively subsidise cotton production on the scheme. This subsidy is ultimately transferred to the government in the form of cotton for which the producer price is artificially low. (This may be one of the reasons why the government has not significantly reorganised the scheme or abandoned cotton production in spite of the low levels of productivity - its share in the profits from the cotton that is produced is so inflated.) However, while the subsidy of farming through the household's off-scheme income permits the continued production of cheap cotton, it also insures that productivity levels will remain low. Farming will not attract the more productive labour which has alternative outlets. And, as cotton cultivation is not rewarded commensurately with the labour it requires, farmers will seek to minimise their labour inputs to cotton. Thus, while the scheme may continue to operate, it will do so at utterly low levels of productivity and will receive little investment from tenants.

On the other hand, the subsidy of household food production from other sources of income keeps the subsistence sector from total collapse. And, as household agricultural production utilises labour that would otherwise be idle, this facilitates the household's intensification of labour output. Furthermore, to the degree that household food production does contribute to the reproduction of labour, value is further extracted from the household in the form of cheap wage labour. Murray argues that even where subsistence agriculture depends on inputs from labour migrants, subsistence production and other services provided in the village, "subsidise capital to the extent that they are the product of unpaid domestic labour" (1978, p. 139).

The complexity of the relationship between household agricultural production and the capitalist economy is much more than simply subsistence farming keeping wages low, or the conversion of peasants into a proletariat. The conditions of agricultural production are themselves altered as are peasants' production strategies. There may be no clear line between peasants and proletarians. It is the involvement in diverse relations of production and exchange within the same household economy that facilitates transfers of value to the capitalist sector from peasants and proletarians alike. While such households appear perched between a peasant economy and full proletarianisation, they are not necessarily a transitory apparition. Limited employment opportunities and low wages, coupled with poor agricultural conditions, may reproduce this type of household economy over time. Gregory and Piche assert: "an ever greater number of people find it impossible to subsist entirely from precapitalist production or entirely from capitalist production" (1978, p. 48).

Conclusion

At Wad al Abbas the interaction between the market economy and household agricultural production has shifted the role of agriculture in household economy and altered the composition of the household agricultural labour force. It has led to an intensification of household labour output and increased transfers of value from the household to the commercial/industrial economy. At the same time, agricultural productivity levels have been depressed and investment in agriculture inhibited.

Many thousands of Sudanese farm on schemes very similar to the one at Wad al Abbas. Furthermore, my own observations on the Gezira, Rahad, and Suki schemes and on White Nile pump schemes, as well as the available literature, suggest that participation of tenants and their household members in off-scheme strategies is widespread. I do not think the conditions I have described here are unique to people on the Wad al Abbas scheme. Rather, I think the extent to which Sudanese tenants and their families depend upon off-scheme incomes has not been fully recognised.

However, there are probably differences between Wad al Abbas villagers and those on other irrigated schemes in Sudan due to several factors. There is some variation in scheme policy and operation. For example, sorghum cultivation is not allowed on the Suki Scheme, gravity irrigation water is available to Gezira tenants for a longer period than irrigation water on pump schemes, and the Rahad Scheme is more mechanised than most other schemes. The composition of the tenant population and the history of settlement also vary. The village of Wad al Abbas was not a creation of the scheme as are many Rahad and New Halfa settlements. Wad al Abbas tenants were sedentary agriculturalists prior to the establishment of the scheme, while newly settled pastoralists make up part of the tenants on many other schemes. Factors such as educational opportunities, proximity to regional markets and other circumstances that might affect the range of off-farm income opportunities also vary from village to village within schemes. Each of these has consequences for household economy and farming strategies. Furthermore, while the scheme at Wad al Abbas certainly contributed to villagers' increasing dependence on trade and wage labour, such a process could occur under other conditions.

Rural populations elsewhere face different configurations of conditions in agriculture and labour and commodities markets than those described here. This case study points to the importance of the larger regional economy in shaping forms of household production. It also draws attention to the interplay between the various economic strategies pursued by one household.

Comparative research would shed further light on the issues raised here. Longitudinal studies of the evolution of the total spectrum of household economic strategies would be particularly useful. They would provide more detailed knowledge of how households respond to changing conditions in the regional economy and how various types of economic activities impinge upon one another within household economy.

Notes

1. The research on which this paper is based was supported by grants from the National Science Foundation and the Social Science Research Council and the American Council of Learned Societies. Ronald Cohen, Karen Hansen, Tekle Woldemikael, Jay O'Brien, Jim Faris, and Lenny Markovitz offered constructive criticism of this work at various states. The conclusions, opinions, and other statements included in this publication are those of the author.

2. I choose to use the term 'peasant', here, rather than 'farmer', 'cultivator', or 'tenant' because unlike the other terms, 'peasant' is clearly more than simply an occupational category.

3. Households were defined as the residential, domestic group that contributed to and/or ate from common stores. Labour migrants and others absent from the village were counted as members of the household they had resided in prior to departure and to which they would return should they return to the village.

4. The wives of polygynous men each have distinct households, generally not in close proximity to one another. It is general practice for all couples to reside with the wife's parents for an initial period (often a number of years). Later they establish an independent household, often but not necessarily near the husband's family.

5. While sorghum production has been an integral part of many Sudanese schemes, it has received little attention from management or from researchers. For example, the ILO (1976) report discusses cotton yields and their possible improvement, but does not even cite average sorghum yields. Gaitskell presents five tables giving a breakdown of Gezira cotton yields, costs, and profits (1959, pp. 267-271). He provides no such data on sorghum. Oesterdiekhoff, in an otherwise comprehensive and stimulating article, also devotes little attention to sorghum production on the irrigated schemes, even though he mentions its importance to tenants (1980). This is one example of how research on Sudanese schemes has been shaped by the orientation of management and narrowly defined national interests, rather than by the concerns of the agricultural producers. The studies of Said (1968) and Versluys (1953) stand out for their attention to costs of production and yields of sorghum as well as cotton.

6. The Sudanese pound was officially worth $1.25 in 1980 and 1981 and was later devalued to $1.11 by June 1982.

7. Of the remaining 10 production units in the sample, 4 let relatives use their land for free, 3 had the land cultivated by sharecroppers under an agreement whereby the owner received no share in the sorghum crop, two left the sorghum plot fallow, and one planted peanuts instead.

8. Ethnicity is an important determinant of job opportunity in Sudan. Southern Sudanese, Western Sudanese, Nuba, Sudanese of

Nigerian or Chadian descent, and the descendants of slaves or former slaves experience restrictions in access to education, training, employment and even tenancy ownership in the region studied. This is not a major factor in the occupational distribution among the tenant households at Wad al Abbas, however, because almost without exception they are members of the more privileged Northern Arab Sudanese ethnic groups.

References

Adam, Farah Hassan and Apaya, William Andrea (1973), 'Agricultural Credit in the Gezira', Sudan Notes and Records, 54, pp. 104-15.

Affan, Khalid(1977),'Wage Determination and Structure in Sudan', Sudan Journal of Development Research, 1, pp. 61-83.

Anthony, K., Johnston, B.; Jones, W. and Uchendu, V. (1979), Agri cultural Change in Tropical Africa. Cornell University Press, Ithaca.

Arnould, Eric J. (1984), 'Marketing and Social Reproduction in Zinder, Niger Republic', in E.J. Arnould, R. McC. Netting and R. R. Wilk (eds.), Households:-Comparative and Historical Studies of the Domestic Group, pp. 130-62, University of California Press, Berkeley.

Asad, Talal (1974), 'Market Model, Class Structure and Consent', Man, 7, pp. 74-94.

Barnett, Tony (1977), The Gezira Scheme: An Illusion of Development, Frank Cass, London.

Bennholdt-Thomsen, Veronika (1982), 'Subsistence Production and Extended Reproduction: A Contribution to the Discussion about Modes of Production', Journal of Peasant Studies, (9) 4, pp. 241-54.

Bernal, Victoria (1985), Household Agricultural Production and Off-farm Work in a Blue Nile Village, Sudan, PhD. Northwestern University.

Bernstein, Henry (1977), 'Notes on Capital and Peasantry', Review of African Political Economy, 10, pp. 60-73.

Bodemann, Y. Michael and Allahar, Anton (1980), 'The Micro-Organization of Backwardness in Central Sardinia: A Reappraisal of Luxemburg's "Three Phases" of Underdevelopment', Journal of Peasant Studies, (7) 4, pp. 458-76.

Brausch, Georges, Cooke, Patrick and Shaw, John (1964), Bashaqra Area Settlement 1963. A Case Study on Village Development in the Gezira Scheme, University of Khartoum Press, Khartoum.

Buttel, Frederick H. and Gillespie, Jr., Gilbert W. (1984), 'The Sexual Division of Farm Household Labour: An Exploratory Study of On-Farm and Off-Farm Labour Allocation Among Farm Men and Women', Rural Sociology, (49) 2, pp. 183-209.

Chayanov, A.V. (1966), The Theory of Peasant Economy, edited by D. Thorner, B. Kerblay, and R.E. Smith, Richard, D. Irwin, Publishers, Illinois.

Chibnik, Michael (1978), 'The Value of Subsistence Production', Journal of Anthropological Research, (34) 4, pp. 561-76.

Cohen, Robin, Gutkind, Peter C.W. and Brazier, Phyllis (eds.), (1979), Peasants and Proletarians: The Struggles of Third World Workers, Monthly Review Press, New York.

Cook, Scott (1984), 'Peasant Economy, Rural Industry and Capitalist Development in the Oaxaca Valley, Mexico', Journal of Peasant Studies, (12) 1, pp. 3-40.

Donham, Donald L. (1981), 'Beyond the Domestic Mode of Production', Man, (16) 4, pp. 515-41.

Duffield, Mark (1983), 'Change Among West African Settlers in Northern Sudan', Review of African Political Economy, 26, pp. 45-59.

Durrenberger, E. Paul ed., (1984), Chayanov, Peasants, and Economic Anthropology, Academic Press, New York.

Friedmann, Harriet (1980), 'Household Production and National Economy: Concepts for the Analysis of Agrarian Formations', Journal of Peasant Studies, (7) 2, pp. 158-84.

Gaitskell, Arthur (1959), Gezira: A Story of Development in the Sudan, Faber and Faber, London.

Ghai, Dharam and Radwan, Samir eds., (1983), Agrarian Policies and Rural Poverty in Africa, ILO, Geneva.

Goodman, David and Redclifft, Michael (1982), From Peasant to Proletarian, Capitalist Development and Agrarian Transitions, St. Martin's Press, New York.

Gregory, Joel W. and Piche, Victor (1978), 'African Migration and Peripheral Capitalism', African Perspectives, 1, pp. 37-50.

Guyer, Jane (1981), 'Household and Community in African Studies', African Studies Review, (24) 213, pp. 87-138.

Halim, Fatimah (1983), 'The Major Mode of Surplus Labour Appropriation in the West Malaysian Countryside: The Share-Cropping System', Journal of Peasant Studies, (10), 2 & 3, pp. 256-78.

Hart, Keith (1982), The Political Economy of West African Agriculture, Cambridge University Press, Cambridge.

Hill, Polly (1982), Dry Grain Farming Families: Hausaland (Nigeria) and Karnatka (India) Compared, Cambridge University Press, New York.

Hoyle, Steve (1977), 'The Khashm al Girba Agricultural Scheme: An Example of an Attempt to Settle Nomads', in P. O'Keefe and B. Wisner (eds.), Land Use and Development, pp. 116-131, International African Institute, London.

International Labour Office (1976), Growth, Employment and Equity: A Comprehensive Strategy for the Sudan, ILO, Geneva.

Kahn, Joel S., (1974), 'Imperialism and the Reproduction of Capitalism', Critique of Anthropology, 2, pp. 1-35.

--- Marxist Analyses and Social Anthropology.

Kerblay, Basile (1971), 'Chayanov and the Theory of Peasantry as a Specific Type of Economy', in T. Shanin (ed.), Peasants and Peasant Societies, pp. 150-60, Penguin Books, New York.

Lebrun, Olivier and Gerry, Chris (1975), 'Petty Producers and Capitalism', Review of African Political Economy, 3, pp. 20-32.

Lewis, John van Dusen (1981), 'Domestic Labour Intensity and the Incorporation of Malian Peasant Farmers into Localized Descent Groups', American Ethnologist, (8) 1, pp. 53-73.

Long, Norman and Richardson, Paul (1978), 'Informal Sector, Petty Commodity Production and the Social Relations of Small-scale Enterprise', in J. Clammer (ed.), The New Economic Anthropology, pp. 176-209, St. Martin's Press, New York.

McLoughlin, Peter F.M. (1963), 'Labour Force Participation Rates in the Sudan's Nine Economic Regions', Nigerian Journal of Economic and Social Studies, (5) 3, pp. 354-63.

Meillassoux, Claude (1981), Maidens, Meal and Money, Cambridge University Press, New York.

Millar, James R. (1970), 'A Reformulation of A.N. Chayanov's Theory of Peasant Economy', Economic Development and Culture Change, 18, pp. 219-29.

Minge-Kalman, Wanda (1978), 'Household Economy During the Peasant-to-Worker Transition in the Swiss Alps', Ethnology, (27), 2, pp. 183-96.

Murray, Colin (1978), 'Migration, Differentiation and the Development Cycle', African Perspectives, 1, pp. 127-43.

--- (1979), 'The Work of Men, Women and the Ancestors: Social Reproduction in the Periphery of Southern Africa" in S. Wallman (ed.), The Social Anthropology of Work, pp. 337-63, Academic Press, New York.

O'Brien, Jay, (1980), Agricultural Labor and Development in Sudan, PhD, University of Connecticut.

--- (1984), 'The Social Reproduction of Tenant Cultivators and Class Formation in the Gezira Scheme, Sudan', in B. Isaac (ed.), Research in Economic Anthropology, Vol. 6, pp. 217-41, JAI Press, Greenwich, Connecticut.

Olsson, Lars and Keddeman, Willem (1978), 'Cotton-picking Labour' in Ali Abdel Gadir Ali and Willem Keddeman (eds.), Employment, Productivity and Incomes in Rural Sudan, pp. 15-26, Economic and Social Research Council and ILO, Khartoum.

Oesterdiekhoff, Peter (1980), 'Der Agrarsektor Des Sudan', in R. Tetzlaff and K. Wolhlmuth (eds.), Der Sudan: Probleme und Perspektiven der Entwicklung, pp. 257-382, Alfred Metler Verlag, Frankfurt am Main.

Orlove, Benjamin (1977), 'Against a Definition of Peasantries: Agrarian Production in Andean Peru', in J. Dow and R. Halperin (eds.), Peasant Livelihood: Studies in Economic Anthropology and Cultural Ecology, pp. 22-35, St. Martin's Press, New York.

Roseberry, William (1978), 'Peasants as Proletarians', Critique of Anthropology, 11, pp. 3-18.

Rothstein, Frances (1983), 'The New Proletarians: Third World Reality and First World Categories'. Paper presented at the annual meetings of the American Anthropological Association, Chicago, Illinois.

Said, Yousif Hassan (1968), The Role of Agriculture in the Economic Development of Sudan, PhD, University of Wisconsin.

Scott, James C. (1976), The Moral Economy of the Peasant, Rebellion and Subsistence in Southeast Asia, Yale University Press, New Haven.

Smith, Alan K. and Welch, Jr., Claude E. (1978), Peasants in Africa. Crossroads Press, Waltham.

Sørbø, Gunnar M. (1972), Economic Adaptations in Khashm al Girba, African Studies Seminar Series 14, Sudan Research Unit, Faculty of Arts, University of Khartoum, Khartoum.

--- (1977), 'Nomads on the Scheme - A Study of Irrigation Agriculture and Pastoralism in Eastern Sudan', in P. O'Keefe and B. Wisner (eds.), Land Use and Development, pp. 132-50, International African Institute, London.

Taha, El Jack Taha (1973), 'Land Tenure and Size of Holding: Toward a New Strategy for Economic Studies of Tenancy Farming in the Gezira Scheme', Journal of Administration Overseas, (12), 4, pp. 211-18.

Tait, John (1978), 'Divisifizierung, Mechanisierung und Kapitalisierung der Produktion im Sudan Gezira Scheme: Auf dem Weg zur Uberwindung kolonial deformierter Agrarstrukturen?', Afrika Spectrum, 13 (2), pp. 165-78.

Taylor, John G.(1979), From Modernization to Modes of Production, Humanities Press, New Jersey.

Vergopoulos, Kostas (1978), 'Capitalism and Peasant Productivity', Journal of Peasant Studies, 5, pp. 446-65.

Versluys, J.D.N. (1953), 'The Gezira Scheme in the Sudan and the Russian Kolkhoz: A Comparison of Two Experiments', Economic Development and Culture Change, part one, (2) 1, pp. 32-59, part two, (2), 2, pp. 120-35, part three, (2), 3, pp. 216-35.

Voll, Sarah P. (1980), 'The Gezira Development Project in Sudan' in Research in Economic Anthropology, 3, pp. 265-90.

8 Merchant capital, the state and peasant farmers in southern Kordofan

ABDEL BASIT SAEED

This paper documents important changes in the relations of production in Southern Kordofan which resulted from transformation to capitalist production in this century. The analysis emphasises the mechanisms through which rural direct producers have consistently been more and more incorporated into and exploited by capitalist production in addition to state and mercantilist appropriation; i.e. processes of capital accumulation by the capitalists and the simultaneous alienation of the producers from instruments and products of their labour. These are at the same time mechanisms by which peasants not only transfer their limited 'surplus', but also products of their labour socially necessary for the survival and reproduction of their families. An emphasis on state policies in South Kordofan will provide a framework within which the discussion is carried out.

The agricultural lands in Wadi Shalango and Wadi Durungas water systems (i.e. Lagawa People's Rural Council) provide the specific area from which examples are drawn. This discussion demonstrates that colonial and post-colonial state policies, and specifically state/direct producer relations in cotton agriculture (commonly perceived as share-cropping), coupled with exploitation by merchant capitalists and dynastic tribal leaders, determined the conditions under which the poverty of direct producers is maintained and perpetuated. Thus, peasants and pastoralists find themselves helplessly stranded in a dilemma maintained by dominant relations which they cannot reverse. This is represented in the consistent usurpation of their land (see Saeed 1982) and deterioration of their animal resources; hence their inevitable tendency to resort, particularly in Wadi Shalango, to migration elsewhere to find work. Historically, this has much to do with the expropriation of communal land by the colonial state and a relatively small group of tribal and sufist religious leaders in the central Nile valley. This process involved many factors: the stabilisation, expansion and eventually concentration of private property; the rise of speculation in real estate; the greater role of money; and the simultaneous placing of private property on firmer juridical foundations. The privatisation of property and commoditisation of the economy were facilitated by the spread of communications, the transformation of key villages into towns, the spread of Westernised educational ideas and the advance in the countryside of territorial relations at the expense of kinship relations, mainly in towns.

It is important to note that from the late 1960s throughout the 1970s the different elements of the competing politically and economically dominant groups seemed to have "clarified", for themselves, common interests on crucial issues; that is, on such matters as providing for the exemption of tribal Nazirs from taxation, the exclusion of categories of non-owners from important state offices (by the mere fact of their illiteracy), and later from acquiring agricultural schemes; and before everything, their consensus on the need to defend the social order from which they all benefited. Hence, we find the relegation of social conflict to "disturbance of public security" and the definition of the suppression of conflict as "the need for maintaining law and order."

To put such developments into perspective, the history of capital accumulation in South Kordofan is periodised into three phases. The first took place under Anglo-Egyptian rule between 1925 and 1945. The second phase, 1945 to 1964, was shaped by the Condominium Government just before the end of the Second World War through the self-determination period of 1953 to 1955. It was then continued by those fractions of the client bourgeoisie who inherited political power at independence and later perpetuated capitalist development programmes up to the fall of the military regime of General Ibrahim Abboud in 1964. The third phase, 1965 to 1980, was engineered in its totality by the nationalist state, rationalised under the ideological pretext of the modernisation of traditional agriculture, and executed by national apparatuses represented here by the Agricultural Bank of Sudan (ABS) and the Mechanised Farming Corporation (MFC). Important foreign institutions, such as the World Bank, also have played important roles, but the analysis here focusses on the mode of functioning and operation of capital within the local economy, and the social impact of such development on rural direct producers in South Kordofan.

State Policies and the Early Transformation of Agricultural Production in South Kordofan

The central role of the state in promoting capitalist development in 20th century Sudan is the most important aspect of colonial and contemporary political economy and social history of this dependent socio-economic formation - a feature which conventional bourgeois analyses depict but fail to explain. The resulting social structure is viewed in terms of social conflicts - particularly in the form of ethnic or tribal rivalries in the context of rapid social change. Emphasis is on the relations direct producers of cotton and food grains enter into with state apparatuses, merchants and among themselves in the production and exchange of these and other products.

British colonial policy in Sudan was guided initially by the desire to find ways and means to relieve the metropolitan and Egyptian treasuries of the financial burden imposed as a result of the conquest (Barnett 1977, p.4). This was done by seizing upon readily available exportable commodities and encouraging their production under the supervision of the colonial administration (Mustafa 1977, pp. 19-25). Another important consideration was to produce those commodities whose availability for import in Britain would lessen or remove what British entrepreneurs and statesmen regarded as dangerous dependencies upon insecure foreign sources of supply in a context of imperialist competition for overseas resources. These considerations determined the colonial policy first to promote cotton plantation agriculture in the central Nile valley, and then to extend cotton production to Kordofan in 1924-25.

In terms of the phases of capitalist accumulation noted above, the establishment of cotton agriculture in South Kordofan between 1924 and 1945 marks the beginning of the first phase of the penetration of capitalist production and the attendant introduction of new production relations. Early in this period efforts were made to isolate the non-Arab populations of the region from Islam and Arab nationalism through the Closed Districts Policy, with the result that capitalist penetration was restricted. The second phase (1945-64) is marked by the re-establishment of cotton agriculture after a short period of discouragement of cotton production by the colonial state during the Second World War aimed at increasing the production of food grains to feed its armies stationed in the region. The return to cotton cultivation in 1948 took place under conditions of a heightening nationalist and anti-colonialist movement in the country. A few cotton-related industries were also established which attracted more and more seasonal wage labour. The 1950s were also characterised by the return of soldiers released from the colonial army after the War.

The third phase (1965 to 1980) was foreshadowed by the promulgation of Sudan's First Ten Year Plan for Social and Economic Development for the period 1961-2 - 1970-1. One major proposition of this plan in relation to South Kordofan was the establishment of mechanised cotton agriculture by individuals, which heralded the commercialisation of agriculture under the domination of the merchant class backed by the banks and foreign capital and protected by state law.

Development of Cotton Cultivation

Experimentation on rainfed short staple cotton in the Nuba Mountains was started by the colonial administration in 1918 to determine the suitability of cotton as a commercial crop (KCMTA 1979). A 1939 report observed that cash returns to the cultivators from the cotton crop were used primarily to pay taxes imposed by the government, and that most of what little remained was invested in purchasing cattle (see Saeed 1982). It was also noted by other reports in the early 1930s that at the time cotton was being introduced (1924-1930) the majority of the population directly produced all their main items of consumption, including vegetable oils pressed from locally grown groundnuts and sesame, salt from sorghum stalks, palm leaf mats, charcoal, clay pots, agricultural tools, beds, etc. (DAS 1979).

The magnitude of colonial intervention in integrating the pre-capitalist economy of southern Kordofan into the mainsteam of cotton monoculture of the central Nile valley was noted by Henderson:

> In the Nuba Mountains, where until recently the aboriginal tribes sat in truculent seclusion ... and cattle-Arabs wandered destructively across the intervening plains, years of patient research and propoaganda by the Agricultural Department and administrative officers had their reward in recent years, when sums amounting to £128,000 in 1938, £103,000 in 1939 and £136,000 in 1940 were paid out for rain grown cotton to an Arab and Nuba population estimated at 400,000 souls (1946, p. 23).

The success of early experimentation triggered a series of government policies for promoting cotton cultivation in the area. The colonial administration instructed Native Administration leaders and notables of both Nuba cultivators and Arab pastoral nomadic groups to pioneer in practicing cotton cultivation, and to persuade as many as possible of their following to take up the practice. In addition, cotton seed was distributed by the government free of charge at the beginning of the rainy season, while in the dry season cotton seed was also distributed free of charge as cattle feed, particularly to pastoralists, to encourage them to take up cotton cultivation.

Furthermore, the government's emphasis on research and experimentation with respect to suitable seed varieties and rotation systems to be followed was facilitated by the establishment, in 1924, at Kadugli of the Nuba Mountains Cotton Administration (hereafter, NMCA), comprised of a director, agricultural experts, engineers and bookkeepers. The NMCA was entrusted with the administration of all land under cotton cultivation in the Nuba Mountains and the purchase of cotton and its subsequent ginning and transportation to the nearest railway collection terminal at Simeih (150 miles to the northeast of Kadugli). This was followed by the establishment between 1925 and 1935 of eight 'inspection' stations whose task was the technical and administrative supervision of mainly cotton and sorghum, and other minor crops.

The success of cotton cultivation and the increased intervention by the state to promote cotton-related industries is also demonstrated, at this early stage, by the fact that as early as 1934 eight ginning factories - the construction of which started in 1927 -with a total ginning capacity of 34,000 metric tons were in operation in the main cultivation districts (IBRD 1976, p. 9). They were handling a total load of three to five thousand metric tons of seed cotton every harvest season. Some of these ginneries were complemented with mills to manufacture cottonseed cooking oil and seedcake as animal feed. For example, in 1937-38 the cottonseed oil manufactory attached to the Kadugli ginnery consumed 2,100 metric tons of cottonseed and produced two hundred tons of cottonseed oil.

The picture would, however, be incomplete without mention of the impact on the regional economy of the Nuba Mountains of the Second World War. As elsewhere in colonial Africa, Sudanese were forced to provide large numbers of men to fight the war for their respective colonisers. Much of the rest of the population which was not physically present in the battlegrounds was compelled to produce food for the troops. In southern Kordofan, farmers were forced to abandon cotton cultivation in order to grow sorghum for the army until 1947. Those who did cultivate cotton between 1942-43 and 1946-47 had to use cottonseed of their own - i.e. kept from previous seasons. The colonial government extended rewards - in cash and in kind - to those cultivators who, while abandoning cotton in compliance with state policies, also produced most sorghum. However, despite the increase in the production of sorghum in those years, the fact that it was used for military purposes and was actually hoarded in state storage houses had by 1947 resulted in famine in some parts of the region (NMAPC 1979).

In the same period, the government established an agricultural scheme on Khor Abu Habil near Simeih primarily for the production of sorghum. The sorghum produced was purchased directly by the government to be used as military supplies. When the government abandoned the promotion of cotton in the Nuba Mountains area in 1942-43, it requisitioned local labour to dig the canal system (Haroun Canal) for irrigating the Abu Habil Project. The project was administered by NMCA from Kadugli and became operational in the 1944-45 season in a total area of 13,000 feddans (1 feddan = 1.038 acres = 0.42 hectare). Four thousand feddans were actually put to sorghum cultivation in the first season, and the cropped area was doubled to 8,000 feddans in the 1945-46 season. When the war effort was over, the colonial government reverted to the policy of promoting cotton cultivation in the Nuba Mountains. Abu Habil Project was put to cotton production in 1952-53 after experimentation between the 1949/50 and 1951-52 seasons. Between 1952 and 1955 the Abu Habil Project contributed 45,000 kantars of cotton worth £S 135,000 to producers.

In three seasons (1945, 1946 and 1947) the Abu Habil Project produced two hundred and ten thousand kantars of sorghum, almost all of which was appropriated for the British armed forces and the war effort. The KCDKR reports show that this volume of sorghum saved one million pounds sterling for the British government which would have otherwise been invested to import food for the army. The government paid the direct producers in Kordofan £48,000, or only about 5 percent of the market value of their product. In the critical years of the war, the colonial government increased the price of one kantar of sorghum from 18 pt in 1942 to 24 pt in 1944.

The price had been 5.5 pt per kantar in 1925. This indicates the extent to which state policy accelerated the incorporation of the hitherto primarily subsistence producers into the circuits of merchant capital.

In 1948-49, with the Second World War now history, the colonial administration started to argue against the production of sorghum in Abu Habil area, by arguing that swarming insects and pests (locally known as massah bug) that had infested sorghum crops during the previous two seasons had mainly been attracted by sorghum, and that going back to cotton cultivation was the best solution in the interest of the cultivators. The government, henceforth, instructed that only 500 feddans - out of the 8,000 feddans that had been under sorghum - would be allowed to be put under sorghum to meet the farmers' subsistence needs, while the rest would be reserved for the cultivation of cotton.

Rising prices immediately after the Second World War, however, as much as this new drive for cotton cultivation, brought higher and higher yields in subsequent seasons. Cotton prices jumped from 42 pt per small kantar in 1941-42 to 85 pt in 1948-49, and to 150 pt in the 1949-50 season (an increase of 357 per cent over the 1941-42 season), thus returning cotton to its prominent place as a cash crop. Cotton prices, the total cropped area, and the volume produced developed side by side until cotton production hit its peak record prior to independence in 1956. In the 1950-51 season, which coincided with the Korean war, 117 thousand feddans produced about 300,000 small kantars and cotton prices reached an all-time high of 520 pt per kantar. Prices have never again attained that level.

In terms of the classification into phases of capital accumulation suggested earlier, this high point in cotton production also represented the most favourable circumstances for merchant capitalist accumulation in the vulgar form of money-lenders, and in the shayl system of individual indebtedness (see below). In anticipation of higher prices, following the high point of 1950-51, cotton production reached 900,000 kantars in 1954-55, but prices fell to 240 pt, and they subsided even further to 185 pt by 1957-58. Since that time cotton production has fluctuated widely, but with a general downward trend. Cotton prices remained virtually unchanged for the following twelve years.

Migration as an Index of Capitalist Expansion and the Problem of Labour

Changes in the division of labour among pastoral nomadic groups were apparent in two major aspects: firstly, in their relation to the sedentary grain-producing Nuba whose offspring formerly herded cattle for the Arabs, and secondly, in their relations to their former slaves who were set free in the early 1920s by Government decree.

By 1924 the colonial government was finally able to put an end to domestic slavery; slaves were freed in State courts and were issued "certificates of freedom". Having nothing at their disposal to live on, some former slaves deserted the Lagawa area and established their own villages. Some of those villages were established on unclaimed land while others were established on land extended to them by their former owners. Another category of former slaves deserted Dar Misiriyya altogether and migrated to the Eastern District of South Kordofan and settled as agriculturalists in the vicinity of Talodi.

The fact that those former slaves who stayed in Dar Misiriyya were given land to cultivate and live on in the vicinity of Abu Zabad in the northern part of Misiriyya territory is explainable in terms of the new economic developments which took place in the 1920s in the southern parts of Dar Misiriyya, namely the introduction of cotton cultivation in the vicinity of Lagawa. When cotton was introduced the Misiriyya deserted the area around Al Sunut and began cotton cultivation along Wadi Shalango. Now that they could not make the former slaves do the cultivating for them, the Misiriyya did not want to let them share the fertile clay soil suitable for cotton cultivation. At the same time, some slave owners did not want to leave their northern lands near Al Sunut altogether. Thus they chose to let the former slaves stay and cultivate for their own benefit. The Misiriyya came back around 1965 to the northern areas around Al Sunut and started cultivating sesame and groundnuts as cash crops after the prices of these crops had risen and the price of cotton had dropped. Here some of them tried to expel the descendants of former slaves, and others, from land their fathers had deserted over 30 years earlier. They also wanted to take away from the descendants of former slaves the administrative positions conferred upon some of them by government authorities by virtue of their long residence.

The Misiriyya Arabs would not accept the proposition that descendants of their former slaves had rights over land that had been given to them by their former owners, and they would not accept the fact that the descendants of former slaves now established their own legal position as far as state laws and policies would define such rights over land or occupancy of local administrative office. This situation now constitutes important antagonistic interests in the area around which many of the conflict situations involving Misiriyya and descendants of former slaves, and for that matter Abu Junuk Hill Nuba and some Burgo (West African immigrants) in Al Sunut, Al'Ifaina and Dabket areas in the northern parts of Lagawa People's Rural Council.

When the Misiriyya lost the free labour of domestic slaves, they turned to the neighbouring Hill Nuba groups to fulfil the subordinate function of cattle herding - though with slightly different terms. Nuba youngsters were contracted on an annual basis, and they were paid in kind. More recently, Nuba youth have not been available for year-round herding and the Misiriyya have turned to employing their poorer kinsmen or Takari youth on similar terms. When wage labour cannot be found, herd owners often take their own sons out of school to do the work.

Another government policy of significant import was the abandonment in 1929 of the Closed Districts Policy with respect to the Nuba Mountains. This move was prompted by the successes shown in the first few years of the introduction of cotton, which also triggered several internal migrations and resettlements of both Nuba and pastoral Arabs. As a result, the Nuba Mountains came under the jurisdiction of Kordofan Province. One such form of migration was reported by Nasr (1971, p. 30), who notes that between 1920 and 1940 migration from the Nuba Mountains into the cotton plantation enclaves and into the cities in central Sudan became an established phenomenon. Nasr (ibid) reports 200 Nuba, 131 of them from Dilling District, passing through Kosti on their way to find work in 1927. Ten years later the estimated number of emigrants from Dilling District was 800.

The second form of movement by larger groups was represented by an influx of Misiriyya into Wadi Shalango basin in the north-western fringes of the Nuba Mountains. Later they left the Al Sunut and Birdiyya areas along Wadi Al Ghalla, where they had established a "home territory" for shifting cultivation of millet as a supplement to herding. A third movement was by the Hawazma pastoralists into the northern and central Nuba Mountains for purposes of cultivation. These latter two movements were motivated primarily by the initial success of cotton cultivation and the new avenues for the accumulation of wealth, primarily to be invested in cattle, made available by returns from cotton sales. These two movements and the taking up of land by the nomadic groups for cultivation brought them into conflict with Nuba cultivators over land. But the new situation also gave birth to agreements between Nuba and incoming nomadic Arab groups. These agreements, besides aiming at ending the intermittent battles between Nuba and Arab nomadic groups over land, also stipulated the release by Nuba leaders of part of their land to those nomadic groups who opted for cotton cultivation and peaceful neighbourly existence. However, while these agreements extended to the newcomers the right to utilise land, the Nuba did not surrender their right to repossess those lands if and when the Arabs decided to desert them in favour of other more fertile land.

This process of mediation and accommodation of Arab-Nuba differences (which was spearheaded by Native Administration leaders) also at the same time consolidated the status and prestige of dynastic leaders. At this time (particularly prior to 1950-51) it was the cultivator's own responsibility to secure or obtain for himself (and his family) a piece of agricultural land in Wadi Shalango and Wadi Durungas water systems, or for that matter, in any part of areas under the command of the NMCA. However, since all land had been made the de jure property of the state as far back as 1905, and since it was the state that was planning and executing the cotton-based agro-industry in the region, dynastic leaders who were assigned "tribal land" were disposed to give in to demands by individual cultivators, lest they be charged with obstruction of state policy. These dynastic leaders became more and more instrumental in mediating conflicts over agricultural land and in arbitrating pacts and agreements in favour of new cultivators. Such a spirit of accommodation, while in effect an execution of colonial state policy to promote cotton agriculture, also imparted prestige and enhanced their power. This became more apparent in the area of imposing and collecting taxes from cultivators (now demanded in money form) primarily because an increase in the numbers of cultivators in a shaykh's area of jurisdiction gave the shaykh a larger commission from taxes collected.

In addition to relocation movements within the region and development of local wage labour, increasing competition for land and rising cash needs led many people to leave the province in search of wage work. Table 8.1 shows that Khartoum, Blue Nile, and Kassala Provinces, which comprised the major enclaves of capitalist development in agriculture, had by 1973 attracted huge numbers of people from rural areas. The western hinterland of Kordofan and Darfur provided the Nile Valley with thousands of workers, primarily unskilled migrants who performed the most difficult tasks of cultivation, weeding, thinning and harvesting of cotton and grain crops and unskilled, unorganised, cheap urban labour. By the late 1960s, as shown in Table 8.2, about a third of the cotton picking labour force in central Sudan was coming from Kordofan and Darfur. Further, the young and most productive are disproportionately represented in the migrant population, resulting in the deprivation of local production of a crucial segment of its labour force (see Saeed 1982).

Merchant-Direct Producer Relations

The introduction of cotton as a cash crop in southern Kordofan attracted large numbers of traders, some of whom moved on donkey-back as hawkers among village communities and nomad camps, while others established retail shops in townships in the vicinity of cotton plantation districts. The town of Lagawa, presently the headquarters of a rural council, presents a good example of this process. Said to have been established by a group of pastoral nomads in the 1880s, Lagawa grew in response to the introduction of cotton in the 1920s and the construction of the first ginnery in 1931 (the second in 1954) and the influx of people and growth of commercial activity. This resulted in its promotion to a township with schools, town councils and an organised market place by 1959.

Lagawa township is comprised of two thousand residential plots, one thousand planned, surveyed and registered by provincial housing authorities. The provincial housing authority charges an annual tax estimated for the 1979-1980 fiscal year at £S6,041. However, records at Lagawa Rural Council show that only £S1,031 (17 per cent) was actually collected. Lagawa market is comprised of sixty shops for which annual tax revenue was estimated in 1979-80 at £S1,365, of whichonly £S262 (19 per cent was actually collected). There are also sixty corrugated metal sheds (owned by Lagawa Rural Council but rented on 25 year leases) for which annual tax revenue was estimated at £S500, of which only £S75 (15 per cent) was actually collected in 1979-80. There are also ten coffee shops and two bakeries for which the government charges £S156 annually, but only £S48 (31 per cent) was actually collected in 1979-80. Comparing collection of taxes for town merchants and pastoral nomads (see Saeed 1982, Appendix No. 43) one notices that while about 79 per cent of taxes

Table 8.1

Migration in the Six Northern Provinces (in ,000 persons)

Province	Migration to Province 1956	Migration to Province 1973	Migration from Province 1956	Migration from Province 1973	Net Difference between Locations 1956	Net Difference between Locations 1973
Khartoum	100	364	42	69	+58	+295
Blue Nile	123	352	52	142	+71	+210
Kassala	71	188	19	68	+52	+120
Northern	14	36	117	263	-103	-227
Kordofan	41	86	65	319	-24	-233
Darfur	22	46	71	237	-57	-191

Source: 1956 and 1973 Population Censuses, Department of Statistics, Khartoum.

Table 8.2

Migration from Western Sudan to the Central Nile Valley

Item	1965-66	1966-67	1967-68
No. of Migrants	21,087	64,921	67,475
% of Total	10%	37%	34%
% of Kordofan migrants to those coming from outside the Gezira region	35%	81%	88%

Item	1968-69	1969-70	1970-71
No. of Migrants	79,053	97,358	95,572
% of Total	31%	31%	31%
% of Kordofan migrants to those coming from outside the Gezira region	81%	49%	59%

Source: Founou-Tchuigoua (1978:45)

Municipal Records Office, May 1980).

imposed on nomadic groups in Lagawa People's Rural Council is collected every year, only about 18 per cent of taxes imposed on town merchants is collected. But such tax revenues go mainly to pay salaries for state employees (estimated by the resident local government officer at £S40,000 per month) rather than services to rural producers (Lagawa People's Rural Council Bookkeeping and Municipal Records Office, May 1980).

Records show that in 1980 three merchant families and three dynastic families owned about 20 per cent of registered residential plots in Lagawa. The merchant families of Mekki Al Sadia, Mahmoud Hashim and Muhammad Doleeb owned 16, 20 and 12 residential plots, respectively, while the dynastic families of Farajallah Tabago of Kamdang, Muhammad Dafa'allah of the Direihmat, and Izzeddin Hummeida of the Ghazaya section owned 30, 50 and 55 plots, respectively. In addition, these families and a handful of jallaba merchants own virtually all of the commercial property and business establishments in town. Of the sixty retail shops in the marketplace, 75 per cent are owned by immigrant merchants from northern Sudan who are also known to own shops and multiple businesses in other towns in Kordofan Region and in other parts of Sudan. Four of the merchants and the dynastic ruling family of Mohammad Dafa'allah also own all six flour grinding mills spread in several locations in Lagawa People's Rural Council. Thus the merchant class and dynastic rulers own considerable residential land and have concentrated into their hands most available avenues of business enterprise in the local economy.

Traditionally, village shop-keepers concentrated their efforts on retailing consumer goods such as sugar, tea, salt, cloth and cooking oil. Payments for these were accepted both in cash and in kind. Village shops were run mostly by immigrant traders from the north. In the 1940s and 1950s, Misiriyya traders were featured in the region, particularly in small villages. Both village shopkeepers and town merchants depended on the exchange of market goods and the marketing of agriculture products. The returns from this activity plus those from the shayl system furnished them with capital necessary for investment in commercial activities and agriculture. Town merchants and village shopkeepers appropriate a large part of the direct producer's produce through this system. Direct producers obtain loans to cover their subsistence needs, mostly during the rainy season when economic activity goes primarily to cultivation of crops. The merchants advance loans in the form of consumer goods, and in fewer cases, cash, against redemption from the next cotton harvest in cash, or sorghum in kind. Profits on shayl lending have been estimated as high as 200 per cent in some cases in Sudan (Agabawi 1968). The shayl system established a relation of dominance for creditors and subordination of borrowers in various ways. The system works as follows: the direct producer borrows his household consumption items and some petty cash in pre-harvest months (usually between July and September) with the option of repaying at any time he has cash. But usually the lender extends the loan with a keen eye on the benefits accruing from redemption in grains, or cash from cotton. This pattern of exploitation has many stages of extraction of the direct producer's labour. For example, a producer may borrow a sack of grain at a price above the usual market price because he is taking it on loan. Here the merchant has already made a profit over and above the usual market price - say selling the sack to the borrower at £S20 rather than the market price of £S18. At harvest time the direct producer shall not only return the sack of grain at harvest prices, which might be only £S10 per sack, but he has to return an amount of grain equal to the value of the first sack he borrowed at £S20. Thus, the producer returns twice as much sorghum at harvest time as he borrowed. The magnitude of this exploitation becomes more apparent in the following cultivation season, a time at which the merchant will be looking forward to selling the two sacks he obtained from the poor producer at harvest time and obtain £S40. The merchant then makes a net profit of over 120 per cent above the original market price of £S18 on the sack he advanced one year earlier.

Through the shayl lending system the village shopkeeper guarantees that the direct producer is a permanent customer because the direct producer cannot change lenders at will without being denied this privilege the next time he needs to borrow. He is also maintained as a supplier of grains which the shopkeeper collects from the villages and takes to the town merchant. Thus the sources of the village shopkeeper's profits are twofold: the distribution of consumer goods and the collection of and siphoning-off of agricultural products from the direct producer. This system exploits the direct producer not only in the sphere of production, but also in the shayl lending relationship.

The role of the town merchant is central in the collection and distribution of goods. Merchants have larger capital and are able to supply a number of shopkeepers in the villages, thereby controlling the shopkeepers themselves. This process of capital accumulation shows how this pattern of exploitation operates to subordinate non-capitalist forms of production to capital and thus distinguishes certain social cetagories as owners of capital and means of production, and other categories as non-owners.

A questionnaire administered to 231 direct producers of nine villages in Wadi Shalango basin indicates that 60 per cent of the respondents went into debt at one or another point of their lives (see Saeed 1982). However, 75 per cent of those who had ever contracted debts were in debt at the time of the survey. Half of those in debt were indebted to merchants, 32 per cent to relatives, 13 per cent to the owner of the land they cultivated, and four percent to "others". 62 per cent borrowed cash while 33 per cent borrowed in the form of commodities for consumption. Asked about the reason why they went into debt, 80 per cent of the respondents related that they needed money to buy consumer goods and other necessities, four per cent to pay taxes, another four per cent to pay for marriage expenses, and six per cent to pay school fees. When asked whether they expected to be able to repay their debts in the current year (1980), 54 per cent answered affirmatively while the rest doubted that they would be able to do so. 83 per cent said they would repay in cash, ten per cent in kind and three per cent would perform work for their creditors in lieu of repayment. The magnitude of indebtedness varied from as little as £S10 to as high as £S300. The majority of those in debt (76 per cent) were indebted in the range of between £S10 and £S75.

Thus, indebtedness under merchant capitalist appropriation underlies the situation of poverty in Wadi Shalango basin, the majority of direct producers being forced to sell the larger part of their cotton crop at harvest time in order to repay debts incurred throughout the year. In cases where the sale of cotton does not cover the producer's debts, he has to sell some of his sorghum to repay. Thus if there is any remaining grain or sesame, it is soon exhausted, making it necessary for the producers once more to go into debt to sustain themselves and feed their families. Other options are forced onto the producers by the mounting pressure of economic necessity to provide for their families. A man may supplement his consumption needs by cutting firewood to sell in the local market or carrying water to sell to townspeople, while a woman may make mats of dom-leaves, or clay pots, and boys may work as houseboys in merchants' homes in Lagawa. Alternatively, older boys may migrate to the cities or agricultural schemes and work for wages and send money home to the villages.

This is how the shayl system of lending and individual indebtedness perpetuates relations of subordination of rural direct producers and functions as an avenue for the transfer of value to the merchant. The expansion of involvement in wage earning and chronic indebtedness not only results in the fact that the single household becomes the basic unit of production and consumption among the direct producers, but also affects relations within the household. In particular, these have a negative cumulative effect on the ability of the father to retain the cohesion of the family unit in rural areas. Thus, the expansion of capitalist production in South Kordofan in general, and in Wadi Shalango basin in particular, has resulted in a tendency for family relations among the poor producers to break down, with the consequent transfer of labour from the subordinate household form of production to those sections of the economy dominated by capitalist forms of production, particularly in cotton agriculture (see below). This tendency also forms the first phases of the creation of a reserve army of unemployed youth in the countryside who are forced to migrate to the cities for jobs.

State-Direct Producer Relations in Cotton Agriculture

During the first twenty-five seasons (1924-25 - 1949-50) the relationship between the NMCA and cotton cultivators was limited to the provision of free cottonseed to the producers at the beginning of each season and the purchase of the harvested crop. Prices were set by the state for each season separately on the basis of international prices. This relationship remained virtually unchanged, in form and in substance, until the 1950-51 season when, due to high world prices stimulated by the Korean War, new variables were introduced to enhance the position of the colonial state in this relationship. In 1950-51 the colonial administration instituted the Farmers' Reserve Fund (FRF). In view of the high prices to producers (£S5.2 per small kantar - small kantar = 100 rotl or about 99 lbs), the government also unilaterally decided that only £S3.2 per small kantar would be paid to the direct producer at the time and site of purchase of the harvested crop. The remaining £S2 per kantar (39 per cent of the selling price) would be put in the FRF as security against declines in the world market price. The Director of Agricultural Services noted in a 1979 report that "... the loss of records concerning the Farmers' Reserve Fund made it impossible to know how much of these monies had been put into this account prior to 1962" (KCMTA 1979). This report also states that a 1960 study to evaluate NMAPC's financial situation showed that "... in the 1962-63 season a total sum of £S324,514 was put into the Farmer's Reserve Fund, and was calculated at the rate of 2 per cent per kantar."

A report by the Public Corporation for Agricultural Production ignores the fact that the colonial state had established the FRF in 1950-51 and claims that:

> The Farmers' Reserve Fund was instituted in the 1962-63 season when cotton-sale prices were high compared to the purchase price from cultivators. This fund is calculated by deducting 2 per cent of cotton proceeds after the joint or common charges account has been settled. The total sum of funds put into the FRF account in 1962-63 was £S 34,500.[1] The purpose for instituting this fund was (a) government's policy to stabilise prices, and (b) as a contingency fund for meeting any future discrepancy or losses the farmers' share in the joint charges account may face or enter into, either due to a decline in international cotton-sale prices, or due to the need for raising cotton purchase prices from the cultivators (KCMTA 1979, Original in Arabic, author's translation).

This quote indicates that the FRF was not intended as a reserve fund for the benefit of the cultivators. Instead, it functioned as a form of indirect tax on the producers. Evidence does not show that the Nuba Mountains cultivators obtained services from this account until they were informed a few years later that their account had run into debt because differences between international prices and those offered to the producer by the state had been redeemed from monies in the FRF (KCMTA 1979). Moreover, the FRF provided a guarantee that the state not bear the costs of fluctuations in the international cotton market while at the same time concealing the real problem of declining cotton prices in world markets.

While the colonial state deducted about 39 per cent per kantar in the 1950-51 season, the post-colonial state restricted deductions to two per cent per kantar. However, the differences between the colonial and post-colonial states in the magnitude of appropriation is far less than these raw figures suggest. As I show below, the two figures are calculated on substantially different bases. In any case, the important point here is that the direct producers neither benefited from this fund nor had any voice in its implementation and management - before and after independence. The absurdity of the Government's designation of the FRF as a reserve fund for the farmers may be seen in the fact that NMCA and NMAPC have not maintained records by which they might trace the cultivators to reimburse their contributions if they withdrew from cultivating cotton in following seasons. Furthermore, there is no contractual arrangement which determines the legal status and positions of the farmers, either collectively or as individuals, towards monies in the FRF account or as noted below, in its twin procedure known as the Joint Charges Account (hereafter, JCA).

From 1962-63 - the second year of the Ten Year Plan - other variables were introduced by the state to regulate the manner in which cotton proceeds would be distributed between the state and direct producers. While these relations are officially classified as relations of share-cropping between the state and cultivators, they put much of the burden on the producer in shouldering expenses and, in effect, enhance the share which is appropriated by various state organs involved in the production and marketing of the cotton crop. These variables are included in the JCA (see Table 8. 4). When NMAPC was established in 1967 to replace the NMCA, such bases for sharing cotton proceeds were included in the statute (see Saeed 1982, Appendix No. 40).

The determination of cotton prices for each season is carried out by state organs operating at two levels. The first set of state organs is comprised of central ministries and public corporations, including the Public Corporation for Agricultural Production (PCAP), the Public Cotton Marketing Corporation (PCMC), the Ministry of Finance and National Economy, and the Ministry of Foreign Trade. These state organs have representatives in the London Stock Exchange, and operate at the level of the world market. The decision whether or not to sell Sudanese cotton of a particular season, therefore, rests with these organs but is determined by the position of cotton in the international market.

A subsidiary of PCAP, NMAPC has the regional monopoly of cotton production in South Kordofan. International world prices of short staple cotton are conveyed to NMAPC by PCMC. NMAPC then calculates the sale price per kantar of seed-cotton and the purchase price to be offered to the direct producer on the basis of four more variables for which estimates are made. These include: the total gross production of cotton; the total expenditures on agricultural and other related operations listed under the JCA, which are deducted from the Gross World Market Prices (GWMP); Marketing Expenses (ME); and estimates on the ratios of the internationally standardised cotton grading system.

One important variable that NMAPC does not even consider in the determination of the purchase price offered to the direct producer is the amount of costs the cultivator incurs directly in the process of production. What NMAPC is doing is actually exploiting the producer by first not considering the costs of production he incurs, while at the same time making him share in all the costs of marketing, transportation, ginning and agricultural operations carried out by NMAPC, as well as salaries of NMAPC's employees. These employees and many of the agricultural and related operations are decided upon by NMAPC's top officals and subsequently imposed on the cultivator.

The determination of the local purchase prices is carried out by

NMAPC in the following accounting procedure:

(a) Cotton is usually graded by NMAPC officials at cotton collection centres into first, second and third grades. The practice of previous seasons has led NMAPC to assume that usually 66 per cent of the total product is purchased from the producer as first grade, 28 per cent as second grade, and six per cent as third grade. A 1980 report on the decline of cotton prices shows that the average ratios for cotton grades for the three seasons 1977-78, 1978-79 and 1979-80 were 77 per cent, 20 per cent and 2 per cent for first, second and third grades respectively, thus making NMAPC's previous assumptions inaccurate (see below), and further reducing the producer's share. NMAPC also takes the average ginned fibre content of each small kantar of seed-cotton to be 31.15 lb., with 68.47 lb. cotton seed component and 0.48 lb. of impurities.

(b) The average purchase price per kantar for all three grades from the producer is calculated in terms of the average grade ratio and the average set price for previous years. For example, cotton prices stagnated between 1962-63 and 1972-73 at purchase prices of £S2 for first grade, £S1.90 for second grade, and £S1.60 for third grade, per small kantar of seed cotton, while the average international sale price for the 1966-67 season for one small kantar of ginned fibre-cotton was £S8.50. Cottonseed was priced at £S15 per ton. Therefore, the average purchase price in 1967 was calculated on this basis as £S1.948 per small kantar. The average world market price of short staple cotton was calculated as follows: ginned fibre per kantar of seed cotton, £S2.647, and cottonseed per kantar, £S0.461. The sum of these values gave an average world market price of £S3.108 per small kantar of seed cotton. The estimated gross world market value of the southern Kordofan cotton crop of 450,000 kantar in 1966-67 was thus set at £S1,398,600, from which total JCA expenses were deducted in setting producer prices.

(c) The JCA expenditures deducted from the estimated total value of cotton purchased by NMAPC are set by law. Joint expenditures are assumed to be fixed and necessary for every season (Table 8.5 depicts the breakdown of JCA for 1979-80 season). How much the direct producer will be offered for his crop is calculated by NMAPC by deducting the average joint charges per small kantar of a particular season from the average price of one small kantar of seed-cotton.

Once the Gross World Market Price (GWMP) for a particular season is estimated, a chain of additional deductions from this figure, representing taxes and fees not included from this in the JCA, are deducted: 1) 5 per cent State Development tax; 2) 1 per cent Export Company charges (the F.O.B. Port Sudan price reflects the deduction of this six per cent (i.e. items 1 and 2 from the GWMP, thus making the price at Port Sudan equal to GWMP-JCA-6 per cent); 3) 2 per cent to the PCMC for services rendered to NMAPC; 4) 2 per cent deducted as FRF; 5) 2 per cent Balance Fund; 6) 0.5 per cent Price Stabilisation Fund. The deduction of this last 6.5 per cent (items 3,4,5 and 6) gives NMAPC the price of one small kantar of ginned fiber cotton which shows in this form:

[(GWMP - JCA) - 6%] - 6.5%

Using this formula, the price of one small kantar of ginned fibre cotton for the 1979-80 season was calculated as £S30.469 (KCDKR 1980). At a ratio of 31.15 lb. of ginned fibre and 68.416 lb. of seed per small kantar of seed cotton, this worked out to a GWMP per kantar of seed cotton of £S11.26. The estimated GWMP of the total crop of 105,000 kantar was £S1,182.300.

The final step in the determination of producer prices is the distribution of revenues between the cultivators and the state. Between 1962-63 and 1966-67 the percentages in which the distribution of the proceeds was administered ran as follows:

1. 82 per cent was the direct producer's share from net returns, the latter obtainable after the deduction of the JCA and taxes and commissions, which on average ran between 50 and 75 per cent of the GWMP;

2. 2 per cent was deducted from the producer's share and kept in the custody of the State treasury as FRF;

3. 18 per cent Government share went to the state over and above what was already obtained through the JCA (about 60 per cent);

4. 0.5 per cent was deducted for the Social Services Fund.

From 1967 to 1975 - as a result of the restructuring of PCAP and the subsidiary status relegated to NMAPC as the official successor of NMCA in 1967 - the government's share was renamed as "NMAPC's share", and the percentages were also revised: the Social Services Fund was raised to one per cent; the Farmers' Share was reduced to 80 per cent; the FRF became deductable from the 'net profits' (i.e. (GWMP-JCA) - 2 per cent); and NMAPC's share was reduced to 17 per cent of the net profits. In addition, Government statutes stipulated that NMAPC's share of 17 per cent should be divided among other state organs involved in the whole exercise of sharing such revenues in the following percentages: central government, 60 per cent; PCAP, 15 per cent; and NMAPC, 25 per cent. However, since 1967 this distribution has not in practice been instituted due to the failure of NMAPC to show any 'profit' over its running expenses.

For the period 1975 to 1980 the statutory formula for distributing cotton proceeds was further revised. People's Local Government institutions also came to share cotton proceeds, despite the fact that such state organs also levy taxes on their own on the subjects (see Saeed 1982, Appendix Nos. 38 and 39). According to this revised formula the shares are as follows: The producer's share was reduced to 78.5 per cent; NMAPC's share was reduced to 15.5 per cent; FRF remained at two per cent; and People's Local Government was assigned three per cent. Further, the 1975 statute for NMAPC stipulated that its share of 15.5 per cent be divided between PCAP, 85 per cent, and NMAPC's Reserve Fund, 15 per cent.

The manner in which the concept of profit is employed by NMAPC invites comment. First, the situation here is one in which a state corporation argues in its statistical records that it sustained persistent loss in its balance of annual earning and expenditures. When the corporation addresses the issue of sharing the proceeds of cotton with direct producers, it insists in its official documents that what it has been distributing in the above mentioned statutory equations is profit. NMAPC reported 'profits' only in the 1967-68 and the 1969-70 seasons, recording 'losses' in all other seasons between 1967-68 and 1978-79 (KCMTA 1979; NMAPC 1978, 1979). These persistent losses correspond to a period of decline in both the total cropped area and the total amount of cotton produced in the Nuba Mountains (see Saeed 1982). This was also a period in which agricultural machinery was introduced into areas under NMAPC's control on a large scale. Such contradictions make it apparent that the explanation cannot be sought in the producers' laziness, but rather in the production relations to which the direct producer is subjected in cotton 'share-cropping' with the state. The producers turned to other crops (grain, sesame, groundnuts and watermelons) from which the state gets no immediate revenue, but which are more lucrative for the producers. However, even in cultivating alternative crops the producer is still confronted with another appropriator - in the form of the crop merchant or the <u>shayl</u> system. Nevertheless, the fact that the merchant offers comparatively higher prices (see Table 8.5) than accrue to the producer in his relationship with the state leads the producer to prefer dealing with the merchant as the "lesser of the two evils". The rural producers' inability to confront either the state or the merchant has forced them into competition with other producers over local resources (pasture, cultivable land, watering sites) in the process of 'making a living'.

Table 8.3 indicates that during the six seasons 1974-75 to 1979-80 the ratios of the JCA to the gross world market value of cotton produced by traditional cultivators and purchased by NMAPC were respectively 75 per cent, 40 per cent, 38 per cent, 50 per cent, and 48 per cent. The average percentage of funds so apropriated for the years noted is 50 per cent of total returns from sale of seed and fibre cotton. However, official reports state (KCDKR 1980):

> Joint expenditures amount to 60 per cent of cotton returns. This is a very high percentage if we bear in mind that the Joint Charges Account does not include expenses incurred by the producers.

One must also add that about 12 per cent of the gross world market price of each kantar is lost to the direct producer in taxes, bank charges and commissions to companies (see Table 8.4) over and above JCA appropriation. Therefore, one can deduce that percentages varying from a minimum of 50 per cent to a maximum of 72 per cent of the gross world market value of each kantar of raw seed cotton are appropriated from the direct producer by state organs and/or banks and companies in processes of production and of marketing.

Table 8.4 shows items and corresponding charges entered in the JCA prescribed by Government statutes. These charges go beyond recovery from the producers of costs of production incurred by state

Table 8.3

Estimates of NMAPC Cotton Purchases

Joint Charges Account and Net Returns from the 1974/75 to 1979/80 Seasons[a]

Season	A	B	C	D	E	F	G	H
1974/75	211	0.9	0.70	75%	4.8	3.4	1.3	1.1
1975/76	319	2.6	1.03	40%	7.1	2.9	4.1	3.4
1976/77	311	2.7	1.04	38%	8.9	3.4	5.1	4.2
1977/78	247	1.8	0.89	50%	7.0	3.6	3.6	2.9
1978/79	247	2.1	1.02	48%	8.6	4.7	4.5	3.5
1979/80[b]	106	1.9	0.73	58%	12.0	7.0	5.0	3.2
Average	240	2.0	0.90	51%	8.1	4.2	3.9	3.1

Abbreviations:

A: Total purchase by NMAPC in (,000) small kantars.
B: Total returns from the sale of seed and fibre cotton in £S million.
C: Total joint charges and expenditures in £S (,000).
D: C as per cent of B (i.e. percentage of monies appropriated by the JCA to the Gross World Market Price of Nuba Mountains cotton).
E: Gross returns per kantar of seed cotton in £S.
F: Joint charges per single kantar of seed cotton in £S.
G: Net returns per kantar of seed cotton in £S.
H: NMAPC's purchase price offered to producers per kantar of seed-cotton (in £S), which includes the 2 per cent FRF to be deducted at the time and location of purchase.

Notes:

a: In 1979 the Central Government issued Ministerial Decree No. 200 constituting a committee to study the causes of the decline in cotton production in the Nuba Mountains. The committee submitted its report in February 1980 which proposed raises in cotton prices for the 1980-81 season.

b: NMAPC's estimates for the 1979-80 season of 106,000 kantars were not realized. Instead production was only 50,000 kantars.

Source: Adapted from the Proceedings of the Kadugli Conference for the Development of Kordofan Region, Kadugli, October 1980.

agencies: 3.4 per cent of the JCA (item 11) is provided to contractors to sign agreements with the state so that they may recruit cheap seasonal labour. In this instance the recruitment of labour is not left to supply and demand, as conventional theory would suggest, but is encouraged, legalised and financed by state funds appropriated from the direct producer. Furthermore, notice that 6.1 per cent (item 5) went to the banks; 3.5 per cent to merchants who monopolise the business of commercial trucking (item 10) and usually enjoy contracts for transporting ginned cotton to the railway terminal at Simeih. 21.1 per cent goes to cover salaries for NMAPC employees who administer cotton markets (item 8); and only 1.4 per cent goes as daily wages for labour (item 9) recruited by contractors (who had just received 3.4 per cent to recruit them in the first place!). In this way the state indirectly over-taxed the cotton cultivator by making him pay over 50 per cent of costs entered into JCA on behalf of the state to pay salaries for state employees. All of the charges levied on producers are over and above the direct taxes paid to the state and local governments. In this relationship the producer is also made to pay for miscellaneous supplies (such as stationery), and all services needed for preparing and marketing cotton.

One further aspect of the process of the transfer of value is that the costs the producer incurs in the process of production (as shown in Table 8.5) are neither accounted nor compensated for in the JCA. The problem is twofold: on the one hand, the producer is underpaid (i.e. his commodity underpriced by the state); on the other hand he has to invest part of what little returns he gets (only 23 per cent of the gross world market price per kantar of seed-cotton in the 1980 season) in producing for the following season. Hence the process of state appropriation, coupled with the highly priced consumption goods which must be purchased, further result in the perpetuation of the cultivator's poverty.

Table 8.5 compares the costs of agricultural operations per feddan for the producers of major crops in 1980. Cotton cultivation appears the least expensive, but it is at the same time the lowest priced and the second lowest in productivity. It is also the only commodity whose cultivator sustains negative returns at harvest. Such declining returns from cotton to the producer in comparison to other crops (on the sale of which the state gets no direct revenue) explains why a producer encompassed by capitalist production as the dominant form would tend to cultivate those crops (in this case sorghum and groundnuts) which may fetch him relatively more income - hence the marked movement since the mid-1970s away from cotton cultivation in favour of other crops, sold mainly to the merchants, and the decline in cotton productivity.

State Modernisation Policies and Capitalist Exploitation

State policies in the 1960s and 1970s furnished merchants, civil servants and dynastic tribal leaders with new opportunities for private ownership of land and allowed them access to loan capital from the banks for investment in agribusiness and in commercial

Table 8.4

Costs of Operations Entered in NMAPC/Cultivator Joint Charges Account for the 1979-80 Season

Item	Charges in £S per Unit	Estimated Costs in £S (,000)	Cost of Operation as Percent. of Total
1. Railway transport of ginned cotton	0.900/kt.	33.075	4.5%
2. Loading/unloading charges	0.100/kt.	3.675	0.5%
3. Bale packing materials	0.421	44.100	6.0%
4. Ginning charges	2.65	98.306	13.5%
5. Bank charges	x*	45.000	6.1%
6. Opening seasonal bush roads	x	35.000	4.8%
7. Clearing cotton stalks	x	15.000	2.1%
8. NMAPC purchase employees	x	154.150	21.1%
9. Daily wage	x	10.500	1.4%
10. Commercial transport by truck contractors	0.710	26.092	3.5%
11. Wage-labour recruitment contracts	0.236	24.780	3.4%
12. Stationery, office supplies	0.025	2.625	0.3%
13. Warehouse supplies	0.025	2.625	0.3%
14. Insecticides	1.344	141.120	19.3%
15. Spraying of bugs	x	16.000	2.2%
16. Opening fire lanes	x	50.000	6.9%
17. Renewal of thornbush fences	x	25.000	3.4%
18. Guarding cotton against animals	0.025	2.625	0.3%
19. Guarding cotton at weighing sites	0.025	2.625	0.3%
Total Joint Charges & Expenditures		732.298	100.0%

Source: KCDKR, 1980.

* Items marked 'x' are charged to the producer as flat rates. The problem is that not all peasant cultivators of cotton (there are some who don't cultivate) are reached in the rainy season due to soaking clay soils, but at the time of sale and balance of JCA all such producers are charged the prescribed amounts whether they received the services (e.g. insecticides, etc.) or not - thus some producers are made to pay for services they have not received.

transport activities. These policies resulted from a rise in the organic composition of capital and the import of machinery which intensified the rate of exploitation of direct producers and ushered in a new phase of capital accumulation for the rural bourgeoisie and proletarianisation of direct producers.

In December 1959 the Military Governor of Kordofan proposed opening the Nuba Mountains to private investors in order to increase cotton production. He said:

> On release of cotton prices for the 1959-60 season (185 pt per small kantar), all the high hopes of the producers were dashed and crushed. The higher prices of cotton compared to other main agricultural products, which used to orient and stimulate the farmers, have been changing so sluggishly - of late - that no cultivator seems to have any basis on which to make any future projections for possible successes or failures in cotton agriculture. As for sorghum the price has plunged to a record low of only two pt per malwa (7 lb. weight, i.e. 60 pt per sack of 210 lbs) whereas it was 16 pt per malwa in 1954-55. It is our intention to consolidate cotton production for strengthening our foreign exchange position (OCNKP 1960) (Original in Arabic, author's translation).

This proposal was sanctioned in state policy in April 1960 - the month in which land preparation for the following season usually starts. The Governor instructed all District Commissioners in South Kordofan and the Director of NMCA to start carrying out the following policy:

> It has been determined that the government will establish spinning and weaving factories which manufacture textiles from American Upland short-staple cotton. And since present levels of production of raw cotton are much below the projected annual capacity of such factories, and in view of the frequent fluctuations in the volume of production, the government has decided to make available to them reasonably sizable land which is also suitable for such private investment both in terms of soil fertility and area. However, the experimental nature of such projects should be made clear to individuals who may be chosen.
>
> Areas selected for this purpose include the following:

District	Area(s)	No. of Projects	Size of each Project
Dilling	Habila	Two	1,000 feddans
Kadugli	Kadugli, Buram Tash	Two	1,000 feddans
Rashad	Gardud and Tusy	Four	1,000 feddans
Al Fula	Durungas	Two	1,000 feddans

Table 8.5

Cost/Benefit Statistics for Major Crops During The 1979-80 Season (in £S/feddan)

Operation	Cotton	Sorghum	Groundnuts	Sesame
Land clearing	1.0	1.5	1.0	1.0
Clearing of stalks	2.0	-	-	-
Seedlings	Free	0.4	5.0	1.0
Sowing	1.0	1.0	2.0	1.0
Weeding (3 times)	5.0	5.0	5.0	3.0
Harvesting & packing	3.4	2.0	4.0	6.0
Packing material	0.8	2.5	6.0	1.0
Porting & transportation	1.8	2.0	7.2	1.5
'Usher & Gibana, i.e. Rural Council Charges	-	2.8	1.8	1.8
Total Cost of Operations	15.0	17.2	32.0	16.3
Average Production/ feddan	3 small	5 sacks	12 sacks	1.7 sacks
Average Unit Price in £S	3.987	5.5	4.0	15.0
Estimated Gross Return	11.961	27.5	48.0	25.2
Net Returns	-3.539	+10.8	+16.0	+7.9
Cost/Benefit Status	Loss	Profit	Profit	Profit

Source: NMAPC Statistical Files (1980)

Please send me your recommendations regarding those individuals who, in your judgement, have the financial capabilities and are able and prepared to undertake this venture. You are requested to consult with the Director General of the Nuba Mountains Cotton Industry (KCDKR 1980, original in Arabic, author's translation).

This statement, while outlining general state policy, also signalled the beginning of the end of the traditional small-scale direct producer, or rather the redefinition of his class position. For example, anyone who applied for land "leases" in the Nuba Mountains was required to satisfy provincial authorities that: (a) he was a Sudanese citizen; (b) he had or could obtain the necessary agricultural machinery; (c) he had sufficient capital to finance agricultural operations; and (d) he had sufficient agricultural knowledge. Conditions b, c, and d immediately and automatically exclude peasant producers. These restrictions limit the eligibility to a small class of Sudanese - mostly merchants, bureaucrats and dynastic tribal leaders - who had hitherto been availed of various avenues for the accumulation of wealth.

The minimum "agricultural machinery" required was one tractor, one wide level disc and seeder-box, worth more than £S 2,000 (Agabawi 1968). Those who could fulfil these requirements were the merchants and contractors who came to constitute the majority of lease holders. In most cases these people did not fulfil eligibility condition "d" concerning agricultural knowledge but hired managers to look after their farms. The result is that many such schemes were acquired by absentee lessees.

Thus, a new phase of larger scale capital accumulation - dominant in South Kordofan up to the present - was begun in the late 1960s. The Mechanised Farming Corporation was established as an autonomous government agency to supervise its expansion, the Agricultural Bank of Sudan was reoriented to service this sector and established new branches in the region, and the IBRD extended a series of loans to the MFC to finance machinery imports. Yielding annual profits to investors as high as 100 percent, such mechanised farming expanded rapidly (see Saeed 1982; O'Brien 1983). By 1980, one million feddans had been demarcated for mechanised farming in South Kordofan, about half of which was under cultivation by that time. To make way for these huge projects, villages of peasant farmers were forcibly resettled and the herders were evicted at gunpoint from prime grazing lands.

A transformed programme to "modernise traditional agriculture" dovetailed nicely with this reorganisation of the countryside in its emphasis on regrouping dispersed cultivations into larger projects for greater efficiency in government supervision and provision of services. The impact of these initiatives on rural direct producers in South Kordofan was increased proletarianisation through dispossession of some of their land, increased subordination to "share-cropping" relations with the state, and increased participation in direct wage labour in the expanding schemes. The essence of the development programmes implemented by the state in South Kordofan in all periods is thus revealed in the results of the last period: a process of class formation producing a small number of wealthy capitalists and a mass of producers proletarianised in different ways and to varying extents.

Note

1. Note the immediate contradiction in the statistical evidence provided in this quote and the one preceding it. The sources are official reports of NMAPC and PCAP. The PCAP quotation of the value of FRF is less than the NMAPC by a factor of more than ten.

References

Agabawi, K.S. (1968), 'Some developments in rainfed agriculture in Central Sudan', Sudan Notes and Records, 50.

Barnett, Tony (1977), The Gezira Scheme: An Illusion of Development, Cass, London.

DAS (1979), Report of the Director for Agricultural Services. Presented to the Kadugli Conference for the Modernization of Traditional Agriculture, Kadugli, 17 January 1979. Office of the Director General, NMAPC, Kadugli, File Series No. MGNZ-2-A-S-4-M-1.

Founou-Tchuigoua, B. (1978), 'De-facto wage-earners in the Gezira Scheme (Sudan)' Africa Development, 3 (1), pp. 25-50.

Henderson, K.D.D. (1946), Survey of the Anglo-Egyptian Sudan, 1898-1944, Longmans, Toronto.

IBRD (1976), Southern Kordofan Agricultural Development, unpublished report, Nairobi.

--- (1977), Third Mechanized Farming Project: Sudan, IBRD, Washington DC.

KCDKR (1980), Proceedings of the Kadugli Conference for the Development of Kordofan Region, October 1980, Kadugli.

KCMTA (1979), Proceedings of the Kadugli Conference for the Modernization of Traditional Agriculture, 17 January 1979. Office of the Director General, NMAPC, Kadugli. File Series No. MGNZ-2-A-2-4-M-1.

Mustafa, Abdel Mohsin (1977), 'The Structural Malformation of the Sudanese Economy', Part II, Bulletin No. 54, Economic and Social Research Council, Khartoum.

NMAPC (1978, 1979, 1980), Statistical files of the Nuba Mountain Agricultural Production Corporation, Kadugli.

Nasr, A.A. (1971), 'British policy towards Islam in the Nuba Mountains, 1920-1940', Sudan Notes and Records, 52.

O'Brien, Jay (1983), 'The political economy of capitalist farming in the central rainlands of Sudan', Labour, Capital and Society, 16 (1), pp. 8-32.

OCNKP (1960), File No. A.G.N. 1960, Office of the Commissioner of North Kordofan Province, El Obeid.

Saeed, A.(1982), The State and Socioeconomic Transformation in the Sudan: The Case of Social Conflict in Southwest Kurdufan, PhD, University of Connecticut.

9 Some aspects of change in commodity production in southeast Kordofan[1]

JAMES C. FARIS

Southeast Nuba, the only Kordofanian linguistic system (cf., Schadeberg, 1981) I can speak of with authority, has an interesting discriminatory logic for some of the types of social relations here discussed. There is a term [nur] that may be glossed as rest, which is a supraordinate for more specific terms for sleep or simply sitting idly -- denoting a lack of activity. Another term [an] may be glossed as activity, which is a supraordinate for normal local activities, production, dances, sports, onerous brideservice, weeding parties, individual production, enjoyable or even difficult acts of voluntary effort, and so forth. The degree of difficulty and/or pleasure involved can be specified, but all local productive efforts and activities may be glossed by this term. This term has, for example, quite the same meaning as English things, as in I have things to do, actually suggesting projects derived from productive forces or acting on them or involving activities stemming from local social relations.

In addition, there is a third supraordinate [ēnōn], which glosses enslavement, such as the forced capture known from the last century at the hands of Turkish raiders or Mahdist military recruitment (cf. Faris 1972). And, significantly for this essay, it also refers to any activity for which there is a wage payment. If a person leaves the community for work elsewhere for cash, whether seasonally or otherwise, this term [ēnōn] - slavery - is used. Hiring oneself to others for weeding or threshing, now a more common arrangement than a decade ago, is described with the term [ēnōn]. The rate of return, the onerousness of the work, is irrelevant. Indeed, some of the endeavour labelled [an] - activity - is extremely onerous, such as the heavy brideservice, and individuals complain loudly and try where possible to avoid it or to ease it. Moreover, the drudgery of weeding, harvesting, etc. is sometimes quite heavy. But it is glossed [an], or activity. Painful to me, of course, was that a young man I had engaged to assist me in local research, at what was a guilt-inspired exhorbitant return, and universally envied by others, was nevertheless referred to as [kēnōn ka Jim] - Jim's slave, as he sold labour time. The wage/slave equation is thus not patented by Marxist rhetorical usage - it is clearly recognised elsewhere.

Commodity production itself, of course, is not new in Kordofan. The production of commodities is as old as the major population groups in the area. Documentation and oral tradition substantiate extensive trade in all directions (cf. Spaulding 1984). It is thus not a new phenomenon, and the issue addressed here is not indeed so much commodity production vs. something that has been called 'domestic production' (production for use), but more properly the dramatic changes in the past ten years or so in the types of commodity production, in the appearance of items previously only produced for use - now produced for exchange, and, increasingly, in the more common appearance of labour time itself as a commodity - as available for exchange. The appearance of the [enon] form (labour time) as an acceptable commodity is new, and has considerable significance.

Valorisation (for exchange) in terms of labour time consumed in production has also long been the case in South Kordofan, so neither are we dealing with the absence of commodity-labour time valorisation. My own research with non-commodity exchange within a village or between adjacent villages confirmed that value has been roughly premised on labour time consumed in production for a long time. That is (see Table 9.1), the value of goods or services for sale or exchange within the local population indicates that the time consumed in the production of, say, a pot, or a bracelet, or a basket, is relevant to its exchange worth in the community. This indicates a long history with mercantile forms of capitalist value reckoning. Labour time itself, however, is not traditionally sold, and that is the critical difference more recently, and the hallmark of a distorted form of mature capitalist social relation.

Confining myself to the Nuba hill communities of southeast Kordofan, I want to focus on conditions at the time of my research, changes in the past decade, and some political commentary. First, let us define commodity production as that production for which some essential aspect of decisions about it rests outside the community - outside the local planning nexus. This says nothing about any other social relations of production, and carries, in my view, no necessary exploitative connotations. In reality, of course, such social relations very commonly are exploitative when power differentials are present between the exchange parties.[2]

Table 9.1

Value of Goods (Services) for Sale (Exchange) Within Local Community, 1969-70

Item	Time in Production*	Div. of Labour**	Value
knife scabbards	1/2 day total labour	I, M, E	10 Pt (skin supplied by maker)
bracelet attachment (wrist & anklet)	up to 1/2 day in heating to expand, fitting, closing	I, M, E	5 Pt hands, 10 PT feet
brass fighting bracelets	acquiring brass, casting & finishing, approx. 1/3 days labour	I, M, E	£S 1-£S 1.5 each excludes price of brass
personal bracelets	1) simple, no casting: 1/2 day total labour; 2) complex, requires casting, approx. 3 days labour	I, M, E	1) 10 Pt (excludes cost of brass 2) up to 50Pt each (cost of brass
stools, girls' beds	stool: 1/2-1 day labour carving bed; 2-3 days labour carving	I, M, E	25 Pt-stool; 50-75 Pt-bed
stools, woven seat	1/2 day frame, 1/2 day seat	I, M, E	15-20 Pt
male beds, woven	1/2 day frame, 1 day seat	I, M, E	25-30 Pt
local tobacco (Nicotiana rustica)	season's labour (approx. 2 hrs/day for 15 days: effort yields average of 25 sm plugs)	I, M, F, E	10-12 Pt dry season-sm.plug; 20 Pt large wet season-small plug
pottery	1 day in clay prep, construction, 1/2 day in firing (3 pots)	I, F,E	15 Pt small open sauce vessel, 25 Pt large H_2O or beer making vessel
blade sharpening (knife/hoe)	1 hour maximum	I, M, E	5 Pt each
baskets	1) coil grain basket, 2 days gathering, drying, weaving	I, F, E	50-75 Pt

(Table 9.1 continued on next page)

Table 9.1 continued)

	2) loose harvest basket, 3 days shaping frame, constructing, leather supplied	I, M, E	75 Pt-£S 1
	3) woven liner to harvest basket, or small woven baskets; all approx. 1/2 day	I, F, or I, M, E	15-20 Pt
sandals	giraffe skin, including tanning - 1/2 to 1 day/pair	I, M, E	25 Pt

* 1/2 day is approximately 2.5-3 hours.

** M = male; F = female; E = elder; I = independently produced (even though efforts may be undertaken jointly with others).

In southeast Kordofan commodity production classically involved a series of items (See Table 9.2), mostly gathered, but some produced in more complicated ways, which left the area into the hands of part-time traders who migrated through, such as nomadic Arabs, or by mercantilists who came to the region in the dry season to secure these items in trade from time to time (see Spaulding 1980; James 1971; Manger 1984). These items were produced by individuals, principally on demand at the time of each individual trader. A trader might request a certain commodity one season, but not the next, and production of this sort was thus appropriate to the specific temporal demand (or items that could be stored for long periods of time without decay), and individuals only produced when normal 'domestic production' (production for local use) was not required, such as during the dry season when such production was least demanding. Although such production was for exchange, planning never interfered with local production for use in very significant ways. Commodities were commonly altered plant products (such as rope from bark, dried palm strips, trimmed bamboo, gum arabic, okra, skins, ivory, and more recently, honey [see Table 9.2]). At the time of my initial research (1966-1969), trade in ivory had stopped, bamboo was coming under Government control, whereas crops, domestic animals, and items of manufacture for local use were very rarely sold or traded outside the community.

This is manifest in the value forms (see Table 9.3) for such non-commodities, where values are generally below those to be found at the time elsewhere in Kordofan. The items of Table 9.3 and their values reflect local trade within the community - any valorisation in terms of labour time is clearly difficult, and values are almost arbitrary. Transmission of all such moving property is within the matriline, even though any individual possessor has rights of disposal or transfer to cash, which he or she may spend or transmit to heirs. Changes in these arrangements are discussed below.

Table 9.2

Indigenous Commodity Production and Value, 1969

Item	Time in Production*	Div. of Labour**	Value
cotton	entire growing season (on Govt. prepared land near Talodi)	M, E, I	£S 4/kg x 100 (1 cotton, 1st matured, 1st picked - £S26.5 av. seasonal return (£S 18 low, £S 37 high)
gum arabic	if easily available, 1/2 day/kg	M, B, E, I	5.5 Pt/kg average best grade gum (8-12 Pt value Khartoum)
tanning bark (Acacia Arabica)	1/2 day gathering, 1/2 day splitting & packing yields two bundles	M, E, I	5 Pt/bundle (10 Pt value in Khartoum)
palm strips (Dombeya quinqueseta)	1/2 day gathering, 1/2 day splitting & drying yields 5 bundles	F, A, C, I	1 Pt/bundle (5 Pt value in Khartoum)
bark rope (Adansonia digitata)	1/2 day gathering, 1 day twisting, drying, sorting, braiding, makes 2 five meter length ropes	M, E, I	10-12 Pt/rope length of five meters)
bamboo (Osytenan-thera abysinica)	25 stalks in 1/2 day	M, B, E, I	.5-1 Pt/trimmed stalk - now Government controlled
skins	variable - little processing, skins scraped, pegged and dried only - 1/2 day	M, B, E, I	snake (3 meters) - £S3; leopard, mature, unmarked, - £S30
ivory	notsecuredduringmy research		now Government controlled

* 1/2 day is approximately 2.5-3 hours.

** M = male; F = female; E = elder; B = post adolescent male, marriage probably unconsummated; C = adult female; A = post adolescent female, marriage not yet consummated; I = independently produced, no necessary co-operation.

Table 9.3

Non-Commodity Production and Value, 1969 (April)*

Item	Value in Cash**
harvested and threshed sesame grain	average of 2.22 Pt/litre (calculated from 10 Pt/midd)
harvested and threshed sorghum grain	average of 1.11 Pt/litre (calculated from 5 Pt/midd)
cattle	mature bull-£S 12-15 mature cow, not with calf, nor in milk £S 8-10 bullock-£S 6 heifer-£S 5-6
pig	mature sow-£S 1.5
goat	female-£S 1.5 male-£S 1.5-2
chickens	5-10 Pt (depending on size)
sheep	ram-£S 3-5 ewe-£S 2-4
beer	5 Pt/litre (liquid form)

* No distinction is made in production for exchange or for use in general (see discussion). No distinction is made in types of grain or animals which may affect value.

** Here I have ignored any season variation in price-average value used.

This all meant that production of classical commodities (to be exchanged outside the community) was nearly always planned in tandem with other local production, or adjunctive to it. There was no exclusive specialisation in commodity production (save some gender-specific items, as noted in Table 9.2), even though there are specialisations beyond gender in local production for exchange within the community (production for use). It should be noted, moreover, that local commodity production was simple - in that neither extensive processing nor complicated production techniques were required, and commodities were principally gathered (produced) by individuals, and thus did not require work organisations of kin, nor developed rules of access to means of production.[3] It should also be mentioned that since no individuals pursued any of this commodity production as a speciality, only a few pounds were made each year. Increasing pressures for cash, increasing privatisation of means of production, Government encroachment on traditional land,

and altered movements of nomadic herders all will probably change this essentially 'free' attitude toward the means of production of such gathered commodities.

Nevertheless, even in 1980, my last visit to the area, no essential specialisation had emerged for this old type of commodity production, and local social relations had not yet changed by virtue of the expansion of this traditional form of commodity production. Although markets are now steadier and more reliable, and access is easier, this does not seem as yet to have much affected specialist production of these commodities. I do not know what effect the more recent disturbances to the south will have. And I should also mention that there has been a slight expansion of commodity production in the form of decorated gourds for tourist consumption - but this too is a seasonal market, principally pursued by the same individual efforts (both young and old) and adjunctive attitude as with other commodities.

Before continuing, let me note that production of commodities traditionally generated means of exchange for goods brought by traders, though increasingly exchange is for cash. Cash has always gone for a series of market items either brought to the area by the commodity traders, or sought by local people at the nearest Jellaba market (which is Kologi, some 45 kilometers northwest). Other cash was commonly put into livestock, and attitudes towards livestock by the Southeast Nuba peoples have generally been dictated by their convertability and their potential as meat. People are principally agriculturalists, and not fundamentally animal keepers. In practically all cases, animals are kept as a supplement to cultivation, with cattle, goats and sheep cared for by boys and young men, pigs and chickens being the responsibility principally of girls and women. Though this might suggest animals as an ideal commodity, the general lack of skills in their keeping, the precarious climate at this latitude, and the agricultural requirements all act against this. Animals are a source of possible cash, a temporary investment, or a meat store.[4]

Now all of the above is the classical pattern of commodity production locally. It is not recent, nor is the valorisation of local production in terms of labour time. But new elements are at work and today have significance for change in the area. Not only did the settlement of the north/south conflict in 1972 mean the opening of the area (for the Southeast Nuba settlements are along the ancient Kordofan route to Malakal, and trucks could go south or north for the first time in many years), but it made the area accessible to tourists. This fact, combined with Numeiri's rightward political swing, had meant a trafficking in exotica (see below). Thus, from two or three trucks in the entire dry season in commodity exchange before 1972, until recently there were up to ten each day during this season.

More rainfed mechanised agricultural schemes have also been established within a day's walk of most of the southern Nuba groups. This makes possible both migration to these schemes for sale of labour to lease-holders, as well as - at least theoretically - actual production tenancies. But let me stress at the outset the essential lack of participation of the Southeast Nuba in these schemes. As noted in Table 9.2, a few individuals from the total population of over 3,000 sought employment in these schemes or took up cotton cultivation on them, but never more than this. And this tendency does not seem to be changing. I documented but two cotton farmers on the schemes near Talodi in 1969, and Iten (1979 and cf., Iten 1977), a decade later, found no more. This will probably not increase much, and even the few young men who might, in groups of two or three, travel north to thresh or harvest grain for ten days or so at the nearest Arab farms or schemes, are now doing so less frequently as a consequence of tourist money now available for exposing their bodies in decoration (another form of wage labour - see below).

The events of the past decade have, however, inaugurated an even more sinister series of experiments in local commodity production which are really at the heart of concern here. Nuba farmers, except for the few noted, have realised that taking up tenancy in a Government scheme away from home to grow cotton for sale at the current Nuba Mountain Agriculture Corporation price is uneconomic (cf. Saeed 1982 and this volume), given the prices of grain they must purchase as a result. What has happened with increasing frequency and evermore problematic consequences is that local agriculturalists, lured by the ever-greater demand for grain at ever-greater prices (as a consequence of declining national production for consumption, if nothing else), are now beginning to plant in excess of the capacity of the traditional production organisation to cope.

Grain sale, as noted, was never a planning strategy in production traditionally. People planted for a certain amount of insurance, hopefully to harvest a small surplus which could always be turned to beer with the abundant opportunities to host rituals and celebrations when such beer is available. Access to means of production was by kin group membership, land was abundant and essentially unlimited, and both males and females undertook such work. Organisation of production in the various tasks was by reciprocal work groups based on age or kinship, or even mutual assistance in bride- service requirements by a group of betrothed. When individuals take decisions to plant in order to harvest surpluses for sale, compromises occur in all directions. Traditional rights to usufruct are put into dispute, for though land is not limited, the best land is near water sources. This means that individuals who plant to sell must exploit more marginal land at greater distances from water sources. This has many ramifications - and in 1980, there were still individuals harvesting such commodity grain in late March and April, at least two months late. This is well into the dry season, and water is no longer available except at great distances. These individuals were paying £S5 for a drum of water delivered to them by merchant truck. Money came from the sale of all remaining animals, and for some, the efforts were abandoned entirely; for others, they yielded to the merchant-dictated buying price for grain at harvest in order to secure the money necessary for water to finish the harvest.

But it was not simply a case of land at greater distances from water sources - the lateness of harvest was a function of the breakdown of traditional labour recruitment mechanisms in the form of reciprocal work parties for harvest, weeding, threshing and other labour-consuming tasks. It also resulted in the attempt by a few of these individuals to hire locals in wage labour forms. The few young men who each year go north to sell their labour were ostensibly available, but local Nuba farmers had neither the existing cash nor credit access to effect very much of this sort of labour hire. However, where it was possible for a few wealthier farmers, the beginnings of at least some of the class implications of this were clear. There were also gender implications: whereas classically women often planted in their own right and secured labour help through the traditional reciprocal work-party means, only men were engaged in this expanded production - which, if the class implications develop, imply even greater sexism in social relations of production (see also O'Brien 1980 for similar implications elsewhere in Sudan). While such capitalist social relations are not the origins of local sexism, certainly such problems are compounded in this circumstance.

This was not happening to many individuals, but it was happening. I have data on eight such individuals, some of whom felt that the problems were merely logistic and the practice had a future, others of whom argued that this ended their failed experiment in the commodity production of grain. It should be emphasised that a decision to plant grain for market is not simply taken without some planning. In the first place, it requires securing and clearing extra land. Secondly, it requires certain types of seeds - those most resistant to early deterioration, those easiest to thresh, most resistant to bird damage (as the grain would remain longer in the fields), those with greatest bulk to winnowed product yield, and a series of other decisions which are not so constrained when the grain need not sit in the fields so long. Former decisions, such as the best beer grain, the best porridge grain, etc., no longer come into play as when producers planned for specific use.[5]

From my limited more recent queries, there is no question that perceived market price is the prime motivation to produce a commodity grain, to produce for exchange. Unfortunately, this is often a motivation based on the selling price for grain at a time of scarcity (when planning for planting is taken), when demand drives the price in the closest Jellaba markets to extremes. After harvest, when supplies are great, prices for grain are, of course, very much lower. Southeast Nuba farmers are not unaware of these fluctuations, but they are naive in marketing security and subject to Government propaganda about price supports and credit regulations, and to Jellaba promises of post-harvest prices for grain.

This indigenous cropping of grain for market is the most significant commodity shift in the area. As noted, each year a few individuals are lured to participate in cotton production or to work for wages in the mechanised schemes; it is usually different people each year, and the total number involved each year did not grow between 1966 and 1980. There are, of course, wholesale migrations of young men (and occasional young women) out of the community today to permanent wage labour in the towns of Kordofan or even Khartoum. And there are also a few local cash opportunites as merchant helpers note that the area has opened up.

The most significant labour-time commodity shift (until war in the South discouraged it) was to be seen in the appearance of exotic modelling. Since at least 1974 European tourists rushing to capture the "vanishing" African "experience" of earlier visitors to the area, such as Leni Riefenstahl (cf. Riefenstahl 1976), had offered cash to Southeast Nuba for modelling exotic body decorations. This caused considerable local unrest, as non-decorating Nuba and local Arabs resented this intrusion (for details of such debate, see Faris 1976, 1980, in press, forthcoming; DeVillez, 1982; Usama, 1982; Loizos, 1982; Ryle, 1982). Moreover, the flamboyant personal art tradition of the young Southeast Nuba had been compromised, as young men were seen to decorate by the hour, using only design forms that can be infinitely expanded so to lengthen the time spent before the cameras. Appropriate design forms and rules of proper use have thus been violated. This was detailed in a BBC-TV documentary in 1982. Other social dislocations could result, as with all wage labour. For example, some young men insist on purchasing cattle with their new cash to give to the parents of their betrothed rather than undertaking the traditional brideservice requirements which a girl's parents had counted on, and which formed an important part of the traditional labour recruitment system. Cattle do not weed, thresh, build huts, or bring gifts; cattle die, get absorbed by fines imposed in local courts, or are commandeered by local state representatives (omda, shaykh) for <u>karama</u> on the visits of dignitaries, or are quickly converted to cash (at times not to the advantage of the owner) for perceived market necessities.

Let me be clear about Southeast Nuba producers and commodity production. Government schemes, of the mechanised sort, for either cotton or grain, have not drawn significant numbers of local cultivators as tenants, and they have been only slightly more successful (except for recent wage labour interference by European tourists before the recent war) in seasonally drawing young men into temporary wage labour. Even here, however, the arrangement is precarious, and should not be the basis of labour planning by authorities (unless, of course, local producers are forced off their lands). If local producers do not feel the need to migrate seasonally, the nearest schemes are simply without help, or without help from this source.

But this is not to suggest complete cynicism for commodity production in grain, for there may well be room for considerable expansion of production locally for the consumption of Sudanese elsewhere. From my point of view this might best be achieved if the State involved itself minimally in actual production - that is, to avoid advice in various appropriate technology schemes (traction innovations, Chinese ploughs, etc.) - but to secure better drinking water arrangements, secure reliable marketing arrangements, and the like. This would help "lengthen" the season at far farm sites (that is, water would be available so that people might harvest and process grain much later in the year than usual), and insure that grain so produced was paid for by something other than usual mercantile opportunism (from shayl to robbery). Thus, I am not arguing against production for exchange, nor some inordinate return to producers at the expense of consumers, but simply for an efficient way of letting producers do what they do best - produce in the circumstances they have worked out. As I see it this is the only way to minimise the potential destructiveness of commodity production. In such manner, local divisions of labour and relations of production might be preserved, even to the involvement of mutual work parties of all those who chose to expand production. The Government's role ought to be to stabilise and guarantee the price, the marketing, the exchange itself.

The consequence might be significant (particularly if combined with a ban on European tourism): grain surpluses with minor infrastructure expense, rural repopulation (as the Southeast Nuba region still has abundant good land), and stable productive communities with acceptable relations of production (in that both women and men produce on their own, by choice). And such strategies must be free of big planning - of the predatory schemes so characteristic thus far of commodity production in Sudan. This avoids turning producers into wage labourers, preventing - in the Southeast Nuba nomenclature with which we began this short essay - producers from becoming slaves.

Notes

1. Research first began in 1966, was most intense from that time until 1969, and has been intermittant until a last six-week visit in 1980. As always, it only proceeded with the help of many persons - of the University of Khartoum, of various Ministries of the Government, and with the firm generosity of local people everywhere.

2. This definition differs somewhat from the orthodox notion of commodity production as that production for exchange (rather than use). It is my view that the use/exchange distinction is, for the social forms discussed here, problematic, so I have focussed on the exterior demands as a definitional condition of the concept commodity production.

3. The means of production of such commodities were usually widely available (or at least, in most cases, randomly available). Dom palm litters the area, and gum trees of the best quality are not cultivated, but are found in the forest - where gum is free to the person who taps the tree each year, usually nearest his/her far farm field. There are some traditional rights to a portion of some gathered materials - specific priesthoods in control of such phenomena.

4. One of the few traditional means by which grain was traded was in exchange with West African herders (Takari) who, if they are this far east (the Southeast Nuba are only some 45 kilometers from the White Nile), are usually desperate for grain. And, late in the season, this means they will undoubtedly lose cattle in travelling west again during the rains. They are thus usually willing to trade a heifer for a midd or so of grain. This is a peculiar example, but nevertheless a circumstance local Nuba took full advantage of, for even if the cattle died (no local Arabs would buy or trade in Takari cattle, as they are known to be weak and diseased at this latitude), they were a source of meat.

5. Indeed, I found in such planning for local use, a developed selection that discriminated some 27 categories about a single species of grain - certain decisions involving, I later learned, selection about a single gene locus. And international advisers think they can teach local producers how to cultivate grain! Most of these selection decisions were, of course, functional to a variety of demands - all relevant to production for use in very great detail.

References

BBC-TV (1982), 'Southeast Nuba', ethnographic documentary film, British Broadcasting Corporation, Bristol.

DeVillez, P. (1982), 'Qualifying for a Permit', Sudanow 7 (3), pp. 35-6.

Faris, J. (1972), 'Southeastern Nuba Age Organization', in I. Cunnison and W. James (eds.), Essays in Sudan Ethnography, Hurst, London.

--- (1976), 'Fascism and Photography', Newsweek, 88 (24), p. 4.

--- (1980), 'Polluted Vision', Sudanow, 5 (5), p. 38.

--- (in press), 'The Significance of Differences in the Male and Female Personal Art of the Southeast Nuba', in A. Rubin (ed.), Art of the Body, University of California Press, UCLA Museum of Cultural History, Los Angeles.

--- (forthcoming), 'Southeast Nuba: A Biographical Statement', in J. Rollwagon (ed.), Anthropological Filmmaking.

Iten, O. (1977), 'Bilder and Zerrbilder der Nuba', Tages Anzeiger, 50 (17), pp. 6-11.

--- (1979), Economic Pressures on Traditional Society: A Case Study of the Southeastern Nuba Economy in the Modern Sudan, European University Studies, Social Economics No. 8, Peter Lang, Berne.

James, W. (1971), 'Social Assimilation and Changing Identity in the Southern Funj', in Y. F. Hasan (ed.), Sudan in Africa, University of Khartoum, Khartoum.

Loizos, P. (1982), 'Review of Southeast Nuba', Royal Anthropological Institute Newsletter, 52 (10).

Manger, L. (1984), Trade and Traders in the Sudan, University of Bergen Occasional Papers in Social Anthropology, 32, Bergen.

O'Brien, J. (1980), Agricultural Labor and Development in Sudan, PhD. University of Connecticut.

Reifenstahl, L. (1976), The People of Kau, Harper and Row, New York.

Ryle, J. (1982), 'Invasion of the Body Snatchers', New Society, 549.

Saeed, Abdel Basit (1982), The State and Socioeconomic Transformation in the Sudan: The Case of Social Conflict in Southeast Kurdufan, PhD., University of Connecticut.

Schadeberg, T. (1981), A Survey of Kordofanian: The Heiban Group, Volume 1, Sprache und Geschichte in Afrika, Beiheft 1, H. Buske, Hamburg.

Spaulding, J. (1980), 'Toward a Demystification of the Funj: Some Perspectives on Society in Southern Sinnar', Northeast African Studies, 2 (1), pp. 1-18.

--- (1984), 'The Management of Exchange in Sinnar, c. 1700', in L.O. Manger (ed.), Trade and Traders in the Sudan, University of Bergen Occasional Papers in Social Anthropology 32, Bergen.

Usama Ibrahim (1982), 'The Children of Kau', Sudanow, 7 (3), p. 49.

10 A strategy for the transformation of the pre-capitalist part of Sudanese society[1]

IBRAHIM KURSANY

The elapse of more than a quarter of a century since the political independence of Sudan has produced no radical improvement in either its social or economic structure. To the contrary, the general living standard of the mass of people has actually deteriorated. The state has failed to provide the basic services which are essential ingredients of any dignified human life, such as housing, clothing, food, education, drinking water and medical services for the working mass of people. This is so because the post-colonial state has been following a capitalist path of development whose success depends on two major factors: (a) a solid basis for free competition, and (b) a capitalist class which is able and willing to invest in the country. Both of these factors were non-existent in Sudan.

Capitalist development in the underdeveloped countries of today mostly starts from a leading sector enjoying a monopolistic position - like that of mechanised farming in Sudan - in both industry and agriculture. The strategy adopted by most underdeveloped capitalist countries in their post-independence period usually calls for heavily protectionist policies on the part of the state. This in the case of Sudan has led to the increase in the cost of production, the deterioration in the quality, and the selection of products which suit the needs of the small elites.

The absence of both political and economic democracy in the under-developed capitalist countries gave birth to the parasitic capitalist class which depends on the bureaucratic apparatus of the state for increasing its income and rate of capital accumulation. Corruption and blackmarketeering replace productive investment as the major sources of income.

Due to political and economic instability, this class usually avoids investment in the productive base of the economy, which is a long-term and risky proposition, and leans instead towards directing its investible surplus to 'quick' profiting projects like residential buildings. This class tends to transfer most of its economic surplus to the places where it thinks political and economic stability are well maintained, mostly to the advanced capitalist countries, where their partners - the owners of big multinational companies - live and invest, and upon whom they depend for their technology and hard currency. This is why this class constitutes a comprador class. It is the 'mastermind' behind all the malpractices which lead to the political repression and economic impoverishment of the working mass of people.

This picture must not blind us to the other face of the coin, namely the existence of another section of the Sudanese capitalist class who generated their income and capital from investment in the productive sectors of the economy during the era of liberal democracy between 1964 and 1969 and have continued to do so till the present moment. This section of the Sudanese capitalist class has genuine interests in investing its economic surplus in the productive sectors of the Sudanese economy and has no intention of either emulating the life-style of the capitalist class of the advanced countries or spending most of its money and time outside Sudan. The interests of this section are, to a great extent, in direct contradiction with the interests of the parasitic comprador capitalist class as well as the interests of foreign monopoly capital.

This is why I think it will be a serious mistake to formulate a development strategy for Sudan which is built on a wrong and misleading conclusion, as Mahmoud does when she claims that all of the Sudanese capitalist class is a comprador class (Mahmoud 1984). In making this claim, Mahmoud has failed clearly to recognise the differences which do exist between the different fractions of the Sudanese capitalist class. Instead of correctly rejecting the capitalist path which has failed to generate rapid economic as well as social development, Mahmoud has rejected the Sudanese capitalist class altogether and denied them any role to play in the socio-economic development of the country at this stage.

The failure of the capitalist path in generating the desired level of economic and social development is not something peculiar to Sudan because:

> since the Second World War no country has attained development, in the all-embracing sense of overcoming mass poverty, illiteracy and rampant disease, through a capitalist strategy (Malima 1978, pp. 45-51).

What is needed in the context of Sudan is a development strategy which will transcend the capitalist one - a strategy capable of mobilising all the natural, financial and human resources, including those of the 'national' bourgeoisie, and commit them to the development of the country at large. The envisaged development strategy is different from the capitalist one because it does not give the leading role of the development process to the existing parasitic capitalist class. The state sector and the nationalised public sector at large should play the leading role in this process. The major objective of this process would be to increase the rate of accumulation of productive assets, which may be regarded as the lever of economic development, and the rational utilisation and sectoral allocation, irrespective of its absolute or relative magnitude.

This increase in the rate of accumulation coupled with its rational utilisation for the economic and social development of Sudan is unattainable without a sustained move in the direction of comprehensive scientific planning. Since the concept of comprehensive scientific planning differs from that of capitalist programming and planning, it must be based on an alternative development strategy to that of capitalism. This strategy is a national democratic one. In order not to be used merely as an ideological weapon in the hands of the conservative classes of Sudanese society for blackmailing the working mass of people, as has been the Sudanese experience so far, a national democratic strategy must be a concrete plan of action for the liquidation of the phenomenon of underdevelopment. The only guarantee for the successful realisation of this objective is the progressive class nature of the state. The new state must have as its leading force the broad alliance of the workers and peasants of the Sudan who constitute 90 per cent of the total population. This characteristic would represent the most democratic state possible in a Sudanese context.

This state must take as its strategic goal the movement towards the industrialisation of Sudan. The building up of a heavy industrial sector, that which produces the means of production and the intermediate goods (Department I in Marx's schema), should be its objective. History has shown us few countries, capitalist or socialist, which have achieved an advanced level of development without developing their industrial base, especially heavy industry. To do so, the maximum effort should be devoted to the mobilisation of all the national resources for further accumulation, the most crucial factor in the process of development. This accumulation must be put under utmost rational utilisation to serve the interest of the whole people through comprehensive plans.

Most of the utilised and under-utilised national resources which need mobilisation lie initially within the agricultural sector. Even in this sector, the national resources lie to a large extent within its precapitalist part. This is why I consider any talk about the industrialisation of Sudan without reference to its agricultural potential as wishful thinking. As industrialisation proceeds, the surplus product of the industrialised sector becomes the source for accumulation. Therefore, the reorganisation of the

Sudanese agricultural sector, especially its precapitalist part, along new lines, is an imperative and necessary condition for the industrialisation of the country.

A Proposed Strategy for the Transformation of the Precapitalist Part of Sudanese Society

A first step in this process of transformation will be the changing of the negative attitude and the wrong interpretation by the Sudanese planners about petty commodity producers. This attitude and understanding can best be demonstrated from the statements of A.R. Mirghani, the Under Secretary of the Ministry of Finance and Economics, which was responsible for planning, at the inception of the Ten Year Plan in the early 1960s. He adopted the following position and understanding towards the 'traditional farmers' of the precapitalist sector:

1) The 'subsistence farmer' is very conservative. He and his family live so close to subsistence level that they cannot afford to experiment with new crops or new farming practices.

2) It is the social value of goods and services that is important to him and not their economic value. There is often a high preference for leisure and also propensity to save.

3) Because the individual farmer often places a premium on social conformity, it is difficult to change his individual values without changing the values of the group. In many high income countries as recently as fifty years ago, simple change in agricultural techniques, such as use of fertilisers, contour ploughing or new rotation cropping patterns were often ridiculed by neighbouring farmers.

4) Through trial and error, 'subsistence farmers' have often worked out a harmony with their environment which is acceptable to them and their tribe or village and therefore the individual sees no advantage to change (Mirghani 1966, pp. 99-100)

This interpretation shows the wrong approach adopted by the Sudanese planners towards the 'traditional' peasants, namely that in order to develop the precapitalist sector one must change the individual peasant himself so as to manipulate and change his social position.

This attitude of the Sudanese planners towards the petty-commodity producers, if it is put in philosophical terms, implies that people's consciousness determines their social existence. It follows therefore that if you want to change the social relations between people, you have to start by changing their consciousness in the first place. This I consider to be the major philosophical weakness underlying bourgeois economic analyses which governed the formulation of all the development plans in the history of Sudan and their failure to acknowledge the problems facing the inhabitants of the precapitalist sector. It leads most senior planners, like

Mirghani, to a stage of desperation whereby they complain that:

> Because lack of knowledge, lack of capital, desire for social conformity, and low living standard are all interrelated, it is difficult for governments to know where or how to attack this problem, or how to make its assistance effective (Mirghani 1966, p. 100).

This statement represents the acute conceptual confusion of the Sudanese bourgeois economists and planners. They should be reminded in the words of Marx that:

> It is not the consciousness of men that determines their social being, but, on the contrary, their social being that determines their consciousness (1955, p. 362).

Accordingly, the process of transformation in the precapitalist part of the Sudanese society must take as its starting point the transformation and development of the productive forces and the production relations as a necessary precondition for the development of the peasant himself, and not the other way round as our planners appear to think. This is so because:

> Peasant farmers, though often illiterate, are usually numerate and are commonly neither stupid nor conservative, their apparent reluctance to adopt innovations is oftendue to their being better judges of the risks than their official advisers (ILO 1976, p. 36).

In view of this, a necessary condition for any successful attempt at formulation and implementation of a development strategy for the transformation of the precapitalist sector is the re-education of the 'educated' Sudanese official advisers to change their negative attitudes towards petty commodity producers and their problems.

An Interim Strategy

The following measures are imperative and must be adopted promptly in order to curb the horizontal extension of mechanised rainfed farming, under its present domination by private capital, into the areas now belonging to the precapitalist sector of Sudanese society:

1) Economic, social and political policies must be carried out so as to regulate rainfed mechanised farming in the areas which belong to the precapitalist sector in such a way that the public and the co-operative sectors should play the leading role in the development process. Private capital should be given a subsidiary role, though very important, within the framework and objectives of the national development plan.

2) Foreign investment - both private and governmental - must be persuaded towards investing in the areas belonging to the precapitalist sector, through the adoption of the rational policies, incentives, concessions and acts which will be designed by the Sudanese State with the prime objective of serving the

Sudanese people.

3) In order to eliminate the antagonism between cultivation and the other uses of land, such as pasture, forest and game, and to resolve the problems which arise out of this, a detailed and comprehensive survey of Sudan's natural resources is badly needed for the determination of the type of projects which are most capable of accelerating the development of the different sectors and regions of the country.

The interim strategy outlined above is capable of preventing any further decay of the precapitalist sector, and of conserving its natural as well as human resources. But the mere stoppage of this process is not sufficient to put this sector on the path of self-generating and self-perpetuating development. This interim strategy is necessary just to halt further deterioration in the agricultural sector. But in order to improve the situation there, some short and long-term strategies related to both precapitalist and capitalist sections must form the basis of the development plan directed towards them. The short and long-term strategies are based on principles of co-ordination and subordination. We must determine what are the essential and less essential targets, by relating the necessary measures to be adopted to the economic base - i.e. production (e.g. property ownership), exchange (e.g. prices) and distribution (e.g. tax subsidies, credit) relations - or to the superstructure (e.g. education) of Sudanese society. The measures relating to the economic base form the primary basis and those related to the superstructure the secondary basis of our development strategy. Within the primary category, those measures which are related to the production relations are considered as prior to those related to the productive forces because the former constitute the basis for the development of the latter.

A Short-term Strategy

The short-term strategy is directed primarily towards the eradication of the exploitative social relations which exist in the precapitalist sector. The first step towards changing these relations is related to land reform. A scientific programme for agrarian reform, based on the survey of natural resources and the land tenure system, should be designed and implemented in order to improve and develop both productive forces and production relations. The ultimate objective is to liberate and mobilise the unutilised and underutilised energies of the seventy five per cent of the labour force which toils in that sector. This should be done by eliminating the institution of Native Administration - the major exploitative institution originally designed by the British as a form of indirect rule in the countryside. The objective is not just the elimination of its administrative role, which was carried out in 1970, but the liquidation of its economic as well as social strongholds which form the basis of its administrative and political domination. It also plays a major role in the subordination of this sector to the interests of both domestic and foreign capital. The major step which will be adopted is the nationalisation of land and animal wealth and their redistribution to the poor peasants.

Another major measure related to the first is the elimination of the other exploitative institution known as the 'shayl system'. It is a system through which the poor peasant mortgages his product in advance of harvest to merchants who resell it at up to 300 per cent of its original price. Of course the first measure will help in the execution of this one because some of the village shops are owned by Native Administrators. Therefore, the first measure is just a necessary condition for the success of the abolition of shayl. The sufficient condition is the provision of credit. The state must provide agricultural credit to the poor peasants. This is important especially in the knowledge that the shayl system mostly develops with the development of capitalism in the agrarian sector. Therefore, a well-adapted credit policy will alleviate the possibility of the poor peasants resorting to the rich peasants and merchants for their financial requirements. This will also halt the flourishing of usury capital by removing the objective factors which condition its rise and development. It requires radical change in the policies of the banking sector and especially of the Agricultural Bank of Sudan so as to serve the interests of the poor peasants. This demands the fulfilment of two conditions. The first is related to either the abolition or reduction of the high value of security demanded by the banks for the provision of their credits - something which could not be afforded by the poor peasants. The second is the mobility of banks so as to reach the poor peasants in their villages. The demand for a relatively luxurious building to accommodate the staff must be abandoned and replaced by mobile units which will cover the whole countryside and make the credit facilities accessible to the whole farming community.

The state must also take the responsibility of marketing the products, fixing the prices and determining the profit rate for the peasants through the formation of specialised state corporations so as to reduce and gradually eliminate the role of the 'Jellaba' who play the role of middlemen and monopolise almost all mercantile activities.

The petty-commodity producers' prime objective is to satisfy their immediate consumption needs. The desirable trend towards commodity production must be consolidated through various means. The most important of these is the role played by the state in the field of distribution. The state should sell to the poor peasants the manufactured articles for their daily consumption and buy their agricultural and animal products. This will help improve the situation in the precapitalist sector on two levels. Firstly, it will reduce the role of the Jellaba in the retailing process, hence getting hold of some of the economic surplus which is appropriated by them, and use it for more productive purposes by the state for the development of the precapitalist sector. Secondly, getting hold of the retailing process will reduce the racial tension which stems from the fact that most of the Jellaba in the precapitalist sector originate mainly from Arab ancestry.

The successful implementation of the above measure is unlikely to be realised without the design of appropriate organisations to carry them out. The most important of these bodies are the producers' co-operative societies. Co-operatives must be formed so as to help the poor peasants increase their productivity and their marketable surplus. The past experience of the co-operative movement in Sudan has shown that co-operatives have tended to serve the interests of the rich peasants. Since the content of this particular sphere of production was subordinated to the dominant mode of production in Sudan as a whole, this is hardly surprising. Under the envisaged national democratic strategy, the co-operative movement must serve as a means of socialising small-scale production and services. It must act as a catalyst whereby the precapitalist sector can be integrated into the national economy. Therefore the present content of co-operatives, which resembles that of a private company rather than a co-operative society, must be altered. This could be achieved through confining the membership to the local residents who are living from the tilling of the land. By doing this, the co-operative movement, instead of being a source for private capital accumulation, would become a vehicle for collective accumulation and contribute to the development of the national economy. But, as was pointed out by O. Lange, the transformation of co-operative ownership into the sector of collective ownership requires the inclusion of the co-operatives in the planned economy and the implementation by the co-operatives of the general political and economic tasks laid down by the national democratic state. Without the fulfilment of this condition co-operatives have no progressive content (Lange 1970, p. 445).

In order for the co-operative movement to be effective, it must be democratic in its structure. That is to say, all the executive bodies must be elected by the peasants. One way of accelerating the democratisation process of the co-operatives is the formation of a representative body for the peasants. The state must help in the formation of a farmers' general union. This body should be democratically elected from among the peasants themselves and not from outsiders, especially the elite group. The peasants' union should be respected by the local authorities and must be represented in all the policy-making bodies and the organisations responsible for the implementation of this strategy. To perfect the democratic process which is necessary for the successful implementation of this strategy, those who are elected to leading positions should be liable to removal if a vote of no confidence is passed on them by the electorate. In this manner the election and removal of local leaders will depend only on the judgement of the local inhabitants without interference from any outside bodies.

The implementation of the above measures will transform the backward and exploitative relations which exist in the agricultural sector and pave the way for the development of the productive forces in that sector. In order to accelerate the process of developing the productive forces certain additional measures should be adopted.

The state must play the leading role in rainfed mechanised farming through the formation and running of public sector schemes. The system of shifting cultivation, on a large-scale basis, as practiced in rainfed capitalist schemes should be abandoned. Mechanised schemes in the public and private sectors should follow a scientific crop rotation which is efficient in increasing the productivity of land and keeping high its fertility level. Not just that, but in order to maintain this fertility level, the state should sell fertilisers to the poor peasants. The state should also sell, through the co-operatives, the necessary and scientific crop protection methods, such as insecticides, which will improve the quality and increase the volume of their agricultural produce.

The peasants of the Nuba Mountains, although dependent on agriculture for their livelihood, do possess a large amount of animal wealth. Care must be given to livestock so as to increase its contribution to the peasants' income. This could be achieved through two measures. Firstly, the state must give the necessary veterinary services and, secondly, fodder must be introduced in the agricultural rotation in both the public and private farms so as to provide the animals with the necessary food lost due to the construction of the mechanised schemes in place of natural pastures.

Of course the implementation of the above strategy depends largely on the volume of labour power available to the peasant. The major source of labour is the family of the peasant himself, therefore a good health standard of the poor peasant and that of his family is a necessary condition for improving the quality of labour power. The state must provide him with the necessary ingredients of medical services, specially preventive medicines. This strategy would restore social justice in the rural areas, improve the quality of life for both people and their animals, and would form a sound basis for the long-term strategy which would absorb this sector, on a permanent basis, in the development process.

A Long-term Strategy

The construction of mechanised schemes in the Nuba Mountains interrupted the traditional routes of the nomadic tribes of Western Sudan. Livestock production constitutes the mode of life for the nomadic population. Therefore, in order to guarantee a good quality of life for them, nomadic tribes must be settled. The necessary measures which will encourage and help the nomads to settle include digging out the maximum number of wells so as to provide them with drinking water. These wells must be distributed in such a way that they should be developed as production and settlement centres providing drinking water, cultivation, especially of fodder, natural pastures which will be provided with scientific means of maintenance, and warehouses.

Change which is imposed on peasants will face fierce resistance. The conviction and consent of the peasant to the change are necessary for the implementation of the strategy. Therefore, the strategy and change must be in the interest of the peasants so as to persuade them to co-operate. To achieve this, demonstration of the better alternatives must be one of the methods used in that process. Successful alternatives depend on scientific research, which should be encouraged so as to provide the peasants with the alternative mode of life best suited to their social and economic conditions. Also, scientific research should be directed towards finding improved seeds and the most rational and efficient methods of cultivation which will revolutionise the productive forces of agriculture.

In order for scientific research to be of much benefit, its results must be diffused to peasants through a well organised and developed system of extension services. Extension officers should be carefully selected and trained. They should be of great calibre in respecting the mode of life of the petty commodity producers. In order to be of benefit to the poor peasants, they must refrain from any practice which might provoke or irritate them. The maintenance of mutual respect between the poor peasant and the extension officer is of great importance to the successful implementation of his rather delicate objective.

The implementation of the results of scientific research requires a minimum degree of education for the peasants. This minimum degree constitutes the eradication of illiteracy among the poor peasants which is imperative for the grasping of advanced and scientific agricultural knowledge. The elimination of illiteracy and the provision of education for the sons and daughters of the poor peasants should be regarded as one of the noblest objectives of the national democratic state.

The eradication of illiteracy would also help in eliminating the backward social and tribal institutions, traditions and values which stand as barriers to the development of this sector and would help prevent the wastage of an already meagre economic surplus. Among these traditions are the high cost of wedding, circumcision and funeral ceremonies. The change of these conservative traditions could be achieved through educating the people, providing them with the experiences of others and increasing and promoting their consumption levels so as to induce them to market more of their products.

The whole agricultural sector in Western Sudan is facing a serious ecological problem. The construction of mechanised rainfed farms involved the cutting down of millions of trees, accelerated desert creep towards the most fertile lands of Sudan. Desert encroachment should be stopped and reversed through avoiding the cutting of trees on this large scale. Desert creep also affects water sources. The provision of quantitatively and qualitatively good supplies of drinking water for both animals and humans on a permanent basis is crucial for the development process in the whole area.

The reorganisation of agricultural production on these lines will form the basis for the construction and development of light industries which will utilise the local raw materials, such as meat, milk and hides. The construction of these industries and their success depends largely on efficient and well-connected transport and communication facilities. These systems should be constructed so as to facilitate the movement of people and animals and the flow of the technical knowledge which will help in improving their lives.

Finally, two independent, but interrelated problems must be solved so as to realise the full potential of the agricultural sector.

The first involves reducing the level of fluctuation in the food supplies for the poor peasants resulting from the seasonality of agricultural production in order to guarantee stable sources of good quality grains. To achieve this, the state should build the necessary efficient warehouse facilities. The second problem results from the fact that agricultural production in the Nuba Mountains depends entirely on highly variable rainfall and climatic conditions. In order to reduce the heavy dependence of agricultural production on the fluctuations of a marginal climate the state should conduct research aimed at finding alternative permanent sources for the irrigation of agriculture.

If these strategies are implemented successfully, they ought to improve the quality of life of the poor peasants and raise their standard of living. A considerable amount of economic surplus will be generated and rationally allocated for the integrated development of the national economy as a whole. In fact, in real life, there is no mechanistic separation between the two strategies. Both of them reinforce each other.

An Epilogue

The implementation of the above outlined strategy should succeed in transforming, gradually but effectively, the precapitalist part of Sudanese society, and would lead ultimately to its positive incorporation in the development process of the country at large. But to help in building an independent, integrated, self-sustaining and self-perpetuating economy on the national level, these measures must be accompanied by, and their success largely depends upon the following three factors:

1) In order to make full use of the resources which will be released due to the development of the agricultural sector and rationally utilise them, industry must develop alongside agriculture so as to absorb these resources.

2) So as to be able to develop both industry and agriculture, the state must resort to comprehensive planning techniques and the leading role in the implementation of this plan should be assigned to the public and co-operative sectors, with the private sector playing a subsidiary but important role. In order to do so, the state must control the necessary means of production. Therefore, the nationalisation of key sectors of the economy seems to be indispensable for the implementation of the above strategy. The elimination of the malpractices of the parasitic petty bourgeois class, which is supported by the bureaucracy of the capitalist state, will enhance the process of the socialisation of the means of production and the development of the country.

3) The state apparatus which will be responsible for the implementation of the above strategy must be democratic and progressive in its class nature. By democratic I mean the provision of the basic democratic rights to the working people of Sudan, including the right of free speech, free association, free assembly, free trade unions, free press, formation of political

parties and the right to strike. All the state legislative and executive bodies must be freely elected. The choices of the electorate should be respected by the different state bodies. This will be assured only if the electorate has the right not just of electing its leaders but removing them from office as well in the event of corruption, inefficiency or betrayal. This mechanism is the only one, in the context of Sudan, which will form a built-in system of checks and balances to safeguard the interests of the poor working mass of people, release and develop the creative abilities of the Sudanese people and prevent the development of any bureaucratic tendencies within the state machinery. To be progressive, the state must be secular. That is to say, the Sudanese state should be based on a non-religious constitution and must respect all the religious and ideological beliefs of its citizens, irrespective of their race or geographical location. This democratic and progressive state apparatus, in order to be effective in carrying out the national democratic strategy, must be based on the broad alliance of the workers and peasants of Sudan and upon their positive participation in all the economic decision making and executing bodies. This is so because the real choice which is facing the Sudanese people is no longer between national democratic development and capitalist development, but rather between national democratic development - which forms the basis for the transition to socialism - and capitalist underdevelopment.

Note

1. The author wishes to thank Ron Bellamy and W. Davies of the School of Economic Studies at Leeds University for their invaluable comments on the ideas presented in this paper.

References

ILO (International Labour Office) (1976), Growth, Employment and Equity: A Comprehensive Strategy for the Sudan, ILO, Geneva.

Lange, O. (1970) Papers in Economics and Sociology, Pan'stowowe Wydawnitctwo Naukowe.

Mahmoud, Fatima Babiker (1984) The Sudanese Bourgeoisie, Zed Press and Khartoum University Press, London and Khartoum.

Malima, K. A. (1978) 'Overcoming underdevelopment', World Marxist Review, (May), pp. 45-51.

Marx, Karl (1955) Preface to A Contribution to a Critique of Political Economy, in Marx and Engels, Selected Works, Foreign Languages Publishing House, Moscow.

Mirghani, A.R. (1966) 'Problems of increasing productivity in the traditional sector', in D.J. Shaw (ed.), Agricultural Development in the Sudan, Vol. 2, Philosophical Society of Sudan, Khartoum.

11 The structure and operation of urban wage–labour markets and the trade unions

SALAH AL-DIN AL-SHAZALI

Studies of urban labour markets in Sudan are relatively few and focus almost exclusively on the situation in Greater Khartoum. With the exception of a handful of relatively early pioneering studies (Fawzi 1954, 1957; McLoughlin 1965, 1970; Suliman 1974), the main body of literature has appeared since 1976, and following the arrival in Sudan of the ILO/UNDP Employment Mission which, upon an official request, sought to formulate a comprehensive development strategy for the country. In undertaking its task, the Mission organised a series of research projects to obtain information on the various aspects of the Sudanese economy. One of these projects dealt with urban labour markets. The larger part of the literature has thus emerged either as findings of research financed and/or conducted by the Mission (e.g. ILO 1976; Kannappan 1977a; Mustafa 1976; Mustafa & Affan 1977; Affan 1977), or as a critique of the Mission's conception and recommendations (e.g. Chase 1977; Galal-al-Din 1978, 1979a, 1980).

With the notable exception of the inspiring, albeit brief critique by Chase (1977), however, these contributions pose serious constraints on our understanding of the structure and operation of urban labour markets. These limitations, I believe, are underlain by flaws inherent in the basic conceptual framework shared by both the ILO studies in Sudan (in which the basic conception is elaborated) and the contributions purporting to criticise them. In this respect, one is tempted to assert that the 'mass of data', which the ILO Mission has gathered, has been fed into the strait-jacket of the ('formal-informal') dualist concept of labour markets in third world cities popularised by the ILO Mission to Kenya (1972), and which has subsequently been incorporated, with minor modifications, into the analysis of country and city studies organised by the ILO as part of its World Employment Programme (cf. Bromley 1979; Moser 1978a). The result in Sudan has been a set of 'theoretical' formulations that are in direct conflict with the 'facts' described in muted terms in the same work.

The dualistic conception of the ILO-studies is based on a distinction between 'formal' and 'informal' segments of the urban labour market. The ILO Mission informs us that:

> Urban labour markets (in the Sudan) differ for the formal and informal sectors. The former ... is characterised by large scale operation, a high degree of capital intensity, relatively high levels of remuneration, and a degree of legislative protection relating to hours of work, working conditions, minimum wages, overtime rates, bargaining and grievance procedures, and compensation and pension schemes; in other words, employment in this sector is similar to that found in the urban centres of industrialised countries. By contrast, the informal sector is characterised by small-scale operation, a primitive level of technology, a relatively low level of earned income, high dependency on family labour, and few regulatory measures of any kind... (ILO 1976, p. 109).

In the so-called 'formal' segment of the labour market, we are told, the employers comprise government departments, public concerns and large-scale private enterprises. Basing itself on the returns of the National Population Census of 1973, the Mission estimates 'formal' employment in Greater Khartoum at under 30 per cent of the Khartoum urban labour force. This percentage, it should be noted, represents 'formal' employment of civil servants, white-collar workers as well as blue-collar workers.

As far as the 'formal' wage labour market is concerned, the ILO studies note that it is far from 'perfect'. Thus neither productivity considerations, nor the forces of supply and demand seem to play prominent roles in the determination of the relatively high wages. "Pressure by trade unions" is said to be the crucial determinant (cf. ibid; Affan 1977, p. 62ff). The underlying assumption here is that establishments in the 'formal' sector are large in size, thus facilitating effective trade-unionism. But, almost all establishments in the so-called 'formal sector' employ large numbers of wage-workers on a temporary or casual basis.

Casual employment in large-scale establishments in Sudan is commonly identified with construction. The case of casual unskilled construction workers in Khartoum has been vividly documented by Kameir (1980a; 1980b). He has demonstrated that resort to casual employment on a daily basis is viewed by contractors as an efficient, flexible, and economical way to obtain the required labour while simultaneously coping with the fluctuations in production schedules. In a similar manner, the Ministry of Construction is also known to engage unskilled construction workers on a non-permanent basis (cf. ILO 1976, p.

365).

Casual and temporary employment in Sudan is not, however, confined to the construction industry; or even to those other large establishments and government departments in which the pace and intensity of production fluctuate with the season. Even in large-scale manufacturing establishments - where employers are expected to be most concerned with developing a 'durable' relation with workers - 'non-permanent' employment is extensive. The following quotation, extracted from the relevant parts of the ILO Report (1976), succinctly provides an overview of the situation:

> Employment in the formal sector in the Sudan, whether private or public, is characterised by an unusually large proportion of workers who are classified as "temporary" and who may be laid off without legislative interference (p.109) ... Data for 1973 for a group of concerns in the public industrial sector employing 22,000 workers suggest that as much as 40 per cent were "temporary" workers, the percentage being even higher if we exclude the white-collar workers... (p.365).

According to Kannappan (1977a, p. 88n), the data for 1973 mentioned above, indicate that 8,791 out of 21,964 employees in that group of concerns were classified as "temporary". Kannappan, moreover, cites statistics which show the number of employees by category, as given here in Table 11.1.

Table 11.1

Number of Employees in a Group of Public Industrial Concerns in Khartoum According to Category

Category	Number	Percentage
Skilled	3,554	16
Unskilled	7,003	32
Temporary	8,791	40
White-collar	2,616	12
TOTAL	21,964	100

It should be noted that the category of temporary workers listed in the table are exclusively unskilled. Excluding the white-collar and skilled workers, who are always 'permanent' employees, we find that temporary workers constitute actually around 60 per cent of the total unskilled labour force (i.e. 8,791 out of 15,794 unskilled workers). Large as it is, however, that percentage does not seem to show the actual total non-permanent employment in these concerns - and cannot be taken as indicative of non-permanent employment in the so-called formal sector as a whole. This is so because there is no reference in the table to the "totally casual" workers employed on a daily basis and who, given day-to-day fluctuations, are indeed very difficult to include in any survey.

In relation to non-permanent employment in large-scale establishments, it should also be stressed that Table 11.1 provides an overview of the situation in public industrial concerns. The proportion of such employment in private large-scale industry could be even higher.[1] The ILO Mission (1976, p. 365) contends that the same survey which estimated manufacturing employment in Khartoum at 33,000 "places 'temporary' manufacturing employment at 31,000."

In describing the magnitude of non-permanent employment in the manufacturing industry in Greater Khartoum, we should not overlook the position of the Conurbation as the industrial centre of Sudan. By the early 1970s the Three Towns had 77 per cent of Sudan's large-scale industrial establishments, and 73 per cent of the entire industrial labour force in the country. It is also important to stress that permanent employment is not confined to large-scale establishments and government departments. Labour legislation in the country stipulates that a permanent post be created if continuous employment is offered for more than 90 days; and accordingly, permanent employment could be encountered in the smallest of enterprises. The classic example of the latter is perhaps that of the employed shop-keeper who runs the shop on behalf of an owner who pursues other interests.

Casual and temporary employment in the 'formal sector' are in fact recognised by the ILO studies. It is also recognised that the wage labour force as a whole constitutes around only a half of the entire labour force in Greater Khartoum. The Mission (1976, p. 111) indeed points out the "very small size" of the category of permanent wage-workers and contends that, "As elsewhere in the Third World this is the labour elite, and we need constantly to keep in mind what a small proportion of the labour force they are."

Both the ILO Mission (1976, p. 365) and Kannappan (1977a, p. 88) attempt to explain the pattern of heavy reliance on non-permanent workers by 'formal' employers. Two factors have been advanced to account for it. First there are considerations of flexibility to cope with the fluctuations in production schedules. This - as I shall explain later - is underlain by the pattern of peripheral-capitalist urbanisation in Greater Khartoum and, for that matter, in third world cities in general. Secondly, the two studies maintain that even where fluctuations in schedules are not as marked, non-permanent employment is observed; and this might be explained in terms of the desire by employers to avert the alleged more expensive commitments associated with permanent employment. The ILO studies seem to emphasise the costly nature of permanent employment, whether in remuneration (the high wages) or legislation relating to it (legislative protection). These contentions I believe to be far-fetched.

If a large proportion of formal wage-employment is actually non-permanent; and if permanent employment is also observed in small-scale enterprises, then the formal/informal conception of the labour market becomes not only meaningless, but also a distortion that blurs the facts of non-employment in the so-called formal sector (cf. Chase 1977). The insertion of non-permanent employment in the formal segment of the labour market as a hazy borderline between the two segments fulfils exactly that function.

The flaw in the dualist conception of the urban labour market in Greater Khartoum does not stem solely from the point that all classification is necessarily arbitrary, but also, and even more significantly, from the attempt to identify the permanent workers as a labour elite upon which privileges are alleged to be conferred. In this respect, it is my central contention that the ILO studies on Sudan have grossly misunderstood the nature, origin, and implications of the distinction between permanent and non-permanent employment. That misunderstanding, moreover, is by no means confined to the ILO studies which initially introduced the distinction and its alleged implications into the analysis of labour markets in Sudan. The otherwise very illuminating comparative study of factory workers and unskilled construction workers in Greater Khartoum by Kameir (1980b), for example, has been carried out with an uncritical acceptance of the alleged implications of permanent employment. Kameir thus adopts the basic dualistic view and sets out to show how the differences in the terms and conditions of permanent employment of factory workers contribute to the stabilisation of the latter while the insecurity of the casual unskilled construction workers creates conditions conducive to circular migration between Greater Khartoum and the home villages. A conspicuous feature in Kameir's study is the silence concerning "temporary" employment in the two factories studied.[2]

A detailed assessment of all aspects of the terms and conditions of permanent employment in Sudan is of course an enormous task that cannot be undertaken here. In order to corroborate my criticism of the ILO studies, however, I will deal with three, closely related, aspects of permanent employment which are said to constitute the vital implications of the distinction between permanent and non-permanent workers. These aspects are:

1) The alleged legislative protection which permanent workers (as opposed to non-permanent workers) are said to enjoy;

2) The alleged high wages, after-service benefits and other expensive commitments associated with permanent employment;

3) The alleged role of trade unions in collective bargaining and its effectiveness in raising the living standards of union workers who are exclusively permanent workers.

What I would like to stress in connection with these three aspects of permanent employment is that the ILO studies seem to have been based on first impressions about labour legislation in Sudan. This is very clear in the overview which the Mission (1976, p. 117) presents in relation to the position of the trade unions in the country and its contention that:

> The organised labour movement in the Sudan has secured an impressive armoury of legislation protecting its right to organise workers and providing the machinery for the orderly settlement of labour disputes. From the Trade Disputes Act of 1966 to the Employer and Employed Persons Ordinance Act of 1971,

Sudanese workers are furnished with collective bargaining procedure that bear comparison with those achieved by organised labour in advanced countries. However, a Presidential Order of 1974 prohibited the right to strike, as well as the employers' right to lock out, without ministerial approval; in consequence, the Sudan has been almost free from strikes in recent years. Far from this creating resentment among union leaders, the view seems to be that prohibition of the right to strike has not hampered organised labour in securing better wages and better working conditions for its members.

But even if labour legislation in Sudan does provide for the protection of the right of the labour movement to organise, bargain, and settle disputes in an orderly manner, such a protection should not be conceived as the simple consequence of legislation issued by a charitable or impartial state. This is particularly so in a country like Sudan where the state assumes the role not only of the protector of the interests of employers, but also that of the largest single employer of workers in the country.

The single most important point to raise here is that the view of labour laws as an initiative taken by the state[3] does not only overlook the basis of labour legislation in Sudan as a reaction by the state to the initiative of the labour movement, but also blurs the status, functions, and implications of such legislation in the arena of class struggle which the phrase industrial relations actually denotes - albeit in muted terms. When viewed in the wider context of class struggle, labour legislation constitutes little more than the outcome of the struggle by workers against unacceptable terms and conditions of work on the one hand and, on the other, the attempt by the state (representing employers) to avert the radical consequences that could arise in the course of the struggle. Labour legislation in Sudan has in the main been intended to pacify the labour movement rather than to advance the cause of workers. In this connection, labour legislation between May 1969 and November 1970 stands as an exception.

Job-Security:

The notion that permanent workers in Sudan enjoy job security seems to be underlain by the existence of some laws that ostensibly provide these workers with legislative protection against unlawful termination of employment by employers. This illusion is further reinforced when the apparent situation of permanent workers is compared to that of temporary and casual workers whom the law excludes. In propagating that illusion, however, two crucial points are usually overlooked:

(a) What the law stipulates as lawful termination against which no protection is provided;

(b) The nature of the circumstances under which employers would wish to terminate the employment of workers.

In relation to the issue of the nature and scope of lawful termination, it should be noted that when lawful is defined in elastic terms, employers can always act within the law and legislative protection becomes a mockery of the concept. This, I believe is the status of the kind of legislative protection stipulated in labour laws in Sudan. The ILO Mission (1976, p. 393) has touched on this issue and contended that:

> We wish to draw special attention to at least one other area of protective legislation, namely that relating to the conditions under which workers may be laid off by employers. Legal provisions pertaining to the termination of employment are contained in the Employer and Employed Persons Ordinance of 1949, as amended in 1969 with only the questions of due notice and compensation. There is no provision in that Act which seeks to provide any measure of security for emloyed persons form arbitrary and unfair dismissal by an employer ...

It is not uncommon though to find temporary workers who have actually worked for the same employer for more than six years! This is not to deny that many other temporary and casual workers do get the sack. The case of the construction contractors mentioned above is perhaps the classic example - although no systematic study has been undertaken in relation to the conditions of the casual construction workers who do get sacked - i.e. do they get employed by other contractors?

The case of the temporary workers who work for years for the same employer is relevant to the point here, insofar as it dramatises my argument concerning the conditions under which employers tend to terminate the employment of their permanent workers. In this respect we should note that a permanent position is usually offered only in those establishments which do not normally experience marked fluctuations in production schedules - otherwise employers would tend to engage casual workers. In other words, the desire of employers to terminate the employment of workers should not be construed as an innate characteristic of employers; and whether the latter employ permanent or non-permanent workers, the question of termination arises in specific circumstances. These may relate to factors such as total or partial dissolution of the establishment, desire to sack incompetent workers, or the wish to get rid of militant workers and trade union activists. Accordingly, the issue of legislative protection should not be assessed at a high level of abstraction; rather our focus should be on the nature of the circumstances under which the question of termination arises, and the relation of the former to the concept of lawful termination against which no protection is offered.

It is noteworthy that despite decades of post-colonial government the current labour laws in Sudan have largely retained the basic concepts and structure of the oppressive colonial legislation (cf. Abu-Eisa, 1981, p. 5). The current law regulating termination of employment (The Employer and Employed Persons Act, 1976) thus constitutes very little more than a minor amendment of the colonial Employer and Employed Persons Ordinance, 1949.

According to Taha and El-Jack (1973, p. 9), the purpose of the 1949 Ordinance was:

> the regulating of terms of employment in both private and public establishments. It set minimum standards relating to hours of work, overtime, holidays, rest periods, sick leaves, the payment of after-service benefits and other terms of employment. It also contained rules regulating the termination of employment dealt with under Section 10 of the Ordinance.

The Ordinance, however, was not intended as a universal law covering all wage-earners in the country. Article (3) of the Ordinance thus stipulated the exclusion of agricultural and temporary workers from the jurisdiction of the Ordinance. It is that stipulation which has created the illusion of the legislative protection provided for permanent workers in Sudan.

In its original formulation in the 1949 Ordinance, Section 10 (1) stipulated that:

> Subject as hereinafter provided, every contract of service wherein no agreement respecting notice of longer duration is expressed not being a contract to perform some specific work without reference to time, shall be terminable by either party:
>
> (a) Where the employed person is engaged on the basis of a monthly wage, at the expiration of one month's notice which may be given at any time;
>
> (b) Where the employed person is engaged on the basis of a weekly wage: [i] if he has completed less than 2 years of continuous service, at the expiration of two weeks notice which may be given at any time.
>
> [bA] Where the employed person is engaged on the basis of a fortnightly wage and has completed less than five years of continuous service, at the expiration of two weeks' notice which may be given at any time.
>
> (c) Where the employed person is engaged on the basis of a daily wage, whether paid daily or not:
>
> [i] if he has not completed six months of continuous service at the close of any day without notice;
> [ii] if he has completed six months but less than two years of continuous service, at the expiration of one week's notice which may be given at any time;
> [iii] if he has completed two but less than five years of continuous service, at the expiration of two weeks' notice which may be given at any time;
>
> (d) Where the employed person is engaged on the basis of a daily, weekly or fortnightly wage and has completed not less than five years of continuous service, at the expiration of one month's notice which may be given at any time (cf. <u>idem</u>:9/10).

After giving due notice employers (and employees) were not required to justify their wish to terminate the contract. Likewise, while notices were stipulated where employees had spent a minimum of six months of continuous service, no after-service payment or gratuity was to be provided for a worker unless he/she had spent a minimum of five years of continuous service (Section 25 of the Ordinance dealt with gratuity). Though the after-service payment was (and still is) not an expensive commitment, an employer could nevertheless manage to avoid it by simply notifying the worker one month before the completion of the five years of his desire to terminate the contract.

Section 10 (2) went even further than the first article by enabling employers to terminate contracts without giving notice or gratuity:

> an employer may dismiss without notice an employed person for wilful disobedience of a lawful order or gross misconduct in or connected with his employment or serious negligence or wilful misconduct calculated seriously to injure the employer's business.

Whenever employers wanted to reduce, for economic reasons, their labour force, but in such a way as to avoid payment of gratuity, or simply to get rid of a militant worker or trade union activist, the provisions of Section 10 (2) could be invoked. Summary dismissals in particular were resorted to by employers in order to inhibit the formation of trade unions; and it was for this reason that the labour movement in Sudan had singled out Section 10 of the Ordinance and raised its amendment as a demand of the highest priority (cf. Abu-Eisa, 1981, p. 11).

The first amendments in the Ordinance, however, did not materialise before February 1969 - only three months prior to the military takeover which brought Numeiri to power. Of particular relevance among the amendments are four points:

Firstly, the minimum period to require giving of notice was amended to become three instead of six months of continuous service. The basic stipulation of Section 10 (1) of giving notice without the requirement of justification, however, was left intact.

Secondly, the amendment introduced Section 10 (2b) which recognized for the first time the right of an employed person to terminate a contract without giving notice to the employer. The cases under which such termination could be effected were laid down in terms of four clearly formulated reasons. There was no provision in the amendment, however, to recognise the right of workers who thus terminate contracts to gratuity, although Section 26 was amended to recognise the right of employed persons to after-service payments. This latter, however, stipulated such payments under difficult conditions and after many years of continuous service reaching in some cases a minimum of 15 years.

Thirdly, the original Section 10 (2) dealing with summary dismissals for serious misconduct was amended to formulate in more specific terms the reasons for which employers could sack their workers immediately, and without notice or gratuity. The amendment stipulated summary dismissals when an employed person:

1) clothes himself with the personality of another or presents forged documents;

2) due to gross negligence commits a wrong resulting in a heavy financial loss to the employer;

3) in spite of being notified in writing, does not comply with any instructions made for the safety of employed persons and of the place of business; provided that such instructions are in writing and fixed in a conspicuous place;

4) omits to carry out his obligations under the contract of service concluded between him and the employer;

5) discloses any industrial secrets;

6) is convicted of an offence against honour or involving moral turpitude or if he commits in the place of business an act inconsistent with morals;

7) during the hours of work is found in a state of evident drunkenness or under the effect of a narcotic substance provided that a medical officer whenever possible testifies to that;

8) assaults his employer or the responsible manager or if in the course of, or due to a cause attributed to, the business he commits any grievous hurt on any of his superiors.

Though this amendment seems to provide greater protection than the original provisions stipulated, in practice the difference between the two is negligible. In particular, the stipulation of dismissal if the employed person commits, in the place of business, an act inconsistent with morals leaves a lot to be desired. Who is to determine whether an act is consistent with morals? Obviously no other than the employer or the responsible manager. In addition, what is the standard for such an evaluation of the act?

<u>Fourthly</u>, Section 10 (2c) was introduced to regulate termination of contract by either party without giving notice. This stipulated that all cases of termination without notice should be referred to the Commissioner of Labour whose consent was decreed essential to the validity of the termination. The Commissioner was required to consider the case and make his decision within a period of not more than seven days. Section 10 (2d), moreover, stipulated that if an employed person is summarily dismissed before the Commissioner of Labour makes his decision, the employer would be forced either to reinstate the employed person and pay him the full wage for the period of suspension, or to pay him in addition to any gratuity and other entitlement a compensation equalling three months wages.

The attempt to regulate summary dismissals, however, resulted in a contraction in the provisions of the different parts of Section 10 which was very difficult for workers to understand. As Eisa (1981, p. 15) notes, Section 10 (2a) stipulated the right of an employer to "dismiss any of his employed persons immediately and without notice or gratuity," while Section 10 (2d) required that "an employer shall not dismiss the employed person and the employed person shall not cease to work unless the dispute is referred to the Commissioner of Labour."

Section 10 of the Ordinance (as amended in 1969) was suspended on 18 October 1970, when the Council of Ministers issued its executive Order No. 993 dealing with the dismissal of employed persons and trade union officials (cf., Taha and El-Jack 1973, p. 13).[4] The provisions of the Ministerial Order were incorporated into the Consolidated Labour Code of November 1970 that repealed all existing labour legislation in Sudan. Of particular significance to this discussion are the provisions contained in Sections 85 to 87.

The most significant difference between the Code (and its precursor, the Ministerial Order) and previous legislation is that employers were required in the former to justify their desire to terminate a contract even with due notice and payment of gratuity (where this last is applicable). Likewise, all cases of dismissal were to be referred to a tripartite committee formed of the representatives of the Labour Office, trade unions and employers; the decisions of these committees, which were to be made within ten days, were considered as both binding and final (Section 85). It is interesting to note in this connection that whereas the Ministerial Order stipulated the penalty of confiscation of establishment in case of non-compliance by employers, the Code stipulated the reinstatement of the employee who was also given the full wage for the period of his suspension.

In relation to the former Section 10 (2) concerning the specification of the conditions of summary dismissal, the Code retained most of the provisions under Section 87 (1) which comprised seven instead of the former eight cases. The right of employers to dismiss an employee if he "omits to carry his obligations under the contract of service", or if he "commits in the place of business an act inconsistent with morals," however, were dropped in the Code. A new provision was introduced stipulating that an employer could apply to dismiss a worker if the latter absented himself for more than 20 days during the last three months or for more than fifteen consecutive days (cf. idem:14). The Consolidated Labour Code was described by employers as an infringement of their (natural?) right to hire and fire workers; and given the sympathetic feelings and attitudes between the government and trade unions on the one hand and between government and some former members of the Sudanese Communist Party on the other, the Code was described in terms of a plot that would destroy the fabric of Sudanese Society (cf. idem., esp. pp.25-35). Despite the self-professed socialist policy of the May regime during that phase, however, the job security of permanent workers was no better than it had been previously. Section 86 (1) of the Code stipulated that employers could apply to the tripartite committee to terminate the service of employees if: (a) the establishment was partially dissolved; (b) the machine on which the worker was engaged broke down; (c) raw materials were not available; (d) or the job was cancelled. I do not need to discuss the scope of freedom to hire and fire left by that provision for employers, particularly given the elasticity of the concept of job cancellation. It should be noted, however, that Section 86(2) stipulated the payment to the worker whose contract was thus terminated - a compensation amounting to one month's wage.

The Consolidated Labour Code was short-lived; only two months following its promulgation it was suspended and the previous 1969 amendment was reinstated, pending new legislaton. Section10 (amendment) continued to be operational until 1973 when a further amendment was made, and it is this last amendment which is still operational in the country.

The 1973 amendment repealed the former Section 10 (1) stipulating termination of contract with due notice and introduced a new provision stipulating that:

A contract of service shall be terminated due to any of the following reasons:-

(a) in case of the disability of the employee to perform his work or if he is so ill that he would cease to work even after the completion of the sick leave and normal holidays to which he is entitled, whether with or without pay, provided that the disability or illness is certified by the employer's Doctor or by the Government Hospital, or if any dispute arises by the Medical Commission;

(b) the completion of the work contracted for;

(c) the total destruction of the establishment.

The provisions of Section 10(2) were left intact while a new provision (Section 10[3]) stipulating that in case of contravention of the notice requirement by either party a payment equalling the wage for the specific period of notice should be made to the injured party.

It is interesting to note that the 1973 amendment did not touch the provisions of 1969 relating to the conditions for summary dismissal for serious misconduct, and retained the very eight points which the Ministerial Order and the Code had modified. Even the same legal paradox concerning the stipulation of immediate summary dismissal and the requirement to refer the dispute to the Commissioner of Labour were retained. Finally, under Section 12(a) of the amendment a new elastic provision was introduced stipulating that:

> A contract of service is terminable due to the inefficiency of the employee or due to a reduction in the labour force for economic reasons.

From the foregoing account of legislation regulating termination of employment in Sudan it should now be clear that the so-called job security of permanent workers is an illusion.

Wage and Other 'Expensive Commitments':

Notwithstanding the enactment in Sudan (in 1974) of a standard minimum wage,[5] the recent literature on the wage structure emphatically asserts the existence of significant intersectoral as well as intrasectoral wage variations in the country. In the discussion of these latter, distinctions are usually made between; (a) the public and the private sector; (b) government departments and parastatal concerns; and (c) large-scale and small-scale private enterprise. A typical statement of the implications of these distinctions is furnished by Kannappan (1977a, p. 90) who contends that:

> Wages rates in Government are higher than in private employment... Within Government, established state enterprises like the Sudan Railways pay better than other branches of Government. However, one must note the practice of employing casual and temporary staff and of contracting out work through others... The position as regards private employment is more complex because of greater variation in size, activities undertaken, skill employed, the influence of government regulations, the pressures of unionisation, and so on. The small number of foreign firms are at the top of the wage hierarchy, even topping the Government. A few of the larger Sudanese firms, including public enterprises, appear to be in this category, carried over from the days prior to nationalisation, and the rest, although among the better paying employers, perhaps trail the government scales of pay. Our information is rather scanty on the smaller enterprises ... (but) it is widely believed that (they) ...pay wages well below the government level.

Suliman (1974, pp. 33-4) reservedly quotes a statement by the Labour Minister in 1969 that whereas the minimum monthly wage in the public sector was £S 13.90, the relevant figure for the private sector did not exceed £S 4.50. A more recent estimate of the wage differential is provided by Affan (1977, p. 75; but cf., Mazloum 1974), who contends that, on average, wage-earners in the public sector receive earnings that are 25 per cent higher than in the private sector.

The message which the literature attempts to convey is clear. Permanent employment in the formal sector is not only more highly paid than casual and temporary employment, but also better remunerated than both employment and self-employment in the numerous smaller private enterprises. This contention underlies the characterisation of formal permanent workers as a labour elite. My intention here is to refute this contention by documenting two main points. The first is that wages for manual work in Sudan are basically uniform for skilled and unskilled workers. The second point is that though differentials are observed between the wage of highly-skilled manual workers and that of unskilled workers, manual work in Sudan is generally poorly remunerated; the really significant and far greater differentials exist between, on the one hand, the wages of skilled and unskilled manual workers and, on the other, the real earnings of the so-called classified staff (civil servants and professionals). I will, start the discussion with a brief account of the wage structure in government employment since the colonial period.

The Wage Structure in the Colonial and Post Colonial Period

The first successful attempt by the colonial government to introduce a measure of control (as opposed to co-ordination) over the wage rates was the sytem of "Block Grants" adopted in 1937 (cf., Fawzi 1954, pp. 159-61). Under this system, the head of a government department was to be given an appropriation (grant) for a definite purpose which might contain provision for pay of individuals only, or which might provide for a service or a new project, and might, therefore, include both pay of employees and cost of materials and machines. The head of department was thus his own policy-maker and, within the financial limits of the Block Grants, had full autonomy over decisions relating to both the number of wage-workers to be employed and the wage rate to be paid to them. The outcome was a hybrid wage structure in government employment - a salient feature being variation in wage rates for similar jobs in different departments on the one hand and, on the other, a stark wage differential between the unskilled general labourer and that of the skilled artisan. During that period the majority of skilled artisans were expatriates. With progress in the recruitment of Sudanese into the ranks of skilled workers, the differential was progressively narrowed.

The emergence of a relatively unified or uniform wage structure and/or policy in government employment is thus a relatively recent development. More precisely, it dates back to the end of 1951 when the colonial Executive Council accepted the system recommended by the Unclassified Staff Commission (better known as the Wakefield Commission, after its Chairman). According to Fawzi (1954, p. 165), the "Group system" recommended by the Wakefield Commission aimed towards the creation of seven groups

> covering the variations in skill and responsibility in jobs undertaken by all categories from the unskilled general labourer (Group 1) to the skilled artisan (Group 7). Into these new groups were to be assimilated the then existing categories of labour. Comparatively short ranges of pay were attached to the various groups - and no overlapping between adjacent scales was allowed. Moreover, the range of pay applicable to any job was to fall within the range of pay allotted to a single group only. The various groups thus constituted separate but consecutive steps in one ladder representing various stages of skill, experience and seniority.

Though by means of the group system the Commission created a uniformity of scales in government employment, its proposals effectively perpetuated the hybrid wage structure. In the determination of the actual amount to be received in wages, the Commission decided to adopt the principle of a subsistence wage for the lowest-paid (Group 1) worker calculated on the basis of the subsistence requirements of a family of four. In recognition of regional variations in the cost of living, the Commission thus divided the country into regions each of which was supposed to have a different level of cost of living. The main regions with a relatively high cost of living comprised what we may generally characterise as "Northern Sudan". The lower-productivity lower-cost-of-living regions, on the other hand, comprised the Southern Region and a few districts in Dar Fur, Kordofan and Blue Nile Provinces (Fawzi, 1957). According to Suliman (1974, p. 35):

> In the North, Group One started with a monthly wage of £E 5.800 ... In (type a) districts in the South ... Group One started with £E 1.300 ... and in (b)districts Group One started with £E 1.750... (while) in (type c) districts (the starting wage was) £E 2.500 ... (My translation).

In adopting the principle of a subsistence wage, the Wakefield Commission showed sensitivity to probable increases in prices in the long run. For this reason it recommended that the wages paid should be formed of two components: (a) a basic wage and (b) a cost of living allowance (COLA). In the event of price rises it was thus envisaged that there would be no need to revise the whole structure of wage rates; adjustments in the COLA, which was to be tied to a price index, would suffice to compensate workers for increases in prices.

The hybrid wage structure introduced by the Wakefield Commission encountered many practical problems in its implementation (cf. Fawzi 1954). Likewise, it induced resentment by both individual workers and the trade union movement. To mention but one of its stark anomalies, workers transferred from the main to the low-cost-of-living regions would experience a reduction in their wages. It was not until 1968 when the recommendations of the Cadre Commission were accepted, however, that a policy of equal pay irrespective of region and sex was, at least in principle, adopted by the government (cf., Suliman 1974).

The 1968 Cadre Commission introduced minor modifications into the Group System introduced by the Wakefield Commission. In recognition of the probable increase in productivity of workers (compared to 1951), for example, a new group (Group Eight) was introduced. Likewise, the Cadre Commission attempted to deal with the complaints of workers who do not get promoted to a higher group and, consequently, get stuck at the wage-ceiling of their respective groups which, according to the original system, was to be reached in six years (i.e. only six annual increments in the basic wage were given to each group irrespective of the number of years a worker would remain in that group). Suliman (1974) notes that many of the unskilled general labourers (Tulba) had actually remained in Group One for over thirty years. The Cadre Commission allowed the annual increments to continue for nine, instead of six, years. Table 11.2 shows the wage structures recommended by the two

Table 11.2

Wage Rates in Government Employment, 1951 & 1968

Group	1951 Starting £E	1951 Ceiling £E	1968 Starting £S	1968 Ceiling £S
One	5.800	7.800	12.500	18.800
Two	6.600	9.000	15.000	22.650
Three	8.300	12.300	18.000	27.000
Four	10.500	16.500	21.600	32.400
Five	14.500	23.500	26.000	39.050
Six	23.500	29.500	31.350	46.650
Seven	23.500	37.500	45.000	67.500

Source: Suliman 1974, p. 36.

commissions.

Though the Cadre Commission retained the formula of basic wage plus COLA, the COLA was no longer tied to any price index (cf. ILO 1976, p. 368).

In 1978 the distinction between Classified and Unclassified Staff in government employment was abolished, and a new Group System comprising 18 groups covering all types and grades in government employment (from the unskilled general labourer to under secretaries) was introduced. In this new system COLA no longer formed a component of the wage (or salary) received. Before discussing this new system, which is still operative in the country, some crucial points relating to the foregoing account should be noted.

The first point relates to the wage differentials between skilled and unskilled workers which is apparent in Table 11.2. While the differential had narrowed between 1951 and 1968, all categories of workers actually experienced a decrease in their real incomes. It is noteworthy here that this reduction has been observed not only in the period 1951-1970, but also in the period 1938-1954. In other words, wage-earners in government employment were better off in 1938 than in 1970.

The wage differential between skilled and unskilled workers has progressively narrowed, but it should be emphasised that the highest-paid workers represent an insignificant proportion of manual workers (a mere 0.3 per cent of all government employees in 1962 were classified as Group Seven), while by far the largest single group in government employment was that of the lowest-paid manual workers (24.1 per cent of all employees in 1962), and as we go up the hierarchy of unclassified staff the percentage gets smaller (cf. Taha 1976, p. 132). Given the few ports of entry into the ranks of the unclassified staff (cf. Kannappan 1977b), only a tiny minority of relatively well-educated (General Secondary and above) manage to start at other than the bottom of the hierarchy. For the ordinary skilled worker, it takes over 20 years to be promoted to a supervisory position (Group Seven); and as such the highest-paid are not only skilled workers, but also those with the longest record of continuous service.

The point about the differential between unskilled and skilled workers leads directly to the differential between manual workers in general and the classified staff in government employment. It is noteworthy that the average wage of a skilled worker (Groups 4-7) is well below the average salary of the clerical employees - not to mention the comparatively much higher paid civil servants and professionals. The average basic salary of the four highest-paid classified staff (£S 130) is four times the wage of the highest-paid unclassified staff, and over six times the average wage of all skilled workers. The highly-inflated basic salaries (i.e. excluding 'fringe benefits' - see below) have for long been identified as relics from the colonial days (cf., Suliman 1974).

The present scales structure in goverment employment in the Sudan has abolished the distinction between classified and unclassified staff. By so doing, however, neither the distinction between 'mental' and 'manual' labour, nor differentials in their remuneration have been, or were even intended to be dissolved. Thus, though at present I have no information whether any manual workers in supervisory positions are in Groups Fifteen and Fourteen, it is certain that over 90 per cent of the (former) unclassified staff are encountered in Groups Eighteen, Seventeen and Sixteen. This is particularly so because of the number of years a worker is expected to spend in any one group and for which he is given annual increments before reaching the ceiling of the group. Thus, provided that a worker is promoted in the same year he reaches the ceiling of a group, it would take at least 25 years to move from the bottom of Group Eighteen to the ceiling of Group Sixteen. A University graduate with BA (Honours), on the other hand, is recruited directly into Group Nine, and within less than ten years he would be promoted to Group Seven at least. If he reads for an MA or PhD, his promotion prospects are even better.

Furthermore, while Table 11.2 shows the differentials in basic pay, we should not overlook the fringe-benefits which the civil servants and professionals receive. These latter groups are usually given a government house (the rent of whose equivalent in the private market is well over £S 1,000 per month) or,because of the recent shortage in government houses, a Housing Allowance (varying between £S 200 and £S 350). Every official is entitled to this housing allowance, even those who have received loans to build their own houses. One further and rather striking set of benefits concerns cars and transport allowances. Those officials who do not own cars are entitled to a Transport Allowance of approximately £S 40 per month, while those who own cars and use them in connection with their work are given a Mileage Allowance of around £S 105. Car loans are also made available to officials and in settlement around £S 40 are deducted from the salary each month.

In comparing the earnings of civil servants and professionals with those of manual workers I should stress that I am not unaware of the fact that in recent years even the highest-paid government employees have experienced a sharp decline in their real income. Inflation in Sudan during the last decade, and since 1978 in particular,[6] is experienced by all those who opted to stay and work in the country, rather than migrate to the oil-rich Gulf states (see Chapter 13, this volume). For the period 1970-1980 the rate of inflation is estimated as 400 per cent (cf.Legum 1978-80, p.121).

In relation to the low-income group, the minimum wage in government employment in 1970 was £S 13.900. Irrespective of whether or not that amount sufficed to meet the requirements of the general unskilled labourer, the deterioration in the living standard experienced by him up to 1979 was to be bought for £S 4.869. In order to maintain in 1979 the <u>same</u> living standard the general unskilled labourer had enjoyed in 1970, the minimum wage in 1979 would have had to be £S 67.679. In reality, however, the minimum wage in 1979 was £S 28.000 (the minimum wage was raised from £S 15 in 1973 to £S 16 in 1974 to £S 28 in 1978).

The rise in the price-index for the period 1980-84 is even worse than that of the 1970s. No official statistics are available, but most estimates point to a probable 300 per cent increase. After the November 1983 revision of the wage-rate, however, the gross annual wage of the lowest-paid was £S 430, or £S 35.833 per month - nearly half what the minimum wage would have had to have been in 1979 in order to enable the general unskilled labourer to maintain a living standard equal to that he used to enjoy back in 1970.

From the foregoing account of the wage structure of the so-called labour elite it should be clear that the wages of manual workers in government employment, and unskilled manual workers in particular, are far from being a 'privilege' for workers, or an expensive commitment for employers. It is indeed because of this wage structure than Sudanese workers are involved in what Chase (1977) calls "an extended urban labour market reaching to the Gulf region." Thus whereas migration to the oil-rich Arab countries had initially involved technocrats, civil servants and skilled workers (cf. Galal-al-Din 1979b), in recent years the numbers of unskilled manual workers migrating from Sudan are increasing very rapidly (cf. Al-Ghoul 1982; Galal-al-Din, this volume). By 1980, no less than 15 per cent of the economically active Sudanese were working in the Gulf (cf. Birks and Sinclair, 1979).

The discussion so far has focussed mainly on issues relating to the level of remuneration in government employment. To acquire an overview of the wage structure in the labour market as a whole, however, we need to consider the wage level for the other two main sections of the urban wage labour force: viz. (a) workers employed by the wage-leaders - the parastatals and the large-scale private enterprises and (b) workers employed (or self-employed) in the numerous smaller private enterprises of the so-called urban informal sector.

In relation to the contention that the so-called wage-leaders pay higher wages than government departments, one basic observation should be spelled out. I could not find in the literature either a precise statement on the level of remuneration paid by the parastatals and/or the large-scale private enterprises, or any comparative figures showing wages in parastatals and government departments. The contention that the former constitute wage-leaders seems to have been given weight by assertion rather than empirical investigation and is most likely based on assumptions concerning the relative strength of trade unions in enterprises with large numbers of workers. In the next section I will deal with the issue of trade unions and their alleged role in collective bargaining. Suffice it here to maintain that though differences in wage rates could once be noted between parastatals and government departments, at present - and indeed since 1970 - all distinctions between the two concerning wages and other terms of employment have been dissolved. This statement, however, should not be taken to mean that the pay rates for all public workers are identical. I have already noted that in certain 'specialised' government institutions (such as the Agricultural Research Corporation, Khartoum University and the National Council for Research) workers are paid a little more than in government departments.[7]

In relation to the issue of earnings in the so-called informal sector, the data I have gathered suggest a rather different situation from that conveyed in the ILO studies. Generally speaking, the findings of my research suggest no significant overall differences between the wages of permanent government workers and paid-workers in the so-called informal sector. In numerous cases of informal employment the daily wage of unskilled workers is actually higher than that of goverment workers. But given the other benefits which government workers are entitled to, such as after-service payments, paid annual holidays, etc. the differences observed between the daily wages of the two groups seem to disappear. I should stress, however, that this generalisation is not intended as a comparison of the total earnings of the two groups of workers. An amalgam of factors renders such a comparison very difficult, if not impossible. To take one of the most important among these factors, the earnings of government workers may not be the same as their wages and other benefits. Quite a number of government workers are observed to engage in 'informal activities' which effectively increase their total income. Many government drivers (as well as junior clerks), for example, work as taxi-drivers in the evenings, and some own taxis. Moonlighting for other categories of government workers is also known to be a normal practice sometimes even undertaken during official work hours. What my generalisation is intended to convey, rather, is that the rewards to labour are basically uniform whether in government or in 'informal' employment.

One objection I could anticipate concerning the presentation of my findings as a critique of the ILO studies is that my data relate to the period 1981-83 and as such are not readily comparable to the situation described in the literature of the mid-1970s (Al-Shazali 1985). In reply to such an objection, it is my central contention that although some quantitative changes have taken place, particularly since 1978, the basic relation between the two levels of remuneration compared above is virtually identical to the situation described in the ILO studies.

According to the Mission (1976, p. 383), the "approximate average monthly revenue" in the so-called informal manufacturing and repair was £S 60, ranging from

> a low of £S 30 for footwear to a high of £S 150 for metallic products ... The value of average capital assets was about £S 129 with a low of £S 14 and £S 15 for leather products and beverages respectively to a high of about £S 250 for wood products, indicating that capital as such may not be a barrier to entrance in some of these handicrafts... The average monthly earnings of employees in these establishments reaches about £S 20 which is more than the statutory minimum wage. However, a low of £S 8 for footwear is reported.

The findings of the Mission, however, not only suggest that in the overwhelming majority of cases of informal employment paid workers actually earn higher than the statutory minimum wage but, when compared with other data furnished by the Mission, also corroborate my contention that the earnings of informal workers could be relatively higher than the wages of their formal counterparts. In a table summarising, inter alia, data on average daily earnings of paid workers in 'informal manufacturing and repair', the Mission (p. 381)reports an average daily income for all informal manufacturing workers of £S 0.80. In another section in the Report, however, the Mission presents a table showing, inter alia, average earnings of workers in a sample of 'formal sector' manufacturing establishments with five or more workers surveyed in 1973 in which the average daily wage of workers (overtime included) is reported to be £S 0.60 (ILO 1976, pp. 367-8; but cf. Sudan Government 1973).[8] Had the mission compared these two averages, its logical conclusion would have been that wages in the formal sector could well be lower than in the so-called informal sector. This same point has been made by Chase (1977) in his critique of the Mission's views on the 'labour elite':

> We can consider the privileged wage standards ... of formal sector urban labour by reference to the average monthly earnings (March 1973) of surveyed formal sector urban manual workers. For the approximately 36 per cent of workers in establishments employing fewer than 100 workers, the average monthly earnings, overtime included, approximated £S 16; while for the approximately 64 per cent employed in firms of 100+ workers the relevant figures would be £S 21.

The minimum wage in government employment in 1973 was £S15 (cf. Suliman 1974). Calculating the average monthly earnings of informal workers from the data furnished by the Mission, the relevant figures would be: £S 17.10 for food and beverage manufacture; £S27.60 in manufacture of leather and leather products; £S9.00 in manufacture of footwear; £S27.60 in manufacture of wood products and furniture; £S23.10 in manufacture and repairing of metallic products; £S37.20 in electrical repair; £S16.20 in repair of motor vehicles and motor cycles; and finally, £S18.00 for "others" - e.g. clothing (cf. ILO 1976, p. 381). It should be emphasised here that these averages are of earnings of paid informal workers and not the self-employed who are reported to have a much higher level of revenue (an average of £S60 per month).

One criticism that might be levelled against the foregoing comparison concerns the frequency of employment and unemployment for informal workers which might reduce their actual monthly earnings. It is generally assumed in the ILO studies that informal workers experience discontinuous employment and frequent spells of unemployment. In none of the ILO studies, however, are there any data on unemployment among the so-called informal workers. In this respect, however, I do not intend to deny that in many cases informal workers may experience unemployment which, if experienced for a period to be assumed as sufficiently long, may lead to return migration. Circular migration for unskilled migrants is in the overwhelming majority of cases not only the norm or normal, but also the original intention of the small farmers and pastoralists who come to the cities as target migrants. Migration is a means to supplement the income from the productive activities pursued in the context of the domestic form of agricultural production. It is only in relatively exceptional circumstances when an unskilled migrant is lucky enough to find himself in a well remunerated position that he tends to give up interest in the productive activities he used to pursue in his home village.

In pointing out the intentions of unskilled migrants, however, it is not my objective to endorse the view that informal employment is as discontinuous as generally assumed. Thus, even when employment is available, a migrant may decide to go back home in a case where he realised the target sum for which he initially came to the city. Leaving aside the findings of my own research (Al-Shazali 1985), the case of the unskilled manual construction workers studied by Kameir (1980b), which is taken to be by far the most extreme case of discontinued employment in the urban setting, may be taken as evidence.

The unskilled manual workers, tulab, studied by Kameir are totally casual workers employed by building contractors. According to Kameir (1980b, p. 170):

> Every contractor has a gang of "semi-stable" workers. The number of workers varies according to the number of contracts undertaken by the individual contractor. I refer to them as "semi-stable" because, while they usually stay with one employer during their stay in town, they are not permanently employed and can be fired without notice ... The pace of work depends on

cooperation between the builders and the tulab... it is because of this that contractors normally prefer to employ groups of builders and tulab that have previously worked together.

Kameir reports a situation of feast and famine experienced by the tulab and how members of the different accommodation cells, who are all Nuer from Southern Sudan, are engaged in constant visits that facilitate the flow of information about employment opportunities throughout the Three Towns (pp. 231ff). To corroborate his view of the discontinuous employment experienced by the Nuer tulab, Kameir presents a table showing the level of employment by one building contractor over a period of 30 consecutive days and how the workers were deployed on seven different sites. The number of workers taken on daily varied a great deal from the low total of six on one day to the high total of 23 on three days; and over the 30 days there was constant chopping and changing of building operations between different sites. Table 11.3 is compiled by Kameir showing the fluctuations in production schedules for the contractor.

The table presented by Kameir can be interpreted in a fashion that reveals a fairly continuous pattern of employment not only in the building industry as a whole, but also in the case of the specific contractor in relation to whose production schedule the table has been compiled. In the case of the industry as a whole the unemployment experienced by members of a gang associated with any one contractor may be compensated by employment by other contractors - given the flow of information among members of the different accommodation cells reported. But even in the specific case of the contractor surveyed by Kameir, unemployment is not a serious problem and, certainly, the level of wages received by the members of the semi-stable gang is by no means lower than that of government workers. The membership of the "semi-stable" gang is reported as being fourteen workers. The average frequency of employment in the month surveyed for each member of the gang can be calculated as the average of person/days deployed by the contractor excluding those person/days in excess of 14 (the number of the gang members) deployed in any one single day. In those three days when 23 workers were employed, for example, the figure to be taken will be 14 only. The assumption here is based on the report by Kameir that contractors tend to employ workers from within the membership of the semi-stable gangs. The total frequency of employment during the 30 days can be calculated in the following steps:

1) the lowest number of workers employed continuously is 6, and this gives us 180 person/days.
2) one additional worker was given employment for 29 days (this is the additional worker in those days when only seven were employed).
3) one worker was given employment for 26 days (when 8 or more workers were employed).
4) one worker was given employment for 24 days (when 9 or more workers were employed).
5) one worker was given employment for 16 days (when 10 or more workers were employed).

Table 11.3

Employment of Day Labourers by One Building Contractor and the Transference of Workers Between Seven Sites over a period of 30 Consecutive Days

Days	Number of Workers on the Different Sites							Total No. of Labourers
	Site 1	Site 2	Site 3	Site 4	Site 5	Site 6	Site 7	
1	6	-	-	1	2	-	1	10
2	6	-	-	1	2	-	1	10
3	4	-	2	1	2	-	1	10
4	2	-	2	1	2	-	1	8
5	-	-	2	1	2	-	1	6
6	2	-	4	1	2	-	1	10
7	1	7	-	1	-	-	1	10
8	-	-	-	23	-	-	-	23
9	-	-	-	23	-	-	-	23
10	-	-	-	23	-	-	-	23
11	4	-	2	3	2	-	1	12
12	4	-	1	1	2	-	1	9
13	2	2	1	1	-	-	1	7
14	2	2	1	2	-	2	1	10
15	2	2	-	3	-	4	1	12
16	-	2	-	2	-	4	-	8
17	-	2	5	2	-	4	1	14
18	-	6	-	3	-	4	-	13
19	4	2	-	2	1	2	-	11
20	3	-	-	2	2	4	1	12
21	3	-	-	2	2	4	1	12
23	-	-	-	2	-	4	1	7
24	-	2	5	-	-	4	-	11
25	4	2	-	2	1	4	-	13
26	3	-	-	2	1	4	-	10
27	2	-	7	2	-	-	-	11
28	4	-	2	2	-	5	-	13
29	4	-	2	2	-	5	-	13
30	4	-	4	2	-	1	-	11

Source: Kameir 1980b, p. 170.

(That there are no figures for day 22 in the original table may be due to an omission in typing as Kameir does not mention that the work has completely stopped in any of the days surveyed. I give a low estimate of 7 workers for that day as it is explicitly reported that it was in only one day that 6 workers were employed.)

6) one worker was given employment for 16 days (when 11 or more workers were employed)
7) a twelfth worker was given employment for 13 days (when 12 or more workers were employed)
8) a thirteenth worker was given employment for 8 days (when 13 or more workers were employed)
9) a fourteenth worker was given employment for 4 days only (when 14 or more workers were employed).

The total person/days worked by the gang is 180+29+26+24+23+16+13+8+4, which is 323 person/days. Given the arduous nature of the work no one worker could be expected to work each of the 30 days; and because of this I calculate the actual days worked in terms of the average frequency of employment for all members of the gang which is around 23 days in the 30 consecutive days surveyed (i.e. 323/14). This calculation, it should be noted, assumes that the member of the gang rests rather than seeks re-employment through his contacts in other building sites.

On the basis of the calculated average frequency of employment we can go further to calculate the average monthly earnings of the members of the gang. Kameir maintains that the average daily wage is £S0.60; but in two stages (digging of foundations and concrete enforcement) the wage is double the average, or £S1.25. In the 30 days surveyed, 3 days are reported to be on concrete enforcement on the ceiling (these are when 23 workers were employed); and it is assumed that digging of foundations was for two days only. Calculating on this basis, the average earnings for each worker during that month were as follows:

(i)	18 days on'average wage':	18x60	£S 10.80
(ii)	3 days on enforcement:	3x125	£S 3.75
(iii)	2 days on foundations:	2x125	£S 2.50
	Total earnings in 23 days		£S 17.05

When Kameir conducted his survey in 1977, the minimum wage in government employment was £S16.50 (cf. Affan 1977, p. 72). In other words, even the most vulnerable of casual workers could earn more than the minimum wage for the permanent government workers!

This comparison of earnings in the formal and informal sectors is intended to counter the conventional wisdom pervading studies on urban wage-labour markets in Sudan. It should not, however, be taken to denote a virtual identity in the terms of employment experienced by the two groups of workers. I refer here to the so-called benefits associated with permanent employment: the paid annual holidays and sick-leave and the after-service payments together with the stipulated compensation in cases of death or injury in the course of work.

When their money-value is calculated, however, the so-called 'privileges' associated with permanent employment are small. Nevertheless, we should not overlook the relative security which some of these 'privileges' provide - a security which the so-called legislative protection does not provide. This is particularly true of sick-leave. A permanent worker, in case of illness, may stay for a period ranging from three to six months (though not with full wage throughout) and comes back to find his job waiting for him. Neither the temporary workers nor the totally casual informal workers are entitled to anything resembling paid sick-leave, or an assured position upon return to work. The role of trade unions in achieving this modest but nevertheless positive gain for permanent workers could hardly be ignored. It is to avert strong trade union activity in those branches of production, such as manufacturing (which do not experience marked fluctuations in production schedules) that prompts a heavy reliance on temporary and casual employment.

Collective Bargaining

Prior to the military take-over in 1969, the forces of supply and demand, productivity considerations and collective bargaining played minimal roles in the determination of wages (cf. Affan 1977, p. 62ff). Wages were almost exclusively determined through administrative and/or legislative action (cf. Taha 1977, p. 193ff). I have already described how the present wage structure in government employment has emerged and the role of the two Commissions of Wakefield in 1951 and the Cadre in 1968. The only exceptions were a handful of large-scale, mainly foreign, companies (e.g. Shell and Mobil Oil) and a few public concerns such as Sudan Railways and the Gezira Board. In relation to these exceptions, it is generally recognised that the adoption of collective bargaining was a function of the size of the workforce and, by extension, of the relative strength of the trade unions. In the case of the multinational corporations and the foreign companies in particular, a desire to avert the emergence of widespread nationalistic feelings was probably a relevant additional factor. By virtue of their strength trade unions in these few establishments managed to obtain for their members higher wages and better terms of employment than in either government departments or the small-scale private enterprises.

While prior to 1969 a form of collective bargaining was observed in a few single enterprises, trade unions and trade union federations were virtually totally excluded from the higher level of national wage policy. More than once the government not only refused to negotiate with the Sudan Workers Trade Union Federation, but also declined even to recognise the federation as the legal representative of workers (cf. Taha 1977, p. 195). The only occasion in which a pre-1969 government actually engaged in negotiations with the Federation, in January 1968, was in response to a desire by government to avert widespread industrial action by union workers (ibid.).

Until the take-over by the Free Officers in May 1969 only a few relatively strong trade unions in some large-scale private enterprises and a few public concerns were able to involve themselves in negotiations with their employers at the level of a single establishment. For the large majority of workers the terms and conditions of employment were decided unilaterally by government; the workers could only indirectly (through industrial action rather than negotiations) influence decisions. The Numeiri regime passed through two distinct phases in its relations with the labour movement. In the first (May 1969–February 1971), the Free Officers adopted a socialist programme and proved, in the main, to be sympathetic to the demands of the labour movement. This phase culminated in the promulgation of the Consolidated Labour Code of November 1970 and witnessed the closest coordination and understanding in the history of the relations between government and trade unions in Sudan. With the suspension of the Consolidated Labour Code in February 1971, the second phase began.

The sympathetic attitude of the May regime during the first phase should not, however, be construed as resulting in improvements in the general conditions of workers. As Taha (1977, p. 122) puts it, in return for sympathy "workers were asked to forego wage demands, to increase production and lend political support for the regime ... (In consequence) .. workers ... not only froze their wage demands, but were subjected to a heavy tax burden." The sympathy referred to concerned measures that effectively increased the number of trade unions and their membership. At the same time, the regime not only undermined the effectiveness of trade unions by prohibiting strikes by means of a Republican Order, but also through its measures to regulate some public concerns brought to an end collective bargaining in the few establishments in Sudan where the relatively strong trade unions managed to involve themselves in the determination of wages. This was the Order suspending the internal rules and regulations of some 18 public concerns pending their revision. The establishments affected included Sudan Railways, the Gezira Board, the Central Corporation for Electricity and Water, and the Rural Water Development Corporation - all of which had the strongest trade unions in the country (cf. Abu-Eisa 1981). The Republican Order thus denied the workers in these establishments gains for which they had fiercely fought, and subjected them once more to the general rules and regulations operating in other government departments. In the large-scale private enterprises, on the other hand, collective bargaining had come to an end as a result of the ban on strikes. Private employers could thus ignore workers' demands without fears concerning disruption of production through industrial action.

The Trade Union Movement in Sudan

Though the trade union movement in Sudan consists of both blue- and white-collar workers, it is the former who initiated the movement historically. Since several contributions dealing with aspects of the history of trade unionism are readily available, I do not need to repeat all the historical account here. The most important contributions are those by Fawzi (1957), Beshir (1974) and Lobban (1975; 1982). In addition to these, a few contributions to the study of labour legislation in Sudan have also emerged in recent years (Taha and El-Jack 1973; Abu-Eisa 1981; and Abdel Karim 1981), among which the contribution by Abu-Eisa is particularly useful in understanding the laws issued in relation to trade unions.

My one important reservation on the historiography of trade unionism in Sudan concerns the tendency of most scholars to equate the origin of the trade union movement with the legislation issued by the colonial state in 1949 (The Trade Unions Ordinance) which recognised the right of a small sector of wage-workers to organise. Most scholars have thus tended to assert that the movement is a creature of the recent past dating back to the strikes of 1947/48 staged by railway workers. These strikes, it is often claimed, were induced by the increase of prices following the Second World War (cf. Fawzi 1957, p. 22; Taha 1972, p. 14); and their success resulted in the promulgation of the Employer and Employed Persons Ordinance and the Trade Union Ordinance in 1949. Despite this assertion all scholars have, in the actual course of their accounts, dealt with some of the events that had occurred at least a decade earlier and which are relevant to the understanding of Sudanese trade unionism. As expressed by Musa (1959, p. 147) in his review of Fawzi's The Labour movement in the Sudan, "instead of telling the story chronologically", these scholars "chose the other way ... (They) started at the point where the workers' consciousness crystallised in a clear cut attempt to form trade unions, and from there went on to tell the story in detail."

Rather than a concern with sheer chronology, however, it is my conviction that in emphasising the events of the 1940s and the attempt to equate the birth of the trade union movement with the legislation of 1949, two basic points have in effect been overlooked. The first concerns the relationship between trade unions and the Trade Union Ordinance. In this respect, the Ordinance marked neither the birth of trade unions, nor even the crystallisation of workers' consciousness to form unions. It was, rather, a capitulation by the colonial state to an already established and well-organised - albeit 'illegal' - trade union movement that forcefully asserted itself. This point has been hammered home by Abu-Eisa (1981, p. 6) who maintains that:

> The 1949 Ordinance recognised the right of workers to organise in trade unions that could serve their objectives and regulate their relations with employers ... Well before that Ordinance, however, Sudanese workers had established their own unions and engaged in union activities despite the opposition of the colonial government to, and lack of laws to legitimise, such organisations and activities. In the face of the intensive pressure applied by the labour movement through industrial action, however, the foreign administration had no alternative but to concede the right of workers to organise ... The Ordinance thus followed in order to 'regulate' an already established trade union movement. This is a crucial point which has to be recapitulated; the right of workers to organise is not a 'gift' from anyone. It is a right of which workers had been deprived, but which they forcefully seized through a long and protracted struggle. (My translation).

As the workers gained recognition for their trade unions through their own struggle, they also engaged in fierce battles in order to assert the right of trade unions to organise in a federation. The Workers Affairs Association which railwaymen established in 1946 as their national organisation thus formed the first stage in what was unilaterally declared by workers in 1950 as the Sudan Workers Trade Union Federation (cf. Fawzi 1957; Taha 1970; 1972). In the face of opposition by the colonial government, the newly established Federation organised in August 1951 one of the most successful strikes in its history.

The initiative of the labour movement to form trade unions found its first successful expression in the formation of workers' clubs in Sudanese towns, starting with Atbara and Khartoum in 1934 and 1935 respectively. The establishment of these clubs (ostensibly for social and recreational purposes) not only illustrates the organisational skills of Sudanese workers, but also, and even more significantly, points to the workers' crystallised consciousness of their common class position and interests. From their inception the clubs constituted bases from which the labour movement waged the struggle to obtain recognition for its right to organise in trade unions. As these clubs were formed, not only the leadership of the trade unions emerged from among their membership, but the clubs themselves were identified with the trade union movement. This last is clearly corroborated by the case of the workers' club in Khartoum which launched in 1946 its own magazine, El-A'mil El-Sudani (The Sudanese Worker). From its first issue, the magazine advocated the need for the establishment, and recognition, of fully-fledged trade unionism to represent Sudanese workers nationally (cf. Fawzi 1957). Thus in no way could the origins of trade unionism be equated with the colonial Trade Union Ordinance.

Most scholars, in fact, tend to trace the origin of the trade union movement to the strikes of the 1940s, and contend that the rise in prices following the Second World War was the main factor behind the militancy of workers. In contrast it is my contention that trade unionism, defined as the concerted effort by workers to unite in their struggle to obtain better terms and conditions of work, is an integral aspect of the process of the emergence of a wage labour force in the country. Unity, however, is a process. It starts from the level of the single establishment, through industrial or sectoral levels, to the national (and international) levels. At all these levels the principle underlying workers' organisation is that of trade unionism, that is to say, of the need of workers to unite in order to be effective in their pursuance of better terms and conditions of work. Trade unionism in Sudan, which could only be meaningfully conceptualised in the terms proposed, could thus be traced not only to the establishment of workers' clubs, but as far back as to 1903 when workers from the forestry department went on strike in protest against the conditions of work (cf., Beshir 1974, p. 190). From that date on, the militancy of workers never ceased throughout the colonial period as evidenced by the incidence of strikes that increasingly involved larger numbers of workers drawn from the different regions of the country (cf., idem., pp. 190 ff; Musa 1959).

In accounting for the struggle waged by the labour movement during the colonial period, many scholars have tended to over-emphasise the nationalist nature of the movement in colonial Sudan to a virtual disregard of its working class origin. In stressing the class, or 'partisan', character of the labour movement, of course, I do not deny that almost all wage-earners in Sudan did, and continue to, subscribe to the ideology of nationalism.[9] Nor is it my intention to belittle the crucial and decisive role which the labour movement played against the British colonial administration in the country. As Taha (1972, p. 15) puts it, the industrial action by Sudanese workers "must have shaken the colonial government and destroyed the facade of invincibility that surrounded it." What should be stressed in connection with the apparently nationalistic or anti-colonial character of trade unions in colonial Sudan, however, is the position of the colonial state as the largest single employer of union workers in the country. In other words, the conflict between the trade unions and the colonial state was, above all, underlain by the former's search to improve the terms and conditions of work on the one hand and, on the other, the unwillingness of the latter (both as employer itself and as guardian of the interests of employers in general) to concede such improvements. Such was the situation between government and trade unions in colonial Sudan, and such is the situation in the post-colonial period. In both periods, the trade unions entered into conflict with the state by virtue of class interests.

It is worth noting that the conflict with the colonial state, coupled with the ideology of nationalism among workers, created conditions conducive to the fostering of an alliance between the labour movement and the educated elite that was seeking to control an independent Sudan. Despite the persistent efforts by the elite to mobilise the support of indivdual workers, however, an alliance between the labour movement and the Graduates Congress led by the elite was never consummated. A more convenient alliance was instead formed between the latter and the various fractions of the (commercial and agricultural) bourgeoisie along with the religious and tribal leaders (who in many cases were also part of the bourgeoisie). With the disintegration of the Graduates Congress and the formation of the traditional political parties in Sudan, the various fractions of that alliance came to constitute the leadership of the political parties which gained power after flag Independence in 1956. The only allies that the labour movement could find were, and still are, a small minority of petty bourgeois elements (a few professionals, a handful of academics, students, etc.) and the Communist Party of Sudan which, though with a small membership compared to the traditional parties, nevertheless has more than proportionate political weight. As soon as Independence was achieved and the nationalist movement started to subside giving way to sectarian loyalties, the post-colonial state proved no less compromising with the labour movement than its colonial predecessor.

The conflict between the labour movement and the state was thus carried over into the post-colonial period. The crisis accruing from the intensification of the conflict between the labour movement and its progressive allies on the one hand and, on the other, the national government controlled by the rural-based Umma Party culminated in a general strike in October 1958 (cf. Beshir 1974, p. 198). With the escalation of the crisis the first parliamentary democracy in the Sudan came to an end. The military junta of General Abboud was literally handed power by the civilian Prime Minister in November 1958. Among the first measures undertaken by the junta was the arrest of union leaders and the dissolution of all trade unions in the country. These measures, of course, were met by stiff opposition from workers, and the military government had to submit to the blue-collar workers' right to organise. Thus, early in 1960 an Ordinance was issued recognising trade unionism for blue-collar workers; white-collar workers were not given that right. As with the original Trade Union Ordinance, the new law imposed many constraints on the movement. Thus, not only was no federation allowed but also the minimum number of workers to form a trade union was increased from 30 to 50. As unions could only be established by workers on the basis of the same employer, the new law resulted in a drastic decrease in the number of both the unions and their membership. According to Taha (1972:, p. 8), the total union membership decreased from 86,355 workers organised in 135 unions in 1958 to 61,959 members organised in 71 unions in 1960.

The attempts by the Abboud Regime to pacify the trade unions resulted in an intensification of the struggle by workers to overthrow the government. The labour movement, however, was not the only target of repression by the junta. As opposition to the military gained strength, the general strike (which was followed soon after by total civil disobedience) in October 1964 effectively guaranteed the success of the October Revolution. The revolutionary elements that assumed power in 1964 had the full backing of the labour movement in Sudan which took the "unprecedented step of suspending wage demands so as to help the government cope with the economic crisis it was facing" (Taha 1972, p. 20). By June 1965, the traditional political parties once more assumed power in Sudan; and with their ascendency there was a renewal of the antagonistic relations between the government and the labour movement. With the exception of the brief period from October 1964 to May 1965, the trade union movement in Sudan was in constant struggle to assert its sheer existence as the legal representative of workers. Only in a few public and large-scale private establishments could trade unions (at the level of a single establishment) involve themselves in collective bargaining. When the Free Officers rose to power in May 1969, the labour movement lent support to the self-professed socialist programme of the Revolutionary Command Council.

The initial sympathy of that government is most clearly corroborated by the creation of the Ministry of Labour (in place of the former Labour Department) and the attempts to involve the trade union movement in the process of labour legislation and policy-making. Following brief negotiations between the Labour Minister and the Trade Union Federation, the May regime authorised the former to form a competent committee led by trade unionists to review all labour legislation, and to present recommendations for new laws (cf. Abu-Eisa 1981).

The new provisions introduced constituted a severe constraint upon the manouevres employers used to adopt in the attempt to obstruct the formation of trade unions in their respective establishment, for example, by firing, from time to time, a number of workers to reduce the size of the workforce to under 30 workers (which is the minimum legal size to form a union). Another Order reduced the procedure for the compulsory registration requirement to the simple filing of papers by unions and the prompt checking of number of workers by the Registrar. The most significant Order, however, was the one stipulating a new principle for the formation of trade unions (cf. Abu-Eisa 1981). By means of this last, workers in small establishments who could not form a union on the basis of the same employer were allowed to organise on the basis of the same industry at the level of the same town or district. The Consolidated Labour Code even went further than the Orders and recognised the right of apprentices to join trade unions. In consequence, the first phase of Numeiri's regime witnessed a dramatic increase in the numbers of both the trade unions and their membership. The Code also stipulated the necessity of unity in the trade union movement, and accordingly prohibited the formation of more than one federation each for blue-collar and white-collar unions whether at the level of a single industry, a sector, or nationally. Likewise, whereas the Code recognised the right of teachers to have their separate national federation, the right of the national federations to form a single confederation was also recognised. The identification of the Code with trade unions was most explicit in its definition of worker which effectively abolished the distinction between manual and mental labour and as such recognised the rights of blue- and white-collar workers to form a joint trade union; affiliation to the higher levels in such cases was left to be decided by the members concerned. The position of trade unionists was also consolidated. The Code stipulated many guarantees for union leaders against dismissal because of union activity. Transfer of union leaders, except with the consent of the union, was also prohibited. Finally, the Code stipulated paid full-time union activity, leave relating to union activity for non-full-timers, etc., which had previously been at the discretion of employers.

In relation to the involvement of trade unions in policy-making, moreover, the Code stipulated the creation of three Councils formed of the representatives of workers, employers and the government; and in each council the representatives of workers were to comprise at least half the total number of members. The first of these Councils, the Supreme Labour Council, headed by the Minister of Labour, was to be responsible for the formulation, in accordance with the general policy of the state, of policies concerning all aspects of work organisation and industrial relations. The other, and lower, two councils headed by the Under-secretary for Labour were the Manpower and Training Council and the Work Relations Council. These latter were to be specialised councils advising the Supreme Council. Subject to the consent of the Labour Minister the decisions of the Supreme Council were to be automatically operational; and in cases of disagreement, the policies were to be submitted before the Cabinet for a final decision.

The Consolidated Labour Code was thus a landmark in the history of the labour movement in Sudan - not least because it recognised the class basis and interests of trade unions and unionists. Only two months following its promulgation, however, the Code was suspended and all the pre-1969 labour laws it had repealed were reinstated. The suspension of the Code heralded the beginnings of the second phase in government-trade unions relations in the era of Numeiri.

Whereas evidence of class struggle in Sudan could be pointed to in the pre-1969 period, the rise of the Free Officers to power had not only unmasked, but also intensified, that struggle at a number of levels. The self-professed 'socialist' aspirations of the new regime shattered the myth of the impartiality of the state which the post-colonial regimes had previously claimed. Coupled with the measures undertaken to end the domination of foreign, mainly finance, capital in Sudan, the nationalisation and confiscation of large-scale industrial and commercial enterprises, and the forceful assertion of state control over all banking and foreign trade in the country, the Free Officers effectively engaged in an offensive against the bourgeoisie (despite the inclusion of the national bourgeoisie as one of the forces of the alliance). The Consolidated Labour Code was thus only one among many measures that antagonised the bourgeoisie who, in return, sought not only the assertion of their privilege to hire and fire workers, but also to restore their control over the commanding heights of the Sudanese economy - foreign trade in particular. Likewise, the secular orientations of the Free Officers challenged the authority and power of the various tribal, sectarian and political leaders who, as in the incidents of the Ansar in Abba Island in March 1970, opposed the new regime and attempted to bring about its collapse. In short, in the process of keeping pace with the consequences of the measures undertaken by the Free Officers, a struggle over power exploded and had to be resolved one way or the other. The Free Officers, however, were not themselves a homogeneous group; and in the absence of a mass organisation to resolve the disagreements in the Revolutionary Command Council, friction developed among the Free Officers themselves. The commonly held contention that the conflict within the ranks of the Officers was between communists seeking transformation and social democrats and nationalists pursuing reforms, however, seems an over-simplification. The same conflict was observed within the ranks of the communist leadership and that contributed to the split in what had once been the strongest and most organised Communist Party in Africa and the Middle East. Numeiri and the reformists eventually resolved the question of power following the abortion of the counter coup by the communist officers - albeit at the cost of retreating from virtually all the socialist measures previously undertaken. This retreat was, and continues to be, reflected in the reinstatement and further entrenchment of foreign banks and multinational corporations.

The Trade Union Act, 1971 (and its amendment in 1976) typifies the retreat in relation to the trade union movement. Thus, not only the union rights of apprentices have been withdrawn and the distinction between mental and manual labour reintroduced, but also the very objectives of trade unions recognised by the state have been emptied of their class basis and interests. In Section Two, Article (5) of the Act - which defines the objectives of unions - priority was given to increasing production over the role of unions in defending the rights of members "within the limits of union laws, and the imperatives of the national economy."[10] The attempt to restrict union activity through the insertion of the nebulous imperatives of the national economy hardly needs any emphasis. Article (6) of the same Section which deals with the legitimacy of union activity, moreover, goes even further than the former article. It states that unions and federations are entitled to adopt all the means suitable to the realisation of their objectives in accordance with the Act, but it stipulates exceptions for activities considered to "constitute a crime against the security and peace of the state, or against the security of its basic institutions, in accordance with the current laws." As pointed out by Abu-Eisa (1981 p. 52), this last clause constrains the legitimacy of union activity, and accords undue discretion to the state to define, and change from time to time, what is to be construed as touching on its security.

The observation that the regime in this second phase had attempted to constrain union activity does not, of course, posit any new experience for the trade union movement. Virtually all governments in Sudan, colonial and post-colonial alike, did what they could to that end. What really constituted a new experience in this second phase, was the persistent effort to bring trade unions under the direct control of the state. Up until 1971 the trade union movement in Sudan had developed independently of state control and supervision. The Trade Union Act of 1971, however, not only stipulated a new structure and organisation for trade unions that conferred unlimited powers to the Minister of Labour but also accorded to the General Registrar the authority to suspend the activities of any union organisation.

The weakness of the trade unions was most evident in their inability to undertake industrial action. Strikes were prohibited in Sudan; and any person and/or union activist found enticing workers to strike was liable to prosecution under the State Security Act. Times have changed, but we need not consider other provisions of the Trade Union Act, which were detrimental to trade unionism, to understand why the trade unions in Sudan were weak. It is this weakness that explains the deterioration in the living standards of union workers. In view of the foregoing discussion it is therefore more than surprising to encounter assertions that the trade union movement in Sudan "has secured an impressive armory of legislation" and that "Sudanese workers are furnished with collective bargaining procedure that bear comparison with those achieved by organised labour in advanced countries" (ILO 1976, p. 117).

Notes

1. A study carried out by the Sudanese Communist Party on manual workers in the Sudan Textile Factory in Khartoum North corroborates this assertion. The purpose of the study was to analyse why the manual workers in the largest private factory did not join the caucus of communists in which the members were virtually all white-collar workers. Turnover of manual workers, according to the study, was the single most important factor; and it is suggested that the manual unskilled labour force in particular is totally changed every two years. Owing to the circumstances in Sudan relating to the position of communists, however, I could not find any copy of this study, which I know of only from previous experience.

2. Had Kameir studied the conditions of temporary workers in the two factories and compared them with those of permanent workers, he would have noted how little, if any, difference exists in wages for the two groups. Basing my analysis on the wage rates for the casual workers in the construction industry reported by Kameir, I will attempt a comparison later.

3. Such a view has been advanced by Taha and El-Jack (1973, p. 38) who, with the utmost contempt for the Sudanese workers, maintain that:

   > We believe that the regulation of termination of contract, and for that matter all labour legislation, should be designed to fit the socio-economic environment of the particular country in question. We propose that in this stage of our economic development it might not be wise to place too many restrictions on the freedom of employers to run their establishments effectively. The industrial labour force in the Sudan is an infant creature. It lacks discipline, skill, and commitment to industrial life. Under such circumstances employers justifiably need more freedom to handle their labour force ...

4. This suspension was undertaken during what I call the 'first phase' of Numeiri's regime that was established in May 25, 1969. In order not to distract attention from the discussion of termination of employment, however, I will postpone the consideration of aspects of government-trade unions relations under this regime, and deal with it later in the chapter.

5. According to Affan (1977, p. 72), "this law excludes three quarters of the labour force in Sudan since it does not cover seasonal agricultural labourers or workers outside 'stipulated' urban areas or workers in establishments that employ less than ten employees or workers whose age is below 18 years."

6. The deterioration in the value of the Sudanese Pound since 1978 is one indicator. Until June 1978, one Sudanese Pound was equal to 2.87 US dollars; in 1979 it was devalued to £S = $2.00, and after a series of devaluations between 1979 and 1984 it stood (April 1984) at £S = $0.55.

7. In making this comparison, it should be emphasised, the intention is not to assert the uniformity of remuneration for all categories of employees. The white-collar workers and professionals working in state-owned banks and corporations earn in some cases several times what their counterparts in government departments earn. The lowest-ranking bank clerk, for example, is known to earn roughly the equivalent of the salary of an under-secretary or director of a ministry.

8. The data on the 'formal sector' manufacturing establishments quoted by the Mission are part of a survey conducted by the Department of Statistics in 1973. As the Minimum Wage Order to equate wages in private establishments to those in government was enacted in October 1974, I anticipate no methodological problems in comparing the 1973 data with the findings of the Mission's survey of 1974. This is particularly so because, on the one hand, government workers are assumed to have earned well above the statutory minimum wage before the enactment of that legislation (cf. ILO 1976, p. 111) and, on the other, private employers in the 'stipulated' medium-sized and large-scale enterprises which the legislation concerned were given two years (i.e. up to 1976) to comply with the stipulations of the Order (cf. Affan 1977, p. 72).

9. A specifically Sudanese nationalism is of course lacking if the term nationalism is to be construed as denoting the phenomenon that furnished the ideology when nation states emerged in Europe. The fact that the present boundaries of Sudan are a colonial creation that cut across the human frontiers of race, religion, and language hardly needs recalling. The current turmoil in Southern Sudan (not to mention the 17 year war in the South that ended in 1972 along with the regional movements that gained political weight in the mid-1960s such as those of the Beja of the Red Sea, the Nuba of Kordofan Province and the Darfurians of the West) clearly points to the unresolved national question(s) in the country. In using the term nationalism I thus denote what binds the different groups in the country to one another. I refer to this bond as an ideology because it masks the structure of asymmetrical (class and other) relations which comprises the essential component of that bond.

10. According to Abu-Eisa (1981), the listing of the objectives of trade unions in that order was not incidental. It does not only accord credibility to some current calls to have increasing productivity as the primary target of trade unions, but also attempts to constrain the class basis and interests of trade unions. Given that the state is the largest single employer of union workers in the country, moreover, whatever action unions undertake in pursuit of the class interests of workers would be interpreted as contrary to their basic objective (of increasing productivity).

References

Abdel Karim, Hashim Rufa'i (1981), 'Labour Laws', paper presented to The First Law Seminar organised by the Sudanese Lawyers Association in honour of the Silver Jubilee of the Independence of Sudan, Khartoum (in Arabic).

Abu-Eisa, Farouk (1981), 'Labour Laws in the Sudan', paper presented to The First Law Seminar organised by the Sudanese Lawyers Association in honour of the Silver Jubilee of the Independence of Sudan, Khartoum (in Arabic).

Affan, Khalid (1977), 'Wage Determination and Structure in Sudan', Sudan Journal of Development Research, 1 (1).

Al-Ghoul, Abdallah El-Sharif (1982), 'Mulahzat a'n el-hijra al-kharijiya (Observations on Emigration), Economic and Social Research Council, Bulletin 93, Khartoum (in Arabic).

Al-Shazali Ibrahim, Salah Al-Din (1985) Peripheral Urbanism in the Sudan: Explorations in the Political Economy of the Wage Labour Market in Greater Khartoum, 1900-1984, PhD, University of Hull.

Beshir, Mohamed Omer (1974), Revolution and Nationalism in the Sudan, Rex Collings, London.

Birks, S. and Sinclair, C. (1979), 'Aspects of International Labour Migration in the Arab Near East: Implications for USAID Policy', U.S. Agency for International Development, Washington, D.C.

Bromley, Ray, ed. (1979), The Urban Informal Sector: Critical Perspectives on Employment and Housing Policies, Pergamon Press, London.

Chase, H. (1977), 'A Review of the ILO's Report on the Sudan with Respect to the Operation of the Urban Labour Market', paper presented to the symposium on The ILO Report organised by the ILO, Ministry of Public Service and Administrative Reform and Development Studies and Research Centre, Khartoum University, 2-5 May 1977.

Fawzi, Sa'ad El-Din (1954), 'Social Aspects of Urban Housing in the Northern Sudan', Sudan Notes and Records, 35.

--- (1957), The Labour Movement in the Sudan, 1946-1955, Oxford University Press, London.

Galal al-Din, Mohamed El-Awad (1978), 'Ba-dh Qadaiya Al-Sukkaan wa Al-Tanmiya fi al-Sudan wa al-A'llam al-Talit', (Some Issues on Population and Development in the Sudan and the Third World), Development Studies and Research Centre, Development Books Series 1, Khartoum University Press, Khartoum (in Arabic).

--- (1979a), 'Al-Hijrat al-Dakhiliya fi al-Sudan' (Internal Migrations in the Sudan), in Mohamed El-Awad Galal al-Din and Mohamed Y.A. El-Mustafa (eds.), al-Hijra al-Wafida ila wa al-Hijra al-Dakhiliya fi al-Sudan (Immigration and Internal Migration in the Sudan), National Council for Research, Khartoum.

-- (1979b) Hijra al-Soudaniyin ila al-Karij (Emigration of Sudanese), Economic and Social Research Council, Khartoum.

--- (1980), 'The Nature and Causes of Labour Migration to the Khartoum Conurbation', in V. Pons (ed.), Urbanization and Urban Life in the Sudan, Development Studies and Research Centre, University of Khartoum and Department of Sociology and Social Anthropology, University of Hull.

ILO (1976), Growth, Employment and Equity: A Comprehensive Strategy for the Sudan, ILO, Geneva.

Kameir, El Wathig (1980a), 'Nuer Migrants in the Building Industry in Khartoum: a Case of the Concentration and Circulation of Labour', in V. Pons (ed.), Urbanization and Urban Life in the Sudan, Development Studies and Research Centre, University of Khartoum and Department of Sociology and Social Anthropology, University of Hull.

--- (1980b), Migrant Workers in an Urban Situation: A Comparative Study of Factory Workers and Building Site Labourers in Khartoum (Sudan), PhD, University of Hull.

Kannappan, S. (1977a), 'Urban Labour Market Structure and Employment Issues in the Sudan', in S. Kannappan (ed.), Studies of Urban Labour Market Behaviour in Developing Areas, International Institute for Labour Studies, Geneva.

--- (1970b), ed., Studies of Urban Labour Market Behaviour in Developing Areas, International Institute for Labour Studies, Geneva.

Legum, Colin, ed. (1979-80), Africa Contemporary Record: Annual Survey and Documents, African Publishing Company, London.

Lobban, R.A. (1975), 'Alienation, Urbanization and Social Networks in the Sudan', Journal of Modern African Studies, 13 (3).

--- (1982), 'Sudanese Class Formation and the Demography of Urban Migration', in H. I. Saffa (ed.), Towards a Political Economy of Urbanization in the Third World, Oxford University Press, Delhi.

Mazloum, K. R. (1974), Draft Report on Labour Statistics, UNDP/ILO/SUD, 71/002.

McLoughlin, P.F. (1965), 'Labour Market Conditions and Wages in the Gash and Tokar Deltas', Sudan Notes and Records, 47.

--- (1970), 'Labour Market Conditions and Wages in the Three Towns, 1900-1950', Sudan Notes and Records, 51.

Moser, C.N. (1979), 'Informal Sector or Petty Commodity Production: Dualism or Dependence in Urban Development?', in R. Bromley (ed.), The Urban Informal Sector: Critical Perspectives on Employment and Housing Policies, Pergamon Press, London.

Musa, Abdel Wahab (1959), 'The Labour Movement in the Sudan, 1946-1955', Sudan Notes and Records, 40.

Mustafa, Mohamed El-Murtada (1976), 'The Sudanese Labour Market: An Overview of its Characteristics and Problems with Special Emphasis on the Urban Market', Manpower and Unemployment Research, 9 (2).

Mustafa, Mohamed El-Murtada and Affan, Khalid (1977), 'The Sudanese Labour Market: An Overview of its Characteristics and Problems with Special Emphasis on the Urban Market', in Ali Mohamed El-Hasan (ed.), Growth, Employment and Equity: A Selection of Papers Presented to the ILO Comprehensive Employment Strategy Mission to the Sudan, 1974-1975, Khartoum University Press, Khartoum.

Sudan Government (1973), Department of Labour Survey, Statistical Abstract, Khartoum.

Suliman, Ali Ahmed (1974), 'Al-jour wa Mashakil il u'maal fi al-Sudan', (Wages and Labour Problems in Sudan), Khartoum University Press, Khartoum (in Arabic).

Taha, Abdel Rahman E. Ali (1970), The Sudanese Labour Movement: A Study of Labour Unionism in a Developing Country, PhD, University of California, Los Angeles.

--- (1972), 'The Political Role of the Labour Movement in the Sudan, 1946-1969', ADAB (A Journal of the Faculty of Arts), 1, University of Khartoum.

--- (1976), 'The Sudanese Development Path', in V.G. Damachi et al (eds.), Development Paths in Africa and China, Macmillan Press, London.

--- (1977), 'The Industrial Relations System in the Sudan', in Ali Mohamed El-Hassan (ed.), An Introduction to the Sudan Economy, Khartoum University Press, Khartoum.

Taha, Abdel Rahman E. Ali and El-Jack, Ahmed (1973), The Regulation of Termination of Employment in the Sudanese Private Sector (A Study of the Law and its Application), Khartoum University Press, Khartoum.

12 Elite Nubians of Greater Khartoum: a study of changing ethnic alignments[1]

SONDRA HALE

Introduction

When I began my research among urban Nubians[2] in Sudan, I intended to limit my investigations to post-relocation[3] change in ethnicity among Greater Khartoum Nubians. Following Cohen, I regarded ethnicity as "the socio-political manifestation of the formation of new political groupings...the result, not of ethnic groupings disengaging themselves from one another, but of increasing interaction between them, within the context of new...situations" (1969, p. 2). In the Sudanese Nubian case this process referred to Nubian sub-groups increasing in their interaction, and to Halfawi Nubians, in particular, manifesting new group identity in Greater Khartoum. My major emphasis was to show how, in order to function effectively in the Sudanese nation-state, Nubians defended their interests through cultural elaboration and adaptation. Consequently, they moved in and out of particular categories of self-identification: one can be Nubian in one situation, Halfawi in another, or "pass" as Arab. During the period of relocation this changing ethnic identity was to be one of the most effective mechanisms of adaptation (Hale 1973).

I observed that in the private domain endogamy, language, and social network (including such institutions as rotating credit associations) served as primary mechanisms for maintaining ethnic identity and creating social order in urban areas. Although the private society of Khartoum Nubians is extensive and flexible, it is simultaneously, but in different domains, closed, self-protective, and self-perpetuating. I observed that in the public domain Nubians articulated and maintained their identity through informal residential segregation, occupational exclusiveness in the forms of nepotism and patronage, and through voluntary associations (Hale 1979a).

Much of what I found in the field seemed to contradict the Egyptian Nubian patterns. These contradictions were not easy to resolve for, although extensive ethnographic fieldwork was carried out in much of Egyptian Nubia before the inundation of the area (Fernea 1966), very little ethnography took place in Sudanese Nubia. Consequently, we are reliant on a great deal of extrapolation from Egyptian sources. Nonetheless, the scant information we do have on contemporary Sudan is useful in helping us understand the strikingly different stratum occupied by Nubians in Sudan in contrast to the stratum occupied by Nubians in Egypt.

Sudanese Nubian Elites

Historically, Sudanese Nubians have been a study in contradictions: a thriving, well-entrenched urbanised group ("effendi"), on the one hand, and a disprivileged urban migrant group on the other; a highly Arabised category in one sphere, and a closed, unassimilated non-Arabised group in another. Yet, on another level, Nubians and Arabs, together, form the dominant, so-called "core-culture" of North-Central Sudan, commonly referred to as "the central riverain culture" (Hale 1979b). All this ethnographic research and ethnographical guessing was interesting. But beyond it, what fascinated me - and ultimately propelled me into another level of research - was the recognition of the manipulation of ethnicity for economic gain - the complicity of Nubian elites with the national bourgeoisie in relation to working class and peasant Nubians and the spoils or gains of relocation. In fact, what began to be obvious is that a significant section of the national bourgeoisie is Nubian.

This should have come as no surprise, as Nubians had been clients of the Turks, Egyptians, and British (see Dafalla 1975) and were automatically in an advantageous position during the Sudanisation process of 1955-56. In fact, since the 1950s, the increasing propensity for education and urban white collar occupations has propelled Sudanese Nubians into the position as one of the dominant elites in the country. Their urban propensity was demonstrated in the 1955-56 census in which, although constituting only 2-3 per cent of the total Sudan population, their number in Greater Khartoum was some 16-18 per cent - increasing even more after relocation[4]. Their demographic power in Greater Khartoum was matched only by their virtual control over certain sectors of the economy, or perhaps even more significant, the belief by non-Nubians and Nubians alike in Nubian "control" over these sectors.

Much of this economic power had originally accrued from a constant flow of resources and personnel to and from the rural homeland. The question in the mid-1960s was: once the waters from the High Dam flooded much of Sudanese Nubia (especially Wadi Halfa, the hub of Sudanese Nubian commerce), would Nubian elites experience a politico-economic decline? It was not long before the question was answered. Relocation, instead of diminishing the fortunes of the older settlers and some post-relocation migrants, was made to serve the interests of some of them and enhanced the class position of the dominant group even more - most notably Halfawi patrons and their respective clientele. New neighbourhood units formed; occupational ranks closed tighter than ever; and the Wadi Halfa Sons Club hived off from the older Nubian Club (dominated by "Egyptian Nubians") and thrived under the patronage of the Nubian power-holders in the form of government sanction in the face of the banning of all other ethnic clubs in 1969.

It was said by nearly everyone I talked with over a period of some fourteen years (at that point) that Nubians monopolise certain jobs and that once one of them "gets in", he will hire only Nubians thereafter. In the 1960s Sudanese frequently repeated to me that most household servants, doormen, guards, and waiters were Nubians. By the 1970s I was being told otherwise - that Nubians monopolised most of the civil service positions in addition to personal service occupations. By 1971, in fact, the positions said to be all Nubian or dominated by Nubians were many. Some of these claims are more difficult than others to document, as they are locally scattered (e.g., household servants), and I had to rely on estimates from officials in the Department of Labour, my field interviews and observation and interviews carried out by my Nubian Research Assistant. Some of the economic sectors pointed out to me by both Nubians and non-Nubians alike as "Nubian-monopolised" were: (1) transport and communications (e.g. Department of Posts and Telegraphs, Sudan Airways, Sudan Railways, Steamers Department); (2) catering (e.g. transportation, bakeries, restaurants/coffee shops, hotels); (3) civil service (e.g. Ministries of Health, Interior, Finance, Education, Planning; Department of Housing, junior and senior clerical; and government ministers and deputy ministers); (4) banks and other financial apparatuses; (5) Central Electricity and Water Administration (CEWA); (6) companies such as Shell, Imperial Chemical Industries (I.C.I.), General and Sudan Insurance Companies; (7) other private businesses, especially commerce; (8) the University of Khartoum; (9) legal positions; (10) religious officials; and (11) personal services.

Clearly, since all these sectors of the Sudanese urban economy represent a large portion of the occupational structure, Nubians cannot dominate all of them. We can assume that stereotyping, exaggeration, and prejudicial attitudes reflecting resentment of the "effendi" affected my research data. But let us look more closely at selected spheres where information could be obtained. For example, in checking out the claim that Nubians dominate hotels and catering services, I took a survey of one of the five first-class hotels in Khartoum in existence in the early 1970s to see if, indeed, the hotel was managed and maintained by Nubians. The five-floor Oasis hotel, when not government-controlled, was owned by the Kronfli family, Catholic Syrian Sudanese. This hotel (called El-Khayam in 1972), had been nationalised and at the time of the survey was government-controlled. That meant that the staff was technically appointed by the Department of Restaurants and Hotels. However, our informant, a Mahas/Sukkot (Nubian) employee, claimed that personal recommendations usually superceded the Department's. That is, there is de facto monopolisation. This informant and my Research Assistant claimed that the Department of Restaurants and Hotels is, itself, dominated by Nubians. The Manager of the Oasis was a Dongolawi, as was the chief cook. The total number of employees was sixty, out of which thirty-five were Nubians - or 58.3 per cent. There were nine at the level of manager or white collar (such as receptionist), six of which were Nubian, or 66.7 per cent. Out of fifty-one labourers (e.g. baggage carriers), twenty-nine were Nubian, or 57.6 per cent. In the case of the Oasis, then, the percentage of Nubians, mainly Mahas, Halfawiyyin, and Danagla, is not only disproportionate to the Nubian population in Sudan as a whole, but also to the 16 per cent Nubian population of Khartoum.

As for education and government, Nubians moved into "effendi" positions as teachers and other civil servants in the field of education by being the best trained when the British began to recruit "locals" for such posts. But it was not just education, but Western education which was important. Because Nubians were among the first group educated in a western mode and in western terms were the best educated in Sudan (Shaw, 1967, p. 487), they were early equipped to move into many middle and higher level positions in education and government. After all, a bureaucracy requires literacy first and foremost. Using Department of Statistics figures for 1960, Shaw tells us that:

> The level of literacy (defined as a person who has attended any school) is far higher for the population of (Old) Wadi Halfa district than for the Sudan as a whole. Sixty-six per cent of the male population between 16 and 20 years of age, some 45 per cent of those between 21 and 30 years and some 26 per cent of those over 30 years went to elementary school. Fourteen per cent of the male population between 21 and 30 years and 5.5 per cent over 30 years went to intermediate school (Shaw, 1967, p. 487).

It has long been said that the Ministry of Education, for example, is dominated by Nubians. It is a difficult claim to prove, but there are strong clues which point to a large number of Nubians engaged as administrators, teachers, and clerks in the Ministry. For example, I was informed that there were four hundred school teachers attached to the Ministry of Education who originated from one small island of some few thousand people in the Mahas/Sukkot area of Nubia. At that time the Minister was Mohi El-Din Sabr (1969-72), an ethnically conscious Mahas Nubian, and many of the administrators under him were Nubian. During the early 1960s the Ministry was nominally headed by a military appointee (Talaat Farid), but it was really the Deputy Minister, a Nubian, who had the most influence in the Ministry.

Nubians moved into these positions as teachers and other civil servants in education by being the best trained when the British began to recruit "locals" for such posts. My Research Assistant and I took an informal survey of selected villages in Khashm el-Girba (the relocation area). In a village such as Ishkeit (Village 12), with a population in excess of only some two thousand residents, we found only twenty-six illiterate women and fifty-six illiterate men, in a society where literacy is generally only around 10-15 per cent. From that same village were two university lecturers and a number of senior civil servants. In Argean (Village 8), with a population of just over 3,000, thirteen people were doing postgraduate studies, and in Halfa Deghaim (Village 21), with a population just over 10,000, residents claimed that there were over two hundred university graduates who claimed Deghaim as their permanent village.

Nubians, then, played a major role in creating, through at least one apparatus of the State - the educational system - the dominant ideology of the society.

No one institution reflects the dominant ideology of the State more than the first and still most important national university, the University of Khartoum. With such a background of educated people, Nubians were bound to be prominent in the highest academic institution in Sudan. In fact, the first two Sudanese to hold powerful positions at the university were Halfawi Nubians. In comparing two University of Khartoum catalogues a decade apart, one finds an amazingly high number of Nubians in important positions. From the 1973 listing, for example, in the Department of Agricultural Botany, I estimate that nearly 80 per cent of the Sudanese faculty were Nubian; the Department of Geography, 57 per cent. Counting only regular Sudanese faculty, the Department of Economics was 33 per cent Nubian. These are faculty figures under the Vice-Chancellorship of Mustafa Hassan, who is an old Mahas settler who does not claim Nubian identity. The officers of the University at that time numbered sixteen Sudanese, 44 per cent of whom were Nubian. In the University Senate Nubians comprised 25 per cent of the officers. As for the administrative staff (academic, personnel, accounts, development, student affairs, physical education, catering, lodging) thirteen out of twenty-eight Sudanese were Nubian, or 46 per cent (Hale 1979a).[5]

In 1975 there were approximately twenty-three top posts at the University of Khartoum, six of which were held by Nubians, or 26 per cent. However, non-Nubian impressions of Nubian domination of the University are not based on numerical predominance alone (which Nubians readily admit to), but on the power which Nubians wield in key posts. For example, two of the most powerful and influential posts in the administration are held by Halfawiyyin - the Vice-Principal for Academic Affairs and the Vice-Principal for Staff Affairs. Also, the medical faculty is the most prestigious and powerful at the University and for some time had been headed by a Halfawi.

When these Nubians hold positions of power in the University, there is a tendency for many of the lower clerical and labour positions also to be filled by Nubians - often kin of their patrons. But this is also a reflection of Nubian preponderance in service occupations in the general population.

Non-Nubians charge that Nubians are dominating the government, and Nubians themselves often boast of it. The topic was too sensitive for me to attempt to document, but we do know that, although Sudan has had many governments, it has had only nine heads of government since independence in 1956. Out of those nine, there were two Kenzi Nubians, one Dongolawi Nubian, and one Hashmab (part Jaali and Mahas, although not identifying as "Nubian"). In 1967 the high posts in the pre-military government were: the President; the Prime Minister; the Council of Ministers; and the Supreme Council, nineteen persons. Not including Southerners, there were sixteen, nine of whom were of Nubian descent, or 56 per cent.

Class and Choice

One of the propositions suggested in my longer work (1979b) is that the resurgence of Nubian ethnic identity in the 1960s was led by the Nubian bourgeoisie in pursuit of their class interests. The most striking examples of manipulation and collaboration for economic gain were among two urbanised groups: (1) wealthy Halfa Deghaim merchants and white collar residents and (2) Nubian residents of Greater Khartoum, many of whom were also originally from Halfa Deghaim. Whether a merchant or businessman attempting to expand his clientele or a politician wishing to enlarge his constituency with "brothers" and "kin", these patrons chose a course of action which would benefit them and their class. Many of these elites surfaced for the first time as "Nubians" during the crisis and recruited a following formed on a "moral basis" (Bailey 1969, p. 36).

The crisis was relocation, a situation in which resources were limited: some would gain a great deal; others very little; some not at all; and still others would lose. The struggle for control of available resources was not limited to Old Halfa. Once relocation itself seemed inevitable, leaders shifted their focus to the resources of the potential resettlement sites.

In general I found that the wealthier a Nubian, the more politically active he[6] was during relocation. Also, the more his original village had to lose, the more a wealthy individual had to lose. The closer a village was to Halfa Town, the wealthier it was and the better educated the people. Among those better educated migrants to the towns was greater political awareness. The better educated the migrant, the better job he held and the more wealthy he became. The wealthier he was, the more politically active because he had more to lose.

To be a successful leader is to gain access to more resources than one's opponents, to use them with greater skill (Bailey 1969, p. 36), and to have a class backing. A Nubian leader was also able to influence and direct his followers' course of action through the expenditure of resources. This expenditure was often in the abstract form of commitment in energy to being more Nubian than the next leader. However, in the case of Nubian politicians there were advantages "in translating even moral interactions into the language of resources" (Bailey 1969, p. 36).

The manoeuvres, expenditures, and rewarding of followers were highly complex combinations of abstract political rewards and concrete economic rewards. Most of all, however, the ideology of the brotherhood was evoked, "an extremely diffuse system of norms which may be used by an individual to suit his own purposes as the occasion demands" (Parkin 1969, p. 126). These leaders, some of whom had mainly the gaining of political office as their rationale for action, made use of these special kinds of interaction - such as locality or brotherhood. In the Nubian case one can contrast the morality of leaders when relocation in general was being rejected (i.e. all relocation sites) versus when relocation became a given and choices were offered. The introduction of the possibility of new resources created new factions. Both Bailey and Parkin point out the use of ceremony and symbol in recruitment and manoeuvring. To Bailey moral teams are held together by a shared ethic. "The main political capital of the leader of a moral group is his monopoly ... of the right to communicate with or to symbolise whatever mystical value it is that holds the group's devotion" (1969 p. 82). For Nubian leaders the important tactic was use of the symbols of Nubian-ness, because "spiritual and moral leadership in political groups is a matter of manipulating symbols" (Bailey 1969, p. 83). Certain distinct cultural institutions were brought to the fore by leaders to generate solidarity in the face of crisis. This crisis was both moral and economic.

Nubian leaders expressed ceremonial brotherhood in the public arena, some for the first time as residents in the urban area. Urban sophisticates, as ceremonial gestures, attended meetings at the ethnic club for the first time. If their children married during this period, they forewent the hitherto western weddings of an urban elite to re-assert their Nubian-ness through traditional Nubian weddings - making these weddings conspicuous in the public domain.

The moral cause around which to rally the brethren was the Dam and the loss of the homeland; the tactics of minimising the loss involved a re-immersion into Nubian culture, a public display of brotherhood and solidarity. Parallel to Peter Geiser's analysis of Egyptian Nubians, the rewards to the followers were of an abstract nature, a rationalisation for leaving their home for the riches and appeal of an urban life. Sudanese Nubian leaders, like the Egyptians that Geiser interviewed, offered that rationale by repeating the often heard "but for the Dam." The social transformation of Nubians was accomplished in part through the use of cultural symbols to preserve collective identification (Geiser 1973, p. 186). Khartoum Nubian leaders gave their followers myths and ceremonies of Nubian-ness which mediated a contradiction with which Nubians had had to live for more than half a century: during the process of radical social transformation (each heightening of the Dam) Nubians found it necessary to maintain their identification with the collective sentiments directed towards the village while engaged in behaviour which established them as an integral part of the urban complex.[7] The Dam was one of many symbols Nubian leaders used - but one which had its rewards for their followers in the form of being able to reconcile village/ethnic sentiments and urban commitment. The rewards for the leaders, too, were, to some extent, abstract. The Dam and the ensuing crisis allowed urbanised

Nubian elites to relax about their Nubian identity and the display of it. They could stop "passing". No Arab could be justified in charging a Nubian with "tribalism" at such a time. And Arabs of the same class would benefit anyway. Any self-respecting person would be expected to display loyalty to his brothers and sisters and to his homeland under such circumstances. The situation was conducive to the manipulating of ethnic symbols in the public domain without loss of rewards built up through decades of public accommodation and the formation of a powerful fraction of the national bourgeoisie.

Conclusion

Research which had begun as a study of ethnicity developed into an analysis of "patron-client" relationships and then evolved into an analysis of class dynamics during a particular period in modern Sudan history. Too often in anthropological studies of Middle Eastern political processes, the integrative appeal of a "patron-client" approach causes scholars not only to sacrifice a view of the class structures of those societies, but even to forego a stress on conflict. "Patrons" and "clients" are often viewed as if their relationships form a coherent system which transcends the local level and explains the "national" political process. This approach allows the student of Middle Eastern political systems to avoid an analysis of the organisation of production, the market/cash nexus, and labour relations. Clients are seen as linked to patrons across class lines, if not also across ethnic lines. It is a view contrary to one which sees a conflict between owners and labourers. Opting for a model different from both Weberian and Marxian, while combining revised elements of both, these scholars often maintain that "patronage ... lies equally in the path of Weberian universalistic bureaucracy and Marxian class consciousness" (Waterbury 1977, p. 334).

In the case of Sudanese Nubians, the patron-client network does function at a local level and the actors often see it that way. I suggest, however, that these patrons and clients represent classes which arise out of specific conditions. Following Gilsenan (1977), I suggest that a model of more explanatory value is one which focusses on the access of the state and ruling groups to their subject populations, rather than the reverse, which is suggested by most patron-client models - that is, that the system allows clients access to the state through patrons (Hale 1978).

Nubian data not only raise questions as to the explanatory power of the "patron-client" model, but show the structures of domination which are obscured by looking at that particular level of relations. "Patron-client" relations need to be analysed and then related to the class alliance dominated by the national bourgeoisie and tied to the world economy. In a so-called "patron-client" situation the society is seen as a fragmented system characterised by separate atomised elements between which there are mediators and clients. The society is seen to operate through patronage, linking person to person down the line. The links are seen as running vertically from top to bottom, cross-cutting horizontal ties. This is a very tempting way to view society. And at one dimension it is valid. It is what happens in everyday life. Or, at least, it is how informants conceptualise it for us. It is true that to function successfully in some societies one has to have a connection, manipulate kin and friendship ties, exploit dependence, collect favours, etc. But in the broader framework such an approach obscures an analysis of the organisation of production - the coalescence of power at the top.

Mediators or patrons are not generated by a need for links to lubricate the system, but by transformations of the economic and political systems such that a new class arrives out of specific conditions. I am suggesting we focus on the access of the state and ruling groups to subject populations, rather than on "clients'" access to the state through patrons. This is, then, turning the "patron-client" model on its head. If we look at political process at a micro-level we do see patrons, clients, and factions. At the more significant level we see class alliances and consolidation of power at the top. The patrons have a common and vested interest in keeping their dependents dependent.

The local model and ideology does see face-to-face relationships and we would be wrong to deny their existence. This is the ideology expressed to me by Nubian informants when they often spoke of favours (wasta) and political bosses (zuama). The integrative power of the "patron-client" local ideology is useful in tracing connections among the actors, but completely embracing such a view as explanatory of the dynamics of Nubian and Sudanese politics can obscure the structures of domination from which those ideologies - mine and theirs - were generated.

In a discussion of the Wadi Halfa Sons Club (a gift from a patron), I give only one example of a case where a wealthy Nubian acted out his role of patron by dispensing favours to his clients. At the same time, however, he also formed alliances among other bourgeois Nubians (and we have seen that there were many), further consolidating his standing in his community. But he also crossed ethnic lines and aligned with the military government and the owners of production who supported that government.

Although there had been a general Nubian Club in Khartoum since 1936, and there are mutual aid societies for nearly every Nubian village, it was not until the relocation period that people from Wadi Halfa organised their own club. The club became a symbol of ethnic identity and different positions on relocation in the 1960s, associated by some with a pro-government position favouring a move to Khashm el-Girba (the present relocation site). The club was thought by many to have been a conservative force, allowed by the government to flourish in order to channel anti-government protests. Furthermore, the first president of the new Wadi Halfa Sons Club, whom I will call "Jaffar", "bought" the club for the Halfawiyyin - contributing both the land and the building, and acting as the first patron.

The suspicions surrounding the already wealthy "Jaffar" involve his pre-relocation investment of over a million Sudanese pounds in government contracts for the development of Khashm el-Girba. His sudden interest in 1) being "Nubian", 2) mixing with Nubians out of his own upper-class, and 3) participating in an institution he had always ignored, brought much suspicion to the club as a possible tool of the government and to "Jaffar" as the manipulator of that tool. The club, located in a middle-class Nubian section of Khartoum, was ideally situated for drawing in large numbers of working class and petty bourgeois Nubians, a conservative force of people who had, in general, supported the move to Khashm el-Girba.

During the period of relocation patrons dispensed many goods and services in exchange for support from their clients. The Wadi Halfa Sons Club was just one example of the process, and "Jaffar" only one example of a powerful patron: the builder of a club; a defender of the "little man"; a mediator for more services from the government; and employer of Nubians.

At one level "Jaffar's" gift of the club was part of the patron-client system. At another level, such an interpretation obscures other factors. "Jaffar" was an owner of production and he aligned with other owners of production to force certain decisions on the part of the Nubian masses and to control their production in Khashm el-Girba. It is a case where, instead of "clients" having more access to the state through patrons, we can see access of the state and ruling groups to subject populations as dependent allies in class alliances seeking hegemony. We would better serve our disciplines and the people among whom we carry out our research if we always observed, indeed focussed on this level of analysis.

Notes

1. The early field trips (1971-72; 1973-75), leading to the analysis presented in this paper were financed by Fulbright-Hays; American Research Center in Egypt; African Studies Center, University of California, Los Angeles; and American Association of University Women. I am indebted to them and to my Research Assistant, Omer Baba. He should not be held responsible for these views. I would also like to thank the Department of Anthropology and Sociology, University of Khartoum, for housing me, as well as Sayyid el-Mahdi, then Dean of the Faculty of Law, for acting as my sponsor at the University.

2. "Nubian" was a generic term used mainly by non-Nubians until the 1960s relocation period when Nubians themselves began to see the usefulness of the term in constructing a unified ethnic group to oppose relocation. The term was to be inclusive of all the Nubian sub-groups, but often connotes people from the Wadi Halfa area. For a fuller discussion of this process see Hale, 1979a.

3. By "relocation" I am referring to the dislocation/relocation of Sudanese Nubians during the period of 1959-1970, a result of the signing by the Sudanese and Egyptian governments of the Nile Waters Agreement (1959) and the consequent building of the High Dam on the Nile at Aswan (called the Sadd al-Aali Dam), which was completed in 1970. Construction had begun in 1898 on the Aswan Dam itself. It was finished in 1902, elevated in 1912, and elevated again in 1933. With these first processes only Egyptian Nubians were affected. But with the building of the High Dam, some 53,000 Sudanese Nubians were relocated. Egyptians were relocated to Kom Ombo, Sudanese Nubians to Khashm el-Girba, 375 miles southeast of Sudanese Nubia. The High Dam completely inundated Egyptian Nubia and partially flooded the Wadi Halfa area of Sudan, which included the town itself and fourteen villages (Fahim 1972).

4. Population figures have been taken from Sudan, Department of Statistics, <u>First Population Census of Sudan, 1955/56. Town Planners Supplement</u>, Vol. 1, Khartoum, 1960 and <u>First Population Census of Sudan, 1955/56. Final Report</u>, 3 vols. Khartoum, 1962.

5. It should be stressed that these are only estimates, affected by the interpretation of my informants. Numbers would be affected also by the fact that some of these people may not self-identify as "Nubian".

6. Although there have been a few important Nubian women leaders, mainly I am referring to specific male leaders of this period. In general, where I have used the masculine pronoun I have been referring to men, for men hold most of the power in the society. In another paper I discuss how women made it possible for Nubian men to hold powerful positions in Greater Khartoum (Hale 1985).

7. Geiser 1973, p. 189. Geiser's work influenced my own. In these respects the Egyptian and Sudanese Nubian experiences are parallel.

References

Bailey, F.G. (1969), Strategems and Spoils: A Social Anthropology of Politics. Schocken Books, New York.

Cohen, Abner (1969), Custom and Politics in Urban Africa: A Study of Hausa Migrants in Yoruba Towns, University of California Press, Berkeley.

Dafalla, Hassan (1975), The Nubian Exodus, Hurst, London.

Fahim, Hussein (1972), Nubian Resettlement in the Sudan, Field Research Projects, Miami, Florida.

Fernea, Robert, ed., (1966), Contemporary Egyptian Nubia, 2 volumes, Human Relations Area Files, New Haven.

Geiser, Peter (1973), 'The Myth of the Dam', American Anthropologist, 75 (1), pp. 184-94.

Gilsenan, Michael (1977), 'Against Patron-Client Relations', in E. Gellner and J. Waterbury (eds.), Patrons and Clients - in Mediterranean Societies, Duckworth, London.

Hale, Sondra (1973), 'Nubians in the Urban Milieu: Greater Khartoum',Sudan Notes and Records, 54, pp. 57-65.

--- (1978), 'Turning "Patron-Client" on Its Head: Nubian's and Sudan's Class Structure', Paper delivered for the 77th Annual Meeting of the American Anthropological Association, Los Angeles.

--- (1979a), The Changing Ethnic Identity of Nubians in an Urban Milieu: Khartoum, Sudan, PhD. (2 vols.), University of California, Los Angeles.

--- (1979b), 'The Ethnic Identity of Sudanese Nubians', Meroitica, 5, pp. 165-72.

--- (1985), 'Women, Work and Islam: Sudanese Women in Crisis', paper delivered for the Annual Meetings of the American Anthropological Association, Washington, D.C.

Parkin, David (1969), Neighbours and Nationals in an African City Ward, University of California Press, Berkeley.

Shaw, D.J. (1967), 'Resettlement from the Nile in Sudan', The Middle East Journal, 21 (4), pp. 462-87.

Sudan, Department of Statistics, 1960, First Population Census of Sudan, 1955/56. Town Planners Supplement, Vol. 1, Khartoum.

--- (1962), First Population Census of Sudan, 1955/56 Final Report, 3 vols, Khartoum.

Waterbury, John (1977), 'An Attempt to Put Patrons and Clients in their Place', in E. Gellner and J. Waterbury (eds.), Patrons and Clients - in Mediterranean Societies, Duckworth, London.

13 Sudanese migration to the oil-producing Arab countries

MOHAMED EL-AWAD GALAL-AL-DIN

Sudan and Egypt are potentially the largest exporters of migrant labour in the Arab region (see Galal-al-Din 1979). Among all the Arab countries, these two have over 10 per cent of the total population; if Morocco and Algeria are excluded from the Arab group, the share of Sudan and Egypt would be almost 60 per cent (Halliday 1977). Egypt, with over 40 million, is potentially the greatest supplier both quantitatively and qualitatively. But Sudanese have begun to exceed the numbers of Egyptians in many areas - particularly in teaching and clerical jobs in Kuwait, Qatar, and the United Arab Emirates, and to a lesser degree in Saudi Arabia, the greatest recipient of migrant workers in general. The chief oil state receiving Sudanese workers in particular is also Saudi Arabia. It is obvious from Table 13.1 that more than one-half of all Arab migrants and more than two-thirds of Sudanese migrants were in Saudi Arabia in 1979. Libya is the second most important receiving country with about 19 per cent of Sudanese migrants (Table 13.1). Saudi Arabia is the largest oil-producer, and Libya with its high-quality oil, is the second largest in the Arab region at least in terms of revenue from oil.

Both Saudi Arabia and Libya have very limited export resources beyond crude petroleum. Until very recently the countries also had large Bedouin populations, sparsely distributed in the desert. Each country has extremely low population densities and extremely low participation rates of women in economic activities, and both suffer acute shortages of skilled and qualified labour. As oil-based income rose, supplies of indigenous and imported European technical labour quickly fell. Both countries rapidly sought imported Arab labour. In recent years, however, Saudi Arabia has also attracted an increasing number from Asia (see Keely 1980, p. 2) and Libya has imported a large number from the Mediterranean countries (see Birks and Sinclair 1979).

Both Saudi Arabia and Libya can be expected to continue investing in construction of infrastructure for only a few more years. In the early 1980s about two-thirds of the migrants in Saudi Arabia and more than 80 per cent in Libya were production workers. The majority of these were unskilled workers, and many of them were without legal status. When Saudi Arabia and Libya move beyond the present stage and the relative size of the tertiary sector increases, the demand for unskilled labourers for infrastructure will decline or at least level off. At the same time, demand for highly qualified manpower is likely to continue at present, or greater rates.

The general situation in other Arab oil-producing countries is unlikely to differ from that of Saudi Arabia and Libya. Kuwait does not employ such a large number of construction workers as the Libyans and the Saudis. According to the 1975 Kuwait Census, almost one-half of the non-Kuwaiti labour force were professional, technical, administrative and managerial workers (11 per cent) or employed in clerical, sales, community, social and personal services. In the small important oil states of Qatar and United Arab Emirates, the majority of immigrants are still construction workers (Ecevit 1978, p. 6) but construction seems to be tailing off gradually and the governments of these states are now warning the immigrants that "as soon as the construction projects are finished there will be exodus of immigrants" (Bahrain's Minister of Labour, quoted in Far Eastern Economic Review, 11 May 1979, p. 40).

When, and if, the oil-producing countries convert their oil revenues into industrial production and associated socio-economic development projects, then the demand for skilled labour will increase. But the demand for skilled labour is unlikely to be as large as for construction workers, especially if more capital intensive technologies are adopted. Also to be taken into consideration are the expanding educational systems of oil-producing countries that in a few years might enable them to satisfy their requirements of local personnel for both middle level and high level employment.

It is very difficult at present to give accurate or even reasonable estimates of the number of Sudanese working in oil-producing countries. Sudan's Department of Labour Statistics shows the number of those who left Sudan legally and with contracts certified by the Labour Department. According to these statistics, the total number would be 45,000, with 30,000 in Saudi Arabia, 10,000 in Libya and 5,000 in other countries. But in the Sudanese Embassy in UAE alone, the number registered is more than 5,000 and of those who voted for the presidential election in 1976 more than 3,000 were Sudanese citizens. In Qatar on the other hand, I counted more than 800 Sudanese recruited just in the Police Department, and in Oman Sultanate the number of teachers checked

Table 13.1

Distribution of Sudanese and Other Migrants in Oil-rich Country of Employment

Countries of employment	Sudanese, 1979* No.	%	All migrants, 1975** No.	%
Saudi Arabia	140,500	67.9	773.40	52.0
Libya	39,000	18.8	332,350	18.1
United Arab Emirates	14,000	6.8	256,500	13.9
Kuwait	4,500	2.2	211,444	11.5
Quatar	2,700	1.3	53,846	2.9
Oman Sultanate	2,500	1.2	-	-
Northern Yemen ***	2,000	1.0	-	-
Iraq	800	0.4	-	-
Others	1,000	0.5	29,982	1.6
Total	207,000	100.1	1,657,522	100.0

* The author's estimates from different sources.

** Birks and Sinclair, 1978, p.10.

*** Northern Yemen is not an oil-producing country; in fact, relative to its population, North Yemen is the most important labour exporting country in the Arab region. Sudanese migrate to North Yemen either to fill the gap created by the Yemenese emigrants or to use North Yemen as a transit point to the rich Arab countries.

Table 13.2

Sudanese Migrants in Capital-rich Arab Countries by Year of Emigration

Year of out-migration	No. of migrants	% of migrants to total
1970 or before	244	6.0
1971	72	1.8
1972	115	2.8
1973	174	4.3
1974	237	5.8
1975	399	9.8
1976	549	13.4
1977	993	24.3
1978	1302	31.9
Total	4085	100.0

Source: Compiled from registration cards at the Sudanese Embassies in the host countries.

from reliable sources in both Sudan and Oman is over a thousand. Also, according to the Kuwait Census of 1975, the Sudanese then were more than 4,500, and in 1978 more than 3,000 of them were registered in the Sudan Embassy in Kuwait. Again, according to the official statistics of Sudan Airways and the Sudan Ministry of Interior, the numbers of Sudanese who made a pilgrimage in 1977 and in 1978 (with return tickets) but did not return to Sudan after the pilgrimage season were 10,500 and 13,000 respectively.

On the other hand, the verbal official Sudanese estimates vary considerably. In Saudi Arabia, the Ambassador told me in 1978 that the number of Sudanese was in excess of a quarter of a million while other officials' estimates ranged between 150-200 thousand. The range of these improbable guesses applied also to Sudanese in Libya. In fact, in both Saudi Arabia and Libya the majority of the Sudanese migrants are believed to be illegal.

In order to arrive at a reasonable estimate, during 1978 I visited not only most of the receiving countries but also most regions of those countries where the Sudanese were expected to be found in significant numbers. The statistics obtained from these visits were checked for consistency with statistics obtained from different sources as well as against information obtained from a sample of 500 migrants in the receiving countries.

The sample results show that only 22 per cent of Sudanese migrants left Sudan through official channels and can thus be considered as legal migrants. If this is so, and if the sample is fairly representative, then the number obtained from the Department of Labour should be multiplied by a factor of 4.5 in order to obtain slightly more than 200,000 Sudanese working in the oil-producing countries.

On the other hand, the number of owners, mostly migrants, of foreign currency accounts, mostly migrants in one Sudanese commercial bank in early 1979 was 27,006. At that time there were four other Sudanese commercial banks and at least two foreign banks where migrants had current accounts. If we assume that all other banks had only 50 per cent of the migrants' accounts, then the total number of accounts would have been about 54,000. According to my survey only 24 per cent of the migrants transferred their savings through banks. Accordingly, the total number should be 225,000 migrants.

These statistics were consistent with the number arrived at from different sources in the receiving countries including Sudanese sources in embassies and social clubs. However, that margin of error is likely to be greater in both Saudi Arabia and Libya, and these are the countries where more than 80 per cent of the Sudanese migrants are to be found.

If, however, we assume that the geographical percentage distribution of Sudanese in 1979 is the same as that of all other migrants in 1975 (See Table 13.1), then their number in Saudi Arabia and hence their total number should be drastically reduced. However, the percentages of Sudanese in both Saudi Arabia and Libya are not expected to decrease because of proximity and because much of the migration is clandestine. On the other hand, it would appear from Table 13.2 that most Sudanese migrants left Sudan after 1975. The table shows that two-thirds of them migrated in the years 1976-1978. Table 13.2, however, shows the trends of the stock of the out-migrants - present in the receiving countries - up to the end of 1978. We have no data on trends of returnees although this is very important. Many migrants - especially the illegal ones, return after a short period (1-3 years) although some of them remigrate at a subsequent date.

Before going further, it is interesting to note from Table 13.1 that about 2,000 Sudanese were working in Northern Yemen in 1979. In fact, one source estimates the number of Sudanese in Northern Yemen as more than 6,000 in early 1979 (Ali 1979, p. 9). We believe that this last estimate is unrealistic. But whatever the actual number, it is surprising to find Sudanese in a country which is considered to be among the poorest countries in the world. Because North Yemen is the most important exporting country in both relative and absolute terms, unskilled Sudanese workers may go there either to fill the gap created by the Yemenese emigrants or just to use Yemen as a transit point to the oil-producing countries when they find it difficult to go directly to those countries. However, the majority of the Sudanese in Yemen are semi-professional, clerical and technical workers and over 100 of them are qualified professionals and experts with immense practical experience. Since Northern Yemen has acute shortages in both middle level and high level personnel (e.g. teachers, nurses, clerical workers, social workers, etc.) many of the Sudanese are there to meet some of the Yemeni requirements, although the majority of them would probably hope for a better job opportunity in the rich Arab countries.

On the other hand, Iraq, although an important oil producing country, is receiving a relatively small number of Sudanese. This is in spite of the fact that any Sudanese, or for that matter, any Arab national, can enter Iraq without an entry visa and stay there as long as he wishes. But Iraq, unlike other Arab oil-producing countries, but like most other developing countries, suffers from a surplus population in the rural areas, and hence can easily attract unskilled labour for construction and industrialisation from its rural sector. However, Iraq appears to have some shortages in technicians and skilled workers. This may explain why almost all the Sudanese in Iraq were reported as skilled labourers, mechanics, electricians, welders, carpenters, etc. None of those met and interviewed reported himself as an unskilled or general worker.

Characteristics of Migrants

Although the Sudanese migrants at present constitute about only 1.5 per cent of Sudan's population, they make up almost 7 per cent of the labour force. This is because most migrants are males. Of the male population in the age group 20-34 they constitute about 10 per cent. Therefore, although the migrants constitute a very small proportion of the total population, they are more significant among those who are more able to contribute effectively to socio-economic development (see Table 13.3). This, however, is only a part of the

Table 13.3

Age Distribution of the Emigrants and Male Population Residing in Sudan (%)

Age Group	Emigrants* 1978	Sudan's male population** 1973
Under 20	.8	55.4
20-29	48.8	14.9
30-39	42.2	12.6
40-49	7.2	8.4
50+	1.0	8.7
Total %	100.0	100.0
No.	500	7,137,964

* Emigration survey.
** Calculated from the 1973 Census of the Sudan.

Table 13.4

Educational Characteristics of Emigrants 20-34 Years of Age and Corresponding Age Group of Population Residing in Sudan

	Emigrants		
	In Saudi Arabia	In all host countries	Sudan
Illiterate or Khalwa*	11.0	8.2	65.7
Comp. primary or less	35.9	31.2	22.8
Comp. J. secondary or less	21.2	22.4	5.2
Comp. H. secondary or less	20.9	26.0	4.8
More than high secondary	11.0	12.2	1.7
Total %	100.0	100.0	100.0
No.	345	500	1,166,046

* Religious schools for learning Koran.

Sources: As in Table 13.3.

story. Table 13.4 shows that, although about two thirds of Sudan's male population in the age-groups (20-34) were illiterate in 1973, the corresponding percentage among the migrants in 1978 was about 10 per cent. On the other hand, more than 10 per cent of the migrants have more than high secondary education while the corresponding percentage among male residing in Sudan is under 2 per cent.

The majority of Sudanese migrants are skilled and qualified labour. Table 13.5, for example, shows that, although Sudan has less than 3 per cent of its labour force as professional and technical workers, 31 per cent of the migrants belong to this occupational group. In general, we can say that more than two-thirds of the migrants are skilled workers and highly qualified. Some of the highly qualified workers constitute only a small proportion of the total number of migrants, but a very high proportion of the supply of qualified national manpower. In percentage terms (see Table 13.7), 45 per cent as many Sudanese medical doctors, 46 per cent as many Sudanese engineers, 53 per cent as many Sudanese university teaching staff and as many or more of all Sudanese surveyors are working abroad as work in Sudan. While some medical doctors also work in developed countries like the United Kingdom, almost all other Sudanese skilled migrant are working in the oil-rich Arab countries.

Most of the migrants in general, and almost all the more skilled in particular, were not unemployed when they left Sudan. It can be seen from Table 13.6 that only 6 per cent of those in our sample reported themselves as unemployed prior to emigration. Hence, the proposition that emigration leads to direct reduction of unemployment and underemployment has no support from the available evidence. Sudan may have high levels of unemployment in both rural and urban areas, but it is obvious from the data that most of those who emigrate were not from categories existing in abundance - as the conventional wisdom suggests.

It is, however, well known that very large numbers of persons in the state administration as well as in the public sector are superfluous employees. Any observer can see that most government employees do very little, and many of them do nothing at all throughout their entire working day. Given the existing political and institutional framework, the reduction of the number of employees would usually be accompanied by a reduction in output and services. This is simply because the remaining employees are not likely to increase their efforts to compensate for the departure of the migrants. To this must be added a phenomenon which is not easily measurable but which can be verified; namely the deterioration and almost near collapse of certain governmental service as a result of out-migration. It is an observable fact that those government employees who do very little or nothing in many cases have their own businesses, or they work with private business, making use of their position to give those businesses access to governmental facilities, e.g. credit, licenses, approval, etc. Since these people can supplement their incomes from salaries and wages, they are the least likely to emigrate. It is probably the more hard-working and the more honest ones who will find themselves compelled to leave.

Table 13.5

Distribution of the Emigrants and Male Population Residing in Sudan by Occupational Groups

Occupational group	Emigrants B*	A**	Sudan
Personal and technical workers	30.6	22.8	2.7
Administrative and managerial workers	4.0	1.6	0.4
Clerical and related workers	9.6	8.8	1.5
Sales workers	4.0	1.6	4.8
Service workers	7.2	8.4	8.0
Agricultural and related workers	6.0	-	58.0
Production, transport, equipment operators and labourers	38.6	56.8	12.5
Others, not classified	-	-	12.0
Total %	100.0	100.0	100.0
No.	500	500	2,759,865

B = occupation before emigration: A = occupation in host countries.

Source: As in Table 13.2.

Table 13.6

Emigrants by Industry Before Departure and on Return as Compared to Population Residing in Sudan (%)

	Emigrants B	IR**	AR**	Male population presiding in Sudan
Agriculture	5.8	5.0	3.6	59.5
Manufacturing	9.8	3.8	5.8	4.1
Construction	20.0	2.0	2.4	2.5
Electricity	3.4	-	1.0	1.2
Trade, hotels & restaurants	5.8	31.0	34.4	6.5
Transport, storage & comm.	19.0	16.0	30.4	4.6
Financing	2.0	2.2	-	0.1
Social & personal services	28.0	6.2	16.6	12.4
Other activities	-	-	-	2.3
Unemployed	6.2	-	5.8	6.8
Undecided	-	33.7	-	-
Total %	100.0	99.9	100.0	100.0
	500	500	250	2,759,865

* B = before emigration.
** IR = intention on return.
*** IR = actual on return.

Table 13.7

Emigration of Same Categories of Professionals and Highly Skilled Sudanese in Relation to Those Working in Sudan, 1978

	No. working in Sudan	No. working abroad	% of emigrants to non-emigrants
Medical doctors	2,169	978	45.1
Engineers & architects	1,078	501	46.5
Surveyors	242	245	101.2
University teachers	500	265	53.0

Source: Compiled by the author from different sources.

Table 13.8

Some Other Characteristics of Emigrants and Emigration

	% of migrants
Going abroad	
Through official channels	22
Pilgrim or omra (illegal)	61
Tourism or visit (illegal)	11
Other means	6
Government employees	
On secondment	14
Resigned from work	12
Left work without notice	74
Marital status	
Married	41
Single	57
Others	2
Wives abroad	
Never	81
All or most of the time	13
Sometimes	6
Birthplace	
Khartoum	13
Other areas	87
Residence before emigration	
Khartoum	32
Other areas	68
Residence on return	
Khartoum	49
Other areas	51

Table 13.8 (Continued)

	% of migrants
Most savings transferred	
Through official channels (banks)	24
By himself	23
Sold to 'suit-case merchants' and others	48
Kept in foreign currency abroad	2
By secret means	3
Most savings are spent on	
Agricultural farms	4
Workshops and equipment	6
Weddings and other ceremonies	17
Taxis, "boxes", grocery stores, etc.	23
Housing or land for housing	25
Durable consumer goods	18
Clothing or other non-durables	3
Other	4
Matching of jobs to migrant's skills in host country	
Matching perfectly	20
Matching to some extent	29
Not matching at all	51
Other skills developed or acquired in host countries	
No	43
Yes, some skills acquired	28
Yes, immense skills attained	25

Table 13.9

Passenger Cars Brought into Sudan by Emigrants (1973/74-1977/78)

Years	No. of cars	%
1973/74	180	1.5
1974/75	430	3.7
1975/76	912	7.8
1976/77	4584	39.1
1977/78	5599	47.8
Total	11,715	99.9

Source: Ministry of Finance, Khartoum.

Even among the highly trained technical professionals (in particular certain specialists in medicine and engineering), it could be argued that there is a surplus. This is because some of the skills acquired, whether inside the country or abroad, are neither suited to a real and independent socio-economic and political development nor to the basic needs of the vast majority of the population. The skills of some highly trained professionals might not be required, or at least utilised fully, even under the existing political and socio-economic situations. This is simply because the demand for certain highly specialised skills is necessarily very limited in a poor country where even the small middle class might not be able to afford the services, or in some cases even need the services, of these professionals. The demand for these services by the privileged few is not likely to match the increasing supply from Sudanese and foreign universities.

It is clear that Sudan has been deprived of the more educated, the more skilled and the more healthy workers. In fact, the selectivity of migration as shown so far is only part of the story. It is well known that the Arab employers or their agents in their initial selection of the workers reject in many cases the majority of the applicants for a certain job. More often than not, verbal and/or written examinations were set for applicants having similar characteristics, and of course those who show more competence will be selected.

In the host countries, employers usually restrict contract renewals to those workers who have proved to be more efficient and more productive; more obedient and more disciplined. Those who return to Sudan after shorter periods are in many cases the ones who are physically worn out, tired, sick or injured persons or otherwise have shown bad socio-occupational adjustment, little or no patience or lower motivation and/or initiative.

In spite of these different stages of selectivity, Table 13. 5 shows that a very high proportion of Sudanese migrants is usually assigned low-skilled tasks in the host countries. Comparing column B (i.e. occupation before emigration) and column A (occupational in host countries), it is clear that the proportion of professional, managerial and clerical workers has decreased substantially in the receiving countries. Many of these have no doubt moved to lower occupational groups, particularly to production, and transport, etc.

The results in Table 13.5 have been confirmed by field observations. While visiting host countries I came to know various examples of highly educated people who are assigned a job not matching their qualifications. A few examples are in order. Two primary school teachers, a Sudan railway clerk (the three with high secondary education) and a nurse were working as bricklayers and painters in Tabook, Saudi Arabia; many high secondary school graduates were laying water pipes in different Saudi towns or handling cargo in the sea-ports or doing various casual work; a veterinary doctor is working as an interpreter in the Yemen Arab Republic and, last but not least, an engineer is working as a time-keeper in the U.A.E.

More than half the migrants in the sample claimed that the jobs assigned to them in the host countries were not matching their qualifications (See Table 13.8). More than 40 per cent of the migrants were not developing or acquiring new skills in the host countries. Hence the claim that emigrants may acquire more skills when working abroad has no support from the available evidence. It is evident, however, that high proportions of Sudanese migrants are working as unskilled or general labourers. This is so, in spite of the fact that more than half of them have post-primary education. At the same time, there are no technical schools or on-the-job training programmes for most Sudanese or other migrants in host countries. Those migrants who are likely to develop new skills or acquire more than they already have are usually the ones who stay abroad longer than the others.

Even if we assume that the bulk of migrants develop new skills and assume further that these skills are relevant to the needs of Sudan, the question is whether the new skills acquired are actually utilised in productive and useful work after return. The evidence provided by Table 13.6 suggests that the majority of migrants intend to join the tertiary sector after return (see column IR). In fact the provisional results taken from a sample of 250 returnees (see Table 13.6, column AR) shows that the overwhelming majority are actually in the tertiary sector, especially trade, taxi services, etc. It is believed that the numbers of people in these services have exceeded the requirement of the economy.

Other evidence that returned migrants, whatever skills they have, might not be employed productively can be shown by investigating the uses to which remittances and savings are put. Table 13.8 shows that most savings of migrants are expended on the consumption of imported goods or on land speculation, housing or trade, and a very limited amount has so far been spent on local production. It is therefore obvious that the migrants' savings tend to swell the country's tertiary sector at the expense of, or at least without contributing to, the development of the agricultural or industrial sectors.

Many economists view a large tertiary sector as a major indicator of development. But if this happened to be so in Western Europe and the U.S.A. in the past hundred years, it is not likely to be so in a dependent under-developed country like Sudan. In a country which is not able so far to meet the basic needs for the majority of its population, and where there is deterioration in both the industrial and agricultural sectors, it would be unwise and in fact very dangerous to create a market for non-basic consumer goods or services out of proportion to Sudan's ability to meet the demand created for a significant number of the population. The rapid expansion of the tertiary sector would simply distort the whole economy and sustain the dependence and underdevelopment of the country.

It is also important to note (see Table 13.8) that the tendency of the majority of migrants is to settle in large urban areas - particularly in the capital city, rather than the rural areas from which they originate. This will no doubt accelerate urban growth and lead to more regional imbalance.

One of the main features of Sudanese migration abroad is that most of it (particularly to Saudi Arabia) can be considered as illegal. Table 13.8 shows that only about 22 per cent of those in the sample left the Sudan through official channels. Over 60 per cent of all migrants went to Saudi Arabia as pilgrims. All Sudanese have a right to make a pilgrimage if they so wish, and many Sudanese, including government employees, ask for a short leave or their annual leave at the time of Omna or Pilgrimage. They claim that they are going to Hadj or Omna but with no intention of an early return, unless they fail to get a job. It can also be seen in Table 13.8 that of those who were government employees in the sample, more than 70 per cent of them left their work without notice. It is very difficult to replace these absentees quickly and easily. Even if there are enough people with the same qualifications and experience (an unlikely assumption), it can sometimes take several months to fill a vacant job.

Many employers in Sudan (both in the public and private sectors) say that they are compelled to replace those who have abandoned their jobs with less qualified and less experienced workers. In some cases they replaced a departing efficient worker with two or more less skilled workers and this has obviously increased substantially the cost of the governmental units or private enterprises without even maintaining the level of productivity. The results have been deterioration in (and in a few cases) complete collapse of certain services and manufacturing enterprises. In fact, in some cases, Sudan was not able to replace certain types of emigrants. Some employers were compelled to import Egyptians or those of other nationalities to replace the Sudanese. There were also a few cases of group emigration where all workers in a certain industry (e.g. Coca Cola factory) left together without the knowledge of the employer.

Government Policy and Flow of Remittances

One of the most important and obvious benefits of emigration is said to be the flow of remittances to the labour exporting countries. It is said that these remittances not only raise the standard of living of migrants and their dependents, but also generate local development by providing additional savings and capital formation. Remittances are also expected to reduce the increasing deficits in the balance of payments and provide some foreign currencies which are badly needed in Sudan.

The incomes of the emigrants and their families and other dependents (whether left in Sudan or abroad) do of course rise and correspondingly their standard of living will rise compared with non-emigrants having similar characteristics. It is also true that some of the savings are sent back to Sudan through official channels, and the impact of these savings on the balance of payment is the same as that of other transfers from abroad. But for the remittances, whether in cash or kind, to generate sustained local development will obviously depend largely on the use to which these remittances are put. Table 13.7 indicates that most savings tend to have a consumption effect rather than an investment effect. They are spent on imported consumer goods, not imported capital goods. Emigrants and their families increase local expenditure rather than local production. Some kinds of expenditure (e.g. on weddings) tend to strengthen and reinforce some of the undesirable traditional values (e.g. social prestige) not consistent with the urgent needs of the society.

Excluding remittances in kind, those who send their savings through official channels constitute only about one-quarter of the emigrants. Only about 24 per cent of emigrants (see Table 13.8) reported that most of their cash savings are transferred to Sudan through commercial banks - a number more or less consistent with the number of owners of foreign currency accounts in the country.

Past experience in Sudan suggests that the black market currency rate is always ahead of even any incentive rate. If currency dealing on the black market is to be eliminated altogether, there would seem to be no solution other than to have an entirely free or floating exchange rate in operation. This means, though that more devaluations would be inevitable, but under present conditions it is most likely that the Sudanese pound will continue to float downwards. Accordingly, many emigrants may keep part of their savings abroad in anticipation of other possible devaluation decisions taken. This is likely to be so because there are now very limited investment opportunities in the country and investment by emigrants in the tertiary sector has already resulted in a surplus of services in Khartoum and in many other large urban centres.

Emigrants, Remittances and Inflation

Inflation has been a marked charactertistic of Sudan's economy in the past few years. Although it is not possible to assess with any precision the part played by emigration and the flow of remittances, there is no doubt that these have contributed significantly to the inflationary pressures experienced by the country. More important factors than emigration included the expansionary monetary policy of the government in the past, the exceptional increases in oil prices after 1973, the several devaluations of the Sudanese pound, and the deterioration in both industrial and agricultural output. But most of these factors in the past have been affected to an extent by emigration. The rapid increase in the supply of money was dictated partly by the flow of remittances for which the central bank needs to create an equivalent. One of the purposes of devaluation is to attract more and more of the emigrant's savings through official channels. Reduction in output in both the industrial and agricultural sectors could be a result of increasing out-migration and increasing absenteeism.

Because of increasing out-migration, increasing trade union pressure, and increasing rates of inflation, the government was forced to grant large salary and wage increases to public employees. Increasing emigration of workers, particularly the skilled ones, has also led to substantial increases in wages in the private sector. As a result both government and private firms were forced to raise the prices of goods and services. Thus, the foreign exchange equivalent in local currencies had been accompanied by increasing rates of both public and private expenditure. The additional demands of emigrants and their family members have added to the already increasing demands of government employees, other wage earners and speculators and contractors whose earnings have increased substantially. In short, the creation of a domestic currency equivalent to repatriated earnings, accompanied by increasing wages, government expenditure and rising costs of production have not been paralleled by corresponding increase in the production of goods and services. It would of course, simply mean an increase in both cost-push and demand-pull inflationary pressures.

With limited additional or alternative investment opportunities, there is no doubt that emigrants have played an important role in the dramatic high rate of inflation of land prices in Khartoum and other urban areas. This inflation has resulted not only in diminishing the purchasing power of the lower salaried Sudanese, it has also been disastrous to the poor masses, particularly in the rural areas. In fact, as far as Greater Khartoum is concerned, there has been increasing administrative intervention in the markets for goods in order to restrain price increases. Although these measures have not been effective, they have at least discouraged open dealing in the black market. The rural masses, however, without much political power to put some pressure on the local and central governments, were left largely at the mercy of the flourishing black market.

The devaluation of the Sudanese pound, partly dictated by migrants' savings, is likely to result in a substantial increase in the export of some food items from Sudan to the oil-producing neighbouring countries. The bulk of this export (just like that of emigration) has been, and will continue to be, conducted illegally through the smuggling routes across the Sahara to Libya and through routes across the Red Sea to Saudi Arabia. Since Sudan itself is a food-deficient country, the transfer of these items can only reduce the domestic consumption and add to the suffering of the local consumer by generating more inflationary pressures. On the other hand, the immediate effect of devaluation will be to increase the price of imported goods expressed in Sudanese pounds. The price elasticity of demand for imports (for both capital and consumption goods) is likely to be very low for emigrants as well as for exporters, speculators and other higher income groups. Hence, their consumption of imported as well as domestic commodities will increase. Thus, whatever the level and rates of remittance flows will be, the balance of payments difficulties will persist as a result of the continuing rising import demands.

Summary and Conclusion

It was estimated that by the end of the 1970s about 200,000 Sudanese were working in Arab countries, not counting those in Egypt. Over two-thirds of these were in Saudi Arabia and 18 per cent in Libya. This number had risen from an estimated 30,000 in 1973 to something in excess of 100,000 by the end of 1976 and to well over 200,000 by the mid-eighties.

Sudanese migrants were found on average to be much more educated, more skilled, energetic and potentially productive men than their counterparts left behind in Sudan. Furthermore, most emigrants were employed persons before departure and many of these were not replaced by unemloyed in their absence. Most emigrants, particularly the more skilled ones, originated from the "modern sectors". Both "modern" agriculture and manufacturing industry were badly hit and many services deteriorated or collapsed altogether.

Most emigrants' savings were used for land speculation, weddings, investment in the tertiary sector, or for imported consumer goods (see Table 13.9). This has reinforced certain undesirable traditional social patterns and structures, or in contrast, created tastes for foreign goods in a poor country not likely to meet the demands created for a significant proportion of its population.

The government policies and incentive schemes to attract more and more of the foreign earnings of emigrants (especially the customs relief policy and the land-for-emigrants scheme) seemed to have serious negative effects on the economy as a whole. Emigration has increased substantially but remittances have remained relatively small. They have been accompanied by rapid inflation and a decline in output and possibly employment.

In general it seems that increasing Sudanese out-migration has contributed significantly to the underutilisation of national resources, speculation and improper uses of resources. It seems to be leading, if it has not already done so, to stag-inflation and to a greater distortion of the whole economy.

References

Ali Abdalla Ali (1979), 'Foreign Labour in the Yemen Arab Republic: A Case Study of the Sudanese Migrants', Central Planning Organisation, Sanaa.

Birks, S. and Sinclair, C. (1979), 'Aspects of International Labour Migration in the Arab Near East: Implications for USAID Policy', U.S. Agency for International Development, Washington, D.C.

Ecevit, Zafer (1978), 'Labour Migration in the Middle East and North Africa and Its Economic Implications', Paper presented to UNECWA Seminar on Population and Development, 25 November 1978.

Galal-al-Din, Mohamed El-Awad (1979), Sudanese Migration Abroad, Khartoum: Economic and Social Research Council (in Arabic).

Halliday, Fred (1977), 'Labour Migration in the Middle East', MERIP Reports, 59, pp. 3-17.

Keely, Charles B. (1980), Asian Worker Migration in the Middle East, Working Paper No. 51, The Population Council, New York.

14 Reproductive ritual and social reproduction: female circumcision and the subordination of women in Sudan

ELLEN GRUENBAUM

To outsiders, the practice of female circumcision stands as a classic case of a tradition which is clearly harmful, seems antithetical to humanitarian values, and seems to make no sense, and as such its immediate abolition is in order. Indeed, in Sudan, where a particularly damaging form is widely practiced, these surgeries have long been opposed by Sudanese and foreign reformers.

The practice seems quintessentially cultural, rather than economic or political, based on traditional ideologies and symbols, spoken of as custom or ritual. As Nahid F. Toubia has pointed out, critics have tended to mystify ritual, often assuming that a cultural practice like this is "something inherited from an untraceable past that has no rational meaning and lies within the realm of the untouchable sensitivity of traditional people" (1985, p. 150). I agree that such a view of culture is too limited and too static, and it is my contention that effective policy proposals for change are less likely to emerge when the political and economic aspects of cultures are separated out. Thus, lest reformers fall into the pattern of Fran Hosken, the notorious American anti-circumcision activist whose counter-productive harangues have insulted so many African women, it is important to consider seriously how the practice fits into the contemporary Sudanese political economy and how it affects and is affected by the situation of women in Sudanese society, which is my purpose in this paper. Only then can more effective strategies for change be outlined, and at the same time a more fundamental understanding of the importance of women's issues to the political as a whole can be gained.

Background: Ritual Female Genital Surgeries in Sudan

Various types of female genital surgeries known collectively (and euphemistically) as female circumcision have been practiced in Sudan for centuries. But many are hopeful that this century will be the last, as the amount of attention being given to the problem is growing rapidly. An international conference sponsored by the World Health Organisation on "Traditional Practices Affecting the Health of Women" held in Khartoum in 1979 - which included presentations on female circumcision by several Sudanese scholars - served to mark the great increase in research and activity related to female circumcision. For example, a large-scale survey was conducted among women and men in several provinces to determine current practices and prevalence, which led to the publication of Asma El Dareer's book Woman, Why Do You Weep? Circumcision and its Consequences (1982). A project sponsored by the Babiker Badri Scientific Association for Women Studies included eradication of female circumcision as a goal in the villages where it was conducted (BBSAWS 1985). A Female Circumcision Information and Resource Centre is being established within the Sudan National Council for Research (Fernea 1985, p. 356). Numerous international organisations have become interested in the problem and linkages have been formed with people in other countries affected by similar practices. But before we conclude that circumcision's demise is imminent, an examination of its prevalence and rationale is in order.

The origin of the practice is unknown, though evidence exists that it was practiced by the ancient civilisations of the Nile Valley in Egypt and Sudan. The practice survived the spread of Christianity to the ruling groups of the Nile Valley kingdoms in Sudan in the sixth century. Later waves of Arab migration and intermarriage with indigenous people and the influence of Islamic teachers resulted in Islamisation of northern Sudan by around 1500. Pharaonic circumcision - along with other pre-Islamic beliefs such as the veneration of ancestors and holy men and even spirit-possession cults - was syncretised into the Sudanese Islamic belief system. The practice is deeply embedded in the cultures of northern Sudanese ethnic groups, exhibiting symbolic significance far deeper than its religious associations or other conscious rationales (see Boddy 1982).

Of all types of female circumcision practiced, it is the most severe form which predominates in Sudan. Called pharaonic circumcision, the operation consists of the removal of all external genitalia - the clitoris, the clitoral prepuce, the labia minora, and all or part of the labia major - and infibulation. The infibulation, or stitching together of the opening, results in the occulsion of the vaginal opening and the urethral meatus, leaving only a single tiny opening for the passage of urine and menses.

Another type, known as "Sunna" (which means traditional, or more specifically, following the traditions of the Prophet Muhammad) is practiced by relatively few. It consists of removing only the tip of the prepuce of the clitoris, according to the Sudanese physician-researcher Asma El Dareer (1982). However, the name Sunna is also commonly applied by Sudanese women to other variations of the operation, including simple clitoridectomy, partial clitoridectomy with removal of the prepuce, and several intermediate forms which come closer to the pharaonic. The best estimates of the current prevalence of the different forms are based on El Dareer's survey of several northern provinces, where the research team found that almost 99 per cent of women had some form of circumcision; only 1.2 per cent were uncircumcised, while 2.5 per cent had had the mildest Sunna, 12.2 per cent had an intermediate form, and fully 83.1 per cent had the pharaonic circumcision (excision plus infibulation) (El Dareer 1982, p. 1).

In the northern two-thirds of the country, female circumcision is practiced everywhere, in both rural and urban areas, and among both Muslims and Coptic Christians. Even among the educated urban elites of Khartoum, relatively few families have successfully abandoned the practice entirely. Only the largely non-Muslim southern provinces are relatively free of the practice, except among people of northern origin.

These operations are occasions for celebration. The young girls on whom they are performed are usually five to seven years old, and although they may be fearful of the operation itself, they look forward to circumcision as the first occasion at which they will be treated as important. The girls can expect to receive new dresses, bracelets, and other gifts. An animal will be slaughtered if the family can afford it, and a special meal is prepared for the many guests and well-wishers who are expected to drop by. Wealthy families often arrange musical entertainment for an evening party to which many guests are invited, providing an opportunity for "conspicuous consumption" (Kameir et al 1984).

The operations are usually performed by midwives, either traditional birth attendants or trained midwives who have taken a one-year course; both speak freely of their participation, despite its illegality. There has been some improvement in the methods used in performing the operations, although this has not been uniform. The dangerously unhygienic traditional methods, such as performing the operation with a knife over a hole in the ground, using thorns and leg-binding for infibulation and plain water for cleansing, have been supplanted by the availability of better equipment and knowledge of more hygienic methods. The government-trained village midwife whose practice I observed did the operations on a wood and rope bed covered with a plastic sheet. She used xylocaine injections for local anesthesia, new razor blades for cutting, suture needles, dissolving sutures when available, and prophylactic antibiotic powder. Her equipment was initially sterilised in a bowl of boiling water, however she returned the instruments to the same bowl without resterilising them for a second girl's operation. The midwife purchases most of the necessary supplies and medications out of her earnings; some of the basic equipment necessary for childbirth attendance is provided by the government, however, and some supplies are obtained informally through the local government health centre.

Despite some improvements, it is still common at the time of circumcision for girls to suffer such serious complications as haemorrhage,infections,septicaemia, retention of urine, or shock, complications from which deaths can and sometimes do occur, as people are aware. Later, infibulated girls sometimes experience retention of menses at menarche or have difficulty urinating (due to scar tissue across the opening). At first intercourse, infibulation presents a barrier which is painfully torn or must be cut open by the husband, a midwife, or a doctor. Childbirth is complicated by the inelastic scar tissue of infibulation, which must be cut open by the birth attendant and restitched after delivery. Vasicovaginal fistulae, which can result from such obstructed labour, are by no means rare in Sudan. Such a fistula - or passage between the urinary bladder and the vagina created by damage to tissue between the two organs - results in a most embarrassing condition for the woman, who cannot retain her urine and therefore leaks constantly. Urinary tract infections, chronic pelvic infections, abscesses, and inclusion cysts are other common long-term complications of female circumcision. (For discussion of damaging health effects of circumcision, see Verzin 1975, Cook 1976, Shandall 1967, Toubia 1985, and El Dareer 1982.)

Circumcision and the Subordination of Women

In Sudan, female circumcision forms part of the socio-cultural arrangement for reinforcing the subordination of women. For those groups in Sudan which practice female circumcision, the operations are part of the social construction of the feminine gender, symbolically and actually taming the sexuality of women for social purposes (cf. Boddy 1982; Toubia 1985). Female sexuality is believed to be inherently powerful and potentially dangerous if not controlled. Hayes's statement that in Sudan "virgins are made, not born" (1975) captures the essence of this social construction of gender and the acceptable female role as chaste. Reinforced by modifications of demeanour, dress, and certain limitations on mobility and activities, the Sudanese woman is protected from the catastrophe of a besmirched reputation which would reflect on the men of the family as well as herself. By attenuating the young girl's sexual desire and, when infibulated, presenting a barrier to penetration, the operations serve to guarantee viriginity, hence marriageability. Any girl known to have been properly circumcised in the pharaonic manner - and indeed there are routinely many women who witness and make suggestions as the operations are performed - can be assumed to be a virgin.

The fact that it is women themselves who carry out this practice and serve as its strongest defenders is due to the importance placed on virginity at marriage and to the more dependent social and economic position of women. Women in Sudan generally must derive much of their social status and economic security from their roles as wives and mothers, in spite of the fact that most women are economically active. There is a marked preference to educate sons rather than daughters and under Islamic law, males inherit twice the share of a female. Domestic work expectations placed on married women combined with the lack of such social supports as low cost child care and social security and care for the elderly further constrain most women's ability to work outside the home to provide for themselves.

Hence the social goal of circumcision in maintaining the reputations and marriageability of daughters is not easily challenged, even when the harmful effects of the surgeries are known, since women are protecting themselves and their daughters against the very real risk of social ostracism and economic ruin. Reinfibulation after childbirth has a similar goal: it is considered to contribute to the sexual pleasure of the husband and is therefore valued by wives seeking to preserve their positions in the family, preventing loss of the husband's interest and his taking advantage of his option (under Islam) to divorce or to take an additional wife.

For Sudanese girls, then, femininity - one's proper gender identity - is closely tied to virginity and marriageability, which can only be guaranteed by circumcision. While many observers and activists expect that education about the dangers of the practice as well as a general rise in the level of female education would help to overcome this view, no coherent substitute definition of femininity has arisen to replace it, and thus even well educated people may continue circumcision. For example, in a review of several recent studies, Amna El Sadik Badri concludes that while there is some evidence that attitudes may be beginning to change, there has been no significant decline in the practice of female circumcision, although there may be a decline in the infibulation type among educated women who live in the Khartoum area (1984, p. 14). One survey of secondary school girls revealed that many of them had actually "forced their parents to have them circumcised mainly because they were called names like ghalfa and nigsa (uncircumcised, unclean) by classmates who had been circumcised" (B. Badri 1983, quoted in A. Badri 1984, p. 16). These girls, among the small percentage to receive secondary education, have still felt compelled to conform to the ideal of femininity defined by circumcision.

Alternative images of femininity have not developed. The idea of a chaste but uncircumcised woman does not appear in Sudanese culture, nor is there a clear idea of what an uncircumcised wife might be like or how marital sexuality might become more fulfilling for both partners. Reformers who seek to promote such alternate images of femininity at this point have little to draw on; perhaps more research on uncircumcised women's lives would be helpful. Thus far, a small study by Gail Price (1979) based on only ten families in Khartoum is apparently the only attempt to investigate the social reaction to those women whose families have made the bold decision not to circumcise their daughters. All of the uncircumcised women continued to express positive attitudes about the decision, in spite of some concern about future problems they might have finding a husband or confronting disapproval of in-laws. Others expected to marry educated men who would approve of their not having had the operation. The three who had already married reported much more pleasurable sex than their circumcised friends and their husbands strongly approved of their wives not being circumcised. Although some reported social disapproval, none of the families had found themselves social outcasts as a result of this change.

Although female circumcision is not limited to Muslims in Sudan, nor is it practiced by all Sudanese Muslims, religious identity clearly has been an important contributing factor to the continuation of the practice, since - in my experience interviewing women in central and northern Sudan - it is widely believed to be commanded by Islam. Although the idea that it is a "Sunna" (which would imply some degree of religious obligation) has been challenged by Sudanese religious scholars, the unfortunate term "Sunna circumcision" currently in use for the clitoridectomy and less drastic forms tends to reinforce the notion that some form of circumcision is expected of Muslims. I have even encountered women who have begun to use the term "Sunna circumcision" for intermediate forms which are closer to the pharaonic, presumably to assert that they are good Sunni Muslims who follow the Sunna. Caution should be exercised, therefore, in the interpretation of questionnaire responses, lest findings of increases in "Sunna circumcision" reflect merely a change in nomenclature rather than a shift in the type of surgery done.

Another recent religious influence on the practice of female circumcision has been felt in one Nile village studied by Janice Boddy (1985). There the return of village men after a period of migrant labour in Saudi Arabia - an activity shared by Sudanese men from many areas of the country - has led to requests that their daughters not receive the traditional clitoridectomies and infibulations, but rather be given only Sunna circumcisions. From their exposure to fundamentalist Islam in Saudi Arabia they have come to believe that the pharaonic circumcisions are barbaric and not supported by the authority of the Koran. These men's demands have met with opposition from village women who feel that men should not try to take over what is women's affair. Yet in a period of religious revival among both sexes in the village and with dramatic changes taking place in other aspects of culture (due to television, economic crises, and migration) it may yet be that Sunna circumcision becomes more common and more closely associated with Islam. It is ironic that this should occur as the result of a fundamentalist movement which has at the same time worked against the position of women: Janice Boddy described the effects of the influx of wealth from returning migrants as undermining the complementarity of sex roles in the Nile village she studied, making women less autonomous and more dependent; at the same time these young men have successfully sought to marry very young girls of ten and eleven, taking them out of school. Although such marriages were viewed with shock by many, the men (in their late twenties) justified it on religious grounds (modelling the Prophet's marriage with 'Aisha) and the assumption that women do not need education; the acquiescence of the girls' parents must be interpreted in light of the Sudanese economic crisis and the attractiveness of an alliance with a man of some wealth (Boddy 1985).

In this situation, the gradual abandonment of pharaonic circumcision for Sunna, although it may be an improvement in terms of health effects, may actually add to the long-term tenacity of some form of the practice by more firmly associating it with religion and by further increasing women's economic dependency on men.

Circumcision and Ethnicity

While a number of studies have recognised ethnic differences in the type and prevalence of circumcision, the ideological use of female circumcision in the maintenance of ethnic identity has not received much attention. This is significant not only because this might serve to preserve the practice to bolster ethnic identity in a multicultural society, but also because in a class-stratified society where ethnicity confers privilege, the boundaries of that ethnicity may be guarded and individuals defined by their adherence to identifying customary practices, motivating insiders to preserve and assimilators to adopt them. I believe that circumcision currently serves as such a marker of ethnic identity, associated with class privilege; if I am correct, this can be expected to constitute another obstacle to change or even a motivation for further spread of the practice.

Focussing first on the ethnic differences within the Muslim, primarily Arabic-speaking, majority of the Sudanese population, it is apparent that most of these ethnic groups have practiced some form of female circumcision traditionally and consider it part of their own culture. There is, however, difference among them in the types of surgeries as well as symbolic or ceremonial differences. For example, at least two nomadic groups, the Rashaida and Messeriya, both say they do not infibulate, but perform only the Sunna, because as nomads, they cannot count on finding a midwife for a woman in labour, which is essential for an infibulated woman. More recently, some of these have begun to infibulate, apparently due to influence from contacts with neighbouring peoples (El Dareer 1982), but for reasons which are not clear. Among the Beni Helba, according to El Dareer, the women of the higher status families (the nazir's lineage) were pharaonically circumcised while other women had Sunna circumcisions only, thereby associating the more drastic operations with higher social standing.

A small minority of Sudanese Muslim ethnic groups do not traditionally circumcise, such as the Fur and the Kinin in the far west, which was one of the last areas of Sudan to come under colonial domination, being the site of a powerful Islamic kingdom. The Kinin are said to refuse to circumcise for religious reasons, believing that true Muslims should not do it, but their refusal has resulted in the disdain of their non-Kinin neighbours. Also they have trouble getting trained midwives to stay there since midwives, dependent on collecting payment for births and circumcisions, find they cannot make an adequate income where no circumcisions are performed. As for the Fur, many have begun to circumcise now, especially those who live in towns. It is interesting to note that the Fur in precolonial times did not circumcise girls, except that among the nobility clitoridectomy was "fashionable and constituted another element of their claims to be more proper Muslims than the commoners", according to historian Lidwien Kapteijns 1983, p. 17). The spread of Pharaonic circumcision in this part of the country appears to be related to the influx of a new urban middle class of government officials, police, soldiers and traders from the Nile valley under the colonial administration, whose social and religious practices came to be emulated by local people in the growing urban areas, apparently aspiring to higher class status (Kapteijns 1983, p. 20).

The other major groups which do not circumcise girls, primarily non-Muslim southern Sudanese, Muslim West African immigrants and "westerners" (Hausa and other ethnic groups discriminated against in central Sudan and commonly referred to by the pejorative gloss "Fallata"), Ethiopian and Eritrean immigrants and refugees (present in large numbers in the towns and in rural eastern Sudan), and also European expatriates. With the exception of Europeans, generally represented by relatively prosperous, educated people who seem to be tolerated despite their differences in religion and lack of circumcision, the other non-circumcising groups are not only ethnically different, but occupy generally low social status. It is not uncommon to hear Arab-Sudanese express dislike or disgust for those who do not circumcise, an attitude which, while certainly not universal, is sufficiently widely held that it plays a role in reinforcing the social class and ethnic boundaries.

In such a situation of ethnic group inequality, there must certainly be a temptation for groups and individuals to assimilate by accepting particularly crucial social customs such as female circumcision. A couple of cases serve to illustrate this problem.

In a study in Kordofan, Jay O'Brien found several families of West African origin who had successfully established a new ethnic identity as part of Joama village; their adaptation included adopting the practice of female genital surgeries (O'Brien 1980). Unfortunately, El Dareer's study of female circumcision in several northern provinces did not include people of West African origin in the surveys, so it is not clear how widespread the trend may be whereby younger generations of these people have begun to circumcise girls in order to assimilate; the motivation, however, is clearly there, since important economic and political rights and opportunities (such as access to tenancies on development projects, citizenship papers, and certain licences) are often unavailable to "non-Sudanese" groups (see Duffield, this volume).

Town-dwelling Nuba, not traditionally circumcisers, have apparently taken up the practice increasingly. El Dareer reported that Nuba in towns "want to be like Arabs", and was told by a Nuba woman she interviewed that she had been teased by her Arab neighbours until she finally conformed and had herself and her daughters circumcised.

The large southern ethnic groups such as the Dinka and the Nuer have not been interested in adopting the practice in their home areas, as I found during fieldwork there in the 1970s. However, the practice was not unheard of, since I was told by some of the women I interviewed of a case of a Dinka woman who had married a northern merchant living in a southern village. Through her contacts with wives of her husband's Arabic-speaking friends, she was told that being circumcised was much better, so she tried it. As the story was told, she reported that it deprived her of sexual pleasure and she passed the warning on to others.

What is significant about this example is that it took place in southern Sudan where Arab-Sudanese are the cultural minority, yet as the dominant majority in the country as a whole they exert an ideological hegemony emanating from a strong religious system (Islam asserts its superiority over traditional religions, which do not claim such superiority), reinforced by the economic dominance of the more developed northern Sudan and its wealthy merchant representatives.

What these few examples suggest is that female circumcision is not merely a residual traditional practice, but is rather an important marker of privileged ethnic group status, used ideologically to exclude aspiring lower status groups, who are in turn tempted to adopt it as part of the cultural assimilation necessary to upward mobility. Thus individuals and groups that pursue strategies of assimilation tend to adopt circumcision as a critical cultural marker. Yet for those groups which have not been able or have not chosen to attempt to assimilate, their avoidance of this practice has in some cases become an element of their case for their own moral superiority over their dominators, reinforcing the cultural boundary from the other side.

The Political Economy of Abolition Efforts

The first efforts to eliminate clitoridectomy and infibulation in Sudan came during the British colonial period. The British midwife who, in 1920, was brought in to organise a midwifery training school, enrolled traditional midwives in her programme, and along with obstetrical lessons sought to persuade them to discontinue circumcision, an effort which apparently had little effect.

When the government promulgated an edict prohibiting pharaonic circumcision in 1946, there had already been collaborative efforts between government and educated Sudanese, particularly doctors and religious scholars, to discourage the pharaonic form. In 1945 the Sudan Medical Service had issued and circulated a pamphlet, written in both English and Arabic, that condemned pharaonic circumcision and urged its abandonment. It was endorsed by the highest ranking British and Sudanese doctors and several Sudanese religious leaders, including the Mufti of Sudan whose authoritative Islamic legal opinion stated that female circumcision was not obligatory under Islam (SMS 1945). Another endorsing religious leader advocated the substitution of the Sunna form for the pharaonic, citing the oft-quoted "Reduce but do not destroy" advice attributed to the Prophet Muhammad. This view was reinforced by a poster used in conjunction with a speaking campaign by several educated Sudanese women - teachers and midwives - which suggested that pharaonic circumcision was un-Islamic, ascribing it to "Pharaoh, the enemy of God" but advocating the Sunna form as coming from the Prophet Muhammad (Hall and Ismail 1981, pp. 93-9).

Few Sudanese I interviewed were aware that the religious leaders had ever come out against circumcision, but the effects of the British-enforced ban on pharaonic circumcision were more widely recognised. Seen as an attempt by a foreign power to dictate Sudanese private cultural practices, the law was resented and defied. Residents of the town of Rufa'a still talk about "our Revolution" - the day in 1946 when they tore the government prison to the ground, they say, to free a midwife who had been arrested for circumcising a girl. Government troops fired on the crowd, injuring some, and leaders of the rebellion were arrested and imprisoned. Resistance to the government ban did not require such open rebellion often; it was enough merely to continue the practice as before, since it took place outside British purview in private homes. The government seldom attempted to enforce the law again.

While it is important that Sudanese leaders and not just foreign administrators were involved in early abolition attempts - controverting Hosken's allegation that the problem has been ignored as a "taboo" subject (1980) - most Sudanese reformers in the period after independence considered it virtually impossible, or at best only a very long term goal, to achieve complete abandonment of female circumcision. The result was that health and medical personnel concentrated what efforts they made not against circumcision as such but specifically against the most dangerous form, pharaonic. In fact, until the Khartoum Conference in 1979 the unofficial opinion of several government health service leaders and other medical doctors with whom I spoke in the late 1970s was that "modification" was better than no change and was therefore an acceptable goal. Many doctors in fact were reluctantly willing to promote clitoridectomies - even performing them in their offices if parents requested a circumcision - rather than letting them take their daughter to a midwife whose methods might be much less hygienic and whose surgery would be more drastic.

That the medical profession allowed its members to do this, acting on the assumption that lay people were unlikely or unable to challenge tradition, perhaps can be attributed to the social distance between highly educated, wealthy doctors and their clients. It may also be related to the definition of circumcision as a "women's problem", which in a country of overwhelming medical problems, might well be relegated to a low priority paralleling women's subordination. However, the other relevant factor is that in a country undersupplied with doctors, it is other types of health workers who must do most of the primary health care, particularly in the smaller towns and rural areas. Routine gynecological and obstetrical work has been the province of traditional birth attendants and trained midwives. Being on the front line of circumcision, it is these women who have been looked to as being in the best position to foster change if they are educated on the health risks to their clients.

Midwives, however, cannot be expected to lead a reform campaign. In fact, they face an acute conflict of interest, since the fees they collect for performing circumcisions, together with gifts such as soap, perfume, meat and other foods from the celebration feast, constitute important parts of many midwives' incomes. Government-trained midwives are not paid by the government at all in some areas and in other areas receive only a small monthly sum, much lower than the already small salaries of rural health workers. Untrained, traditional midwives receive no benefits from the government at all; even basic equipment for childbirth attendance is supplied only to the trained midwives, and both groups must purchase their own drugs and supplies, unless acquired informally through local health services facilities. Thus the fee-for-service payment system means that the midwife's income is directly dependent on the number of births attended and circumcisions performed, clearly an economic incentive to continue rather than suppress the practice.

Another impetus for abolition, which can be considered only briefly here, is pressure from organisations outside Sudan to abandon the practice. Perhaps most notorious is the work of Fran Hosken, who has done much to publicise the extent of the practice in various countries. She has recommended that aid missions, international organisations, and even non-governmental and church groups take firm stands "to prevent the operations" (Hosken 1980), even withholding funds until serious work is undertaken against female circumcison. This sort of approach has elicited bitter backlash responses, witnessed at international women's conferences where certain American and European women have clashed with African women on this subject. Nawal el Saadawi, an Egyptian doctor and novelist who has written extensively on women in Arab societies, has criticised the "'them' helping 'us'" approach of foreign groups: "That kind of help, which they think of as solidarity, is another type of colonialism in disguise. So we must deal with female circumcision ourselves. It is our culture, we understand it, when to fight against it and how, because this is the process of liberation" (El Saadawi 1980). In fact, it is very likely that foreign criticism is viewed as a smokescreen, counter-productively blaming the victim while at the same time being unwilling to address the conditions of exploitation, inequality and economic crisis - and the role in them played by the same foreign powers anxious to help stamp out circumcision - which perpetuate conditions of underdevelopment. The recent development of international working groups of women from the affected countries may be more promising.

To expect foreign aid or development agencies to play a leading role is also misguided from another perspective, for such organisations are not ordinarily guided by moral concerns so much as by international political and economic concerns. For example, USAID projects must be demonstrated to have some beneficial effect on U.S. trade, geo-political strategies, or other interests; beneficial effects on the people or economies of the developing country are desirable but secondary, and the acceptability of projects to ruling groups is a prerequisite. Aid must therefore not seem to make the nation or government appear backward or discriminatory, nor must policies appear to foster politically sensitive goals, such as population control. Thus it is unlikely that external aid agencies will play a key role. As I have argued elsewhere (Gruenbaum 1982), the movement against clitoridectomy and infibulation must receive its primary momentum from national movements in which women themselves play a leading role.

Risks and Strategies

What is needed first is to make both men and women more aware of the harmful consequences and the lack of religious compulsion. Secondly adults must be motivated to take the risks - of social criticism and impairment of the marriageability of their daughters - that pioneering non-circumcising parents must face. A public health campaign can only address the former. This is why involvement of a women's movement is needed, since the social and economic risks for children's futures raise complex questions about the role of women in Sudanese economy and society and challenge existing Sudanese conceptions of honour and morality.

The necessary risks could more easily be undertaken if there were alternative sources of security for women who currently can find it only in marriage. I am not suggesting that Sudanese women would ever want to eschew marriage and child-bearing, but there are ways to promote women's economic security and reduce their vulnerability and dependence on husbands which could reduce some of the current pressure for conformity to the cultural ideal of infibulation - and might also ultimately strengthen marriage and make it more satisfying to both partners. In this process, enhancement of women's educational and employment opportunities is especially crucial.

Education for women is valuable not only because of the expectation that it will bring with it better knowledge of health and hygiene, or that literacy will enable women to be more aware of current health advice and more knowledgeable about religious texts, but also because it can enable women to participate more fully in production, as wage-earners and as co-decision-makers in family enterprises.

Sudan has been described as having a "much longer history of female education" than many of the other Arab countries (Al-Sanabary 1985, p. 95), thanks in large part to pioneering efforts of Babiker Badri, for whom the Sudanese women's studies association is named. Still, the percentage of girls in the schools at all levels is greatly behind that of boys, though it has been improving. For example, as of 1975/76, females represented 35.6 per cent of the total students enrolled in the primary grades (1-6), 32.7 per cent in general secondary (grades 7-9), and 28.0 per cent in higher secondary (grades 10-12). In the technical secondary schools girls were only 6.1 per cent of the total, but in teacher's higher secondary there were 42.2 per cent girls (Sudan Government 1976). Each of these figures is higher than a decade earlier, and each is comparable to, though slightly lower than, the average for the sixteen Arab countries compared by Al-Sanabary (1985, p. 96, see Table 1). It is at the post-secondary level that the disparity is greatest; enrolment at the University of Khartoum in 1975-76 was only 12 per cent female, although the total for all available higher educational institutions was 15.9 per cent, considerably lower than the 28 per cent average for the Arab countries.

Of course part of the reason for the smaller percentages at the higher levels is due to the delayed effect of expansion at the lower levels. It is also a problem that even at the primary level most areas of the country try to maintain sex-segregated schools; as a result when a village is building its first primary school or a town its first general secondary school, the new school places made available will almost always be for boys, who are looked to as the families' future security and therefore more in need of education. The building of a school for girls commonly is delayed till after education for boys is well established. It should also be noted that the school places available at all levels are still inadequate, and for both boys and girls Sudan's enrollment ratio (percentage of children from each appropriate age group who are actually enrolled in school) is one of the lowest of the Arab countries: for primary, only 49 per cent of boys and 30 per cent of girls are enrolled, for secondary only 18 per cent of boys and 8 percent of girls, and in higher education it is only a little over two per cent of males and less than one-half of one per cent for females (Al-Sanabary 1985, p. 97).

Although education is necessary for some types of economic opportunity, there are of course many other factors influencing women's economic activities. Sudanese laws and social values already offer some advantages to female labour force participation not found elsewhere - the expectation and legal recognition, for example, that educated women should have careers with the same pay and benefits as men, that maternity leaves are available in government and some other employment, and that often additional unpaid maternity leave with positions held is available. Even so, women's responsibilities for domestic work and social reproduction inhibit women's taking advantage of many desired economic opportunities, and they find it a much greater strain when they do. Working women complain that they must still perform the usual housework after coming home (the well-known "second shift" problem shared by women of many nations) and are still expected to make time for all the traditional visiting and hospitality expected of homemakers. Women college students often find that their neighbours and relatives consider them snobbish if they do not take the time for such visiting, regardless of the demands of their studies, and those whose work requires odd hours (such as medical students who must sometimes spend the night at the hospital during clinical rotations) may jeopardise their reputations in some social groups.

Since childbearing is expected to begin immediately after marriage, the employed married woman must nearly always depend on a mother or other female relative to provide child care. If family members are dependent on her income a woman may find it necessary to continue working even when other obligations conflict, as in cases of illness, family crises, celebrations, or bereavements. Clearly, additional social services such as child care, would help. While government-sponsored child care centres do exist in some areas, many women workers find them unavailable or too costly. Of course women and men share many of the same difficulties - with transportation, inflation, lack of social security in periods of sickness or unemployment - but the effects are different and usually more limiting for women insofar as they interfere with gender role expectations.

The obstacles to security for urban working women are significant, but even more striking is the vulnerability of the women of rural peasant and pastoral communities who are more often uneducated, have access to fewer social services, lack transportation and knowledge of cities and markets, and therefore enjoy fewer income opportunities. Economists in the 1970s often termed rural women as "not economically active" despite hours of daily grain pounding, water carrying, brewing, milking, weaving, and other tasks, and development planners until recently largely overlooked women in their projects, presumably seeing in their daily labours the analogue of the work of housewives in the metropolitan countries. Thus, allocation of irrigated tenancies or training in the use of machines has more commonly gone to males. But as that view has come under critical scrutiny and the importance of women's work in farming, food-processing, handicrafts, water supply, etc., has been more widely recognised, development efforts have increasingly taken women into account. And yet such efforts still result in proposals which seek to improve women's income-earning capacities while neglecting their already heavy workload. They are thus based on a faulty analysis of women's economic vulnerability and consequently deepen rather than alleviate it.

In Marxist-feminist analysis, it is increasingly being recognised that the work done by women in rural areas - regardless of whether they are or are not also engaging in wage-earning or commodity production - is vital to the reproduction of life and the working capacity of the individuals who form the labour force, and as such is most properly analysed in terms of its role in extended reproduction within the capitalist mode of production (see Bennholdt-Thomsen 1984). In fact, in the so-called Third World countries, were it not for the subsistence work performed mostly (but not always exclusively) by women, wage labour for industry and capitalist agriculture would not be available at so low a price. This is especially apparent for the case of migrant and temporary labourers, who are supported by subsistence work for the part of the year when they are not away working for wages, and who are supported by relatives before maturity, in illness, when unemployed, and after retirement. But it is also true for those who have their origins in peasant communities but spend most of their lives in wage labour; indeed it is increasingly rare to find families in which an exclusively "subsistence" strategy is maintained.

Bennholdt-Thomsen (1984) asserts that political economy has incorrectly considered the reproduction of life and working capacity of individuals as given by nature, essentially ignoring the expenditure of labour involved in subsistence production. She recognises and includes in subsistence production the "work related to pregnancy, childbirth, nursing and education of children, as well as that required in the production and transformation of food, clothing, housing, and the physical and psychological demands associated with sexuality" (1984, p. 42). The primary locus of this activity - and the "relation of production central to subsistence production" (Bennholdt-Thomsen 1984, p. 42) - is the family.

While this formulation will seem unorthodox to many, it has an important contribution to make to our thinking on women and family, for it places ideologies which control the physical and social reproductive activities of women squarely within the dynamic of capitalist development. Although rooted in a precapitalist past, ideologies of female subordination and male-dominated family control of women's various labours are not merely "customs" left over from a "traditional" past, but are crucial to the dynamic of capitalist accumulation. For Sudan, that ideology entails female circumcision, by which female sexuality and reproductive potential are socialised and brought firmly under the control of the family. To challenge the surgical ritual by which this control is recognised in fact challenges much more. In the absence of some replacement ideology to preserve that control, undermining circumcision challenges the basic right of the family to control these labours of females.

And yet to detach female labours without changing the economic system is an impossibility, as many women and men must clearly sense. For some women this is understood in terms of the threatened loss of complementarity of gender roles - which at least give subordinated women some basis for influencing the conditions of their lives - and the prospect of increasing their economic dependency, as with the villagers studied by Boddy. These women may then cling to pharaonic circumcision and its associated sex role complementarity for fear of the alternatives, such as increased dependency and increased male control under the influence of fundamentalist Islam. For others, the choice might be to risk independence from family and from men, choosing to remain unmarried and, as a result, facing the possibility of ostracism and/or penury, and perhaps finding themselves unmarriageable should they eventually change their minds.

In this situation, the effort to eliminate pharaonic circumcision cannot succeed as a piecemeal elimination of one practice. It is not a matter of health education comparable to promoting immunisations. Rather, because of its ideological significance - tied up with concepts of gender, religion, ethnicity and ultimately the control of reproductive labour and its role in the capitalist economy - a more dramatic social change will be necessary.

One possibility is that another form of control of reproductive work will be created which preserves the basic relations but with a shift in ideology. It is conceiveable, for example, that pharaonic circumcision might eventually be eliminated at the same time as women become more subordinated (under conditions of increasing economic inequality and the spread of fundamentalist Islam), a situation which might well preserve Sunna circumcision. Such a possible development is consonant with the idea that pharaonic circumcision may be inversely related to female seclusion: where high walls, heavy veils, restricted movements of women and girls, and careful chaperoning safeguard female chastity, the bodily impairment of circumcision is less likely to be resorted to.

For the Sudanese to eliminate all forms of female circumcision, though, requires a quite different sort of development: the cultural change envisioned in the movement to abolish female genital mutilations must be accomplished through improvement of women's opportunities and promotion of their emancipation. This is not to say that "cultural" changes are secondary to fundamental social and economic change and therefore need not be addressed until "after the revolution", as it were; rather, the two are integrated. I agree with Sondra Hale's analysis (1986) of Sudanese women's politics: that for women to challenge the structures of patriarchy in their own lives will challenge the entire structure of exploitation in the Sudanese political economy, and that therefore the subordination or discounting of the importance of women's issues in a political agenda overlooks a tremendous potential force for change.

The issue of female circumcision has long been part of the agenda of the progressive women's movement in Sudan - witness the stand against female circumcision taken by the Women's Union decades ago. Together with more general concern over the role of the family in structuring the capture of reproductive labour in the capital accumulation process, female circumcision deserves a central place in the analyses and debates of the progressive democratic movement in Sudan.

References

Al-Sanabary, Nagat (1985), 'Continuity and Change in Women's Education in the Arab States', in E.W. Fernea (ed.), Women and the Family in the Middle East: New Voices of Change, pp. 93-110, University of Texas Press, Austin, Texas.

Badri, Amna el Sadik (1984), 'Female Circumcision in the Sudan', The Ahfad Journal, (Omdurman, Sudan), 1, pp. 11-21.

Badri, Badria Suleiman (1983), 'Knowledge and Attitude towards Female Circumcision among High School Girls', unpublished paper, Ahfad University College, Ombdurman, Sudan.

BBSAWS (Babiker Badri Scientific Associationfor Women Studies), 1985, Integrated Project for Rural Women, Women, pp. 23-7.

Bennholdt-Thomsen, Veronika (1984), 'Subsistence Production and Extended Reproduction' in K. Young, C. Wollkowitz and R. McCullagh (eds.), Of Marriage and the Market: Women's Subordination Internationally and Its Lessons, Routledge & Kegan Paul, London.

Boddy, Janice (1982), 'Womb as Oasis: The Symbolic Context of Pharaonic Circumcision in Rural Northern Sudan', American Ethnologist, 9, (4), pp. 682-98.

--- (1985), 'Saudi Islam, Egyptian Dramas and Northern Sudanese Women', paper presented at the Annual Meeting of the American Anthropological Association, Washington, D.C.

Cook, Robin (1976), 'Damage to Physical Health from Pharaonic Circumcision (Infibulation) of Females: A Review of the Medical Literature', World Health Organization, Sept. 30 (Reprinted: WHO/Eastern Mediterranean Regional Office Technical Publication No. 2, 1979).

El Dareer, Asma (1982), Woman, Why Do You Weep? Circumcision and Its Consequences, Zed Press, London.

El Saadawi, Nawal (1980), 'Creative Women in Changing Societies: A Personal Reflection', Race and Class, 22, 2, pp. 159-82.

Fernea, Elizabeth Warnock (ed.), (1985), Women and the Family in the Middle East: New Voices of Change, University of Texas Press, Austin, Texas.

Gruenbaum, Ellen (1982), 'The Movement Against Clitoridectomy and Infibulation in Sudan: Public Health Policy and the Women's Movement', Medical Anthropology Newsletter, 13, 2, pp. 4-12.

Hale, Sondra (1986), 'The Wing of the Patriarch: Sudanese Women and Revolutionary Parties', MERIP Report, 16, 1, pp. 25-30.

Hall, Marjorie and Bakhita Amin Ismail (1981), Sisters under the Sun: The Story of Sudanese Women, Longmans, London.

Hayes, Rose Oldfield (1975), 'Female Genital Mutilation, Fertility Control, Women's Roles, and the Patrilineage in Modern Sudan: A Functional Analysis', American Ethnologist, 2, pp. 617-33.

Hosken, Franzeska (1980), Female Sexual Mutilations: The Facts and Proposals for Action, Women's International Network News, Lexington, Massachusetts.

Kameir, El-Wathig; El-Bakri, Zeineb; Salim, Idris and El-Ngar, Samiya (1984), 'The State of Women's Studies in the Sudan', Review of African Political Economy, 27 & 28, pp. 130-7.

Kapteijns, Lidwien (1983), 'Islamic Rationales for the Changing Social Roles of Women in the Western Sudan', paper presented to the conference on Women in Muslim Societies: Is Feminism Possible? Brooklyn College, City University of New York, New York.

O'Brien, Jay (1980), Agricultural Labor and Development in Sudan, PhD, University of Connecticut.

Price, Gail (1979), 'Factors Related to Sudanese Families Deciding Against Female Circumcision', Proceedings of the Symposium on the Changing Status of Sudanese Women, Ahfad University College for Women, Omdurman, Sudan.

Shandall, A.A. (1967), 'Circumcision and Infibulation of Females: A General Consideration of the Problem and a Clinical Study of the Complications in Sudanese Women', Sudan Medical Journal, 5, pp. 178-212.

SMS (Sudan Medical Service), (1945), 'Female Circumcision in the Anglo-Egyptian Sudan', Sudan Medical Service.

Sudan Government (1976), Annual Statistical Report, Department of Statistics, Khartoum.

Toubia, Nahid F. (1985), 'The Social and Political Implications of Female Circumcision: The Case of the Sudan', in E.W. Fernea (ed.), Women and the Family in the Middle East: New Voices of Change, pp. 148-59, University of Texas Press, Austin, Texas.

Verzin, J. A. (1975), 'Sequelae of Female Circumcision', Tropical Doctor, October.

Ideas. Look at GB. 1913 etc. Lancashire etc.

KEY 1913 GB ✓. Kitchener ✓ BUT only removed obstacle.

Sudan govt first. Now use for capital.